SCHULER BOOKS

One of the Midwest's
Largest and
Most Complete
Bookstores

Over 75,000 Titles

942-2561
1-800-331-1727
FAX 942-9238

2975 28th Street Southeast
Grand Rapids Michigan 49512

MICHIGAN

"PARTNERS IN PROGRESS"
BY JAMES F. FILGAS AND
LUTHER JACKSON III

PRODUCED IN COOPERATION WITH
THE HISTORICAL SOCIETY OF MICHIGAN

WINDSOR PUBLICATIONS, INC.
NORTHRIDGE, CALIFORNIA

MICHIGAN

An Illustrated History of
THE GREAT LAKES STATE

GEORGE S. MAY

Windsor Publications, Inc.—History Book Division

Vice President/Publisher: Hal Silverman
Editorial Director: Teri Davis Greenberg
Corporate Biography Director: Karen Story
Design Director: Alexander D'Anca

Staff for *Michigan: An Illustrated History of the Great Lakes State*
Senior Editor: Jerry Mosher
Assistant Director, Corporate Biographies: Phyllis Gray
Editor, Corporate Biographies: Brenda Berryhill
Production Editor, Corporate Biographies: Una FitzSimons
Sales Representatives, Corporate Biographies: Greg Gavrilides, John Swedberg,
    Cal Young
Editorial Assistants: Kathy M. Brown, Nina Kanga, Susan Kanga,
    Pat Pittman
Proofreader: Susan J. Muhler
Designer and Art Director: Ellen Ifrah
Layout Artist, Editorial: Tom Prager
Layout Artist, Corporate Biographies: Mari Catherine Preimesberger

Library of Congress Cataloging-in-Publication Data
May, George S.
    Michigan: an illustrated history of the Great Lakes state.
    "Partners in progress [chp. 13] by James F. Filgas and Luther Jackson."
    Bibliography: p. 286
    Includes index.
    1. Michigan—History. 2. Michigan—Description and travel. 3. Michigan—Industries. I. Filgas, James F., 1934- . II. Jackson, Luther. III. Title.
F566.M454   1987   977.4   87-20961
ISBN 0-89781-181-X

Title page: This detailed lithograph of the fort on Mackinac Island, looking out at the harbor with Round Island in the distance, is one of several Mackinac Island and Great Lakes scenes appearing in Vues et Souvenirs de L'Amerique du Nord *by Francis, Comte de Castelnau, published in Paris in 1842. Courtesy, Michigan Historical Collections, Bentley Historical Library, University of Michigan*

Opposite page: Michigan's 3,121 miles of Great Lakes shoreline are one of the state's greatest and most recognizable natural assets. In the Upper Peninsula, the Cut River Bridge on U.S. 2 west of St. Ignace was part of a highway built with some difficulty along Lake Michigan's sandy shore. It provided the motoring public with the most extensive and magnificent views of Michigan's Great Lakes setting. Courtesy, Library of Congress

Page 6: Michigan's farming economy provided an initial boost to Dexter M. Ferry's seed company, which ultimately evolved into today's Ferry-Morse Company. By the 1880s it was one of the nation's largest seed houses, annually shipping 500 carloads of seed to its dealers and filling orders from recipients of the hundreds of thousands of seed catalogs it mailed out each year.

To the McGinnis girls, Tish and Peg

PORTULACA,

From Seeds put up by D. M. Ferry & Co.
DETROIT, Mich.

(See Over.)

PAINTED FROM ACTUAL SPECIMENS

GROWN ON D.M.FERRY & CO'S. TRIAL GROUNDS

6

CONTENTS

INTRODUCTION
· · · · · · · · · · ·

The Historical Society of Michigan is honored to be the sponsor of George May's *Michigan: An Illustrated History of the Great Lakes State.* As the culmination of a three-year project, this book is one of the Society's many efforts to contribute to the celebration of Michigan's sesquicentennial.

It is thus appropriate that Dr. May's narrative begins by taking us back to the era of Michigan statehood—the 1830s—when the Michigan territory was bursting with pride and settlers eager to tame the land. Out of those heady days Michigan's reputation as a leader in economic development was established. Within a decade, the first exploration of the Upper Peninsula's rich, ore-laden lands began. Lumbering followed, and Michigan soon led the nation in lumber production, a position it would hold throughout the latter half of the nineteenth century. The dawn of the twentieth century saw the advent of the auto manufacturers, and by the 1910s Michigan and its largest city, Detroit, had become synonymous with cars. All the while, Michigan farmers steadily kept the state in the forefront of agricultural productivity. Today, tourism holds an important place among the state's leading revenue-producing enterprises. Areas once left behind in the rush of economic development are enjoying new or renewed financial boosts buoyed by the influx of in-state and out-of-state visitors.

Dr. May reminds us that, throughout Michigan's history, it has been the people of Michigan who have made the state what it is. The quality of its communities, competence of its work force, and level of its civic pride are the hallmarks of its people. And it is to them that the Historical Society of Michigan dedicates this book. Just as the celebration of Michigan's sesquicentennial is a people-oriented celebration, so too should this volume stand as a testimony to Michiganians' depth of resolve, tenacity of spirit, and love of home and family. To them, *Michigan: An Illustrated History of the Great Lakes State* is gratefully presented as a birthday gift that will be a source of pride and information for generations to come.

Thomas L. Jones
Executive Director
Historical Society of Michigan
Ann Arbor, Michigan

The Atlas Mill in Genesee County, erected in 1836 by Judge Norman Davison, was used as a woolen mill, grist mill, and post office before it ceased operation in 1940. Courtesy, The Flint Journal

CHAPTER I

THE NEW STATE OF MICHIGAN

This portrait by Detroit painter Alvin (or Allen) Smith, Jr., suggests the youthful determination with which Stevens T. Mason approached the difficulties Michigan encountered in achieving statehood in the mid-1830s. Courtesy, Michigan Historical Collections, Bentley Historical Library, University of Michigan

On January 26, 1837, an act of Congress "to admit the State of Michigan into the Union, upon an equal footing with the original States" was signed and approved by President Andrew Jackson. Earlier, two future presidents, James K. Polk, who was then the Speaker of the House of Representatives, and Vice President Martin Van Buren, had also signed the legislation that, on this twenty-sixth day of the new year, exactly doubled the number of states from the original figure of thirteen.

From the federal government's viewpoint, January 26, 1837, is the date Michigan became a state. Michigan, on the other hand, had been claiming to be a state and had been operating under a duly elected state government since the fall of 1835, creating uncertainty as to which date to observe when it came time to celebrate the centennial of statehood in the 1930s and the sesquicentennial in the 1980s. The solution was to stretch these celebrations over a three-year period, but in the 1830s the difficulties associated with the issue of statehood were not so easily resolved. Thus, Jackson and his fellow

Democrats Van Buren and Polk must have felt greatly relieved to know that their signatures had officially closed the book on a matter that had been a political embarrassment to them.

The issue of Michigan statehood originated fifty years earlier when Congress, in the Northwest Ordinance of 1787, had created the Northwest Territory to govern the lands north of the Ohio and east of the Mississippi, which then comprised the northwestern corner of the new United States. As these largely undeveloped lands were settled, the ordinance called for eventually subdividing the vast territory into a maximum of five states, whose boundaries were specified. Thus, when Congress in 1805 established the territory of Michigan, the first time the name had been applied to a unit of government, the southern boundary followed the line that Congress in 1787 had said would separate the states on the south from those formed to the north—a line running due east and west from the southernmost point of Lake Michigan.

When Ohio, the first of the states formed in the northwest, was preparing

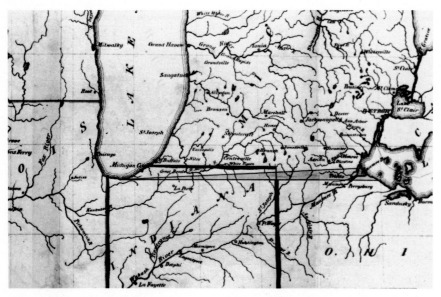

Superimposed on this mid-1830s map is the area in dispute between Michigan and Ohio—the line due east from the southern tip of Lake Michigan, which was the basis of Michigan's claim, and the line drawn at a slight angle so as to hit the north cape of Maumee Bay, the line Ohio claimed. Courtesy, State Archives, Michigan Department of State

to enter the Union in 1802, the delegates who were drawing up that state's constitution were told by a hunter, according to one popular story, that Lake Michigan extended farther south than the maps of that period indicated. This would mean that the boundary line running due east from the lake's southern tip would probably intersect Lake Erie south of the mouth of the Maumee River, the future site of the important port of Toledo. Realizing the desirability of controlling this waterway, the delegates wrote into the constitution a proviso that if, when the state's northern boundary was surveyed, the ordinance line did indeed run south of Maumee Bay, then the boundary should be relocated along a line run on an angle sufficient to place the entire bay within Ohio's borders. Congress accepted the constitution and admitted Ohio to the Union in 1803. When Congress set up the Michigan territory two years later, however, it used the 1787 line in describing Michigan's boundary with Ohio, which seemed to indicate that in accepting Ohio's constitution Congress was not necessarily agreeing with every provision of that document.

The basis of a boundary dispute between Michigan and Ohio had thus been established between 1802 and 1805, but little attention was paid to

the question for some years. Congress in 1812 did request that the line from the southernmost point of Lake Michigan be surveyed, but the onset of the War of 1812 postponed the survey until 1817. In the meantime Indiana, upon its admission to the Union in 1816, persuaded Congress to push its boundary with Michigan ten miles north of the ordinance line. Among other things, it meant that South Bend's Notre Dame University would not be located in Michigan to vie with Michigan's Wolverines and Michigan State's Spartans for the state's top football honors. Michigan's Governor Lewis Cass protested, to no avail, the loss of a slice of southwestern Michigan to Indiana. When in 1817 the federal surveyor (whose boss, the surveyor general, was a former Ohio governor) made sure that the line from the southernmost point of Lake Michigan came out just north of Maumee Bay, Cass cried foul and insisted that the surveyor general do what Congress had requested. The result was a second survey in 1818 in which another surveyor ran his line due east and, as the hunter is alleged to have told Ohio's delegates in 1802, the boundary placed the mouth of the Maumee in Michigan, not in Ohio.

Although the lines had now been established and the pie-shaped area in between that was claimed by both Michigan and Ohio was clearly defined, it was another fifteen years before the area known as the Toledo Strip generated great interest. Ohio made no effort to assert its rights to this land, seemingly content to leave its administration in the hands of Michigan. But by the early 1830s Michigan's days as a territory were numbered. The Northwest Ordinance had set 60,000 as the minimum population figure a territory needed to attain statehood. By 1833, Michigan's population was close to that level, if it had not actually reached it, prompting the territorial government to ask Congress's permission to proceed with the steps necessary to become a state. It was only then that Ohio, now one of the more populous states and a strong supporter of President Jackson and the Democratic party, used its political clout to block Michigan's entry into the Union until it agreed to accept Ohio's boundary claims. Ohio also persuaded Indiana and Illinois, which, when it became a state, had gotten Congress to push its boundary sixty miles north of the Ordinance line, to join in opposing Michigan's bid. Ohio accomplished this by arguing that if Michigan won the boundary case it might put in jeopardy the rights to the land Indiana and Illinois had received north of the 1787 line. As a result, Congress in 1834 refused to authorize Michigan to proceed in applying for statehood.

It was then that Acting Governor Stevens T. Mason moved to make Michigan a state without the prior approval of Congress. Mason, an impetuous young man from Virginia, was only nineteen when Jackson, as a favor to Mason's father, appointed him to be territorial secretary in 1831. George Porter, who had become governor of the territory in 1831 when Lewis Cass resigned to accept a post in Jackson's cabinet, died during a cholera epidemic in the summer of 1834, and Mason, as secretary, became acting governor. Since Jackson and the United States Senate could not agree upon an appointee to succeed Porter, Mason continued as the territory's chief executive during the critical months that followed.

A special census initiated by Mason showed that aside from other parts of the territory Michigan's lower peninsula had a population of 85,856, far more than the amount required for statehood. Mason then drew upon the example of the territory of Tennessee, which, in the 1790s when it had a population of 60,000, had gone ahead on its own to organize a state government and had then demanded that Congress ac-

cept it into the Union. Mason ordered territorial elections in the spring of 1835 for delegates to a state constitutional convention, which met in Detroit in May. Within six weeks the delegates had finished their job. The following October the constitution they had drafted was approved by the voters, who also elected the members of the state government called for by the document, with Mason becoming the state's first governor. He and the other elected officials were sworn in on November 2, 1835.

Andrew Jackson, meanwhile, had grown increasingly irritated at Mason's actions, which he feared might offend Ohio's Democrats to the point that they might not support Jackson's party in the upcoming 1836 presidential election. Jackson thus removed Mason from his job as secretary in the fall of 1835 and appointed John Horner in his place. However, as Michigan, under Mason's leadership, proceeded to set up a state government, the efforts of Horner and the Jackson administration to keep a rival territorial government in power were doomed to fail. Before long Horner had left for the lands across Lake Michigan where a movement was underway to create the Wisconsin territory, and by the summer of 1836 federal authorities were dealing with Mason as the head of the only recognized government in Michigan.

Although Michigan now claimed to be a state, it would remain without the rights possessed by other states until such time as Congress and the President chose to admit it to the Union. The stumbling block continued to be Ohio. Early in 1835, the Buckeye State, alarmed by Michigan's move to ignore the Congressional action of 1834 and proceed with its statehood plans, belatedly sought to assert its authority over the Toledo Strip. Michigan's territorial government responded by declaring it illegal for anyone to assume governmental powers anywhere in the ter-

The respect with which President Andrew Jackson was held in Michigan, as through much of what was then the American West, was reflected in the numerous counties and places named for him and members of his cabinet. Political considerations, however, necessitated the support Jackson gave to Ohio in its boundary dispute with Michigan. From Cirker, Dictionary of American Portraits, Dover, 1967

Above: *The Great Seal of the State of Michigan, adopted in 1835, was designed by long-time governor of the territory Lewis Cass. Tuebor ("I will defend") perhaps referred to Michigan's fight to retain the Toledo Strip, while the longer Latin phrase, meaning "If you seek a pleasant peninsula, look around you," refers to the state's distinctive geographical outline. Courtesy, Travel Bureau, Michigan Department of Commerce*

Below: *Michigan officially became a state on January 26, 1837, after President Andrew Jackson, Vice President Martin Van Buren, and Speaker of the House James K. Polk affixed their signatures to this document and approved Congress's action in admitting Michigan "into the Union, upon an equal footing with the original States." Courtesy, Library of Congress*

ritory except under the authority of the territorial or federal governments. That started a series of moves and counter-moves that culminated in the summer of 1835 with the threat of armed clashes between the militia and law enforcement agents of the two governments. Fortunately, the Toledo War, as this confrontation came to be called, was mainly a war of words. The only casualty was a Michigan deputy sheriff who was stabbed by Two Stickney, son of Benjamin F. Stickney, an eccentric Ohio partisan who for simplicity's sake had named his sons respectively One and Two.

Before the Toledo Strip became an actual war zone, Mason in the fall of 1835 took the lead in shifting the conflict to the halls of Congress. Upon being inaugurated as head of the new state government in November, Mason persuaded his fellow state officials to move cautiously in asserting their authority so as not to upset negotiations in Washington that might resolve the boundary question in Michigan's favor. However, when Michigan's newly elected three-man Congressional delegation arrived in the nation's capital, any thought that such a resolution was in the offing was quickly dispelled. Congress refused to seat these representatives of an unrecognized state, although they were allowed to stay around as unofficial observers. In the debate that followed, Ohio held firm in its insistence that the Toledo Strip was its price for supporting Michigan's admission to the Union. Furthermore, President Jackson made it plain to the Democratic Congressional leadership that nothing must be done that would endanger the party's chances of carrying Ohio, Indiana, and Illinois in the fall election. It made no difference that most of Washington's politicians probably agreed with former President John Quincy Adams, now a congressman from Massachusetts, who stated he had never seen a controversy where

one side was so clearly in the right as Michigan was in this instance. Congressional action approved by Jackson on June 15, 1836, declared that Michigan would be admitted to the Union only on the condition that it give up its claim to the Toledo Strip. As compensation, however, the plan also offered Michigan, in exchange for the loss of this land on its southern border, a vast area to the northwest in what would come to be referred to as Michigan's Upper Peninsula.

In contrast to the attention given to Michigan's boundary on the south, little notice had been paid to its northern borders. Despite the term "Peninsular Michigan," which was frequently used in the years leading up to statehood and implied that Michigan was thought of as occupying only the lower peninsula, the eastern portion of the Upper Peninsula had been part of Michigan since the day the territory was established in 1805. To be sure, some residents of the remote region had subsequently petitioned to be made part of a new territory extending along the southern shores of Lake Superior; others, however, wished to remain part of Michigan and were represented at the state's first constitutional convention in 1835. That first constitution had defined the state as including with the lower peninsula the area in the northern peninsula that lay east of a line drawn due north from the northernmost point of Lake Michigan, a point some thirty or forty miles west of St. Ignace. This area included the fur trading settlements at the Straits of Mackinac and Sault Ste. Marie that had always had close economic ties with the fur trading posts in the lower peninsula. But when Congress proposed to give Michigan, in exchange for the Toledo Strip, the rest of the Upper Peninsula westward to the Menominee and Montreal rivers, the reaction of many in the state was one of outrage. In their view, Michigan was being of-

fered a barren wilderness, devoid of any settlement save a few scattered bands of Indians. The Detroit *Free Press* termed it "a region of perpetual snows—the Ultima Thule of our national domain of the north."

In accordance with the terms of the Congressional proposal, a special convention assembled in Ann Arbor at the end of September for the sole purpose of expressing an opinion for or against the plan. After four days of discussion, the delegates voted against acceptance. But within a short time Democrats from Wayne and Washtenaw counties took the lead in calling for a second convention to reconsider the decision. Unlike the first convention, it had not been officially authorized by the state government and was boycotted by the opposition Whig party because of its undoubted extralegal origins. The second convention met in Ann Arbor on December 6, 1836, and, ridiculed by its critics as the "frostbitten convention," voted to accept Congress's terms for Michigan's admission to the Union. After Governor Mason notified the federal government of the decision, Congress and the president took the appropriate steps that made Michigan an equal member of the Union on January 26, 1837.

As Thomas M. Cooley, Michigan's foremost legal authority of the nineteenth century, observed a number of years later, "it would have been idle to quarrel with or condemn" the process by which Michigan had finally achieved statehood. "The State could not maintain its anomalous position, and for any wrong in its treatment only Congress could give redress ... The State had maintained its honor in standing upon its rights and the compromise which by a species of fraud was forced upon it gave more than it took away, and left the State a decided gainer in the transaction." Cooley was writing in the 1880s when the western part of the Upper Peninsula was experiencing a great boom in the mining of copper and iron ore, making it appear that Michigan had gotten the better of the bargain when these distant northern lands had proven to be not so barren after all. In later years, however, nearly all of the mines were shut down and the Upper Peninsula was beset by economic problems, thereby compounding the task of creating any real feeling of unity between the residents of this peninsula and the far more numerous residents of the peninsula to the south. As a result, there were those who were not so ready to concede that the trade made in the 1830s had been, in the long run, beneficial to the best interests of either peninsula.

But in 1837 all this was in the future. The 175,000 people that were now living in Michigan were eager to develop the 36 million acres of land and the vast resources of the surrounding lakes that were also included within the new state's boundaries. Their accomplishments and those of succeeding generations would be celebrated during the state's sesquicentennial in the 1980s, but any such observance would be woefully incomplete if it did not recognize that this 150-year development is but the latest, and, chronologically, one of the briefest, in a series of historical developments that began many thousands of years ago. It is in that distant and imperfectly known past that Michigan's history had its beginnings and the state's distinctive characteristics began to emerge.

The state seal's wording has remained constant in the 150 years since its adoption, but the figures that form the state coat of arms and the material within the outer circles have varied greatly, as is evident by comparing their appearance on the Great Seal (opposite page) and on the state flag (above), adopted in 1911. Courtesy, Travel Bureau, Michigan Department of Commerce

THE INDIANS

Sometime around 9000 B.C., give or take several hundred years, a few of the ancestors of today's Indians camped for a short while near present-day Flint. There, on the lee side of a ridge that provided some shelter from the Arctic-like winds found at that time in this southern Michigan locale, the families lived by hunting caribou and other game that was then native to the area. Eleven thousand years later, in 1978, archaeologists began to excavate the place where these ancient travelers had stayed, a place that has been labeled the Gainey site. Artifacts that they recovered show similarities to those found at other North American sites where other hunting peoples resided. These stone tools reveal precious little information about the people who made them—exactly who they were, their names, their physical appearance, their language, where they had come from, and where they went after leaving the Gainey site—but to date they are the first human beings who lived in Michigan about whom even this much information exists.

The origins of the people whom Columbus mistakenly labeled Indians will always remain something of a mystery. While many Indians believe their presence in this part of the world is the result of divine action akin to that in the Biblical story of Creation, the more scientifically-based hypothesis points to a migration of people from Asia across the Bering Strait into Alaska, from where these pioneers and their descendants traveled over the Western Hemisphere. How long ago this migration began is still to be determined, with recent evidence suggesting that mankind may have been living in these lands much longer than the earlier estimates of from 20,000 to 40,000 years.

Regardless of what may turn up elsewhere, in Michigan, as in much of the rest of the northern areas, there is little likelihood of discovering anything stemming from human activity that dates back farther than about 11,000 B.C. Prior to that time, glaciers from the last Ice Age had for thousands of years covered most of what is now Michigan, totally reshaping the land and obliterating, under the enormous weight of ice which measured thousands of feet in thickness, whatever evidence of earlier human residence may

Pictographs and other forms of prehistoric artwork that are found fairly often elsewhere are virtually unknown in Michigan, with the exception of these figures. Believed to be of Indian origin, they appear high above the water level on Burnt Bluff, near Fayette in the Upper Peninsula. Courtesy, State Archives, Michigan Department of State

have existed. By 11,000 B.C., as the climate began to moderate, the ice started melting at what must have been a virtually imperceptible rate, and the glaciers gradually began their retreat northward. On the land that was uncovered vegetation eventually emerged, attracting and sustaining animals such as the caribou. In turn, the animals attracted people who lived by hunting them.

Those hunters who camped near Flint 11,000 years ago were only the latest of many such groups who probably had been coming into southern Michigan for 1,000 or 2,000 years. Documenting their presence has been complicated tremendously not only by recent man-made changes that have disturbed or in some instances destroyed evidence of past inhabitation, but even more so by the physical changes that occurred over thousands of years as the land recovered from the effects of glaciers. In particular, as the Great Lakes emerged, many areas where prehistoric camp or village sites could have been found are now submerged under hundreds of feet of water.

By approximately 6000 B.C. (and none of the dates used in this prehistoric chronology are, because of the meager and imprecise nature of the data on which they are based, anything but approximations) the glaciers had left the Michigan area entirely. From then until perhaps 2000 B.C. the climate became increasingly warm, reaching temperature levels by the latter date that have not been reached since then. By that time the Great Lakes as we know them today had appeared, although their water levels were considerably lower than in later times when the climate became cooler and wetter. On land, the Arctic or sub-Arctic tundra-type vegetation of the early post-Ice Age years had long since been replaced by the heavy forest cover that has remained, with the waters of the adjacent lakes, the most obvious

feature of the Michigan landscape.

Of necessity, the people in the area adapted to this changing environment. Most of them continued to live a hunting existence, but as the climate warmed the big game they had hunted either drifted north to colder climates, as in the case of the caribou, or became extinct, as was the case with the mastodon, which had lived in Michigan in the latter years of the Ice Age. The archaeological evidence indicates that some of the early hunters followed the caribou northward while others, perhaps new groups of hunters moving up from areas to the south, turned to hunting the wildlife that began to assume the characteristics that have remained to the present time. In addition, the people took advantage of the edible fruits and nuts, and in some areas such delicacies as wild rice, as these sources of food came to thrive in this wooded, well-watered land. Nor were the fish in the lakes overlooked, and for many inhabitants fish became a more important part of their diet than the game that they or their ancestors had originally sought.

Changes in the design of artifacts found are the basis for archaeologists' postulation of cultural change and progress in the early period. A major breakthrough evidently occurred around 5000 B.C. when some of the early Michiganians discovered that the copper found in the extreme north could be used in making some artifacts, thereby enabling them to become the first people in the Western Hemisphere to move out of the Stone Age level of existence. The discovery of objects made from Michigan copper at sites throughout the eastern part of North America as far south as the Gulf of Mexico testifies to the eventual growth of what must have been a considerable degree of contact and trade between the residents of the Great Lakes and these other parts of the continent.

In the latter part of the pre-

Christian era more advanced cultures developed, using ceramic pottery and interring some group members in burial mounds. The more than 1,000 burial mounds that have been found in Michigan, such as one in Bronson Park in Kalamazoo and a group of about fifteen along the Grand River near Grand Rapids, provide the earliest visible remnants of these long-departed cultures that the layman, as well as the trained archaeologist, can understand and appreciate. But perhaps the most important change that occurred at this time resulted from the development of a primitive form of agriculture. In the Ohio valley south of Michigan, a type of prehistoric Indian culture that has been named Hopewell flourished from the last years of the pre-Christian era through the first centuries after Christ. In addition to elaborate burial mounds, earthworks, artistically decorated pottery, and other evidences of a highly developed society, the Hopewell Indians had learned to supply their food needs not only by the traditional means but also by growing vegetables such as corn, squash, and beans. The Hopewell influence was apparent in southern Michigan at least by the start of the Christian era, although according to James E. Fitting, a leading authority, the Michigan sites that have been discovered are of "an impoverished Hopewell" character, akin to the rather crude frontier outposts of later historical times. Nevertheless, some of the residents of the river valleys of southern Michigan, such as the Kalamazoo, St. Joseph, Grand, and Saginaw, began growing food, thereby becoming less dependent on older sources of food which they were less able to control.

By A.D. 1600, Indians of widely differing levels of cultural development had been in Michigan perhaps as long as 13,000 years, a number worth contemplating when it is remembered that the state of Michigan is a mere 150 years old. These prehistoric peoples had survived as best they could by adapting to the conditions they encountered. Changes in their way of life took centuries before the effects were fully evident. For reasons that are not understood, the various groups living in the Michigan area in the time immediately preceding the 1600s seem to have suffered a cultural decline from the levels reached during the era of the Hopewell influence. In addition, the area's total population seems to have fallen off rather dramatically by the 1500s, perhaps as a result of an epidemic or, more probably, because of conflicts with tribes to the east which caused some of the Michigan Indians to flee to the west. Suddenly at the start of the seventeenth century other people began arriving from the east—not Indians but Europeans. Michigan's long prehistoric era had come to an end and its still brief historic era had begun. For the Indians, change would now be forced on them at a far faster pace than in the past.

As the French and then other Europeans came to Michigan, the meager and inconclusive information that can be gleaned from the archaeologists' findings is suddenly augmented by a growing mass of written records in which these newcomers told of what they found and saw. The information is often confusing and in some cases probably misleading if not erroneous. It is supplied by individuals who were, for the most part, ill-prepared to act as impartial observers of people and cultures totally different from their own. Accustomed only to their own ways, they were puzzled, astonished, and at times outraged by the ways of the Indians, and consequently their reports were often far from being sympathetic or unbiased accounts. The language barrier, furthermore, was a formidable obstacle to understanding. The Indians lacked any form of written language to which the Europeans could refer, and in attempting to phonetically repro-

Above: *The largest of the Norton Indian Mounds at Grand Rapids was excavated by a University of Michigan archaeological team in 1964. Courtesy, Grand Rapids Public Museum*

Below: *Excavating the Norton Indian Mounds at Grand Rapids, University of Michigan archaeologists found the skeletal remains of more than thirty individuals, such as this one, who had resided in Michigan 2,000 years ago. Bodies had been buried along the banks of the Grand River with a wide variety of artifacts. Courtesy, Grand Rapids Public Museum*

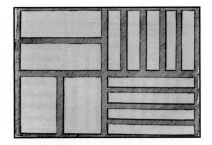

Above: *The most mysterious of prehistoric survivals were the garden beds found in the nineteenth century in southern Michigan. So-called because they consisted of ridges of earth in designs resembling formal gardens, they were found almost nowhere else. Their purpose is unknown and all traces were destroyed by the pioneers' plows. Courtesy, State Archives, Michigan Department of State*

Below: *These pieces of reassembled pottery, about 2,000 years old, were recovered from the Norton Mounds along the Grand River west of Grand Rapids. Courtesy, State Archives, Michigan Department of State*

duce the words and sounds they heard, the Europeans often found it difficult if not impossible to put them down on paper because the Indian way of speaking was so different. Thus, *Chippewa* and *Ojibwa* are two very different attempts to write down the name of one of Michigan's most important tribes. Similarly, the Indian geographical term that is most commonly written as Mackinac or Michilimackinac appears in the early documents in such wildly varying phonetic spellings that students of Indian linguistics are completely unable to agree as to what actual Indian term is represented by these spellings or what the term would have meant.

Inadequate as they often may be, these written records nevertheless provide a far more precise picture of seventeenth-century Indian life in the Great Lakes area than can be gained from the kinds of records available from earlier periods. For the first time we have descriptions of how these people dressed, their housing, what they or others called these people (not terms such as Hopewell, applied to prehistoric peoples by modern scholars), and even in a few instances details of the activities of individuals.

There were, it is clear, few Indians living in Michigan at the start of the historic era, certainly far fewer than the 39,714 listed as Indians in the 1980 census. The lower peninsula seems to have been virtually devoid of any people, save a few who might make occasional hunting or fishing forays into its northern areas for a few weeks out of the year. Those tribes that had lived in that peninsula in earlier years had moved across Lake Michigan to Wisconsin or beyond to escape the wrath of the several Iroquois tribes in New York. In the Upper Peninsula a band of Chippewa Indians was living along the waters of the river that connects Lake Superior with Lake Huron, a river that the French missionaries

would name the St. Mary's, hence the name of the village along the rapids *(sault*, in French) caused by the drop in lake levels: Sault Ste. Marie. The Chippewa were adept at fishing these fast-moving waters, as their ancestors had undoubtedly been doing for many years. Aside from one or two other small groups of Chippewa that may have been found at other points in Michigan's Upper Peninsula, the bulk of this tribe, one of the largest in North America with an estimated population of 30,000, was found scattered over a vast area north of Lake Superior. Living by hunting and fishing, they were scarcely affected by the changes that had resulted from the introduction of agriculture nearly 2,000 years earlier in regions farther to the south.

The only other Indians that can be located with any certainty in Michigan in the early 1600s are members of the Menominee tribe, a relatively small group living in the valley of the river that bears its name. The Menominee were woodland Indians and, like the Chippewa, still heavily depended on hunting and fishing for their food. But they were also famous for their use of the wild rice that grew abundantly in the river valley; from it they took their tribal name, said to mean "gatherers of wild rice."

Several other tribes would begin moving into Michigan by the late seventeenth century, moves that were largely the result of change instituted by white men and their activities. To the east, in the Georgian Bay area of what is now Ontario, lived the Huron Indians, who may have constituted half of the estimated 100,000 Indians living in the Upper Great Lakes area. More than any of these tribes, the Hurons were agriculturalists, and as a result were sedentary, not migratory, Indians. They lived in large villages, necessitating a well-developed system of political and social organization that made them favorites of the French, who felt that the Hurons' way of life came closer to that of the European civilizations. But in the 1640s the Hurons came under attack from the Iroquois tribes of New York, as both groups sought to play a dominant role in the developing trade with the Europeans. The Hurons were nearly wiped out and most of those who survived fled to the west, eventually settling at the Straits of Mackinac in northern Michigan by the 1670s. In the early 1700s the tribe moved near the new French settlement of Detroit, where they lived for over a century before being forced to move once again, ultimately west of the Mississippi.

The Ottawa Indians, neighbors of the Hurons in the early 1600s, were a tribe of a few thousand living on the islands in northern Lake Huron and on the adjacent mainland. Hunters and fishers more than farmers, the Ottawa were also noted for their abilities as traders, and like the Hurons, they were forced by the Iroquois to seek new homes to the west. Unlike the Hurons, however, the Ottawa would remain as permanent residents of Michigan, as many of them still live in the northern parts of the lower peninsula where their forefathers settled in the eighteenth century.

From the west, the Winnebago, Sac, and Fox tribes in Wisconsin would all be involved in events that from time to time affected Michigan, but the Pottawattami and Miami tribes, found in central and southern Wisconsin, moved from those areas to southern Michigan in the latter part of the seventeenth century. Subsequent events would result in the Miami leaving Michigan entirely by the nineteenth century, but although a large part of the Pottawattami tribe was forcibly removed to the west in the 1830s, some members of the tribe were able to remain in southwestern Michigan, where they reside to the present day. Other Pottawattami wound up in the western part of the Up-

per Peninsula on the Hannahville reservation.

For two centuries after the coming of the first non-Indians, the Indian residents of the Michigan area survived and lived according to their accustomed ways much better than did their fellow Indians to the east. There, the newcomers were mainly interested in clearing the forests and farming the land. To them, the Indians were a nuisance, to be moved off the land. In the Great Lakes region, however, the outsiders came to obtain furs, and for them the Indians were essential, since they hunted the fur-bearing animals and provided the desired furs. Thus the Hurons, the Chippewa, the Ottawa, the Pottawattami, and the others were encouraged to continue in their traditional hunting activities. They were vital to the fur trade's survival, and in time of war, when first the French and then the British found their claims to these lands threatened, the Indians were invaluable as allies.

In the early nineteenth century, however, these conditions ceased to exist. Supporters of an agricultural economy rapidly began moving into the Great Lakes region, forcing the Indians off their land and clearing the forests, thereby ending the days of the fur

The clothes they wear and the boats they use are different, but these Chippewa Indians in the late nineteenth century are doing what their ancestors had done for centuries and what their descendants would continue to do—fish the rapids of the St. Mary's River. Courtesy, State Archives, Michigan Department of State

Andrew J. Blackbird (right) *goes farther than necessary in this photograph to emphasize his Indian background. The pride evident in this display and in his face, however, stands in sharp contrast with the sad, defeated figure of Chief Okemos* (far right), *photographed some years earlier in the 1850s. Courtesy, State Archives, Michigan Department of State*

Geologist, explorer, and Indian agent in Michigan in the 1820s and 1830s, Henry R. Schoolcraft married a Sault Ste. Marie woman whose mother was a Chippewa, and strove to help the Indians adjust to the white man's ways. Through a series of scholarly studies he sought to explain the Indian culture to the non-Indian world, studies which were the inspiration for Longfellow's Hiawatha. Courtesy, State Archives, Michigan Department of State

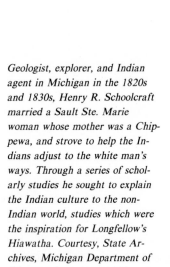

trade. At the same time wars between rival powers seeking dominance over this part of North America came to an end, thus removing the need for a respectful attitude toward Indians who might be allies or enemies in case of such a war. The effect on the Indians was devastating. They had stubbornly opposed efforts to change their ways of thinking to those of the white man, but at the same time they had become dependent on the white man to supply them with the material features of the white man's culture that the Indians had eagerly adopted—blankets, iron kettles, guns, and numerous other things, including, regrettably, liquor. Now that they had ceased to be important to the white man, the Indians frequently had to resort to humiliating tactics to receive these items. In the mid-nineteenth century, for example, Okemos, an elderly Indian leader of either Chippewa or Ottawa background, was a familiar sight in Lansing, where he and some of his fellow tribesmen begged for favors.

To preserve their self-respect or simply to survive, more and more Indians abandoned the life of the past and sought to adapt to the new conditions. Andrew J. Blackbird, an Ottawa

Indian born in northern Michigan, in the mid-nineteenth century enrolled in what is now Eastern Michigan University in Ypsilanti, where he was a student for two-and-a-half years before lack of funds forced him to drop out of school. He then became a government Indian interpreter and later was postmaster for eleven years at Harbor Springs in the area where he had been born. At the same time that he took advantage of the job opportunities in the white man's society, however, Blackbird did not forget the society from which he had come, completing in the 1880s a history of the Ottawa and Chippewa Indians that remains one of the rare accounts of these peoples not written by an outsider.

By the mid-twentieth century the great majority of Michigan's residents of Indian background had moved into the mainstream of the state's population. Many held jobs in the urban areas of southern Michigan where the fact that they were Indians made them no more different in most people's minds than any of the communities' other numerous ethnic and racial groups. Only a minority of Indians continued to live in northern Michigan, where the environment, whether on the four federal reservations or in other parts of this sparsely populated region, was more conducive to the preservation of a more distinctively Indian way of life.

In recent years, some Michigan Indians, affected by the more militant attitudes emerging among Indians across the country, began to assert their rights more vigorously. Through the Indian Claims Commission established by Congress in 1946, they have fought for, and frequently obtained, substantial additional payments for lands which their ancestors had bargained away in treaties signed in the early nineteenth century. In 1980 a federal district court agreed with the claims of northern Michigan Indian commercial fishermen that the terms of an 1836 Indian land treaty exempted them from the fishing restrictions imposed by the state. After disputes between Indian and non-Indian fishermen, an agreement, signed by tribal leaders and state and federal officials on March 28, 1985, established the boundaries of the lake waters assigned to Indian commercial fishermen and those reserved for non-Indian commercial fishermen and sport fishing. Committees comprised of tribal and governmental representatives were set up to administer the agreement and to resolve disputes that might arise. Some Indians expressed dissatisfaction with the agreement, contending that the tribes had given up too much. Other Indians, however, supported the view of one tribal spokesman who declared that, by ending the uncertainty and controversy that had followed the 1980 court decision, the agreement would enable the Indians "to more effectively manage their resource, both biologically and economically, to bring the greatest and most long-lasting benefit possible to Indian fishermen." After nearly four centuries it was clear that Michigan's Indians, like their prehistoric ancestors, had learned how to adapt to change.

Above: *Women and children seeking to eke out a living through basket weaving in a northern Michigan village testify to the wretched conditions Indians had to endure in the late nineteenth century—conditions that would show little or no improvement in the years ahead. Courtesy, Grand Rapids Public Library*

Below: *After three days of intense negotiations, the seated representatives of Indian groups, federal and state agencies, and sportsmen's organizations are visibly relieved as the Tribal Fishing Agreement is signed on March 28, 1985. Looking on are the attorneys who represented each interested party. Photo by Liz Rafaele. Courtesy,* Sault Ste. Marie Evening News

EUROPEANS AND THE FUR TRADE

One of the first Europeans the Michigan Indians met was Etienne Brule, a young Frenchman who began exploring the Great Lakes area shortly after the colony of New France established a permanent settlement with the founding of Quebec in 1608. Samuel de Champlain, the long-time leader of the colony, assigned Brule to find out more about the land and the peoples to the west, and also to see if the waters that emptied into the St. Lawrence might somehow be part of a waterway upon which the French could reach the Orient and its fabled riches. These goals would draw the French ever deeper into the North American continent and would lead them to Michigan in a period when the colonial activities of their English rivals were confined to the eastern coastal areas of what is now the United States.

By around 1610 Brule was making the Huron villages at the head of Georgian Bay his base of operations. From there, he and another Frenchman known only to us by his last name, Grenoble, set off about 1620 to find the largest of the great inland lakes. Traveling northward along the shores of

Georgian Bay and northern Lake Huron, Brule and Grenoble threaded their way through the maze of islands in the St. Mary's River, along whose banks they met the Chippewa Indians. Making their way through the rapids at the site of the present city of Sault Ste. Marie, the Frenchmen went on into Lake Superior, so named by the French not because it was the greatest of these lakes but because it was situated above the others.

Because he was illiterate, Brule left no records of his explorations. The brief references to him in the writings of others do not enable us to positively date this first known visit of a non-Indian to what would become Michigan, or to know how far into Lake Superior he traveled. However, before he met his death at the hands of some Hurons, Brule's discoveries had made it possible for Champlain by the end of the 1620s to greatly improve the maps that he included in his reports on the colony. They showed for the first time the St. Mary's rapids that would be a barrier to the free flow of water traffic between Lake Huron and Lake Superior until the mid-nineteenth century.

Michigan was, for nearly a century and a half, part of an area developed by the French. In this map published in 1632, the man principally responsible for the start of that development, Samuel de Champlain, depicted New France as it was then known to him, including Lake Superior (Grand Lac) and the rapids (Sault) that carried its waters into Lake Huron (Mer douce). Courtesy, Library of Congress

Known as the "Father of Canada," Samuel de Champlain deserves to be called at least the grandfather of Michigan, for it was he who set in motion the explorations that brought the French to Michigan by the 1620s, if not sooner. From Cirker, Dictionary of American Portraits, *Dover, 1967*

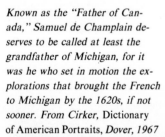

In 1634, Champlain dispatched Jean Nicolet to continue the work Brule had begun, this time in the areas west of Lake Huron. The French had deluded themselves into believing that on the western shores of these freshwater seas they would find outposts of China, if not China itself. Although the sources of information on Nicolet's activities are nearly as vague as those dealing with Brule's, it appears that Nicolet canoed through the Straits of Mackinac, along the Lake Michigan shore of the Upper Peninsula, and on into Green Bay. There, at the site of the Wisconsin city that is so familiar to football fans, Nicolet encountered some Winnebago Indians who were as surprised to see him as he was to see them. They were not, he must have realized immediately, the Oriental people he had been hoping to find.

It took an astonishingly long time before the French were finally convinced that the Great Lakes were not part of a practical route to the treasures of the Indies for which so many Europeans had been searching since Columbus's day. Yet the explorations of Brule, Nicolet, and others, while a failure in that respect, provided a growing body of knowledge which the French began to realize could be put to other uses. Out of this realization would

come the first European settlements in Michigan.

The best documented of the French activities for many years were those of the Catholic missionaries, who as early as 1614 had settled among the Huron Indians in the Georgian Bay area, trying to convert them to Catholicism and the European way of life. By the 1630s this work had come under the control of the Jesuits, and it was from the Jesuit mission among the Hurons that fathers Isaac Jogues and Charles Raymbault in the summer of 1641 retraced Brule's route of two decades earlier. The priests spent some weeks among the Chippewa Indians at Sault Ste. Marie, where they conducted the first Christian services ever held in Michigan. Later that year they returned to the Huron villages, where Jogues was one of several Jesuits killed during the Iroquois attacks later in the 1640s that destroyed the Huron villages and forced the handful of surviving Hurons to flee far to the west. The Jesuits found the survivors on the shores of Lake Superior and established a new mission near present-day Ashland, Wisconsin, on Chequamegon Bay, an impressive Chippewa Indian term whose meaning is again uncertain.

Following this resumption of Great Lakes missionary work, there arrived in the area the most celebrated of the missionaries, Father Jacques Marquette, a sturdy young Frenchman who had been preparing for this kind of life since he was a small boy in France. Now in 1668, after two years in New France, he was sent by his superiors to establish a mission at Sault Ste. Marie. By the end of the year, Marquette and his helper had built a chapel and house enclosed within a wooden stockade, thereby inaugurating the European settlement of Michigan. After some thirty years the Jesuits abandoned this mission, but because its location along the river linking the largest of the Great Lakes was too important to be vacated for long, it would be the site of another French settlement later in the eighteenth century.

Marquette went on in 1671 to establish a second mission, this time on the north side of the Straits of Mackinac at the site of the city of St. Ignace, a name Marquette chose for his mission to honor the founder of the Jesuit order. Marquette's colleagues, especially Father Claude Allouez, were equally diligent in pursuing the goals of the missionaries in the region, establishing other missions at Green Bay and, in the late 1680s, at the site of present-day Niles in southwestern Michigan. Important as their religious

work may have been to these priests, however, French colonial authorities were more interested in how their work could contribute to the advancement of France's imperial goals. Thus in 1671 the Jesuits helped to gather a large crowd of Indians at Sault Ste. Marie, where Father Allouez exhorted them to be loyal to the French king, whose great power Allouez graphically described in terms meant to impress his listeners. Afterwards a French official, the Sieur de St. Lusson, laid formal claim to these interior lands, whose boundaries were described vaguely enough to encompass many areas that the French had yet to explore.

Two years later Father Marquette accompanied Louis Jolliet on the most famous of these French explorations into an area previously known to the French only through what the Indians had told them. With their French canoemen, Jolliet and Marquette proceeded from St. Ignace along the northern shores of Lake Michigan into Green Bay and from there by river and portage to the Mississippi. They followed that river southward as far as the point where it is joined by the waters of the Arkansas, and then they turned around and came back north through Illinois to Lake Michigan. The geographical information that Jolliet

By 1672, when this famous Jesuit map of the upper Great Lakes was published, French explorations since Champlain's time had led to an image of the area that remains recognizable to anyone familiar with the area 300 years later. These explorations had also resulted in the first French settlements in Michigan—the Mission de Ste. Marie du Sault and the Mission de St. Ignace. Courtesy, Library of Congress

Champlain's decision in 1609 to assist Indians from the St. Lawrence Valley in this clash with the Iroquois Indians in New York led to the routing of the Iroquois, who had never encountered guns. For a century the Iroquois would be bitter enemies of the French, with important consequences for Michigan. Courtesy, State Archives, Michigan Department of State

As a passenger in 1679 aboard the Griffin, the first sailing vessel on the upper Great Lakes, Father Louis Hennepin, shown here in a 1694 portrait by an unknown artist, saw the eastern shore of the lower peninsula. Describing what is now the Detroit area, he declared that those fortunate enough "to possess this fertile and pleasant strait will be much obliged to those who have shown them the way." Courtesy, Minnesota Historical Society

brought back forced French cartographers to correct many of their previous misconceptions of America's midsection. Marquette, meanwhile, returned to the Illinois country on what proved to be his final mission, for in the spring of 1675, his once-robust health shattered, he sought to return to St. Ignace where he might die in the company of his fellow Jesuits. Instead, he died along the Lake Michigan shore of the lower peninsula, probably at Ludington, at the mouth of the river that has long borne his name. However, other Michigan cities along this shore have entered their rather ghoulish claims to having been the place where this renowned missionary died.

Marquette's companions on his final journey were two French canoemen, representatives of a new breed of Frenchmen known as the voyageurs, who had learned the time-honored ways the Indians had used to travel in this vast continent. Although their services were vital to the missionaries and explorers, these men were in far greater demand by those engaged in the fur trade.

Some French merchants in the late sixteenth century realized that Canada was an enormous untapped source of furs, which aroused their interest in establishing New France so European trade goods could be exchanged for Indian furs. As the supply of furs, especially beaver pelts, declined in eastern Canada, the traders had to look to more distant areas for their furs. For some years the Hurons acted as middlemen, taking furs from the Great Lakes Indian tribes down to the trading posts on the St. Lawrence and returning with enough trade goods to meet their needs and those of the Indians to the west. The Iroquois attacks on the Hurons in the 1640s are believed to have been motivated largely by these New York Indians' desire to drive away the tribe that was preventing them from assuming a similar role in the trade with the

Dutch in the Hudson Valley. When the Hurons were eliminated, the French were forced to move directly into the Great Lakes region to protect their interests from their rivals the Dutch and the English, who took over the Dutch colony in the 1660s. By the 1670s hundreds of fur traders and their voyageur employees, who provided the muscle power required to bring the trade goods by canoe to the Indian villages and the furs back to Montreal and Quebec, were coming into the Michigan area every year. Sault Ste. Marie, St. Ignace, and the other missions now became convenient advance bases for the trade, located as they always were on important water routes.

In the 1680s the Iroquois sought to terrorize Great Lakes tribes into trading with them and abandoning the French, and the fur trading partners of the Iroquois, the English, came out of New York all the way up to the Straits of Mackinac. The French acted quickly to maintain their monopoly of the Great Lakes trade by stationing soldiers in this area for the first time, both as a means of keeping out the handful of English intruders and to bolster Indian resistance to the continuing Iroquois raids. The southern entrance to Lake Huron at the modern site of Port Huron, Michigan, was briefly fortified in the mid-1680s, and in the mid-1690s a more permanent military post, named Fort St. Joseph after the river it guarded, was established near the Jesuit mission in southwestern Michigan. But the most important of these French forts was that at St. Ignace, guarding the Straits of Mackinac. In its heyday in the 1690s it had a garrison of 100 soldiers.

The French soldiers succeeded not only in turning back the challenge of the Iroquois and the English, but also in stimulating the fur trade with their presence in the Michigan area. As a result, the market in France was soon glutted by a flood of furs being shipped out of New France. King Louis XIV, in response to the pleas of French fur merchants, moved to stem this flow of furs in 1696 by ordering all soldiers and fur traders to withdraw from the posts in the West, save one in Illinois. Within a couple of years the French soldiers at Fort St. Joseph and St. Ignace were gone, as were most of the fur traders, although some ignored the commands of their distant monarch and stayed. Even the Jesuits, who had not been ordered to leave, abandoned their mission at Sault Ste. Marie at the end of the century. Michigan seemed about to revert to the conditions of an earlier day when the area was inhabited only by Indians who, if they wanted the guns, blankets, iron kettles, and trinkets that the fur traders had to offer, would have to travel to the French settlements on the St. Lawrence.

During this same period of the late seventeenth century, however, Europe became engulfed in a succession of wars in which France and Great Britain, together with assorted allies, fought over the desires of Louis XIV and the kings who succeeded him to increase France's power. The first of these wars, which spread from Europe to North America in 1689 and became known in American history as King William's War, had little impact on Michigan. But shortly after its end in 1697, Louis XIV began to see in his North American possessions a means of hemming in the English along the Atlantic coast. Thus, within a few years after ordering the withdrawal of French forces from Michigan and other western areas, the French king authorized the return of French soldiers to the West, this time for imperial, not economic, reasons. To control the continent's interior, strongholds were established in the early eighteenth century on the Mississippi River at New Orleans and upriver in southern Illinois, and at Detroit, on the narrow waterway (the French term for which

Born in Detroit in 1860, Gari Melchers studied and taught painting in Europe for many years but returned to his hometown to paint several murals in the Detroit Public Library. This one depicts the arrival of Cadillac's wife in Detroit a few months after he founded the town in 1701. Courtesy, Detroit Public Library

was *detroit*) that connects Lake Huron and Lake Erie.

Detroit is really Michigan's oldest permanent settlement. It has been continuously occupied since its founding on July 24, 1701, whereas such earlier settlements as Sault Ste. Marie, St. Ignace, and Niles were abandoned after a few years and later reoccupied. In addition, those earlier French outposts had been male communities, occupied by missionaries, soldiers, and fur traders, none of whom, probably, looked upon his residence as more than a temporary one. Detroit, on the other hand, was intended by its founder, Antoine de la Mothe Cadillac, to be a real community that would be home to French families making their living there, as it would be for their children after them. The often high-handed methods Cadillac used to promote his settlement and himself caused a rash of complaints from the new town's residents, who regarded Cadillac with none of the affection expressed in recent years by Detroit history buffs, some of whom have gone as far as to pay for the preservation of Cadillac's birthplace in France. French colo-

Beginning in 1959, archaeologists employed by the Mackinac Island State Park Commission began the systematic excavation of the grounds within the old fort's reconstructed stockade on the Lake Michigan side of the Straits of Mackinac. They unlocked a treasure trove of eighteenth-century materials. Courtesy, State Archives, Michigan Department of State

nial officials, heeding the complaints against Cadillac, transferred him to Louisiana in 1710, by which time Cadillac's plans for Detroit had enjoyed only modest success. They fared little better under Cadillac's successors during the next half century. Relatively few Frenchmen took the opportunity to obtain and farm land along the Detroit River or practice a trade within the narrow confines of the little stockaded town on the river where today's Detroit Civic Center stands. For many of those who did settle at Detroit, the lure of the fur trade and the greater potential for profit that it seemed to offer proved too strong an attraction, and the French hopes of making Detroit the supply point for the scattered outposts of the upper Great Lakes were never fulfilled.

As part of his plans, Cadillac had also sought to persuade Indian tribes from around the Great Lakes to relocate in the Detroit area. This would facilitate French trade with these Indians and make it easier to achieve the long-range goal of assimilating these people into the French culture. Cadillac had much greater success in persuading Indians to come to Detroit than he did in persuading Frenchmen. Shortly after Detroit was established, Ottawas and the remnants of the Huron tribe moved down from the Straits of Mackinac area, where they had lived for some years, and made the Detroit area their home for many decades. Elements of the Chippewa, Pottawattami, and Mi-

ami tribes also settled in the southeast-ern Michigan region where few, if any, Indians had lived for many years prior to the founding of Detroit.

The departure of the Hurons and Ottawas for Detroit forced the Jesuits to give up their mission at St. Ignace by 1705, but within a decade other Frenchmen returned to maintain French control of this strategic avenue of trade. Rather than reoccupy the site of the old fort on the north side of the straits, however, the French chose a new site on the south side to build a fort that they called Michilimackinac, the geographical name of that area. Unlike other sites dating from the French period, that on which the fort was erected, although lying on the outskirts

of the present community of Mackinaw City, remained relatively undisturbed after it was abandoned in the late eigh-teenth century. As a result, an am-bitious and ongoing archaeological examination of the site since 1959 has uncovered an enormous collection of eighteenth-century artifacts and other kinds of data relating to the structures that once stood on the site. These finds and other archival materials have en-abled much of the long-vanished forti-fied settlement to be reconstructed, giving the visitor a feeling for what life must have been like in that French community that is not possible at the modern communities of Detroit, Sault Ste. Marie, St. Ignace, and Niles, where the evidence of early French set-

Within a few years after the transfer of the fort from the south side of the Straits of Mackinac over to Mackinac Island in the 1780s, there was little to remind one of the busy settlement that had existed there through much of the eighteenth century. Courtesy, State Archives, Michigan Depart-ment of State

On the footings of the original buildings that the archaeologists had uncovered, the park commission began the job of re-creating the old Fort Michilimackinac, just to the west of the Mackinac Bridge. Historical accuracy did not, however, necessarily extend to all the materials used in the buildings' reconstruction. Courtesy, State Archives, Michigan Department of State

tlements has been obliterated by subsequent developments.

Because of its strategic position and the efforts made there to encourage a more diversified economy, Detroit was the largest of the French settlements in Michigan in the eighteenth century. For the fur trade, however, Michilimackinac was more important because it was the base for French trading operations far to the west and the north where the best furs were obtained. The threat to these operations from the expanding activities of the English Hudson's Bay Company to the north led the French to establish a small fort at Sault Ste. Marie in the early 1750s. This action, together with the earlier reoccupation of Fort St. Joseph at present-day Niles, rounds out the story of organized settlements in the latter years of Michigan's French period.

Those settlements existed because of the fur trade, since they were designed to give the French control of the main routes that trade followed. Through the middle of the eighteenth century the French continued to successfully fend off the efforts of the English in New York and on Hudson Bay to take over the Great Lakes trade. To be sure, the French had some uneasy moments in the 1740s during King George's War, the American phase of the latest European conflict resulting

from rival dynastic interests. At that time Miami Indians in northern Ohio openly began trading with the English, a move which, had it spread to other tribes to the north, could have undermined French control of Michigan. However, the other tribes remained loyal to the French, and in 1752, after the war was over, a war party of Michigan Indians overwhelmingly defeated the Miami at their village near the present town of Piqua, Ohio. They were led by a French officer, Charles Langlade, a remarkable Michigan native whose father was French and whose mother was an Ottawa Indian. The English traders found at the village were taken prisoner, and the French voyageurs employed by these traders were summarily executed.

Such ruthless tactics sufficiently enabled the French to maintain their century-old control of the Great Lakes fur trade, but they were not enough to deal with a far more serious threat than that presented by a relatively small number of English fur traders. Most of the settlers in the English colonies along the Atlantic were interested not in the fur trade, but in farming. By 1750, these settlers, outnumbering those in New France by about thirty to one, were looking to the lands beyond the Appalachians to expand their agricultural economy. These were the lands that the French had long claimed and where they had carried on their widely scattered trading activities. Several English colonies, however, claimed that their royal charters gave them the rights to portions of these same lands. Virginia claimed most of the American Middle West, including Michigan. It was Virginia's effort to move over the Appalachians into the Ohio Valley and the determination of the French to keep the Virginians out that touched off the final colonial conflict between Great Britain and France, one that started in 1754 in North America rather than as an outgrowth of a war between the home countries in Europe.

English colonists dubbed the conflict "the French and Indian War" because the French and the Indians stood in the way of the English colonies' expansion to the west, and for several years the forces opposed to the English had the upper hand in the fighting. No combat took place in Michigan or anywhere nearby, but Michigan Indians led by Charles Langlade constantly fought on the battlefronts to the east, seeking to defeat those who desired to destroy the wilderness environment upon which the traditional way of Indian life depended. In 1755, in fact, Langlade and his Indian warriors were responsible for the most famous French victory in the war when they ambushed and routed British forces led by General Edward Braddock that were advancing on a French fort at the site of the city of Pittsburgh, guarding the gateway to the Ohio Valley. But eventually the superior power of the British prevailed, and at his surrender of Montreal in September 1760, the governor of New France also surrendered the remaining French lands to the west, including Michigan. Members of the Royal American Regiment, commanded by Major Robert Rogers of Rogers' Rangers fame, were immediately sent west to secure control of the surrendered outposts. On November 29 they arrived at Detroit, where the local

French commander, after being notified of the surrender, turned the fort over to Rogers. The British flag for the first time replaced the French flag that had flown there for nearly sixty years.

The onset of winter delayed the occupation of Michilimackinac and the other French forts until late in the following summer. Finally, in 1763, in the treaty that ended a war that had eventually spread from the colonies to Europe and elsewhere in the world, France formally ceded Michigan and its other possessions east of the Mississippi to Great Britain—an event that is usually said to have ended Michigan's French period. Such was indeed the case if that term refers to the period of French political control that now gave way to the British, represented by the British soldiers who had taken over the forts from their departed French garrisons. But the French civilians remained and until the 1820s would continue to comprise the majority of Michigan's non-Indian population. The fur trade, which the French had introduced in Michigan in the seventeenth century, remained the dominant economic activity until well into the nineteenth century. With the skills acquired through generations of experience in the business, the French were much in demand, even though the fur trade was now controlled by a different nationality. New economic interests in the nineteenth and twentieth centuries would attract great numbers of settlers from different backgrounds and would make the French an increasingly minor ethnic element in Michigan, but the place names encountered—not only Detroit and Sault Ste. Marie but Grosse Pointe, Grand Marais, Presque Isle, Marquette, and a host of others—and the names found today in the phone books of numerous Michigan communities are enough to dispel any notion that the impact of these first European immigrants was in any way minor or forgotten.

In Gros Cap Cemetery just west of St. Ignace, this grave marker for Edward Poupard's wife, Josephine, who died in 1881— "May her soul rest in peace, Amen"—reflects the continuing importance of the French in the northern areas. The cemetery, certainly one of Michigan's oldest, was an Indian burial ground perhaps as early as 1710 and it continues to serve the community to the present time. Photo by Margaret Beattie Bogue

CHAPTER IV

THE AMERICAN ERA BEGINS

General Anthony Wayne, a veteran of the American Revolution, brought the Indians in the Northwest under control and thereby paved the way for the American takeover of Michigan in 1796. He died late that year on his way back east from Detroit. Today, innumerable places, organizations, and businesses in Michigan are named for him. Courtesy, State Archives, Michigan Department of State

On July 4, 1776, the day the United States was born, Charles Langlade was leaving Michilimackinac on an assignment that was part of the British effort to suppress the rebellion of their thirteen colonies to the east. Langlade's willingness to fight for those whom he had so bitterly and capably opposed only a decade and a half earlier dramatically illustrates Great Britain's success in winning support among the residents of the Michigan area. In fact, the British made Michigan their base of operations in the West during the American Revolution.

Gaining that support had not been easy, however. The French residents had accepted the change to British control in the early 1760s with resignation, if not enthusiasm, but for the Indians the adjustment was much more difficult. To them this was still their land. They had for many years accepted the French because the fur traders provided the Indians with material benefits without significantly threatening their traditional life. Had the British heeded the advice of their own fur traders, such as Alexander Henry, Indian acceptance of the British would have

been achieved far more readily. Henry arrived at Michilimackinac in 1761 some months before British soldiers and, after some admittedly tense moments, was able to begin trading with the Indians. But British officials were generally insensitive to the feelings of the Indians, and the Indians feared that their presence heralded the imminent arrival of American settlers who would drive them off their land and transform the wilderness into farms, as settlers had done in the East. Consequently, in 1763 Indians in the Detroit area, led by the Ottawa chieftain Pontiac, sought to expel the British. Foiled in his initial plan in May to capture the British-held fort by catching its garrison off guard, Pontiac launched a six-month siege of Detroit in an effort to force the British to surrender. His actions inspired Indians elsewhere, and within a few weeks the areas from Michigan south to the Ohio River and east to the New York-Pennsylvania frontier were engulfed in the greatest Indian uprising in American history.

In Michigan, the handful of soldiers stationed at Fort St. Joseph were surprised and overwhelmed by Indians

In a mural painted for the Detroit Public Library, Gari Melchers sought to depict the dramatic meeting of Pontiac with the British commander, Henry Gladwin, on which occasion the soldiers standing guard warned Pontiac that the surprise he had counted on was not present. In depicting Gladwin, Melchers could work from an actual portrait, but Pontiac's features were strictly a guess. Courtesy, Detroit Public Library

late in May 1763. Early in June at the Straits of Mackinac, in a classic variation on the Trojan Horse tactic, Indians engaged in a seemingly innocent game of lacrosse, as it is now called, used the excuse of retrieving a lost ball as a way of entering the fort. Once inside, they proceeded to attack the unsuspecting soldiers, killing half of them and making the rest prisoners. This Indian triumph, which non-Indian writers predictably called the Massacre at Michilimackinac, is one of the high points in the campaign to oust the British from these western areas and was shortly followed by a decline in Indian fortunes.

Pontiac's siege operations at Detroit, although exacting a heavy toll of British defenders, could not halt the arrival of some supplies and reinforcements by lake vessels from Niagara. In the fall Pontiac's forces began to dwindle as more and more of his warriors returned to their villages to care for their families during the coming winter. Finally, at the end of October, Pontiac received word that France had permanently transferred its lands to the British earlier in the year, meaning

that there was no longer any possibility, as Pontiac had hoped, of French soldiers joining the Indians in their campaign. Realizing that he was beaten, Pontiac broke off the siege and left the area after sending the local British commander, Major Henry Gladwin, a message in which the great Indian leader showed himself to be a rather gracious loser, expressing hope that the Indians and the British could eventually become reconciled to each other.

Pontiac can not be said to have completely failed to achieve what he had been fighting for. Although British military forces from Niagara and Fort Pitt were used to restore peace in 1764, British colonial officials in London, upon hearing of the violent Indian uprising, had recognized the need to adopt policies that would resolve their grievances. The result was the Proclamation of 1763, which, among other provisions, prohibited any new settlements west of the Appalachians. This action had been strongly advocated by British fur trading interests, who had no wish to see farmers move into these lands and destroy the conditions upon which the traders depended for their

furs. The proclamation removed the major obstacle to improved relations with the Indians, most of whom were soon persuaded that the British, like the French before them, would protect the Indians' rights to the lands. Pontiac himself became strongly pro-British in the late 1760s, and his efforts to convince Indians in the Midwest of the wisdom of such an attitude apparently led to his assassination in 1769 by Indians in Illinois who continued to be hostile toward the British.

The British policy regarding the lands beyond the Appalachians, while pleasing the Indians, highly displeased the colonists along the Atlantic who had thought the defeat of the French would open the door to westward expansion. Many colonists soon viewed the Proclamation of 1763 as the first in a series of British actions aimed at restricting the colonies' development, eventually leading them to seek independence from British control. The American revolutionists' opposition to the British western land policies, in turn, made it easy to convince the In-

dians that their interests were best served by helping the British defeat the Americans. It apparently did not take much persuading either to convince Charles Langlade, who had retired to Wisconsin, to resume his familiar role of organizer and leader of Indians in guerilla-type attacks against the Americans.

Langlade and others led these attacks on the new settlements established by Virginians in Kentucky, which caused Kentuckians under George Rogers Clark to take the offensive in defense of their homes. Clark's ultimate goal was to capture Detroit and Michilimackinac, the bases where the British and Indian raids originated, but initially in the fall of 1778 Clark occupied the advance bases these raiders had used in southern Indiana and Illinois. In 1779 Clark successfully defended the bases, turning back troops led by the British commander in Detroit, Henry Hamilton.

Anticipating an American attack, the British at Detroit and the Straits of Mackinac abandoned the old French

When the seafaring British took over Michigan they immediately made far more use of sailing vessels than had the French. One such vessel was the Welcome *owned by John Askin, a fur trader at Michilimackinac. The British navy took over the vessel in 1779 and used it to transport materials to Mackinac Island, where a new fort was being built. The ship sank in 1781 but was reconstructed by the Mackinac Island State Park Commission in the late 1970s at Mackinaw City. Photo by Margaret Beattie Bogue*

forts built early in the century, moving to new fortifications that could be more easily defended. At Detroit the British built a new fort a short distance back from the river in the area where the Federal Building and the Comerica (formerly Detroit Bank and Trust) headquarters now stand. The change at the straits was more drastic, as the British moved from the fort on the south side of that waterway over to Mackinac Island. There they constructed a fort atop a bluff on the south side of the island, and by 1780 the garrison had transferred to the third and last fort to guard the area during the past three centuries. The fort, with its numerous additions made in later years, remains the center of attention for the hordes of tourists who descend upon the historic island each summer. The fur traders and other residents of the community on the south side of the straits soon followed the soldiers over to the island, leaving the remnants of the old French settlement to be buried under the sands along Lake Michigan.

As it turned out, the British were needlessly concerned about the threat of an American attack because George Rogers Clark was never able to secure the support he needed to launch his invasion of Michigan. The British recov-

ered from the defeats suffered in 1778 and 1779 and reestablished their control of much of the area from the Great Lakes to the Ohio River, even resuming the raids into Kentucky that Clark had sought to end. Thus, when the American and British negotiators met in Paris to draw up the treaty that would recognize the independence of Britain's thirteen colonies along the East Coast, the question of the continued British possession of Michigan would not seem to have been a matter for much discussion. Yet, in deciding on the boundaries of the new nation, the British agreed to include Michigan and much of the Great Lakes region as part of the territory of the United States.

The British generosity partly stemmed from a desire to please the Americans and thereby encourage them to resume the close economic ties they had had with the British in the years before the Revolution. Furthermore, the British gave the Americans the lands north of the Ohio River in order to avoid any chance that some or all of these lands would fall into the hands of Spain. That country's claim was the result of one of the most puzzling events of the American Revolution, one in which a Spanish force from St. Louis had moved up through Illinois and in February 1781 occupied Fort St. Joseph in southwestern Michigan for twenty-four hours before returning to St. Louis. Historians have never been able to agree upon what the Spanish were hoping to achieve by this short-lived capture of a fort where no soldiers had been stationed since Pontiac's War in 1763. But aside from giving Niles the honor of being the only Michigan city over which the flags of four nations have flown, the capture gave Spanish negotiators at the peace talks in Europe an opportunity to declare that as a participant in the war against the British they were entitled to territory east of the Mississippi by reason of conquest. The British foiled this maneuver by giving the Americans everything east of the Mississippi, which had formed the boundary between the British and the Spanish colonial empires in North America.

When the treaty was signed and formally accepted in 1783, the award of the Michigan area to the United States infuriated the British fur traders, since it threatened to end their use of the vital trade route that passed through the area. The Indians also felt betrayed by the action of these Europeans who, like the French twenty years earlier, had transferred control of their lands to the very people they had fought to keep out. As a result, the British government, for two decades a model of indecisiveness in dealing with its North American interests, proceeded to keep its troops in Detroit and Michilimackinac and other Great Lakes posts for thirteen years after it was supposed to have ceded the area to the United States. The action raised false hopes among the fur traders and the Indians that the British, despite what the treaty said, were committed to maintaining the status quo in the Great Lakes.

In 1796, conflicts between the British and the French in Europe helped the United States persuade the British to pull their forces out of Michigan. During the same period the United States, with the emergence of a strong government under the Constitution and George Washington, forced the Indians after a prolonged and bloody war to allow Americans to settle on some of the lands north of the Ohio. On July 11, 1796, members of an American regiment commanded by Lieutenant Colonel John Francis Hamtramck arrived at Detroit and took over the fort from the departing British garrison. Although his name is attached to an enclave in Detroit that has long been known as the most solidly Polish community in America, Hamtramck was not Polish but French-

Canadian, one of the relatively few who sided with the Americans during their War for Independence. General Anthony Wayne, the victor in the war with the Indians, arrived in August, and his name is attached today to a county, a city, a university, and innumerable businesses in southeastern Michigan. With the arrival of American forces on Mackinac Island in September the American occupation of Michigan was complete.

Michigan now became part of the Northwest Territory, the political unit Congress had provided in 1787 to administer the area north of the Ohio River and west of Pennsylvania after the British had agreed to vacate the premises. As the southeastern part of the territory began to fill up, Ohio in 1803 became the first of the new states that the act of 1787 had declared would ultimately be carved out of this huge region. Following Ohio's admission to the Union, the remainder of the old Northwest Territory went through a series of reorganizations out of which emerged a territory in 1805 that for the first time bore the name Michigan, although it included more land in the south and much less in the north than what would be included in the state of Michigan when it emerged in the 1830s. William Hull, a native of Massachusetts, was appointed Michigan's first governor, and on June 30, 1805, he and the territory's other appointed officials began to perform their duties at the territorial capital in Detroit.

In spite of the presence of American officials, American soldiers, and the American flag, American control of Michigan was in actuality quite tenuous. When the British forces left Michigan in 1796 they had taken up quarters just across the border at Amherstburg, across the Detroit River from Detroit, and to the north at St. Joseph Island in the St. Mary's River. From these posts British Indian agents were able to maintain the close ties they

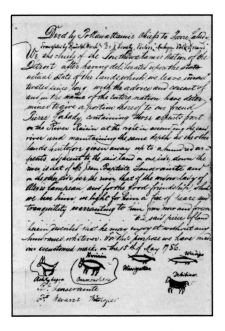

The close links between the French and the Indians are indicated in deeds such as this, dated May 15, 1786, in which Pottawattami chiefs granted land along the River Raisin to "our friend Pierre Labady." Determining the precise boundaries of such grants was the major job of federal surveyors in the early days of American occupation. Courtesy, State Archives, Michigan Department of State

This portrait of Tecumseh, the authenticity of which has been often questioned, shows the great Indian wearing a British officer's coat. To the frontiersmen this confirmed their belief that he was only a tool of the British who wished to prevent the further spread of farming in the Northwest. Courtesy, Bureau of American Ethnology, Smithsonian Institution. From Cirker, Dictionary of American Portraits, *Dover, 1967*

had developed with Michigan's Indians who, despite what had happened since 1783, felt more comfortable dealing with the British than they did with the Americans. The British also continued to dominate Michigan's fur trade, because when the British government agreed to remove its troops from Michigan it had insisted that the lands remain open to British traders.

In 1810, Michigan's non-Indian population was only 4,672, the bulk of it, as it is today, concentrated in the southeast. There, in addition to Detroit, some settlement had spread north along the shores of Lake St. Clair, inland as far as what is now Ypsilanti, and south at scattered points as far as present-day Monroe, known then as Frenchtown after the French farmers who had begun to locate there in the 1780s. In southwestern Michigan a handful of settlers lived at the site of old Fort St. Joseph, while in the north Mackinac Island and Sault Ste. Marie rounded out the pattern of settlement that had shown little change since the French period. The economy remained centered around the fur trade, and about the only Americans coming to Michigan were those with an interest in that business.

To the south of Michigan an agricultural economy was booming by the early years of the nineteenth century. What Indians such as Pontiac a half century earlier had feared would happen was now in fact happening: tribes were constantly pressured to give up their rights to more of their lands in order that they might be opened to farming. Consequently, Tecumseh, leader of the Shawnee tribe that had gradually been pushed from its ancestral home in the East to lands in Indiana, persuaded Indian tribes to join together and resist further demands for their lands. This was an unwelcome development for those Americans wishing to promote agricultural growth in the West, who again saw their wishes threatened by Indian opposition. And again, these Americans were convinced that they were opposed not only by the Indians but also by the British in Canada, who encouraged the Indian resistance with their advice and weapons. Although the fur traders undoubtedly supported the Indian effort to halt the advance of the farming frontier, the evidence indicates that many, if not all, British authorities in Canada discouraged actions that might arouse the anger of the Americans at a time when Great Britain was engaged in a struggle with Napoleon's forces in Europe. However, the American belief that the British were helping the Indians was a major cause of support for the declaration of war against Great Britain approved by Congress on June 18, 1812.

The War of 1812 was the last of a long series of wars that had been fought since the seventeenth century for dominance in North America, and in the West it continued the struggle for dominance between the competing economic interests of the farmer and the fur trader. Unlike the earlier wars, Michigan in this case was in the center of the fighting.

Governor William Hull, a veteran of the American Revolution, had been given command of the American forces in the Northwest. When the war began, Hull, although he had expressed reservations about the wisdom of getting into a war for which the country was clearly ill-prepared, sought to carry out the orders he had been given as part of the War Department's plans. These were based on the assumption that Britain's war with Napoleon would make it impossible for them to divert very many men to the new war across the Atlantic, making it easy for American forces to invade Canada. But the planners did not take into consideration the caliber of the British commander in Canada, the brilliant Isaac Brock. With only a small contingent of British soldiers at his command, Brock augmented his forces by mobilizing the fur traders and particularly by calling upon the Indians for assistance. From his headquarters at Niagara, Brock quite accurately sized up the American

commander in New York, General Henry Dearborn, as a man who was in no hurry to carry out his instructions to invade Canada from the east. Brock therefore decided to move most of his forces across southern Ontario to the Detroit River and meet the invasion there before Dearborn decided to make a move from the east.

On July 12, William Hull crossed the river and occupied what is now Windsor, Ontario, the first step of the American invasion plans in the West. But Hull, an aging and overcautious man, then threw away the chance to quickly overrun the British fort at Amherstburg on the Detroit River south of Windsor and thus clear the way to move inland. Instead, he waited for the arrival of more artillery, which, it soon developed, could not get through because the British and their Indian allies, led by Tecumseh, controlled the route over which this material had to be brought up from Ohio. Already doubting his chances of succeeding in the invasion of Canada because of this problem, Hull abandoned any thought of continuing the offensive after learning of the fall of Mackinac Island on July 17 to an invading force of British soldiers, fur traders, and Indians who had outnumbered the small American garrison by more than ten to one. Envisioning hordes of Indians coming down from the north to add to his grief, Hull

This sketch of Mackinac Island's harbor at the start of the War of 1812 reflects the activity generated by the fur trade. On a bluff rising up from the harbor is the fort which the American garrison surrendered to a far superior force of British soldiers, fur traders, and Indians on July 17, 1812. Courtesy, State Archives, Michigan Department of State

Above: *In this circa 1824 portrait of William Hull, painter Gilbert Stuart suggests the former Michigan governor's stress as Hull sought unsuccessfully to overturn his conviction on various charges resulting from his actions during the War of 1812. Hull died in 1825, but historians are still debating the merits of the case against him. Courtesy, State Archives, Michigan Department of State*

Above right: *This decidedly imaginative contemporary drawing depicts Colonel Richard M. Johnson, part of a regiment of mounted Kentuckians, about to slay Tecumseh, who holds a tomahawk. Johnson was elected vice president in 1836 on the strength of his claim to having killed the great Indian leader, which was impossible to verify. Courtesy, State Archives, Michigan Department of State*

pulled his men back across the river into the fort at Detroit on August 8. Less than a week later, Brock arrived from the east, and when he crossed the river below Detroit on the morning of August 16 and advanced toward Detroit, Hull agreed to surrender without a fight, convinced that he was outnumbered, which apparently was not true. Hull also feared that if fighting broke out Brock would be unable to control his Indian allies, who might kill civilians as well as soldiers. Having disposed of Hull in the West, Brock returned east in time to defeat the American invasion on the Niagara front when it finally came that fall, although he was killed in the battle. But in a few weeks Brock had left the American plans to conquer Canada in a shambles. Rather than the Americans being deep into Canada, the British had seized control of the entire upper Great Lakes. The governor of Michigan was a prisoner of war, and when Hull was returned to America a court-martial in 1814 found him guilty of cowardice, neglect of duty, and con-

duct unbecoming an officer for his actions in the early weeks of the war. He was sentenced to be shot. President James Madison set aside the sentence but not the guilty verdicts, and though some believe they were unjustified, they served as a dismal climax to what had been a dismal American performance at the start of the war.

In January 1813, Michigan was the scene of still another American disaster when about 1,000 American troops were sent on an ill-advised move northward from Ohio to Frenchtown, on the River Raisin in southeastern Michigan. Here they drove off the handful of Canadian militia and Indians guarding the town, only to see them return on January 22 with reinforcements which, after heavy fighting, forced the surrender of the entire American force. The British took their prisoners to Fort Malden at Amherstburg but left behind, unguarded, American wounded who could not be moved. On January 23, 200 Indians, angered by the casualties they had suffered the previous day, roamed through

MICHIGANIAN
OR
MICHIGANDER?

If you do not wish to refer to a resident of Michigan as a Michigan resident, how *do* you refer to such a person? (In polite terms, that is.) Lexicographers who specialize in such matters have found that several terms, based on the state's name, have been used in the years since an area designated as Michigan first appeared. Michiganite and Michiganese, the latter seemingly more applicable to groups of people than to single individuals, were probably never in common usage at any time and have long since ceased to be heard at all, but Michiganian and Michigander both continue to be used.

Michiganian was the first of the terms to appear, evidence of its use being found as early as 1813. It caught on quickly and cropped up in the writings of Harriet Martineau and Charles Fenno Hoffman in the 1830s when they discussed their travels in Michigan. Hoffman spoke of "the pride of a Michiganian in the beautiful land of his adoption." It was in this period that Michigander began to be heard. Although he did not coin the term, Abraham Lincoln no doubt helped popularize it in 1848 when, in a speech on behalf of the Whig presidential candidate, General Zachary Taylor, he referred to "the military tail the Democrats are now engaged in dovetailing on to the great Michigander," meaning, of course, the Democratic candidate, Lewis Cass.

It is clear that Michigander, as Lincoln used it, ridiculed the manner in which Democrats were trying to make Cass's rather modest record of service in the War of 1812 appear to rival that of Taylor, a great Mexican War hero. It is probably because of this usage and because Michigander has a rather silly ring to it that many have opposed its use. The historian Willis F. Dunbar once observed that this terminology would seem to require a female resident to be called a Michigoose. Michiganian, on the other hand, is consistent with the practice in most states where an ending of -an or -ian is added to the state's name, as in Ohioan or Oregonian, and this is why a great many continue to favor its usage. Conversely, it is probably because of Michigander's distinctive character that others prefer it over Michiganian.

The state's largest newspaper, the Detroit *News,* uses Michiganian in preference to Michigander, but in 1985 the Detroit *Free Press* promised to use Michigander when a telephone poll of its readers revealed that it was the favored term. The closeness of the vote (1,435 favoring Michigander, 1,364 favoring Michiganian) indicated, however, that the dispute was far from settled.

Frenchtown and killed the wounded soldiers, whose number, according to different estimates, was from 30 to 100. The event, called with some justification the River Raisin Massacre, prompted cries of horror and outrage in the West. For many, "Remember the River Raisin" had the same emotional impact that "Remember the Maine" and "Remember Pearl Harbor" would have in later wars.

In September 1813, Commodore Oliver Hazard Perry's fleet defeated the British in the Battle of Lake Erie, leading the British to pull out of Detroit, which was reoccupied by American troops on September 29. General William Henry Harrison, who had succeeded Hull as commander of the Army of the Northwest, pursued the British into Canada and caught up with them in the Battle of the Thames on October 4. The British forces soon abandoned the fight, but Tecumseh

From the top of the bluff on which it stands, Fort Mackinac gives an impression of great strength, as seen in this modern view. However, during the British capture of the island in 1812 and their successful defense in 1814, the fort proved to be of little value. Courtesy, State Archives, Michigan Department of State

and his Indians fought on, with Tecumseh finally meeting his death at the hands of Kentuckians who felt this was revenge for the River Raisin Massacre, although Tecumseh had nothing to do with that tragedy.

Although the Americans had regained Detroit, most of the rest of Michigan remained controlled by the British operating out of Mackinac Island. In 1814, the British commander on Mackinac Island, Lieutenant Colonel Robert McDouall, showed how well he and his British colleagues had mastered the guerilla-style war tactics that they, like the French before them, had learned from the Indians. Within a matter of a few weeks McDouall detached some of his mixed force of sol-

diers, fur traders, and Indians and sent them off on a successful mission to oust the Americans from Prairie du Chien, hundreds of miles away on the Mississippi. He turned back an attack on Mackinac Island by a joint military-naval task force that was seemingly far superior in strength to what McDouall had at his command, and when the Americans gave up the attempt to retake Mackinac, the British, with no naval vessels, captured the two ships the Americans had left behind to cut the island's lines of supply.

American control of Michigan was in jeopardy, but by that time the British negotiators who met at the Belgian town of Ghent to discuss peace terms were as anxious as the Americans to

end the war. The British had just ended a terrible war with France that had been going on almost constantly for two decades, and they had no desire to commit themselves to another long and bloody effort to defeat the United States. The result was a treaty, signed on Christmas Eve, 1814, that declared the war had ended in a draw. The boundaries between the United States and the British possessions to the north would remain exactly as they were at the start of the war; neither country gained an inch of territory after two and a half years of conflict.

As a result of the treaty, Michigan would remain part of the United States. American control, which had been at best shaky prior to the war, was soon firmly established. Congress in 1816 prohibited foreign companies from engaging in the fur trade on American soil, giving the New York-based American Fur Company of John Jacob Astor the opportunity to monopolize the business from its headquarters on Mackinac Island. But the record profits Astor earned in the decade following the war represented the last great days of the business activity that had dominated the area for two centuries. American control inevitably meant that the desires of the great majority of Americans who favored farming pursuits could no longer be denied. As the United States and Great Britain increasingly expressed a mutual desire to avoid any actions that might threaten their peaceful relationship, the Indians in Michigan and elsewhere in the upper Midwest soon realized that they could no longer expect any help from the British in resisting new demands for land. For Michigan the day of the farmer was about to begin.

Left: *Following the War of 1812, the British built a fort on the western end of Drummond Island which they later had to abandon when a boundary commission determined that the island fell on the American, not the Canadian, side of the international boundary. A few massive chimneys are all that survive of this last British-held outpost in Michigan. Courtesy, State Archives, Michigan Department of State*

Above: *From his office in New York, John Jacob Astor brilliantly directed a fur trading operation, centered for many years in Michigan, that enabled this German immigrant to amass a fortune that has amply supported his descendants living both in the United States and Great Britain. Courtesy, State Archives, Michigan Department of State*

Left: *Photographed in 1965, these buildings on the southern shore of Grand Island, near Munising on the northern side of the Upper Peninsula, were relics of one of Michigan's last fur-trading posts that had operated here more than a century before. Courtesy, State Archives, Michigan Department of State*

CHAPTER V

THE FARM STATE

Until well into the twentieth century, steam-powered threshing machines and their crews went from farm to farm during the fall harvesting season, as here in Oak Grove in northern Livingston County. Courtesy, Michigan Historical Collections, Bentley Historical Library, University of Michigan

In the early 1830s, John Nowlin, a thirty-nine-year-old farmer in Putnam County, New York, was growing ever more concerned about his prospects for the future. Efforts to expand his small farm were hampered by stony soils, causing poor crop yields and financial problems that threatened his ability to hold on to his farm. As his son William later recalled, "He said it was impossible for a poor man to get along and support his family; that he never could get any land for his children there, and he would sell what he had and go to a better country, where land was cheap and where he could get land for them." So in 1833, Nowlin sold his New York farm and went "to view" the Michigan territory, which he had become convinced was the promised land that he sought.

After two months Nowlin returned and told his wife and children that he had bought eighty acres of land in Dearborn Township, about twelve miles west of Detroit, and after he moved the family west in the spring he planned to buy an additional eighty acres. Obviously Michigan had lived up to Nowlin's expectations. He told

his family that it "was a beautiful country ... the soil was as rich as a barnyard, as level as a house floor, and no stones in the way." (William Nowlin, in reporting this glowing assessment, hastened to add that his father's acquaintanceship with the territory had at that time not extended beyond Dearborn.) Nowlin's family was not so easily sold on the desirability of moving to Michigan. William, at twelve the oldest of the children, declared, "The thought of Indians, bears, and wolves terrified me, and the thought of leaving my schoolmates and native place was terrible." Melinda Nowlin shared her children's anxieties, and her poor health raised fears that she could not survive the arduous trip to Michigan or that if she did, the hardships of frontier life would soon lead to her death. When John Nowlin remained determined to carry out his plans she made him promise that when she died she would be returned for burial in New York, beside her ancestors.

In the spring of 1834 the Nowlins moved to Michigan, traveling via the Erie Canal and then by the steamer *Michigan* to Detroit. From there they

Above left: *William Nowlin's charming recollections of his family's pioneer experiences,* The Bark-Covered House *(1877), included several illustrations which presumably were drawn under his supervision. Certainly this sketch of the* Michigan, *struggling through a storm, depicted one of the most frightening aspects of the family's trip to Michigan.*

Center: *At the Nowlins' first home in Michigan, John Nowlin and his son William rest from their unending efforts to push back the forest that hemmed them in. From Nowlin,* The Bark-Covered House, *1877*

Right: *The house that John Nowlin built in 1854, together with the nearby farm buildings and the surrounding open fields, provided a dramatic contrast with the conditions under which the Nowlins had begun their life in Michigan twenty years before. From Nowlin,* The Bark-Covered House, *1877*

went the remaining few miles to Dearborn by way of the Chicago Road, opened a few years earlier as a military road linking the forts at Detroit and Chicago and surviving today as U.S. 12. For two weeks the family lived with a neighbor who had arrived from New York the previous year, until John Nowlin, with help from the men of the area, built a log house with a bark-covered roof.

At first the Nowlins' progress on their new farm was heartbreakingly slow. John and William struggled to clear enough of the densely wooded land to allow their first crops to receive sunlight from ten in the morning until early afternoon, when the sun disappeared behind the virgin forests to the west. Before long John was forced to mortgage the farm to keep going, while young William worked as a hunter to supplement the family's income. But in an amazingly short time conditions began to improve, especially after the opening of a railroad from Detroit to Dearborn in 1838 made it possible for the Nowlins to take their produce into

the city in the morning, sell it, and return home the same day. By the early 1840s the bark-covered house had been replaced by a far superior family residence, the mortgage had been paid off, and when William married in 1843 John provided his son with land on which to start his own farm, as he did a few years later for his younger son John Jr. By the end of the 1840s John Nowlin had prospered to the point where he was able to buy more land and build a large brick house, referred to as Nowlin's Castle, where he resided for the rest of his life. During the years in their new surroundings the entire family had become confirmed Michiganians, and even Melinda, whose health improved remarkably, had no desire to return to the land from which she had come.

The Nowlins participated in one of history's greatest migrations, the movement of pioneers across the Appalachians. In its early years this migration led to the emergence of the states to the south of Michigan, and by the 1820s it was rapidly changing the land-

scape of the future Wolverine State. What set these settlers apart from most of those who had come earlier was their interest not in the fur trade but in farming and related pursuits. Michigan's land was what they were seeking, and thus there occurred for the first time a large-scale movement into Michigan's interior, away from the handful of outposts the fur traders had established along the peripheries of Michigan's peninsulas.

Since the end of the last ice age thousands of years ago, Michigan's land has been essentially as it is today, and the fact that some of it is admirably suited to agriculture has been known for at least 2,000 years since Indians introduced farming in the southern part of the lower peninsula. Early in the historic period, some of the French settlers, especially those in the Detroit River area, sought to establish farms. A few of the pear trees that they brought in still survive, even in such an unlikely place as the Grosse Pointes, which, before they became Detroit's most fashionable suburbs, were once

French farm country. It was not until the arrival of Americans in the nineteenth century, however, that widespread and continual agricultural development began.

To facilitate this development in the trans-Appalachian area, Congress, beginning in 1785, initiated a policy which in the following years made it ever easier for individuals to buy government land. By the time the Nowlins arrived in Michigan in 1834, it was possible to purchase as little as eighty acres at a cost of only $1.25 an acre. Before any land could be sold, however, Indian claims had to be settled, a process that began in earnest in Michigan in 1807 and which by 1842 had resulted in a series of treaties in which the Indians surrendered their claims to virtually all of the state's land. The land then had to be surveyed according to a simple rectangular system outlined in the 1785 ordinance. Only when that survey had been completed could any land be opened for sale at government land offices. Some surveying was done in Michigan prior to the War of 1812 to determine the boundaries of private land holdings that existed at Detroit and other settlements at the time the United States took possession of Michigan in 1796. After the war federal surveyors began the monumental task of laying out into thirty-six-square-mile townships the vast majority of Michigan that was not part of those earlier holdings.

The federal surveyors completed their job by about 1850, but enough land had been surveyed by 1818 for land sales to begin at the Detroit land office. Additional offices were established at Monroe in 1823 and White Pigeon in 1831, the latter being transferred to Kalamazoo in 1834. By 1836 offices had also been opened at Ionia and Flint. By that time Michigan was in the grip of one of the most spectacular land booms in American history, rivaling the more publicized land developments in Oklahoma in the 1890s or Florida in the 1920s. Sales at Michigan's land offices helped popularize the term "Doing a land office business," describing the kind of sales performances merchandisers dream of achieving. But the fact that land sales had been quite modest until the 1830s led some to wonder why it took so long for people to become aware of the opportunities Michigan offered.

Fears that Michigan might become a battleground probably scared away many potential settlers in the early days of American control. When war came, the sickness that killed many soldiers stationed in Detroit in 1813-1814 was perhaps the origin of a widely circulated verse that warned: "Don't go to Michigan, that land of ills/ The word means ague, fever and chills." Such ideas, although not entirely unfounded (periodic attacks of malaria, or "the ague," would plague many Michigan pioneers for years), also stemmed from the fact that Michigan, even in the early nineteenth century, was still an unknown region and hence the source of numerous unflattering rumors that could well have turned away some who were contemplating a move westward.

Published reports in popular geographies and travel narratives, and word-of-mouth accounts from settlers such as John Nowlin, soon created a more positive picture of the area. Borrowing one of the numerous editions of Jedediah Morse's *American Universal Geography* from a neighbor in New York, Nowlin learned that Michigan "was a very fertile country, that it was nearly surrounded by great lakes, and that wild grapes and other wild fruit grew in abundance." In 1833 Charles Fenno Hoffman was told that in parts of southern Michigan the rich soils were "four feet deep, and so fat that it will grease your fingers." Similarly, a visitor from Maryland in 1836 remarked on the "deep & rich loam which will grease your fingers, and feels in the hand like a finely granulated brown sugar." He declared he had "rarely seen a richer tract of country than that which we are now traversing." Farmers who heard such reports would probably have concluded that for such soils they could put up with an occasional attack of ague, fever, and chills.

By the time Hoffman's account of his western travels was published, residents of the East were coming down in increasing numbers with another kind of fever, "Michigan fever," as it was termed. The reason that few were infected until the 1830s is probably not due to any image problem Michigan may have had but rather a result of the difficulties encountered in traveling to or from that remote northwestern territory. Michigan was far removed from the Ohio and Mississippi rivers that were the economic lifeline of the new settlements in the West. That remoteness began to disappear in 1819, however, when the steamboat *Walk-in-the-Water* arrived in Detroit, marking the

beginning of a faster, more reliable means of transportation on the upper Great Lakes. The opening of the Erie Canal in 1825 provided an all-water route to the Atlantic coast that immediately gave areas such as Michigan far better and cheaper connections with the markets of the East than those provided by the Ohio-Mississippi river routes. These dramatic transportation breakthroughs, combined with improved economic conditions at the end of the 1820s, largely account for the escalating interest in Michigan that was evident by the early 1830s.

In 1820, a quarter century after the United States had acquired control of the area, the majority of Michigan's non-Indian population of just under 9,000 were French in background, reflecting the limited impact of early American occupation. The balance began to shift in the 1820s with the first sizable movement inland. Ypsilanti, Ann Arbor, Tecumseh, and Adrian were founded in mid-decade, joining Pontiac, whose founding in 1819 had first signaled an awakening interest in

the areas beyond the century-old town of Detroit. By 1830 Michigan's population, excluding the areas to the west that had by then been incorporated into the territory, was nearly 30,000, an increase of over threefold in a decade. The new state's population soared to 212,000 by 1840, an astounding ten-year increase of 700 percent. Although such increases could not be maintained in the years thereafter, Michigan's population had a net gain of nearly 200,000 during the 1840s, and increased each decade by about 400,000 during the rest of the century.

By far the largest number of the newcomers were those referred to as Yankees because of their New England origins. Some, like Lewis Cass and Zachariah Chandler, Michigan's preeminent nineteenth-century political leaders, were natives of New England proper. But far more had been born in New York, coming in large part from that state's western sections, which had been settled by New Englanders since the 1780s. In 1850, Michigan's population of 397,654 included 133,756 born

Among the state's first and foremost public universities was the University of Michigan, shown here in 1874, a little over thirty years after the first classes were held on the Ann Arbor campus. Its growth in later years would be so great that none of the academic buildings shown in this engraving have survived. Courtesy, Michigan Historical Collections, Bentley Historical Library, University of Michigan

Top right: *The state had, from its inception, paid great attention to establishing strong public education at the elementary and secondary levels. By the end of the century photographs such as this one, depicting students and staff at Climax in 1894-1895, attested to the pride communities both large and small took in their schools. Courtesy, Regional History Collection, Western Michigan University*

Right: *Schools were not the only sign of cultural stirrings. In 1852 educator Lucinda Hinsdale Stone and other Kalamazoo women organized the Ladies' Library Association, Michigan's first women's club and the third in the nation. Since 1879 the club has met in this building, shown in this late nineteenth-century interior view. Courtesy, Regional History Collection, Western Michigan University*

The Pillar Christian Reformed Church in Holland was built in 1856 to house the congregation of the Reverend Albertus C. Van Raalte, who had founded the city in 1847. One of only two buildings to survive Holland's terrible fire of 1871, the church is a fine example of Greek Revival architecture, which Yankees from the East introduced in Michigan. Photo by Margaret Beattie Bogue

in New York, by far the largest number of York Staters, as they were called, anywhere in the country outside of New York. York Staters and those from New England and the neighboring states of New Jersey and Pennsylvania made up more than 45 percent of Michigan's population. It was these easterners who transformed southern Michigan from a wilderness area into one whose settlements often bore such names as Utica, Brooklyn, Plymouth, Concord, Newport, or Manchester, leaving no doubt as to the origins of their founders. The New England town meeting that was introduced in the pioneer era survives as an element in the government of rural townships, and throughout the area that was settled in the mid-nineteenth century the classical styles of architecture that were popular in the East are evident in innumerable structures dating from that era.

Among these structures are churches built to house Congregationalists, the church of the Pilgrims and Puritans, and the even more numerous Methodists, Presbyterians, Baptists, Episcopalians, and other Protestant denominations that appeared with the

Yankees' arrival in an area where the Catholic church had previously been the only organized religion. Few Catholics were found among the Americans from the East or other parts of the country who became more numerous in Michigan during the last half of the century. However, the ranks of the Catholics were being reinforced by foreign-born immigrants, who by 1850 made up nearly 14 percent of the state's population. By 1870, with 22 percent of the population, they outnumbered the New York natives.

The largest foreign group in 1870 had not traveled far, having moved in from Michigan's neighbor across the international boundary, Canada. Some of these Canadians were of English background, not unlike the New Englanders who arrived in the same period, and the considerable number of French Canadians breathed new life into the French Catholic culture that had remained from Michigan's French period. From Europe the overwhelming majority of immigrants were from four countries. From the British Isles the largest group was the Irish, who, like the French Canadians, greatly

Marshall in particular has capitalized on its wealth of well-preserved nineteenth-century buildings. These include, along with structures in the popular classical architectural style, this oddity, the Honolulu House. It was so named because its builder, Abner Pratt, sought to imitate the house he lived in while serving as American consul to Hawaii. Courtesy, Michigan Historical Collections, Bentley Historical Library, University of Michigan

George Peters and Fredricka Lederman Peters (or Petters, as the name would come to be spelled) posed for this classic nineteenth-century charcoal portrait of a typical German immigrant couple. Settling first in Pennsylvania, they moved westward with their children, some of whom eventually came to Michigan. Courtesy, George Wiskemann and Geneva Kebler Wiskemann

strengthened the Catholic church in Michigan, while the English and the Scots added members to such Protestant churches as the Methodist and Presbyterian. From the continent, the largest of these European immigrant groups, the Germans, introduced the Lutheran church to Michigan, although the majority of Germans were Catholic. The fourth major European element, the Dutch, affiliated with the Reformed Church of America, a Protestant group centered in the East that was rarely found in Michigan until the arrival of the Dutch.

A search for religious freedom provided the initial impetus for the Dutch immigration to Michigan, while a certain number of the Canadians in the late 1830s and the Germans in mid-century were refugees from political turmoil in their native lands. But the great majority of all immigrants, like their counterparts from within the United States, came to Michigan in search of economic opportunity. For nearly all who came from the New England-New York area and for a very substantial percentage of the foreign immigrants, acquisition of Michigan land was regarded as the key to economic advancement. From a total of about 147,000 acres sold in 1830, United States land office sales in Mich-

igan rose to nearly 500,000 acres in 1834 before mushrooming in 1835 with sales of 1,817,248 acres. In 1836 sales hit an all-time record of 4,189,823 acres, more than one-ninth of the state's entire acreage, but a much higher proportion of the available land in the southern half of the lower peninsula where these sales took place. By the mid-1830s Flint, Jackson (also referred to in this era when Andrew Jackson was president as Jacksonopolis, Jacksonburg, and Jacksonville), Battle Creek, Kalamazoo, Grand Rapids, St. Joseph, and a host of other place names familiar to generations of Michiganians dotted the landscape.

Gripped by the prevailing optimism of that day, the fledgling state government in 1837 plunged into an ambitious program to promote even more growth by building three railroads and two canals across southern Michigan and a third canal to the north around the rapids at Sault Ste. Marie. All this was to be financed with a five-million-dollar bond issue to be repaid with revenues from these state-operated facilities. However, the program was far too grandiose, and its timing unfortunately coincided with a sharp decline in the nation's economy that probably killed whatever chances Michigan had of completing any of the

Above: *In 1848 Cornelius Vander Meulen and his Dutch congregation founded Zeeland, named after the province from which they had come. The town, just east of Holland, remains decidedly Dutch in flavor. Courtesy, Julian DePree*

Left: *This appealing young couple stands before St. Mary's Catholic Church in Westphalia, a prosperous Clinton County farming community founded in the 1830s by immigrants from the Prussian province of the same name. Today the town is still solidly German. Courtesy, State Archives, Michigan Department of State*

RUDYARD, KIPLING, AND OTHER PLACE NAMES

Place names often provide interesting clues to an area's history. Kalamazoo, Presque Isle, and New Haven, for example, are readily recognized as originating with Michigan's Indian, French, and New England heritage, while Cass City, Mason, and Monroe are examples of names that honor individuals of some prominence in the state's and nation's development. The map of Michigan, however, is dotted with names whose origins are not quite so apparent, probably because those who chose them shared with the New England founders of the eastern Michigan town of Romeo a desire "to avoid the commonplace."

Singapore, Ganges, Baroda, and Canton are examples of Asiatic place names that caught the fancy of pioneer town and township founders. The fascination of Americans in the 1820s with the Greek War of Independence from the Turks compelled Judge Augustus B. Woodward to fasten on one Washtenaw County community the unforgettable name of Ypsilanti, after one of the Greek war heroes. During the same era the interest in Greek and classical ideas that was also evident in architecture accounts for such names as Athens, Sparta, and Ithaca, as well as such classical-sounding inventions as Cassopolis, Arenac, Alpena, and Iosco. The last three are among the numerous names devised by Henry R. Schoolcraft, the onetime Indian agent in northern Michigan who by mid-century became the country's foremost Indian authority. In addition to marrying Indian and classical or Arabic forms, Schoolcraft persuaded the legislature to attach authentic Indian names or terms to a number of counties. The unpronounceable or unattractive character of such names as Kaykakee, Meegisee, and Kautawbet enabled some of Schoolcraft's enemies in the legislature in 1843 to replace these and several other northern Michigan Indian county names with the names of such Irish counties as Antrim, Clare, Emmet, Roscommon, and Wexford.

Geographical features explain names such as Oakland and Hillsdale, although Lake County in western Michigan is one of the few areas in this famous Water Wonderland where lakes are virtually nonexistent. Glen Arbor, Spring Arbor, and Ann Arbor indicate that some names were selected simply because they had a pleasant sound, although the exact origins of Ann Arbor's name have stimulated more discussion than probably any other place name in the state.

A desire to attract British investments in railroad developments may explain such Upper Peninsula names as Gladstone, Rudyard, and Kipling. When the famed British author after whom the last two hamlets were named learned of the honor bestowed on him he wrote in amusement:

'Wise is the child who knows his sire,'
The ancient proverb ran,
But wiser far the man who knows
How, where and when his off-spring grows,
For who the mischief would suppose
I've sons in Michigan?

The privately financed Erie and Kalamazoo Railroad provided the first train service west of the Appalachians when it began its run from Toledo to Adrian in 1836. This sketch, made some years later, depicts the excitement that the locomotive generated among the pioneer settlers along the route. The Erie and Kalamazoo, which never went beyond Adrian, survives as a corporate entity to the present day, although it has operated no trains since 1849. Courtesy, State Archives, Michigan Department of State

projects. Before the money ran out in the early 1840s, the Michigan Central Railroad had been completed from Detroit to Kalamazoo, the Michigan Southern from Monroe to Hillsdale, and a short section of the Clinton-Kalamazoo Canal from Mount Clemens to the Rochester area—all the state would have to show for efforts that left it mired in a financial morass from which it took years to escape. To its credit, the state program provided an impetus for railroad construction, with private companies completing the work that the state had begun, and it provided a stimulus for other developments. The picturesque town of Vermontville in western Eaton County, for example, owes its location to the desire of its New England founders to be on the route of the Clinton-Kalamazoo Canal.

Private investors were not interested in carrying through the southern Michigan canal projects, and thus Vermontville did not see the Clinton-Kalamazoo Canal come closer than 100 miles to the east. The town sur-

vived this disappointment, but the same could not be said of some other town projects launched at the height of Michigan fever in the mid-1830s. Promoters acquired large tracts of land at the mouth of a river, along rapids that could provide power, or along an important transportation route, platted the land, and offered lots for sale. As real estate developers have been known to do, information to the potential buyers sometimes stretched the truth, promising well-established communities with broad avenues, bustling business sections, and splendid residential areas where little or nothing existed. In 1837 Bela Hubbard visited White Rock City on the Lake Huron shore of Michigan's Thumb, expecting to see "the magnificent harbor," the busy sawmills, the courthouse, churches, bank, and the other features shown on maps which were "executed in the highest style of the typographer's art" and displayed wherever newcomers to Michigan assembled. "We found the entering river," Hubbard recalled. "It hardly admitted our canoe. Harbor

Although Michigan's initial railroad building era under either public or private auspices was scarcely spectacular in the results it achieved, by the end of the century the state was served by a network of some 8,000 miles of tracks. The railroads reached into such remote communities as tiny Bruce Crossing in the western Upper Peninsula, providing access to the world for its residents or diversion for those who came only to watch the arrival of the train. Courtesy, State Archives, Michigan Department of State

there was none. Churches, houses, mills, people were all a myth. A thick wilderness covered the whole site. Even those marks of advancing civilization, the surveyor's marks, were wanting."

More substantial were the plans of several easterners in this same period to develop Port Sheldon on the shores of Lake Michigan, south of Grand Haven. In 1836 they cleared the site, laid out streets and sidewalks, and built a spectacular hotel with eight columns across its front as the community showpiece. Port Sheldon township survives, but the community as its founders planned it does not. An unfortunate location at a river mouth that constantly filled with sand and the onset of the depression of the late 1830s led to the quick collapse of this real estate venture. All that remains of the original town are four of the hotel columns which have graced a building in Grand

Rapids since the 1840s.

Port Sheldon and White Rock City are extreme examples of the speculative mania that drew so many to Michigan to buy land, not for settlement, but as an investment which could be sold later, it was hoped, at great profit. John M. Gordon, a young Baltimore attorney and banker who spent several weeks in Michigan in 1836, typified the more cautious speculator who was careful to examine the lands he proposed to buy. Buoyed by assurances that no one had ever lost money on Michigan land nor had anyone who bought government land at the bargain basement price of $1.25 an acre done worse than doubling their money, Gordon bought nearly 7,000 acres of land in southwestern Michigan. In the process he learned of investors who had made fabulous profits, such as the Detroit boot maker who paid $5,000 for

Left: *The New England origins of Vermontville are evident not only in the town's name but in its distinctly Yankee appearance, as seen here in the plain, austere lines of the interior of the Congregational church. Courtesy, Michigan Historical Collections, Bentley Historical Library, University of Michigan*

Below: *A little of Port Sheldon survives today in the four pillars that were once part of the town's hotel and which then became part of the Abram Pike house in Grand Rapids. For many years the home of the Grand Rapids Art Gallery, the building now houses a commercial business. Courtesy, Michigan Historical Collections, Bentley Historical Library, University of Michigan*

a portion of what became Grand Rapids and eighteen months later sold the property to a New York judge for $105,000. Horace H. Comstock, related by marriage to author James Fenimore Cooper, came to Michigan from Cooperstown, New York in 1831 with $5,000, and by 1836 his land holdings, Gordon was told, had an estimated worth of $500,000. John T. Blois, author of Michigan's first gazetteer, maintained that there had probably "been more fortunes made, more instances of individuals, possessing a mere pittance, sufficient to locate a lot of eighty acres, who have risen to a competence, or state of independence, in a short period of five, three, or perhaps two years only, than can be found in many of the older States in perhaps twenty years."

Although himself a speculator, Gordon never felt comfortable being identified with a group that was "particularly odious to emigrants, and justly so," he had to admit, "for no sooner has a settler established himself than all the lots around him are taken up by these persons who when he desires to enlarge his farm charge him three or four [times the original price]." But if farmers hated the speculators, the speculators depended on farmers to promote the growth of a

FURMAN HUFF

MRS. FURMAN HUFF.

In the 1870s wealthy farmers often were persuaded to pay to have a sketch of their farm and themselves appear in county histories. Furman Huff came to Michigan from New Jersey in 1837, and in the biography that accompanied this sketch he modestly admitted that in the succeeding forty years "ease and comfort have been reached." From Crisfield Johnson, History of Hillsdale County..., 1879

farm economy, which they needed to attain the profits they hoped to harvest.

The farmers cooperated by transforming Michigan almost overnight into a state dominated by an agricultural economy. As early as 1840 the federal occupational census listed 56,521 persons employed in farming, more than six times the number engaged in all other occupations and over a quarter of the state's total population. The feverish development of the mid-1830s was cooled sharply by the depression following the Panic of 1837 and by an economy that remained weak into the 1840s. This was followed, however, by the resumption of growth, and was all the more impressive because it resulted from a steady expansion of the farming economy and was generally not accompanied by the wild speculation that had characterized the earlier boom period.

The state government promoted this growth through publications and through agents in New York and Europe who sought to direct immigrants, particularly Germans, to Michigan, al-

though little effort was actually required to sell prospects. One German later recalled that farmland in Germany in this period cost 200 times the price of land in Michigan, and the fact that most of the Michigan land was densely wooded was not considered a drawback to the hard-working German farmer and his family. For the Yankees, generations of whom had grown accustomed to the arduous task of clearing their land of trees, the lure of Michigan was expressed in a song of the 1830s, one of whose verses went:

Then come ye Yankee farmers,
 Who've mettle hearts like me,
elbow-grease in plenty,
 To bow the forest tree;
Come take a 'Quarter Section,'
 And I'll be bound you'll say,
This country takes the rag off,
 This Michigania.

From 1850, when the first detailed agricultural census figures became available, the number of Michigan farms increased by an average of 3,997 a year over the next three decades, topping 154,000 by 1880. The rate of increase slowed markedly thereafter, but the number of farms continued upwards to a peak of 206,900 in 1910. Farm acreage, which had totaled 4,383,890 in 1850, hit its high point in 1920, at which time farmland occupied 19,031,961 acres, nearly 52 percent of Michigan's entire land area. Farms were found throughout the state but the heaviest concentration remained in the southern half of the lower peninsula, where soils and climate were most suitable to farming. Here pioneers found patches of open prairie lands and areas of widely scattered trees, called oak openings, the title of one of the lesser-known novels of James Fenimore Cooper, who, like his relative Horace Comstock, invested in Michigan land.

Timbered lands, however, were by far the most common type in southern Michigan and virtually the only kind found in the northern regions. This may explain why the average farm size declined from 128 acres in 1850 to approximately 86 acres in 1890 as difficulties in clearing the land forced farmers to be more realistic in the goals they set for themselves. Realism was also dictated by the fact that by the end of the century, when other parts of the Middle West were seeing more and more large farms operated by managers and tenants for absentee owners, Michigan was still dominated by that romantic ideal of an earlier day—the family-owned and -operated farm. In the twentieth century Michigan began coming closer to the national norms but in 1920 the state's number of family farms still ranked sixth in the country. The farm of about eighty acres remained the most popular size, while only 827 farms, four-tenths of one percent of the state's total, had 500 acres or more.

As Michigan farmers moved from the subsistence level of farming to one in which they made a profit from their

efforts, wheat was for many years their leading cash crop. Pioneer farmers in southern Michigan found they got excellent yields of winter wheat and were harvesting over a million bushels by 1837. One farmer in Jackson County who had planted 300 acres of wheat declared at that time that southern Michigan was, "as a wheat country, probably the very first in America." By 1850, with nearly five million bushels of wheat, Michigan ranked sixth among all states in this crop. Bumper crops and high prices encouraged the continuing emphasis on wheat until annual production averaged thirty million bushels in 1880. Then, however, falling prices, lower yields due to a failure to rotate crops and to employ fertilizers, some unusually severe winters, and the rise of huge wheat operations in the West caused more and more Michigan farmers to switch from this old favorite. Wheat production by the early twentieth century declined to less than half the output of the early 1880s.

Wheat would remain an important crop in southern Michigan, but other

Traffic congestion in downtown Eaton Rapids on wheat market day in the mid-1870s indicated the dominance of wheat in Michigan agriculture at that time. Southern Michigan farmers were getting bigger yields per acre than almost any other area in the country and the price they got for their wheat would not be equalled for another half century. Courtesy, State Archives, Michigan Department of State

Above: *Dr. William James Beal's work in establishing the nation's first seed-testing laboratory paved the way for the development of hybrid corn. As the first president of the Society for the Promotion of Agricultural Science, Beal also helped establish the state's agricultural college as one of the leaders in such work. Courtesy, Michigan State University. From Cirker,* Dictionary of American Portraits, *Dover, 1967*

Above right: *State Agricultural College professor Robert C. Kedzie lectures to his chemistry class in 1892. Kedzie's work stimulated more scientific approaches to farming in Michigan, including the adoption of such new crops as sugar beets. Courtesy, State Archives, Michigan Department of State*

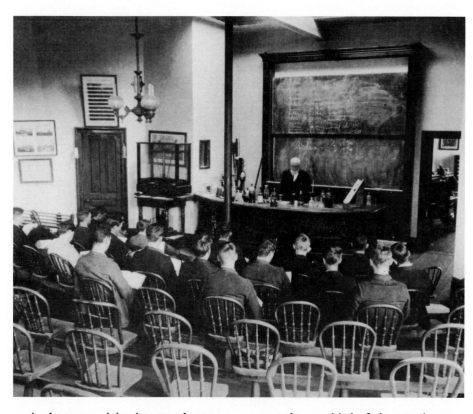

grains began receiving increased attention. Rye, barley, and buckwheat were, on the whole, of limited importance, but oats were much more widely grown, with the acreage planted and the amount harvested sometimes exceeding those of wheat. But no grain has been as important as corn, which has been grown in southern Michigan at least since the time of Christ when Indians introduced it to the area. The pioneers of the early nineteenth century planted corn before anything else because the ground did not have to be plowed. Grains of corn were placed in holes punched in the newly cleared fields, the number of grains often dictated by an old maxim: "One for the blackbird, one for the crow/ One for the cut-worm, and three to grow." Corn, in the form of johnnycake, mush, or hominy, was the staple of the pioneers' diet, and it was only later that it was primarily used as fodder for livestock. With that development, corn production, which in the early years usually equaled that of wheat, forged far ahead of all other grains. Presently

more than a third of the state's cropland is planted in corn, with seven times as many bushels of corn harvested as are harvested of wheat, the second leading grain. What had been known to the pioneer as Indian corn began changing dramatically, however, with the development of the first hybrid corn varieties in 1879 by Dr. William James Beal at the State Agricultural College in East Lansing and then by Beal's student Perry G. Holden at the agricultural college and the University of Illinois.

The work of Beal and Holden with hybrid corn, which has been called the agricultural miracle of the twentieth century, illustrates the leading role of the nation's first agricultural college (now Michigan State University) in promoting the farming economy's growth. Dr. Robert C. Kedzie provided another example of this influence when he and his colleagues in the 1890s were largely responsible for introducing a new product, sugar beets, to the state's farmers. Since that time Michigan has usually ranked among the top five

states in sugar beet production.

Sugar beets, although originally grown in many parts of Michigan, eventually came to be concentrated in the Saginaw Bay area. Since the nineteenth century, the same area around Saginaw Bay and into the northern Thumb region has been the principal souce of dry beans, a crop in which Michigan has long had a near monopoly. Sugar beets and beans typify the tendency of Michigan farmers in later decades to specialize in one or two products, depending on the area where they are situated. With some exceptions in the case of oats, grains were principally grown in southern Michigan after it was discovered that conditions in northern Michigan were unsuitable for these crops. However, when farmers began moving into the northern parts of the state after the Civil War, they found that potatoes did exceptionally well. Although the major share of Michigan's potato crop is grown in scattered areas in the south, it is one of the state's major farm products to which farmers in northern

Michigan, particularly in Presque Isle County, contribute significantly.

In the western part of the lower peninsula farmers were discovering as early as the 1830s that the moderating effect of Lake Michigan's waters made the land immediately bordering the lake ideal for the growing of fruit. A narrow band of land from Berrien County on the south to Grand Traverse Bay on the north soon became famous as Michigan's Fruit Belt, whose orchards, vineyards, and farms made the state a national leader in the production of apples, cherries, grapes, peaches, blueberries, and numerous other fruits and berries. In the same period the adaptability of the mucklands around Kalamazoo to celery cultivation made that area the world's largest producer of this crop and Kalamazoo and celery almost synonymous terms. Peppermint and spearmint production also became centered in this and one or two other areas of southern Michigan. To the west, Allegan and Ottawa counties became the major centers of poultry farming.

Vineyards such as these near Paw Paw have long made that city the center of the state's wine industry. Michigan currently ranks fourth in the country in grape production, and nearly all of the grapes are grown in the two southwestern counties of Berrien and Van Buren. Photo by Margaret Beattie Bogue

THE
WOLVERINE
STATE

Although wolverine is Michigan's state nickname as well as that of the University of Michigan's athletic teams, and the name of numerous businesses such as Rockford's giant Wolverine World Wide shoe company, why this came about remains a mystery. Whether the wolverine, which in modern times has been found primarily in the world's northern polar regions, was ever even a native of Michigan during historic times is a matter of much dispute. After a determined effort to uncover evidence of these animals' presence in the state, longtime Michigan Wolverine football coach Fielding H. Yost reported that the only wolverines he could find that had ever lived in Michigan were a few that had resided in zoos. On the other hand, Michigan State

In the mid-1920s Zeeland was famous as the baby-chick center of western Michigan. Here, farmers from six poultry farms wait for the train that will haul away the boxes of live chicks piled on these wagons. Today the chicks are gone and Zeeland is known for its furniture and clock manufacturers. Courtesy, Zeeland Historical Museum

Livestock, which began to receive more careful attention after the initial pioneer era when most farmers had a cow or pigs on the premises simply to meet the family's own needs, became an area of farm activity that, until recent years, exceeded farm crops in overall value. Sheep raising, in fact, rivaled wheat in the nineteenth century as the leading source of farm income. When sheep raising declined toward the end of the nineteenth century, hogs and, somewhat later, beef cattle, took their place. Hopes that the Upper Pen-

insula and the northern part of the lower peninsula could benefit significantly from their use as grazing lands for cattle have never been realized to any large degree, livestock activities being chiefly concentrated in southern Michigan. But dairy activities, in which the state emerged as a national leader, have been much more widely carried on across the state, including the northern areas.

By the twentieth century, Michigan had long since begun losing the image it once had as a farm state. In this century the number of farms has fallen off by the 1980s to approximately 60,000, less than a third of the number at the start of the century. Meanwhile, the amount of farmland, although not declining so sharply, has dropped to around eleven million acres, off about 40 percent from the record figures in 1920. Some of this decline is the result of urban sprawl. The conversion of the rich mucklands around Kalamazoo into residential and business developments is typical of what has happened throughout southern Michigan as it experienced a mushrooming

University zoologist Rollin H. Baker, in a recent study of Michigan mammals, concluded that limited numbers of wolverines did indeed inhabit parts of northern Michigan as late as the nineteenth century, although he admitted that much of the evidence was hearsay.

If the wolverine nickname could not have originated because of the animal's great abundance in the state, some have assumed that it must have resulted from the great quantity of wolverine pelts shipped out of Michigan during the fur trading days. The records indicate, however, that few if any of these furs passed through Mackinac, Detroit, and the other trading posts. By far the most common pelts were those of the beaver, but Oregon, a later fur trading center, is known as the Beaver State.

It is likely that the wolverine nickname owes its origin to the animal's reputation, whether well-founded or not, as a nasty, ill-tempered beast whose eating habits are expressed in the species' generic name, which is the Latin word meaning "glutton." Michiganians were probably first dubbed wolverines in the 1830s during the boundary dispute with Ohio. Residents of the Buckeye State may have decided that wolverine was an appropriate term to call people who were trying to prevent Ohio from gaining more territory. Such would seem to have been the view of a folksy almanac writer of that era when he declared: "The chaps from the Wolverine state are the all-greediest, ugliest, an sourest characters on all Uncle Sam's twenty-six farms, they are, in thar natur, like their wolfish namesakes, always so etarnal hungry that they bite at the air, and hang their underlips, and show the harrow teeth of their mouths, as if they'd jump right into you, an swaller you hull, without salt."

As oftentimes happens, those against whom the term was hurled in a pejorative sense came to accept the designation, using it with pride. That may be based on the fact that the wolverine, although a disagreeable beast, is also one of nature's most courageous animals.

growth unrelated to the agricultural development of an earlier day. Much of the decline also stems from the attempt to farm land, especially in northern Michigan, that proved so unproductive that the unlucky owners gave up, allowing millions of acres to revert to the state for non-payment of taxes.

But, despite the claims of the tourist industry, agriculture probably remains the second most important element in the state's economy after the auto industry. In the summer the traveler on I-94 just east of Kalamazoo can on occasion smell the celery that a few farmers continue to grow in that area, although most of the state's celery now comes from areas other than that which once had been celebrated for the product. North of Lansing the motorist on U.S. 27 can be reminded by the pungent smell of mint of another crop for which Michigan has been famous in the past. To the knowledgeable traveler along the major throughways, mile after mile of corn fields, spectacular springtime vistas of orchards in blossom, and herds of grazing cattle and sheep indicate the survival of a multibillion-dollar farm economy in a state better known for quite different products. Even today, there is no part of southern Michigan, even in metropolitan Detroit, where those who turn off the main highways are not within a few minutes' drive of open country, dotted with farms and small communities and crossroads towns such as Petersburg and Rives Junction and Overisel where William Nowlin and his father, who would be bewildered by what had happened to their Dearborn homestead, would soon feel at home.

Although located in western Wayne County near the giant Willow Run factory and metropolitan Detroit, Canton was an agricultural township. Only in recent years has urban growth seriously affected Canton's rural character, as typified by its one-room Truesdell School seen here in 1947. Courtesy, Glenna and Richard Kaiser

CHAPTER VI

SLAVERY AND THE CIVIL WAR

An elderly Laura Haviland poses with some of the barbarous objects of the institution of slavery, which had become museum pieces in part through the efforts of individuals such as herself. Courtesy, State Archives, Michigan Department of State

Of the Americans who came to Michigan in the 1830s, 1840s, and 1850s, relatively few were from the South. In fact, in 1850 the number of Michigan's residents born in Connecticut was nearly twice the number of those who were natives of all of the southern states combined. Differences between Michigan's living conditions and those in the South no doubt accounted for some southerners' disinterest, but the fact that it was part of the area in which Congress, in the Northwest Ordinance of 1787, prohibited slavery certainly caused attitudes toward Michigan to differ between northeasterners and southerners.

Although Michigan entered the Union in 1837 as one of the free states of the North, slavery had earlier existed within its borders. At one time a few residents had owned slaves known as "panis," who were Indians captured in intertribal warfare and sold into slavery by fellow Indians. As for the more common black slaves, 183 were reportedly in Michigan when it was assigned to the United States at the end of the American Revolution. Because the Northwest Ordinance's prohibition

of slavery applied only to slaves brought into the area after its adoption and did not free slaves already there, the Michigan territory's first census in 1810 listed twenty-four slaves. Thirty-two slaves were counted in 1830, but only one was found in what is now the state of Michigan, the rest being in areas to the west that were then within the boundaries of the territory of Michigan.

Regardless of any Congressional action, it is unlikely that slavery would ever have developed further in Michigan. In the late eighteenth century William Macomb of Detroit had owned twenty-six slaves, but this was an exceptional case. Most of Michigan's handful of slaveowners had only one or two slaves whom they generally employed as house servants. Michigan's climate, like that of other northern states, could not support the type of agriculture that made slavery such an attractive form of labor in the South. Thus slavery would inevitably have been treated as it had been in the older states to the east—a system of labor not worth preserving.

Black slavery ceased in Michigan

by the 1830s, and blacks were among those settling in southern Michigan in this period. By 1860 blacks totaled 6,799, a number that was less than one percent of the state's population but still exceeded that of one of Michigan's best-known immigrant groups, the Dutch. The availability of potential farmland that attracted whites also attracted blacks, some of whom came from the New England-New York area in the mainstream of pioneer migration. Far more blacks, however, came from the South; Michigan's prohibition of slavery stimulated their interest in the area as much as it discouraged that of southern whites.

Fugitive slaves who had escaped from the South via the Underground Railroad accounted for only a small number of these southern blacks, most of whom were legally free. To discourage the growth of a large free black population, many southern states passed laws requiring slaveowners who freed their slaves to move them out of the state. In 1849 the executor of the estate of Sampson Saunders, a Virginia slaveowner whose slaves were freed upon his death, resettled forty-seven on land purchased for them in Calvin Township of Cass County. He probably chose the rural, southwestern Michigan township because many blacks had been living there since the 1830s, supposedly attracted by the friendship shown them by white Quakers. Calvin Township was largely responsible for the fact that in 1860 one-fifth of Michigan's blacks lived in Cass County; only Wayne County, where Detroit is located, had more.

Whites and blacks in the mid-nineteenth century may have shared an interest in Michigan's farming opportunities, but this did not create any feelings of closeness between them. Most whites, although not wishing to see black slavery in their state, agreed with southern slaveholders that blacks were inferior and did not deserve equal treatment. One writer, discussing the various elements of the state's population in 1838, noted that there were "occasionally seen some of the Negro race, but they are fortunately few in number."

Discrimination against blacks was openly practiced and officially condoned since territorial days, when an 1827 law required all blacks in the territory to present proof that they were legally free and to post a $500 bond guaranteeing their good behavior. When Detroit in 1842 became the state's first school district to provide free public education, black children were from the outset segregated from white children. In 1835 delegates to Michigan's first constitutional convention dismissed with little debate the suggestion that black men be permitted to vote. When a new constitution was submitted to voters in 1850, the question of extending voting rights to black men was included on the ballot as a separate issue, which white voters promptly rejected, 32,026 to 12,840. (Blacks in 1855 were authorized to vote in school elections, a move largely resulting from Calvin Township's predominantly black population. The change did not benefit Detroit blacks because the city's school board members were appointed, not elected.)

In spite of such discriminatory attitudes toward blacks, many northern whites vehemently opposed slavery and sought to abolish it nationwide. Quakers in Lenawee County formed Michigan's first antislavery society in 1832. Especially prominent among its organizers was Elizabeth Chandler, a young poet whose antislavery writings had brought her fame before she settled in Adrian, Michigan, in 1830. She died in 1834, but other women continued the fight against slavery, notably Laura Haviland. Another Quaker who spent her life fighting for black freedom, Haviland and her husband established a school near Adrian, where she sought

to enable blacks to fully enjoy the benefits of their freedom. In the 1850s, the legendary freed slave Sojourner Truth settled in Battle Creek, where she continued the antislavery activities that made her famous.

In 1836 the Michigan Antislavery Society was formed at a meeting in Ann Arbor's Presbyterian church. Lenawee County Quakers were again prominent in this organization, but the Presbyterians' involvement exemplified the interest that other religious groups were now showing. The antislavery views of many northern Methodists, Baptists, and Presbyterians ultimately split these denominations into northern and southern factions. In Michigan some ardently antislavery Methodists in Wayne County opposed the views even of their northern brethren, prompting them in 1841 to help form the Wesleyan Methodist church. The splinter group still maintains a separate identity long after other northern and southern Methodist organizations reunited earlier in this century. Yet by the late 1830s many abolitionists real-

ized that the movement's religious orientation had failed to persuade many slaveholders of the sinfulness of their ways, leading some to consider political action as the more appropriate course to take—and one to which Michigan would significantly contribute.

Political parties were largely unknown in Michigan prior to the 1830s, in part because few offices in the territory were filled by election until the mid-1820s, and in part because modern political party organizations had not fully emerged. From the 1830s to the mid-1850s Michigan was dominated by the Democratic party, the party of Andrew Jackson. His two terms as president coincided with southern Michigan's settlement boom, resulting in the naming of several newly established counties after Jackson and such members of his administration as John C. Calhoun, Martin Van Buren, John M. Berrien, Samuel D. Ingham, and Michigan's own Lewis Cass. The Whig party, which arose in opposition to Jackson, was a perennial loser in Michigan; its policies generally did not

Above left: *Elizabeth Chandler's life ended tragically at a young age shortly after her arrival in the state, but not before her writings had made her the first Michigan woman to become a nationally known leader in the antislavery movement. Courtesy, State Archives, Michigan Department of State*

Above: *Father Gabriel Richard, a refugee from the French Revolution, served his Detroit parish from 1798 until his death during a cholera epidemic in 1832. He was active in educational developments, and in the mid-1820s, with the backing of Michigan's French-speaking voters, served a term as the territory's non-voting delegate in the U.S. House of Representatives. Until the 1970s Richard had the distinction of having been the only Catholic priest to serve in Congress. Courtesy, State Archives, Michigan Department of State*

James G. Birney, as depicted in this typical nineteenth-century portrait of a public figure, clearly was a man whose formidable physical appearance could have helped bring him political victory had he identified himself with more popular causes then abolitionism. Courtesy, State Archives, Michigan Department of State

appeal to westerners. It took unusual circumstances to enable the Whigs to score their only victories in Michigan in the gubernatorial election of 1839 and the presidential election of 1840.

The antislavery societies failed to get any support from the Democrats and Whigs because the parties feared losing their members in the South. Consequently, the abolitionists organized the Liberty party, whose overriding interest was simply to end slavery. In 1840 and 1844 the Liberty candidate for president was James G. Birney, an Alabama slaveholder who had become convinced that slavery was wrong and, at great cost to himself, had freed his slaves, become a leader in the antislavery movement, and moved north. In 1841 he settled in Lower Saginaw, later renamed Bay City. Friends urged him to settle in a less remote, more civilized part of the country, but Birney enthusiastically supported his adopted state. The people of Michigan, he said, were "intelligent, imbued more than is common in their circumstances, with religious sentiments—law-abiding, hospi-

table, and generous. This is the mental and moral soil on which the shoot of Liberty naturally springs and grows."

Birney's candidacy had little impact on the election of 1840, as most voters supported parties whose platforms appealed to a variety of concerns, rather than to just one. In Michigan's 1843 gubernatorial race, however, the 2,775 votes that Birney received, although leaving him a distant third, indicated increasing support for the Liberty party. This support made Birney the deciding factor in the 1844 presidential election, when he was the first Michigan resident to run for president.

The 1844 campaign revolved around the issue of annexing the slave state of Texas, which the Liberty party and many other northerners opposed. The Democrats nominated James K. Polk of Tennessee, who promised not only to acquire Texas but also to gain control of the Oregon country, thereby attracting many northern votes. Whig candidate Henry Clay had hoped to keep Texas out of the campaign, but Polk's promises compelled him to shore up southern support by promising to annex Texas in a way that would satisfy both sections. Many northern Whigs, unhappy with Clay for waffling on the Texas issue, cast their votes for Birney, enough of them deserting Clay in New York to give that state's electoral vote—and the election—to Polk. Birney's critics charged that all he had accomplished was to elect the one candidate whose triumph assured the very thing Birney wished to prevent. His defenders argued that he had laid the groundwork for the antislavery political movement's emergence as a major party.

After 1844 recurrent illness ended Birney's political activity and eventually forced him to leave the rigors of the Saginaw Valley for more comfortable surroundings in the East. In 1848, however, another Michigan political figure,

Lewis Cass, ran for president on the Democratic ticket, the party that in normal circumstances would have been the favorite to win.

In the era of television campaigning, Cass would have had little chance of winning his party's nomination, let alone the election. Although he sometimes showed statesmanlike qualities, he was the very opposite of photogenic, was given to long-winded, boring speeches, and rarely showed any humor or other endearing personal characteristics. In short, he was dull. Nevertheless, Cass had served as governor of Michigan territory, secretary of war under Jackson, American minister to France, and United States senator from Michigan; by the mid-1840s he had achieved a ranking among national political leaders rarely if ever equalled by any other Michigan politician. When President Polk chose to serve only one term, Cass was the acknowledged front-runner for the Democratic nomination in 1848.

The hottest issue this time was whether slavery should be allowed in the area west of Texas, which the country was about to receive as the victor in the Mexican War. Cass, a New Hampshire native and a Detroit resident since 1813, was no defender of slavery, but like many who had grown up in the early days of the republic he believed the preservation of the Union took precedence over all other issues. Thus he sought a middle-of-the-road approach to the question of slavery in the western territories. He proposed that Congress take no stand and allow unrestricted migration into these territories, and when the territory gained self-governing rights its residents could resolve the slavery question. This idea appealed to moderates in the North and South and gained Cass the Democratic nomination in 1848, making him the only Michigan resident until Gerald Ford in 1976 to be the candidate of a major party. But Cass had an-

gered those northern Democrats who favored a congressional ban on any further expansion of slavery. Enough of them voted for the popular old Democratic war horse Martin Van Buren, the candidate of the antislavery party that was now called the Free-Soil party, to enable Whig candidate Zachary Taylor to gain the victory.

Despite Cass's defeat, his approach to the slavery question was adopted in 1850 when Congress created the territories of Utah and New Mexico despite bitter opposition from antislavery congressmen, including Michigan Democrat Kinsley S. Bingham. However, an 1854 proposal to apply the same principle to the new territories of Kansas and Nebraska, thereby allowing the choice of slavery where Congress in the Missouri Compromise of 1820 had said it was forever prohibited, completely unhinged existing political alignments in the North.

Those opposed to the Kansas-Nebraska bill met at Detroit, Grand Rapids, Jackson, and other Michigan towns in February 1854. In addition to

This portrait of Lewis Cass appeared as the frontispiece in a history of Michigan published in 1856. The book was dedicated to Cass, and with good reason. The text consisted largely of translations of documents relating to early Michigan which Cass had obtained from the French Colonial Archives while he served as the American diplomatic representative to France from 1836 to 1842. From Sheldon, The Early History of Michigan . . . , *1856*

Above: *Van Buren County in southwestern Michigan was named for him, but Michigan voters, who were not eligible to vote in 1836 when Martin Van Buren was elected president, did not support him in his losing bid for a second term in 1840. In 1848 Van Buren's presence as a third-party candidate led to the defeat of Michigan's own Lewis Cass. Courtesy, U.S. Department of State. From Cirker,* Dictionary of American Portraits, *Dover, 1967*

Above right: *On June 4, 1910, President William Howard Taft, a Republican, pulls the cord that unveils a plaque commemorating the meeting in Jackson fifty-six years before at which that political party was born. Courtesy, Ella Sharp Museum, Jackson*

the Free-Soil party, strong opposition included a faction of the Whig party led by Zachariah Chandler, the party's candidate for governor in 1852, and Democrats led by former congressman Bingham. These Democrats had broken with the regular Democratic organization of Lewis Cass, who supported the bill. The fact that Congress in May passed the controversial legislation convinced the various factions that only in unity could they effectively resist further demands of those favoring the expansion of slavery. A call went out at the end of May for a convention at Jackson on July 6 for all those who were willing to abandon previous partisan ties and unite as independents determined "to take such measures as shall be thought best to concentrate the popular sentiment of this state against the aggression of the slave power." Ten thousand signatures supported the convention plan and notices were published in newspapers throughout the state; a notable exception was the state's oldest paper, the Detroit *Free Press,* a loyal Democratic mouthpiece that fiercely opposed the antislavery leaders' actions.

The estimated 1,500 to 5,000 delegates (depending on which source you consult) who appeared in Jackson on July 6 could not be accommodated in any of the town's halls. The planning committee therefore provided a speaker's stand and temporary seating in the oak grove in what is now the heart of downtown Jackson. In this idyllic outdoor setting the delegates resolved: "That in view of the necessity of battling for the first principles of republican government and against the schemes of an aristocracy, the most revolting and oppressive with which the earth was ever cursed or man debased, we will cooperate and be known as Republicans until the contest be terminated." A new party was being organized at meetings throughout the Middle West during the first half of 1854, but the one held "under the oaks" in Jackson was the first statewide gathering of this political movement and the one that christened the party. Yet, aside from a 1910 ceremony in which President William Howard Taft dedicated a marker at the historic meeting's site, Jackson has done surprisingly little to capitalize on its legitimate claim to

Left: *In the late nineteenth century, Saginaw-born artist Eanger Irving Couse (1866-1936) became one of the best known painters of American Indians. Here Couse depicts in all his splendor Chief Shoppenegons (a name more commonly appearing as Shoppenagon), who was known to multitudes of visitors of Grayling around the turn of the century and whose name would be attached to that northern Michigan city's principal hotel. ©1987 The Detroit Institute of Arts, Gift of Charles Willis Ward*

Above: *The Indian most frequently associated with Michigan is no doubt Hiawatha, whose exploits, as recorded in Longfellow's epic poem, have long caused tourist promoters to refer to the Upper Peninsula, where Hiawatha supposedly lived, as Hiawathaland. In this 1868 painting, Albert Bierstadt depicts Hiawatha's departure "On a long and distant journey/To the portals of the Sunset," with his followers standing on the shores of Gitchee Gumee (Lake Superior). Never mind that the real Hiawatha was a member of one of the Iroquois tribes who resided in central New York. Courtesy, National Park Service, Longfellow National Historic Site*

Right: *In the 1820s an unknown primitive artist sought with considerable success to depict the furious activity that prevailed around Mackinac Island's harbor near the end of the fur trade era. The painting hangs in the island's historic Mission Church. Photo by Eugene T. Petersen*

Below right: *In 1836 George Catlin became the first major American artist to visit northern Michigan when he was touring the Great Lakes in search of the Indian subjects for which he is famous. While at Sault Ste. Marie he completed this oil painting from the Canadian side of the river, with the American fort, flag flying, visible on the opposite side. On the right are the rapids, and in the distance the entrance to Lake Superior. Courtesy, National Museum of American Art, Smithsonian Institution, Gift of Mrs. Joseph Harrison, Jr.*

Opposite page, bottom: *Few who came to Michigan during the pioneer period attracted as much attention as James J. Strang, who led a splinter group of Mormons to Beaver Island. There he proclaimed himself king and supported polygamy as one of the church's beliefs, actions which led in 1856 to his assassination and the collapse of his kingdom. An artist who obviously had never been near Beaver Island was inspired to depict the bearded monarch luxuriating in the attention of his wives, who in actuality numbered five, not eight as the unknown artist would have us believe. From the collections of Henry Ford Museum and Greenfield Village, Negative No. D-6446*

Above: *In this panoramic 1856 view of Grand Rapids by local artist Sarah Nelson, the Indian encampment on the right was a reminder of a past that was rapidly vanishing with the growth of this town, founded a quarter of a century earlier. On the right is St. Mark's Episcopal Church, built in 1848, which still stands. The large building with a cupola on the top of the hill is a school that was torn down in 1867. Courtesy, Grand Rapids Public Library*

Opposite page, top: *During much of the nineteenth century Detroit's growth resulted from its location on a waterway that linked the upper and lower Great Lakes, a theme that continually fascinated artists. Around 1900, Detroit's most famous marine artist, Robert Hopkin, painted this nostalgic scene, "'Comment Ca Va': A View of Belle Isle," depicting an earlier day when French Canadian farmers came out on the river to sell vegetables to passing ships. Courtesy, Great Lakes Maritime Institute, Dossin Museum*

Opposite page, bottom: *From the Canadian side of the Detroit River, British army doctor Edward Walsh painted this view of Detroit in 1804, a year before the frontier outpost became the capital of the new Michigan Territory. Courtesy, William L. Clements Library, University of Michigan*

An obscure artist, Thomas M. Burnham (1818-1866), incorrectly identified by generations of writers as T. H. O. P. "Alphabet" Burnham because of the way in which "Thos." appears in his signature, gained immortality with this painting of election day in Detroit, November 1837, when Stevens T. Mason, the man on the left with the top hat, was reelected to a second term as governor. The election result was never in doubt, but Mason is believed to be shown padding his victory margin by slipping a bribe to the man with his hand out, while others wait in line for their payoff. ©1987 The Detroit Institute of Arts, Gift of Mrs. Samuel T. Carson

This watercolor, showing Detroit on the far side of the Detroit River, was executed in 1820 by George Washington Whistler, father of the painter whose mother would be the subject of the son's most famous work. In the foreground is the Walk-in-the-Water, whose arrival in Michigan waters began to reduce the remoteness that had earlier separated the area from most of the country. Courtesy, William L. Clements Library, University of Michigan

Sixteen years after Whistler's rendering of the Detroit River scene, the English-born painter William James Bennett (1787-1844) set up his easel at about the same spot and painted this "View of Detroit in 1836." The amount of river traffic (including the Detroit-built, 156-foot steamship Michigan in the foreground) and the number of buildings clustered on the Detroit side of the river testify to the rapid growth that had occurred since 1820. ©1987 The Detroit Institute of Arts, Gift of the Fred Sanders Company in memory of its founder, Fred Sanders

On October 29, 1864, the black abolitionist Sojourner Truth met with Abraham Lincoln, who showed her a Bible that Baltimore blacks had given him. The meeting has been depicted by at least three artists; this painting, done in 1902 by Lottie Wilson, a black painter from Niles, Michigan, lay forgotten for many years in Washington, D.C., until it turned up in the 1980s and was purchased by the Niles Public Library. Photo by Jim Nice. Courtesy, Niles Public Library

An uncompromising foe of slavery, Zachariah Chandler became Michigan's first Republican U.S. senator in 1857. In this portrait, artist Lewis T. Ives of Detroit captured some of the toughness that made Chandler such an effective, although not a very lovable, political leader. Courtesy, Detroit Historical Museum

having been the birthplace of the Republican party.

Michigan's Republicans capitalized on the dissatisfaction caused by the Kansas-Nebraska bill to sweep to victory in the state elections that fall, beginning a nearly uninterrupted seventy-eight-year period of Republican dominance in the state. The Whig party ceased to exist as most of its members joined the new party, as did the members of the earlier antislavery party, the Free-Soilers. The Democratic party, long the majority party in the state, suffered heavy losses to the Republicans but retained enough members to carry on. It remained a minority party whose only chance of winning until well into the next century depended less on the appeal of its candidates and programs than on internal divisions among the Republicans.

Among the leaders of the July 6 convention, Kinsley Bingham carried the party to victory in 1854 and 1856 as its gubernatorial candidate. In 1860 another leader of that convention, Austin Blair of Jackson, was elected governor and would become famous as the holder of that office through all but the last five months of the Civil War. (Elected as lieutenant governor in 1860 was James Birney, whose father did not live to see him share in the triumphs that had escaped the elder Birney two decades earlier.) Bingham went to the United States Senate, succeeded upon his death in mid-term in 1861 by Jacob M. Howard of Detroit, who quickly became one of the more influential Republicans in Congress during the 1860s. Yet towering over all of these Michigan Republicans was Zachariah Chandler.

A native of New Hampshire, Chandler came to Detroit in the 1830s, becoming a highly successful merchant. He also became politically active as a Whig, a natural choice, it might seem, because that party's programs were designed to appeal to business interests.

However, it was as an aggressive, uncompromising foe of slavery that Chandler would make his mark in politics. When Abraham Lincoln, in his sole appearance in Michigan at a Kalamazoo rally in 1856, indicated a willingness to negotiate with the South on some aspects of the slavery issue, Chandler later expressed his disgust with Lincoln's moderate views, which may explain the frosty relationship between the two from that time on. In 1857 the Republican-controlled legislature elected Chandler as Michigan's first Republican U.S. senator. He succeeded Lewis Cass and quickly established his right to be paired with Cass as the two most powerful national politicians to come out of Michigan in the nineteenth century.

In 1860 the decades-old controversy over slavery reached a climax with the election of Abraham Lincoln as president. Surprisingly, Lincoln had not been the first choice of Michigan's Republicans. Their delegation had gone to the party's national convention determined to secure the nomination of veteran New York politician William Seward, a choice not so surprising considering the state's large population of ex-New Yorkers. When the convention nominated Lincoln, Austin Blair, head of the Michigan delegation, was visibly upset at Seward's defeat even while he was pledging Michigan's support of Lincoln.

Michigan Republicans swallowed their disappointment and turned out a solid majority for Lincoln, helping him gain the victory that led South Carolina to secede from the Union in December. Most of the other southern states followed, saying they could not remain in a union governed by a party opposed to slavery. Their secession prompted northern political leaders to unite, even such widely divergent figures as Zachariah Chandler and Lewis Cass. The latter, now in his late seventies, had been serving as secretary of state

This photograph suggests the idealism that propelled Austin Blair into public life, as well as the sensitive qualities that hindered Blair's efforts to overcome Zachariah Chandler's hard-nosed opposition to his ambitions to become a U.S. senator. Courtesy, State Archives, Michigan Department of State

Right: *The original three-month 1st Michigan Infantry Regiment was succeeded by a second unit, also bearing the 1st Michigan name, whose members enlisted for three years. By the fall of 1861 they were camped in the East, as depicted in this lithograph. Courtesy, Michigan Historical Collections, Bentley Historical Library, University of Michigan*

Below right: *By 1862 volunteers were not so eager to enlist as they had been in the early weeks of the war. Inducements were offered, as in Ann Arbor where the lucky recruit in a company of the 20th Michigan Infantry Regiment was promised forty dollars when he signed up, financial help for his family, and 160 acres of land and seventy-five dollars at war's end. Courtesy, Michigan Historical Collections, Bentley Historical Library, University of Michigan*

RESPOND
TO OUR COUNTRY'S CALL!!
WANTED!
100 AblE Bodied Men, to Fill up the Ranks of the
Company being raised in this city, for the
20TH REGIMENT!
$100 BOUNTY!
25 DOLLARS ON BEING MUSTERED INTO
Service; $13,00, the first month's pay and a premium of $2,
MAKING IN ALL $40
That each VOLUNTEER RECEIVES IN ADVANCE. The FAMILY of a VOLUNTEER RECEIVES $5 to $15 a month from the County.

AT THE CLOSE OF THE WAR
160 ACRES OF LAND AND THE REMAINING 75 DOLLARS OF THE BOUNTY.

The last opportunity is now offered to patriots to volunteer in the service of their country. Men must respond speedily to the call or drafting will be resorted to for our country is in danger. The drafted man receives only his $11 per month. Our government has been liberal to us—let us be prompt to sustain it. A Regiment raised in 30 days is worth two raised in 60.

Recruiting Office two doors West of Cook's Hotel in Donelly's new Block, Ann Arbor.

C. B. GRANT, CAPTAIN.

under President James Buchanan. When Buchanan, who was still president until Lincoln was inaugurated on March 4, 1861, did nothing to halt the South's secession, Cass resigned and denounced Buchanan for his failure to carry out his duty to preserve the Union. Returning to Detroit, Cass sorrowfully remarked that he remembered as a boy the celebrations held when the Union was born under the Constitution and now as an old man he was seeing its death. He lived until 1866, however, and thus saw his beloved Union preserved as a result of a war. It was the prospect of such a war that led Senator Chandler in February 1861 to make the comment for which he is best remembered: "Some of the manufacturing states think a fight would be awful. Without a little bloodletting, this Union will not, in my estimation, be worth a rush."

The blood-letting began in the middle of April when Confederate guns forced Union forces to surrender at Fort Sumter in the harbor of Charleston, South Carolina. President Lincoln proclaimed that a state of insurrection existed and called on the loyal states to furnish troops to crush the rebellion. Governor Austin Blair, who had returned to his Jackson home after the adjournment of the state legislature in Lansing, received a telegram from the War Department on April 15 asking Michigan to furnish one infantry regiment. The office of governor, which had been for his predecessors essentially a part-time job, now became a full-time responsibility as Blair and his military aides struggled to meet the successive troop calls the state received throughout the war. All told, some 90,000 men, nearly an eighth of Michigan's total population in 1860, served in the war. Thirty infantry regiments, eleven cavalry regiments, fourteen artillery batteries, and miscellaneous other units carried the Michigan name throughout their tours of army duty.

The first of these units, the First Michigan Infantry Regiment, arrived in Washington on May 16, 1861, as the first unit from the western states to come to the defense of the nation's capital. On July 21 it fought with distinction in the war's first major battle, Bull Run. The Union forces' defeat in that battle convinced firebrands such as Senator Chandler, who expected the immediate collapse of the Confederacy, that the war was not going to be any cakewalk.

When the Confederacy finally did collapse, Lieutenant Colonel Benjamin D. Pritchard and the Fourth Michigan Cavalry Regiment on May 10, 1865, captured the fleeing Confederate president Jefferson Davis. Upon delivering his famous prisoner to Fortress Monroe, Virginia, Pritchard was given a receipt that described Davis as the "late president of the so-called Confederate States of America."

In the four years that separated the actions of these two Michigan regiments, there were virtually no battles or campaigns in which Michigan soldiers were not involved, sometimes at enormous cost. The Twenty-fourth Michigan Infantry Regiment, for example, was virtually wiped out on the first day of the Battle of Gettysburg. The Michigan Cavalry Brigade played a crucial role in the events of the third day of that battle, helping to assure the Union victory that marked a turning point in the war. Commanding the brigade was George Armstrong Custer, whose family had moved from Ohio to Monroe, Michigan, just prior to the war, and whose illustrious—and controversial—military career had its beginnings with his leadership of the Michigan cavalrymen at Gettysburg.

By the end of the war, nearly 15,000 Michigan soldiers had died; two-thirds of these deaths due not to enemy bullets but to disease and other non-battlefield causes. The Sixth Michigan Infantry Regiment, for ex-

Beards were definitely de rigueur *among Civil War soldiers and cavalrymen such as Allegan's Lieutenant Colonel Benjamin Pritchard, captor of Jefferson Davis. Courtesy, State Archives, Michigan Department of State*

Veterans of the Civil War kept alive their memories of that terrible conflict through annual reunions, such as this one decades after the war at which survivors of Company G of the 13th Michigan Infantry sat for a rather grim group portrait. Courtesy, Regional History Collections, Western Michigan University

ample, had the highest fatality figures of any Michigan unit and one of the highest for the entire Union army: 504 men, over a fourth of the regiment's total enrollment, died of disease, and only 78 died in battle.

These soldiers fought and died for the restoration of the Union, a goal on which there was little disagreement. Yet from the outset, the hard-line abolitionist wing of the Republican party, led by Michigan's Senator Chandler and Governor Blair, argued that the war should be fought to rid the nation of slavery forever. Blair, in a message to the legislature on January 2, 1862, expressed his indignation at Lincoln's caution in committing the country to this goal. "To treat this enemy gently is to excite his derision," Blair declared. "To protect his slave property, is to help him to butcher our people and burn our houses. No. He must be met with an activity and a purpose equal to

his own . . . Let us hope that we have not much longer to wait." Nine months later, Lincoln issued his Emancipation Proclamation, which officially took effect on January 1, 1863, a date that Michigan blacks celebrated as the start of a new era.

Many whites, unfortunately, did not greet these developments with enthusiasm. Longstanding racial animosities were reinforced by fears that the South would fight harder and prolong the war now that it was being fought to free black slaves as well as to restore the Union. On March 6, 1863, two young white girls claimed that they had been raped by a black man—a charge the girls later admitted was pure fabrication—triggering a riot in Detroit. A mob of whites, turned back in their efforts to lynch the accused rapist, raged through Detroit's black neighborhoods, killing two blacks, seriously injuring at least a score of others, and

leaving more than 200 without shelter after their homes had been destroyed.

To their credit, Michigan's most prominent Republicans not only supported the ending of slavery as the new objective of the Union's war effort, but also fought for black rights during and after the war. In 1867, former governor Austin Blair filed a writ of mandamus in the state Supreme Court that led to a court ruling striking down the state's school segregation practices. As a member of the state legislature in the 1840s Blair had spoken out strongly in favor of giving the vote to blacks; as a member of Congress after the war he joined with Senators Chandler and Jacob Howard to successfully push through constitutional amendments that formally abolished slavery, guaranteed equal rights to all citizens regardless of race, and finally, in 1870, prohibited race from being a basis that determined one's right to vote. In 1867

a provision in a new state constitution that would have allowed black men to vote was regarded as the main reason why voters refused to ratify it. Even in 1869, after the Michigan legislature had ratified the Fifteenth Amendment to the U.S. Constitution that prohibited such racially restrictive practices, Michigan voters only barely approved an amendment to the state constitution bringing it into line with the federal voting provisions.

It had been a long struggle, but on April 7, 1870, upon the final ratification of the Fifteenth Amendment, William Lambert, a leader of Detroit's black community for over thirty years, could write: "Freedom reigns to-day!" Slavery was a thing of the past; the war that accomplished that objective and saved the Union had been over for five years. To many it now seemed time to deal with new interests that demanded attention.

CHAPTER VII

L UMBERJACKS AND MINERS

Lumbermen delighted in seeing how many logs they could stack up on a logging sled. Seeing this championship load from the 1890s, one wonders what the horses thought as they contemplated the task at hand. Courtesy, State Archives, Michigan Department of State

At midnight, December 31, 1864, Austin Blair's second and last term as governor ended. He would serve in the U.S. House of Representatives from 1867 to 1873, but his longtime ambition of becoming a U.S. senator was frustrated by the opposition of Michigan Republican boss Zachariah Chandler, and thus Blair would always be remembered as the state's "War Governor." Three years after he died in 1895, a bronze statue erected in his honor on the state capitol grounds would again recall this wartime service through which he was "inseparably linked with the glorious achievements of [Michigan's] citizen soldiers."

This linkage was a vital part of the Republican postwar strategy known as "Waving the Bloody Flag," in which it reminded voters that it was the party of Lincoln by frequently nominating as candidates such war heroes as Colonel Benjamin D. Pritchard, the captor of Jefferson Davis, and another well-known Michigan cavalry commander, Russell A. Alger. No other Michigan Civil War veteran reaped more political benefits from his war record than did Alger, who served as governor in

the mid-1880s, secretary of war under William McKinley, and U.S. senator at the time of his death in 1907. However, it is also clear that Alger's postwar activities greatly contributed to his political success.

An Ohioan who first came to Michigan in 1859, Alger settled in Detroit after the war and soon became one of the state's leading lumbermen. He contributed to the emergence of new economic activities that exploited Michigan's enormous timber and mineral resources, making the lumberjack and the miner the symbols of this new Michigan in the same way that farmers, who remained the largest economic group, had symbolized the state's earlier development. Twenty years prior to Alger's tenure as governor, the office was held from 1865 to 1869 by lumberman Henry H. Crapo, the first of a long series of political leaders who attained their positions through prominence in the lumber industry.

Aside from scattered small patches of prairie lands in the south, forests have covered Michigan since the prehistoric era. The Indians had made

At Hartwick Pines State Park near Grayling, one of the state's few surviving stands of virgin timber enables the visitor to see what the forests must have been like when they covered most of Michigan only 150 years ago. Courtesy, State Archives, Michigan Department of State

only limited use of this resource, and the French and the British used wood only to construct buildings, stockades, and, in the case of the British, sailing vessels. Thus it was only with the Americans' arrival in the early nineteenth century that any extensive lumbering got underway, and by the time Michigan became a state in 1837 there were more than 400 sawmills in operation. Yet aside from a few mills in lake ports such as Detroit and Port Huron which shipped limited amounts of lumber to destinations around the Great Lakes, these were small mills built to serve local markets in the rapidly growing southern agricultural regions. Here it was the land, and not what was on

it, that attracted the settlers. The forests, consisting mainly of hardwoods such as oak, maple, hickory, and walnut, were merely something that had to be removed before farming could commence. Eventually some farmers profited by selling the timber rights to their remaining woodlots, but stories of farmers who received for just one fine hardwood tree a price equal to the original cost of all their land indicate the potential wealth that had earlier been destroyed.

To the north of a line stretching roughly from Port Huron to Grand Haven, the hardwoods increasingly gave way to forests of softwood varieties, most notably white pine. The sandy

soils responsible for this change did not prove as suitable to farming as the richer soils farther south. Instead, the great pine forests of the north became for many decades a more than adequate substitute for farming in that region's development. It was here that large-scale lumbering activities were centered.

Northern Michigan's timber was part of a vast band of forests that began far to the east in Canada's Maritime Provinces and swept westward through New England, the St. Lawrence Valley, New York, Pennsylvania and on to Michigan, Wisconsin, and Minnesota. Logging techniques had been perfected by the end of the eighteenth century in New Brunswick and in Maine, the leader of the blossoming American lumber industry. Of the forests' variety of trees, white pine was the most highly prized by lumbermen. Cedar was cut to make shingles and hemlock was sometimes taken because tanners used its bark, but white pine dominated the lumber industry in the same way that beaver pelts had dominated the fur trade. By the 1840s the industry was clearly moving westward, as New York and Pennsylvania pushed ahead of

Maine in lumber output. It was not the lack of timber resources in the East that caused this development. New England's lumber production would not peak until the early twentieth century, but by that time production was based on spruce and other trees that had been passed over in the earlier white pine era. It was the depletion of white pine in the East that turned lumbermen's attention to the West.

By the 1830s Michigan's untapped timber resources were attracting lumbermen to the area. Big-time lumber-

ing first emerged in the Saginaw Valley, and throughout the heyday of Michigan lumbering it remained the state's leading lumber producer. Until late in the century the industry almost totally depended on rivers to transport logs to the sawmills, making the valley an ideal site. Mills located along the Saginaw had access, through such tributaries of the Saginaw as the Tittabawassee, Shiawassee, Flint, and Cass rivers, to the largest watershed in the state, which encompassed some three million acres. In 1834 Harvey Williams installed the valley's first steam-powered mill, using the engine that had once powered the *Walk-in-the-Water*, the first steamboat on the upper Great Lakes. Williams built the

mill for his nephews, Ephraim S. and Gardner D. Williams, who were agents for John Jacob Astor's American Fur Company. Now, in the dying days of Michigan's fur trade, they switched to an industry only in its infancy.

In 1836 Harvey Williams built a second steam mill at Saginaw, which Curtis Emerson purchased ten years later. Emerson was one of those hard-drinking, crude characters so common in a business in which one had to be tough to survive. When Emerson was not invited to the 1859 dedication of the Bancroft House, he proceeded to crash the party. He jumped on a long banquet table at which Saginaw's invited elite were seated, and marched along, kicking and breaking everything in his

path. The result was $2,000 in damages and injuries to a score of guests who were cut by assorted flying objects. Stewart H. Holbrook, an admiring chronicler of lumberjack deeds, called it "a gorgeous incident that tells more about the time and place than half a dozen histories of the Saginaw Valley."

Emerson's lack of the social graces was at least partially offset by his ability as a lumberman. His sawmill, he would later boast, cut enough lumber to have built a privy six feet high and six feet wide from Saginaw to Albany, New York. In any event, Albany, then the lumber capital of the nation, received in 1847 what is said to have been the East's first shipment of Saginaw white pine, which had been cut at

Emerson's mill. It was top grade white pine, what lumbermen called cork pine, and was equal to the best pine from Maine, the Pine Tree State. This quality boosted the East's interest in Michigan as a source of white pine. By 1850 Michigan had risen to fifth place among lumber-producing states behind New York, Pennsylvania, Maine, and Ohio; by 1860 it was in third place. The lumber industry developed through much of northern Michigan, especially in the northern two-thirds of the lower peninsula, which maintained its preeminent role through the remainder of the century. Muskegon, at the mouth of one of the state's longest rivers, quickly became the leading lumber center on the peninsula's western side. Yet it

This racially integrated logging crew poses at Slocum's Grove, east of Muskegon, early in this century. Blacks are not usually associated with Michigan's lumber industry, but since the days of the fur trade they have taken advantage of the same opportunities that attracted others to the state. Courtesy, Grand Rapids Public Library

In the 1870s and 1880s, at the peak of the lumber boom, the river at Saginaw was packed with logs that had been floated down its tributaries. Employees of the Tittabawassee Boom Company handled all phases of the log drive, culminating here in the task of sorting the logs according to their owners' log marks and fastening them together to be towed to the sawmills that lined the river bank. Courtesy, State Archives, Michigan Department of State

never quite matched the production levels of its rival and the state leader, Saginaw. By 1854, Saginaw's twenty-nine mills were struggling to keep up with the demand for its pine that Curtis Emerson had helped to ignite a few years before.

The interest in Michigan land which had earlier focused on the farming potential of the southern counties now shifted to the pine lands farther north and the possibilities they offered for much greater and quicker profits. Among the novice and experienced eastern lumbermen who scrambled to secure rights in Michigan timber was the state's future governor, Henry H. Crapo. A respected businessman in

New Bedford, Massachusetts, Crapo served as secretary of the Commercial Mutual Marine Insurance Company while he invested in a wide range of business interests, including New Bedford's famed whaling industry and midwestern real estate. By about 1850 Crapo's investments centered on Michigan. Contacts with a Detroit land agent during his frequent trips to Michigan led Crapo and two New Bedford business acquaintances in 1855 to acquire 12,000 acres of pine along the Flint River in Lapeer County. Crapo confidently assured his partners that heavy demand for lumber guaranteed a small fortune in profits from the logging of their tract.

On December 26, 1855, Crapo left for Michigan to oversee the logging operations. Crapo, who knew nothing about lumbering, soon discovered to his dismay that his initial expectations would have to be drastically revised. He had thought it would be simple to contract the logging of the Lapeer County tract that winter. In the spring the logs would be floated down the Flint River to the Saginaw sawmills, and by the summer the three New England partners would be pocketing the first installment on their anticipated tidy profit. However, Crapo learned that it was too late in the year to get an experienced crew of workers and supervisors for that year's logging operations, which had commenced earlier that fall. Not only was he thereby forced to delay any logging until the fall of 1856, but his discovery of a series of rapids in the Flint River also raised serious doubts about the practicality of floating logs from Lapeer County down to Saginaw. Finally, when Crapo waded through the snow to inspect the timber that he and his partners had bought sight unseen, he had a sinking feeling that they had been greatly misinformed about both the quantity and the quality of the pine.

Crapo was naturally disheartened and discouraged but he refused to give in to the temptation to abandon the whole project. Instead, in a truly remarkable demonstration of entrepreneurial skills that he probably never dreamed he possessed, Crapo fought back and developed within less than a decade perhaps the largest individually owned lumber company in the state. He began logging operations in the fall of 1856, importing lumber workers from New England. When Crapo became dissatisfied with the loggers' supervisors, he took over their role, teaching himself that phase of the business. To avoid the risks involved in shipping logs through the Flint rapids to Saginaw, Crapo persuaded his partners to purchase mills at Flint, only a few miles from the Lapeer tract. When Crapo again became dissatisfied with the sawmills' operators, he also took over that job to assure the high quality work that he believed was necessary for the operation's success.

In a few years Crapo virtually monopolized the local market for lumber in Flint. Needing larger markets beyond that area to sell his increasing amounts of lumber, Crapo built lumber yards along the Detroit and Milwaukee Railroad, sixteen miles south of Flint. Crapo initially hauled the lumber over a plank road to the yards, but in 1864 he constructed a railroad over the same route. This railroad, along with the other rail connections Flint had by then acquired, enabled Crapo to expand his lumber sales throughout the Middle West and beyond.

Crapo had bought out his New Bedford associates, who lacked his commitment to a venture that was at best only marginally profitable until 1863. In that year, all of the work he had put into the business finally paid off. This success was accomplished only with Crapo's incredible exertion, which, with the added responsibilities he assumed as governor, hastened his death at the age of sixty-five in 1869.

When Crapo died he was, by some estimates, a millionaire, a term rarely applied to a Michigan resident prior to that time. By the late 1860s, however, Michigan had become the number one lumber-producing state in the nation, a position it held until the very end of the century. The work begun by pioneers like Crapo was now pursued with such intensity that by 1880 Michigan's logging camps and sawmills were producing nearly as much lumber as the next three states combined. They were also producing millionaires by the scores—ninety-eight in Saginaw and Bay City, forty in Muskegon, and uncounted others in such lumber centers as Manistee, Ludington, Traverse

When Henry Crapo in the 1860s managed to fit politics into an already hectic business career and was successively elected mayor of Flint, state senator, and finally governor, he had taken on a decidedly Lincolnesque appearance, as befitted one who was a loyal member of Lincoln's party. Courtesy, The Flint Journal

MICHIGAN'S
TERRIBLE CALAMITY.

DANSVILLE SOCIETY OF THE

RED CROSS.

A CRY FOR HELP!

The Dansville Society of the Red Cross, whose duty it is to accumulate funds and material, to provide nurses and assistants if may be, and hold these for use or service in case of war, or other national calamity—has heard the cry for help from Michigan. Senator O. D. Conger wrote on the 9th of September that he had just returned from the burnt region. Bodies of more than 200 persons had already been buried, and more than 1500 families had been burned out of everything. That was in only twenty townships in two counties. He invoked the aid of all our people. The character and extent of the calamity cannot be described in words. The manifold horrors of the fire were multiplied by fearful tornadoes, which cut off retreat in every direction. In some places whole families have been found reduced to an undistinguishable heap of wasted and blackened blocks of flesh, where they fell together overwhelmed by the rushing flames. For the dead, alas! there is nothing but burial. For the thousands who survive, without shelter, without clothing, without food, whose every vestige of a once happy home has been swept away, haply much, everything, can be done. The Society of the Red Cross of Dansville proposes to exercise its functions in this emergency, and to see to it that sympathy, money, clothing, bedding, everything wh'c'l those entirely destitute can need, shall find its way promptly to them. But the society is in its infancy here. It has in fact barely completed its organization. It has not in possession for imme.iate use the funds and stores which will in future be accumulated for such emergencies. It calls therefore upon the generous people of Dansville and vicinity to make at once such contributions, money or clothing, as their liberal hearts and the terrible exigency must prompt them to make. Our citizens will be called upon for cash subscriptions, or such subscriptions may be left with James Faulkner, Jr., Treasurer of the Society, at the First National Bank of Dansville. Contributions of Clothing and Bedding may be left at 154 Main street, Maxwell Block, Sewing Machine Agency of Mrs. John Sheppard.

☞A special agent of the Society will be dispatched with the money and goods to see to their proper distribution. Please act promptly.

EXECUTIVE COMMITTEE RED CROSS.

Dansville, Sept. 13, 1881.

DANSVILLE ADVERTISER STEAM PRINT.

Above: *Fire frequently swept through cutover areas in dry seasons, when piles of cuttings discarded by lumbermen were ignited by the slightest spark. The worst of these fires in September 1881 devastated whole sections of the Thumb region. Among those responding to appeals for help was the newly formed American Red Cross, which made this its first disaster relief project. Courtesy, State Archives, Michigan Department of State*

Above right: *From the sight of piles of logs on the bank of the Muskegon River and men ready to begin the annual log drive, one would hardly have suspected that the peak of Michigan's lumber industry had been passed some ten years before this picture was taken in the 1890s. Courtesy, State Archives, Michigan Department of State*

City, Cheboygan, Escanaba, and Menominee.

Yet the huge, ostentatious mansions built by these timber barons would soon be monuments to an age that had passed. "The modern saw mill is the most perfect devourer of the forest ever known," remarked a speaker at the state's semi-centennial celebration in 1886. The larger mills, he said, could cut 55 million board feet of lumber a year, "and as the average of pine to the acre is about 10,000 feet, one year's work will clear 5,500 acres. At that rate our pine will soon be exhausted." And so it was. At the end of the century the great forests in the lower peninsula were nearly gone, and Michigan had slipped to second place in lumber production. A long period of decline set in, continuing until Michigan reached a level of production that could be maintained by the compara-

tively modest, controlled logging operations that have prevailed in the latter years of the twentieth century.

Nearly all of northern Michigan benefited economically, if only for a relatively brief period, from the cutting of the region's timber. Those areas fortunate enough to also possess significant mineral deposits were much more scattered, but the economic benefits resulting from mining occurred over a much longer period and were sometimes the source of even greater wealth.

The variety of Michigan's minerals is extraordinary and their exploitation has at various times made the state a major source—even the number one source—of salt, gypsum, limestone, sandstone, and sand and gravel; it has also produced less significant amounts of coal, oil, natural gas, and even gold and silver. To most people, however, mining in Michigan immediately

brings to mind the copper and iron ore mines of the western Upper Peninsula, where for many years the most famous and most profitable mining occurred.

Rarely is a single individual responsible for starting a development of major importance, but a notable exception is Douglass Houghton, whose surveys sparked Michigan's mining industry. As a twenty-one-year-old graduate of New York's Rensselaer Polytechnic Institute, Houghton arrived in Detroit in the fall of 1830 to deliver a series of lectures on chemistry. A group of Detroit citizens, including the ubiquitous Lewis Cass, wished "to render the evenings of winter not only pleasant but profitable" and had raised funds to sponsor what must have been Michigan's first adult education program. Unlikely as it would have seemed in that remote frontier community, Houghton's twenty-six talks on

chemistry, followed by a second series on "Mechanical Philosophy and Natural History," were given before capacity audiences. The crowds, it was said, consisted "even of those who had been accustomed to look for enjoyment only in balls and pleasure parties." Houghton liked Detroit as much as Detroiters liked the engaging, enthusiastic New Yorker, and he decided to make the city his home.

Houghton, a frail-looking, little man, hung out his shingle as a physician, and the "Little Doctor," as he was affectionately dubbed, soon had one of Detroit's most successful practices. A jack of all trades, he also dabbled in dentistry and real estate speculation, and in 1842 was elected mayor. There was probably no limit to how far Houghton might have gone in Michigan had he decided to pursue a political career, but geology, rather than poli-

Few people would associate underground mining with a southern Michigan locale, but here, deep beneath the city of Detroit, the International Salt Company from 1910 to 1983 mined immense deposits of salt, most of which in recent years was used to clear snow and ice off highways. Cheaper sources of salt elsewhere caused the mining operations to close. Courtesy, State Archives, Michigan Department of State

These women at the Diamond Crystal Salt Company in St. Clair circa 1910 pack and label table salt. Here the salt was not mined but was extracted by pumping water into underground crystal deposits and then pumping out the dissolved product and removing the water. Courtesy, State Archives, Michigan Department of State

tics, medicine, chemistry, or real estate, became the overriding interest in his life. In 1837 Houghton persuaded Governor Stevens T. Mason and the legislature to create the State Geological Survey. Although the salary was far less than he would have earned had he continued his multifaceted career, Houghton served as the first state geologist, directing a program that was to have canvassed a number of resources but which soon concentrated on the state's minerals.

In 1837 and 1838, Houghton and his staff surveyed various sections of the lower peninsula, awakening an interest that eventually led to the exploitation of coal, gypsum, and salt deposits that they located. Then in 1839 and 1840 Houghton turned to the Upper Peninsula, surveying a finger of land jutting into Lake Superior, the Keweenaw Peninsula. The existence of copper there had been known since pre-

historic visitors had begun fashioning artifacts from this relatively soft metal as early as 5000 B.C. Yet in historic times, except for one halfhearted attempt around 1770, no effort at mining this copper had been made. A brief survey in 1831 had convinced Houghton of these copper deposits' potential worth, and after far more detailed investigations he published his results in 1841. Houghton concluded that copper was the only mineral in the area with commercial possibilities, but he warned that most of these deposits were not of the pure type, known as native copper, which are readily visible on the surface. Instead, the deposits were found in trap-rock formations deep beneath the surface which could be mined only with the expenditure of much time, money, and manpower.

Houghton's warning was largely ignored when his report circulated through the country, as many construed it to confirm earlier rumors that native copper, just waiting to be picked up, was far more abundant in the Keweenaw Peninsula than probably anywhere else in the world. The result was America's first great mining boom. A few prospectors arrived as early as 1841 and 1842, but it was not until 1843, after the previous year's Treaty of La Pointe had transferred clear title to the western Upper Peninsula lands from the Indians to the federal government, that large numbers of get-rich-quick types came by ship from Sault Ste. Marie. By mid-decade, thousands of people had flocked to this area along Michigan's Lake Superior shoreline, uninhabited save for a handful of Indians only a short time earlier, that was now called the Copper Country. Boom towns sprang up on the tip of the peninsula at Copper Harbor (where Fort Wilkins, the last of Michigan's wooden stockaded army posts, was built to prevent disturbances between miners and Indians), at Eagle Harbor, and at Ontonagon at the base of the peninsula. Prostitutes, saloon keepers, and gamblers quickly materialized, previewing conditions that would become better known with the rise of the celebrated boom towns of the western gold rush days. The California Gold Rush of 1849, in fact, probably siphoned off many of the miners in northern Michigan who had not already departed when the realities of the situation in the Copper Country became obvious.

It was not that there was no copper. By 1846 over 100 copper mining companies had been formed in spite of the fact that the federal government retained the mineral rights on public lands sold. Many miners presumably had found copper and thought they could make money, even though they would have to pay the government a 6 percent royalty during the first three years and 10 percent of what they took in thereafter. The expense of mining this copper, however, killed further in-

terest in almost all of these ventures. The boom nearly collapsed, even after Congress dropped the leasing idea in 1850 and allowed both the land and its mineral rights to be sold at $1.25 an acre, the same rate farmers and lumbermen had paid for Michigan land.

Michigan, however, was already the leading source of copper by 1847 (little copper had been mined in the United States), and the profits of its few successful mines in these early years maintained interest in the area. On the tip of the peninsula, the Cliff Mine, with a paid in capital of $110,905, struck a vein of native copper in 1845 that netted stockholders a more than 2,000 percent profit over the next twenty-five years. At the other end of the peninsula in the Ontonagon district, the Minesota Mine (a spelling resulting from a clerical error when the company's papers were filed) likewise benefited from the discovery of native copper, as did the National Mine, where a 500-ton mass of pure copper uncovered in 1857 sold for over $200,000. By 1860 Michigan was producing twelve million pounds of copper a year, and that was only an inkling of the production to be reached when its major area of deposits in the middle of the Copper Country began to be tapped.

Meanwhile, a year before he died in a boating accident off Eagle Harbor in 1845, Douglass Houghton convinced the federal government to combine the state's geological survey with the linear survey that had been laying out Michigan's townships since 1816. On September 19, 1844, this combined survey team, headed by the veteran surveyor William A. Burt, was working west of Negaunee in what is now Marquette County when the needle on their magnetic compass began acting strangely. Houghton's brother, Jacob, who was a member of the crew, recalled:

As we looked at the instrument, to our

This 1835 portrait of Douglass Houghton by Alvah Bradish, one of Michigan's most prolific portraitists, reveals delicate features that one does not expect in a man noted for a rugged career of exploration. Courtesy, Michigan Historical Collections, Bentley Historical Library, University of Michigan

Surveyor William A. Burt invented a solar compass and one of the early versions of the typewriter, but he is remembered primarily for his discovery of a vast body of iron ore near the future city of Negaunee in 1844. Courtesy, State Archives, Michigan Department of State

astonishment, the north end of the needle was traversing a few degrees to the south of west. Mr. Burt called out: "Boys, look around and see what you can find!" We all left the line, some going to the east, some going to the west, and all of us returned with specimens of iron ore, most gathered from outcrops.

Jacob Houghton and his fellow workers had stumbled on the first of several immense bodies of deposits that would make the Lake Superior region the world's leading source of iron ore for more than a century.

In 1845 an Indian who had been a member of Burt's survey party led several fortune-seeking men from Jackson, Michigan, to this mountain of iron. The Michigan men acquired the land and mineral rights and formed the Jackson Iron Company, which began mining in 1846. Other companies soon formed to mine an area of iron ore deposits that was found to extend up to thirty miles west of the Jackson Mine in what became known as the Marquette Iron Range. Little iron ore was mined for a number of years, however, mainly because it was difficult to ship such a bulky product, a substantial portion of which was not iron and hence was worthless. The companies initially concentrated on trying to smelt the ore on site so they could ship out iron instead of ore. Using the area's timber for fuel, a charcoal iron industry developed in the Upper Peninsula. Still, there remained the problem of shipping the

smelted iron to manufacturing centers far to the south and east.

Moving the iron to the shore of Lake Superior from the Jackson mine area, although a trip of only a dozen or so miles, was difficult enough because of the rugged terrain. Yet the biggest obstacle lay ahead at Sault Ste. Marie, where any cargoes carried by Lake Superior ships had to be unloaded, moved around the St. Mary's Rapids, and then loaded on other ships coming up from the south. Not surprisingly, individuals with interests in iron and copper mines promoted the construction of a canal and locks to facilitate unimpeded shipping between Lake Superior and Lake Huron. In 1853 Michigan contracted with the St. Mary's Falls Ship Canal Company to eliminate this barrier to

Great Lakes traffic with the promise that if the job was completed in two years the company would be awarded 750,000 acres of land granted by Congress to aid the project. On June 18, 1855, the first ships passed through the newly completed Soo Canal. The job had proven much more difficult than the company had estimated, but this was more than offset by the awarded right to select the best available timber and mineral lands in northern Michigan as part of its land grant.

The opening of what would be the first of a series of successively bigger locks was followed by other improvements that further eased the transportation problems that had hampered the growth of Upper Peninsula mining. In 1857 a railroad was completed over the

By about 1860, when this picture was taken, the operators of the Jackson Mine had dug deep into the mountain of iron ore to which the company's founders had been led in 1845. The open pit mining technique used here would rarely be possible at other Michigan iron mines, where the deposits could usually be reached only by the more expensive underground approach. Courtesy, State Archives, Michigan Department of State

dozen miles from the Negaunee area to the new town of Marquette on the Lake Superior shore. Ore docks were built at Marquette to load ships that could now carry cargoes by way of the Soo Locks straight through to their destinations to the south. Shipments which had totaled only 1,449 tons in 1855 increased to 114,401 tons by 1860. By 1864 iron ore destined for the Chicago area could be hauled by railroad from Negaunee to Escanaba where it was loaded on ore boats, thus avoiding the long voyage around the Upper Peninsula. Charcoal iron continued to be produced in this northern area for a number of decades, but as transportation costs were reduced iron ore was increasingly shipped directly to the main centers of iron and steel production in the Midwest and the East.

Michigan iron ore output exceeded one million tons a year by the early 1870s. Late in that decade ores along the Wisconsin border, southwest of the Marquette range, began to be mined. Their presence had been noted by surveyors a quarter of a century before but only now had railroad development in this part of the Upper Peninsula made it practical to begin mining operations. The Breen and Vulcan mines near Iron Mountain were first into production in 1877, and in 1882 the mining of ores in the Crystal Falls area started production in the other part of what was

now called the Menominee Iron Range. In the mid-1880s, the Colby Mine at Bessemer, in the extreme western part of the peninsula, initiated mining on the third and last of these ranges: the Gogebic Iron Range (an Indian term of uncertain meaning that was often in this period spelled Agogebic), which possessed a rich body of ores extending westward into Wisconsin for more than thirty miles. The Menominee ores were shipped to the Escanaba port, while the Gogebic ores would go out through Ashland, Wisconsin, forty miles west on Lake Superior.

As the annual production of Michigan's iron mines shot up from two million tons in 1880 to seven million tons by the end of the decade, Michigan moved well ahead of all other iron-producing states. Yet this dominance was not achieved with Michigan investment funds. Throughout its history, Michigan had depended on outside capital to develop its rich resources: French and English capital and Astor's New York-based company built the fur trade; New England financed Michigan's lumber industry; and eastern promoters completed the railroads that the state had started but found itself unable to finish in the 1840s. Although the Jackson Mine had been established by Michigan men, the money and leadership behind subsequent developments came principally from Cleve-

In the early days, when iron ore was loaded by hand at docks such as this one at Marquette, weary sailors sang: "Oh, we're bound down from Marquette, my two hands are sore;/I've been pushing a wheelbarrow, and I'll do it no more./ I'm humpbacked from shoveling, so listen to my roar;/ When we get to Cleveland, I'll shake red iron ore." Courtesy, State Archives, Michigan Department of State

land, Ohio. There, in the 1840s, a group of young business and professional men had been swept up in the interest generated by Douglass Houghton's reports on Upper Peninsula minerals. In 1846, J. Lang Cassel, a geologist hired by some of the Clevelanders to investigate possible Michigan mining sites, met a Jackson Mine official who was bringing samples of the first ores through Sault Ste. Marie. Cassel's new information prompted the Clevelanders to turn their attention away from Michigan copper to Michigan iron ore. The Cleveland Iron Company (later retitled the Cleveland Iron Mining Company) was organized in 1847, staking a claim to iron ore lands at present-day Ishpeming, just west of Negaunee. In 1853 it absorbed the Marquette Iron Company, backed by New England interests, whose claims to the same body of ore deposits had been overruled by the courts.

It was also in 1853 that Samuel L. Mather, one of the original organizers of the Cleveland Iron Mining Company, began to dominate its affairs. From that time until his death in 1890, Mather devoted his attention to building the company into the biggest Michigan iron ore producer. It owned large areas of timber to provide fuel for its charcoal iron production, and a fleet of ore boats to haul its ore southward to Cleveland. Many said that Mather's

company "contributed more than any other to the beginning of Cleveland's industrial prominence."

Upon Mather's death, his son, William G. Mather, merged the company with its principal competitor on the Marquette range, the Iron Cliffs Company, forming the Cleveland-Cliffs Iron Company in 1891. William Mather continued for decades to head this consolidated giant which remains the dominant iron ore producer in the Upper Peninsula. Meanwhile, Mather's half-brother, Samuel Mather, formed Pickands, Mather & Company in 1883. The Cleveland firm leased and operated iron mines in the Upper Peninsula and in the iron ranges of Minnesota, and like Cleveland-Cliffs, had its own fleet of ore boats. During the same period the third of these Cleveland iron mining giants, M.A. Hanna & Company, was formed by Marcus Alonzo Hanna. Hanna divided his time between Upper Peninsula iron mining activities and politics, successfully managing William McKinley's presidential campaigns in 1896 and 1900.

As Michigan became a leading source of iron ore, its copper production continued to grow, benefiting from the opening of the Soo Locks and the construction of railroads into the Copper Country. In 1873 the Portage Lake and Lake Superior Ship Canal was completed with the aid of another federal

Samuel Mather, eldest son of the Cleveland-Cliffs' Samuel L. Mather, founded Pickands, Mather and Company in 1883 with James Pickands and Jay Morse. The company soon ranked second in iron ore production behind Cleveland-Cliffs. Courtesy, State Archives, Michigan Department of State

In 1883 in the westernmost part of the Upper Peninsula, these men were part of a crew exploring for iron ore in the third and last of Michigan's iron ranges—the Gogebic. Within a couple of years the town of Ironwood would begin to emerge on this site, and by the end of the decade it was one of the fastest growing mining towns in the peninsula. Courtesy, State Archives, Michigan Department of State

A steam shovel loads ore cars from the huge piles of ore brought up from a mine shaft at one of the Cleveland-Cliffs mines in Ishpeming in 1903. Courtesy, State Archives, Michigan Department of State

land grant. The canal cut through the middle of the Keweenaw Peninsula, allowing lake vessels easier access to what had become the most important copper mining area.

Unlike the earlier mines at the opposite ends of the Copper Country which had mined great masses of native copper, those mining the middle section found the copper generally embedded in rock formations that had to be crushed so that the copper could be extracted and then smelted into bars for shipping. The added costs of mining this copper and obtaining perhaps a hundred pounds of the metal for each ton of rock mined caused many to initially shun the area. Those first impressions were soon dispelled, however, by the Quincy Mine at Hancock on the north side of Portage Lake. Working a type of porous, copper-bearing rock known as amygdaloid in the mid-1850s, the mine extracted over 300 million pounds of refined copper during the next eighty years. Grateful stockholders referred to the Quincy as "Old Reliable" because of the regularity of

its dividend payments. Yet it was soon overshadowed, as were all other Michigan mines, by the rise of the great Calumet and Hecla Mining Company a dozen or so miles north of Portage Lake.

In 1859 Detroit civil engineer Edwin J. Hulbert discovered a portion of what turned out to be an immense body of conglomerate rock, a solid mixture of sand, pebbles, copper, and other materials, much richer in copper than the softer amygdaloid to the south. During the next five years Hulbert bought some 2,000 acres of land in the area, but he lacked the capital needed to develop these properties. In the mid-1860s he found investors in Boston, which was soon financing Michigan's copper mining in the same way that Cleveland supported the state's iron mining. Yet as a stockholder and manager of the newly formed mining companies, Hulbert, despite his previous copper mining experience, proved totally unable to manage these mines. To protect the investments, major stockholder Quincy Adama Shaw ousted

Hulbert in 1867 and installed Shaw's brother-in-law, Alexander Agassiz, to manage the mines.

Agassiz, son of the great Harvard naturalist Louis Agassiz, set the operations on a sound, profit-making course within two years. By 1871, when the several mines were consolidated into the Calumet and Hecla firm, Agassiz had boosted its share of the state's copper output from 8 percent in 1867 to more than 60 percent, a figure that remained relatively constant through the remainder of the century. By 1884, a 20 percent share of the company's stock would have already earned five million dollars in dividends, while one share of that stock, which was then selling for around $250, would rise as high as $1,000 in 1907.

Alexander Agassiz, meanwhile, devoted more of his time to his real interest, zoology. Traveling to the Copper Country twice a year to keep the operations on track, he spent the rest of the year serving as curator of Harvard's Museum of Natural History. In the 1870s, Quincy Shaw, perhaps

driven by guilt feelings, gave Edwin Hulbert a thousand shares of Calumet and Hecla, which Hulbert proceeded to squander on more unsuccessful projects. Hulbert then spent his last years in Italy (thanks to a generous pension from Shaw), reflecting on the wealth that might have been his and claiming to know of another vein of copper deposits "far richer than the richest part of the Calumet conglomerate."

By the time of Hulbert's death in 1910 the great days of Michigan copper and iron mining were, like the boom days of Michigan lumbering, rapidly fading. Copper output continued to rise for a few years, peaking at nearly 270 million pounds in 1916, while the annual output of Michigan's three iron ranges rose to 18 million tons in the same period. But other areas had long since supplanted Michigan as the leading source of these metals. In the mid-1880s, Michigan lost its dominance in copper to western states such as Montana, Arizona, and Utah; although Michigan's production increased over the next thirty years, its share of the

national output steadily shrank. Likewise, in 1900 Minnesota replaced Michigan as the number one producer of iron ore.

Much of the western copper and the iron ore on Minnesota's great Mesabi Range could be mined by the open pit method, whereas nearly all of Michigan's copper and iron mining companies had long since had to resort to using more costly underground mines to reach deposits that were now being found at depths of as much as a mile. Consequently, Michigan companies could not remain competitive because of their higher production costs, leading to the decline of the state's iron ore and copper production. It signaled the start of troubled economic times for the western Upper Peninsula areas, just as the exhaustion of the pine forests had earlier marked the beginning of hard times for the northern lower peninsula.

In the good years from the 1840s to the 1900s, lumbering and mining had attracted to northern Michigan a population significantly different from the one that had been drawn by farming into the southern counties. The

New England element that had been so dominant in the south provided investment capital for northern developments and much of the lumber industry's early work force, but foreign immigrants formed a much higher percentage of northern Michigan's population.

Some immigrant groups were found throughout the state. The Irish and the Germans, the two largest immigrant elements in the mid-nineteenth-century population of southern Michigan, were often found in northern lumber camps and sawmills. Although Germans were relatively uncommon in the mining areas, Irish miners were a substantial element in most mining towns. Canadians, especially French Canadians, were another familiar group in lumbering areas.

Other immigrants, however, were from areas largely unrepresented in the farming counties. Scandinavians—Swedes, Norwegians, and to a much lesser extent, Danes—were one of the largest groups drawn upon by the lumber industry since the 1850s; a considerable number of Swedes also located in the mining towns. By the 1870s Finnish immigrants formed an increasingly important source of labor in the mines, and many of them used their

earnings to buy farms. The resulting Finnish influence in the rural areas of the Upper Peninsula continues in evidence today.

Many immigrants from southern and eastern Europe were also drawn to the Copper Country and the three iron ranges, but the best known and earliest immigrant group to arrive in the mining areas were peoples from Cornwall. Many Cornish miners were thrown out of work with the sharp decline in the centuries-old copper and tin mining activities in their southwestern English duchy. They flocked to the Upper Peninsula, and their excellent reputation as miners gained them the top supervisory jobs—those officials who were referred to as "Captains"—as well as jobs underground.

Lumbering and mining and the people they involved left a permanent mark on northern Michigan, but by the early 1900s the growth these activities had fostered was at an end. At the same time, Michigan's agriculture had also passed its peak of development in terms of the number of people it could support. But the appearance of a new source of opportunity, in the nick of time, saved the state from an economic decline and instead launched it into another extended period of growth.

Above left: *These Michigan lumberjacks pause from their day's labor in 1917 when, as this photograph indicates, little timber was left to be harvested. Courtesy, State Archives, Michigan Department of State*

Above: *Two young Scandinavian immigrants stopped off in a photographer's studio on October 8, 1889, proudly dressed and equipped for the jobs they had as part of an Upper Peninsula geological survey team. Courtesy, State Archives, Michigan Department of State*

CHAPTER VIII

MANUFACTURING AND THE AUTOMOBILE

In the second decade of the twentieth century the Ford Motor Company made frequent use of this photograph, showing one day's production of Model T chassis at its Highland Park plant, to illustrate the astonishing advances made possible by mass production. Courtesy, State Archives, Michigan Department of State

As writer William Saroyan was driving across southern Michigan on his way back to California during the summer of 1963, his cousin, a fellow Californian who was riding with him, remarked: "I never expected Michigan to be so good to be in ... I mean, whenever I've *thought* of Michigan—and I've never made a point of it—I've thought of the automobile industry, I haven't thought of a big green place, like this."

It is a typical reaction of those visiting Michigan for the first time. Because the national news media tends to focus on Detroit and its industrial achievements and problems, the sight of Michigan's great expanses of green farmland is bound to be a surprise. Given the number of Fords coming out of Dearborn, the Pontiacs from the city of the same name, the Oldsmobiles from Lansing, and the Buicks and Chevrolets assembled in Flint, it is not surprising that the automobile industry is all that visitors think of when Michigan comes to mind. Yet just as it is incorrect to categorize twentieth-century Michigan simply as an urban-industrial state, it has also never been accurate to describe Michigan manufacturing only

in terms of automobiles.

Actually, manufacturing had its beginnings in Michigan decades before automobiles were produced anywhere in the world. In 1850 few significant manufacturing developments had occurred in the state; probably no more than one percent of Michigan's wage earners were employed in what would now be regarded as a factory job (the figure given at the time was considerably higher because the census bureau included sawmill and other lumber industry jobs under the classification of manufacturing). By 1900, however, an estimated one of every four Michigan workers was engaged in a manufacturing occupation—and in that year an automobile industry had not yet emerged in the state.

Nearly all of the manufacturing that developed in the last half of the nineteenth century was confined, as it is now, to the southern third of the lower peninsula. Those seeking to exploit Michigan's timber and copper and iron ore had to go wherever those resources were located; those interested in establishing a factory, however, favored the more heavily populated

Michigan winters annually provided a fresh supply of ice which could be harvested and stored for use in the warmer months of the year. The Knickerbocker Ice Company of Harbor Springs used this tramway in 1889 to carry ice from Little Traverse Bay to the company's storage facilities. Courtesy, Michigan Historical Collections, Bentley Historical Library, University of Michigan

counties in southern Michigan, which provided a ready source of labor, a substantial local market, and easy access to larger markets throughout the Middle West and beyond. To manufacturers, southern Michigan was a more attractive location than the remote, less developed areas to the north.

Factors other than population density and transportation facilities can, of course, determine the location of a factory. The availability of materials needed to manufacture a product may make it necessary or at least desirable to locate close to those resources. For example, the chemical industry which developed in Michigan toward the end of the nineteenth century was based entirely on the processing of the state's

salt and brine deposits. As it happened, the deposits that were of interest to the industry were mainly in southern Michigan.

At Wyandotte the founder of the Pittsburgh Plate Glass Company, Captain John B. Ford, launched an experiment in 1890 to see if the deposits of rock salt found in the Detroit River area could be used to produce soda ash. Ford and other American glass makers generally had to import the chemical, which is needed to make glass. The experiment was a success, leading to the creation of what became the Wyandotte Chemicals Corporation, now a division of the West German chemical firm, BASF. In Detroit Ford's family was soon referred to as the "Salt"

Fords or the "Chemical" Fords, to distinguish them from those other Fords. By 1918, the Wyandotte Company and other firms had made the Detroit area the center of a chemical industry that annually shipped more than 200 million pounds of soda ash.

In the same period, Herbert H. Dow, a young chemist from Cleveland, successfully employed a new process for extracting bromine from the brine deposits found in the Midland area, marking the beginnings of the giant Dow Chemical Company, incorporated in 1897. Few communities of any size are as completely linked with the destinies of one company as are Midland and Dow, and the brine deposits of that area would remain a major element in

Dow's line of products until the mid-1980s.

In the twentieth century Michigan has also become one of the leading sources of portland cement. Although one major company, Dundee Cement, is located in the southeastern Michigan town of that name, this is one industry that also developed in northern Michigan because of the area's limestone, an ingredient in one of the cement manufacturing processes. In 1907 members of the "Salt" Ford family helped establish the Huron Portland Cement Company at Alpena, which capitalized on the area's vast limestone deposits to become the world's largest cement plant. Petoskey and Charlevoix have also accommodated northern Michigan ce-

Established by John B. Ford, the Wyandotte Chemicals facility in Wyandotte produced soda ash for glass manufacturers. In the foreground of this 1960 photo is one of the corporation's Great Lakes vessels. Courtesy, State Archives, Michigan Department of State

Herbert H. Dow rented this well in 1891 to demonstrate the superiority of the method he had developed to extract bromine from underground brine in the Midland area. Courtesy, State Archives, Michigan Department of State

A mid-twentieth century aerial view of the Huron Portland Cement operations at Alpena would seem to support the company's claim that it was the world's largest cement plant. Courtesy, State Archives, Michigan Department of State

ment producers.

One of Huron Portland Cement's founders was Stanford T. Crapo, whose grandfather, Henry Crapo, had declared in the 1860s that

All that Michigan wants is a little time to pay all her debts, and the use of a little capital, a small amount compared with what Massachusetts requires, to set in motion a thousand branches of industry and enterprises, that would at once not only free her from debt, but make her prosperous and rich.

Perhaps the major contribution made by the elder Crapo and other lumber-

men of his day to Michigan's subsequent development was in creating family fortunes. Wealth enabled more than one of Crapo's grandsons, for example, to play major roles in the establishment of new ventures and reduced the state's dependence on outside capital and leadership.

Of course, the timber resources that made these family fortunes also triggered the rise of numerous industries dependent on wood for their products. In the twentieth century, northern Michigan communities such as Munising, Manistique, and Alpena became the sites of paper mills that used the area's remaining forests as a source of wood pulp. Michigan's paper industry, however, originated long before that time in such southern Michigan locations as Monroe, Ypsilanti, and Kalamazoo, whose mills used rags, straw, and other materials instead of wood. The Kalamazoo Paper Company, organized in 1866, became the nucleus around which a host of other diversified paper companies developed in nearby communities such as Plainwell, Otsego, and Parchment, making that area the center of Michigan's paper industry.

The manufacture of sashes and doors, shingles, matches, toothpicks, and many other wood products developed simultaneously with the sawmills

in the major centers of the lumber industry. As early as the 1880s companies in Saginaw and St. Johns were cutting lumber to the exact specifications of a particular building, marking the beginnings of the prefabricated housing unit decades before such buildings achieved widespread notoriety after World War II. The availability of wood in this area also accounted for the rise of companies building wooden carriages and wagons, and by the 1890s Flint referred to itself as "The Vehicle City." The individual most responsible for putting Flint in the forefront of this industry was Henry Crapo's most famous grandson, William Crapo "Billy" Durant. Using extraordinary promotional skills and the prestige and wealth of his Crapo connections, Durant created the Durant-Dort Carriage Company, which vied with the older Studebaker firm of South Bend, Indiana, for the honor of being the biggest company in the business.

Of Michigan's various wood-related industries, none achieved the attention that the furniture industry received by the latter part of the nineteenth century. Although Detroit and a number of other southern Michigan towns had furniture factories, Grand Rapids was the industry's center. In fact, it was probably the first city in the

state to win widespread fame and recognition for a manufactured product.

Unlike most of the industrial developments discussed earlier, Grand Rapids' success was not a result of good location or resource availability. Until the 1870s, the town was poorly situated in comparison with communities farther south that had had good rail connections with the major markets in the Midwest and the East for two decades. Those same southern Michigan communities were also surrounded by hardwoods which were commonly used for the furniture of that period, while Grand Rapids was in an area where the forests were beginning to consist mainly

By 1905 the sprawling Dow Chemical Company in Midland testified to the success of Herbert H. Dow's method of extracting bromine from underground brine. Courtesy, State Archives, Michigan Department of State

These workers in one of the Kalamazoo Paper Company's coating rooms took a break from what was obviously a messy job to have their picture taken, circa 1920. Courtesy, Regional History Collections, Western Michigan University

Above: *Lumbering attracted New Englander Charles C. Comstock to Michigan in the mid-nineteenth century, but shortly after his arrival Comstock switched his interest to a wood-working activity, the furniture industry. Courtesy, State Archives, Michigan Department of State*

Above right: *In the late nineteenth century most of Michigan's approximately 125 manufacturers of carriages and wagons were not big operations, like Flint's Durant-Dort Carriage Company, but were more like Wichers & DeKruif & Company, whose one-, two-, and three-seat buggies are displayed here on Zeeland's Main Street. Courtesy, Zeeland Historical Museum*

of softwood trees. A succession of enterprising pioneers, however, enabled Grand Rapids to overcome such disadvantages.

William Haldane, a cabinetmaker, started it all in the mid-1830s, taking orders from area residents for handcrafted pieces of furniture. As his business grew, he added workers and began to use power from the Grand River for some of his operations, encouraging others to enter the business. In the 1850s, Charles C. Comstock was the first to look beyond the local market and manufacture furniture in relatively large quantities. Until the railroad arrived, he used the Grand River and Lake Michigan to ship the furniture to dealers in the Midwest. In the 1860s, Julius Berkey began emphasizing high-quality furniture, and by the 1870s his firm, Berkey and Gay, was one of the first Grand Rapids companies to tap the large markets of the East. Grand Rapids' position among the nation's furniture centers declined in the twentieth century, but firms such as Sligh, Herman Miller, and Baker in Grand Rapids and the nearby communities of Zeeland and Holland maintained the area's enviable reputation for fine furniture. In recent times, Steelcase, Zeeland's Herman Miller, Holland's

Haworth, the Grand Rapids-based Westinghouse Furniture Division, Stow Davis, American Seating, and Muskegon's Shaw Walker have given the Grand Rapids area a commanding 40 percent share of the office furnishings industry, a field whose rapid growth is based on the fact that over half of America's workers now work in offices.

Not long after Grand Rapids gained prominence, Battle Creek began to achieve worldwide renown as the "breakfast food city." Although cereal production can be classified as a food-processing activity, the origins of Battle Creek's breakfast food companies were not similar to those of the Saginaw Valley's sugar factories or other agriculturally related industries in southern Michigan's farm country. Companies making various kinds of farm equipment sprang up in such places as Port Huron, Jackson, and Albion, and the products of Battle Creek's Advance Thresher and Nichols & Shepard companies gave rise to its claim in the 1890s that it "made more traction engines and threshing machinery than . . . any other city in America." Yet the fact that Battle Creek's breakfast foods are made with local grains had nothing to do with the origins of the companies so famous today for their sponsorship of television's Saturday morning cartoon shows.

Kellogg, Post, and the rest have their origins in a decision made by leaders of the Seventh-day Adventists in the mid-nineteenth century to make Battle Creek their headquarters. The group's spiritual leader, Sister Ellen White, had visions in the 1860s that prompted the leaders to make health and diet important parts of the members' religious beliefs. In 1877 Dr. John Harvey Kellogg, a member of a prominent Battle Creek-area Seventh-day Adventist family, assumed the direction of the Battle Creek Sanitarium, which the church had established to practice its ideas regarding proper health care. Seeking ways to make his patients' meals more interesting while still adhering to the church's insistence on a vegetarian diet devoid of any liquids containing stimulants, Dr. Kellogg began creating new foods, aided by his younger brother, W.K. Kellogg. After first coming up with a hot drink that looked like coffee but had none of coffee's stimulants, the good doctor turned to cold breakfast foods. The patients liked the new items, but Dr. Kellogg refused to authorize

the sale of the products except on a limited mail-order basis to former patients. Thus it was not Kellogg but Charles W. Post, a patient for a few months in 1891, who demonstrated the commercial possibilities of Kellogg's work. In the late 1890s he aggressively marketed Postum, his own version of Dr. Kellogg's coffee substitute, and Grape-Nuts, a copy of Kellogg's first breakfast food.

The huge success enjoyed by Post's company, which is now the Post division of General Foods, led others in the early 1900s to descend on Battle Creek in hopes of stealing more of Kellogg's ideas and luring away those who had worked with him. Dismayed by others getting rich by exploiting the work that he and his brother had done, W.K. Kellogg obtained financing in 1906 to produce a flaked cereal developed by the Kelloggs that had not yet been copied. The Kellogg Company, first called the Battle Creek Toasted Corn Flakes Company, soon became the industry's giant, as it remains today. Early in the company's development, W.K. Kellogg saw the importance of selling children on these cereals in order to pressure parents into buying them, an approach that has seemingly dominated industry thinking ever since.

By 1900 close observers of developments in Michigan were realizing that as one century was giving way to another, an old economy was giving way to a new one. Rather than exploiting the state's natural resources, it was increasingly clear that any hopes for future growth now depended on the kinds of manufacturing activities developing throughout the state. It was at this time that automobiles burst on the scene, and by 1904 Detroit was already recognized as the center of auto production in the United States—indeed, in the entire world.

Detroit had just celebrated the 200th anniversary of its founding by Cadillac in the summer of 1701—an

W. K. Kellogg's advertising gimmick declaring that only his original corn flakes had his signature on the box became the subject of this 1936 New Yorker cartoon (whose seated figure is a recognizable caricature of Kellogg). The caption read: "Historic Moments in the Annals of American Industry. An efficiency engineer discovers that printing will save Mr. Kellogg from having to sign his name on each of the Corn Flakes boxes." Drawing by Rea Irvin; ©1936, 1964 The New Yorker Magazine, Inc.

Left: Dr. John Harvey Kellogg lived to be ninety-one years old, living proof, perhaps, of the kinds of health care he advocated throughout his career. The fact that his name would always be linked with the development of breakfast foods has tended to obscure the important contributions he made in areas such as public health. Courtesy, State Archives, Michigan Department of State

D. M. Ferry and Company had built the huge six-story warehouse on the right in 1887, but by the time this engraving was made in the 1890s the seed company's rapid growth had already compelled it to build the even taller warehouse on the left. From Headlight magazine

event that probably accounts for the name of one of its best-known cars, the first models of which went on sale early in 1903. For more than a century after its founding, Michigan's oldest permanently settled city had grown at a painfully slow pace when it was a fur trading and military outpost. Shortly after the War of 1812, the tempo picked up considerably as Detroit became the principal entry point and trading center for the booming interior regions of southern Michigan. Then in the last half of the nineteenth century the city's growth, though not up to that of such comparative newcomers in the area as Buffalo, Cleveland, and Chicago, was spurred by the rise of manufacturing. By the 1890s Detroit's factories employed about a seventh of the city's total population of 280,000 and annually produced goods worth approximately $100 million.

In sharp contrast with later developments that saddled the city with such nicknames as "Motown," Detroit at the end of the nineteenth century had an exceedingly diversified industrial economy. The fact that it was a major Great Lakes port helped make its shipyards and those of its immediate Detroit River environs among the busiest in the country. In turn, shipbuild-

ing, introduced by the British in the 1760s, was largely responsible for the development of the city's paint and varnish companies, engine manufacturers, and brass works. Similarly, Michigan's farming economy provided an initial boost to Dexter M. Ferry's seed company, which ultimately evolved into today's Ferry-Morse company. By the 1880s it was one of the nation's largest seed houses, annually shipping 500 carloads of seed to its dealers and filling orders from recipients of the hundreds of thousands of seed catalogs it mailed out each year. Furthermore, Michigan's timber resources spurred Detroit's furniture industry, second in the state only to that of Grand Rapids, just as the city's underground salt deposits gave rise to its chemical industry.

Yet the standard economic factors do not adequately explain the presence of other elements among Detroit manufacturers. Take the tobacco industry, the value of whose output in the 1880s exceeded that of any of Detroit's other industries. Tobacco has been grown in Ontario, some distance east of Detroit, since the prehistoric Indian era, but it has never been a crop of any significance in Michigan. Nevertheless by the 1880s Detroit was turning out an eighth of the nation's fine-cut tobacco

This 1890s engraving of the Parke, Davis pharmaceutical operations in Detroit depicts its main offices and laboratories facing the river and its four other buildings to the rear. According to Headlight *magazine it was "easily the most extensive plant in the United States or, indeed, the world." From* Headlight *magazine*

and nearly a tenth of its smoking tobacco. In addition, the millions of cigars it produced would lead to the city being termed the "Tampa of the North." A successful chewing tobacco company operated by Israel Miller and his sons in the 1840s provided the training ground for five big companies operating toward the end of the century. One who prospered from the lessons he learned in Miller's shop was John J. Bagley, Michigan's governor from 1873 through 1876. Bagley's Mayflower chewing tobacco made him a millionaire, prompting him to remark to a Detroit clergyman: "You and I thrive on the sins of the people."

Whatever the churchman may have thought of Bagley's sense of humor, it may have brought to his mind the distillery business that another Detroiter, Hiram Walker, was operating across the border in Windsor, Ontario. Closer to home, numerous Detroit breweries contributed a major share of the more than 400,000 barrels of beer produced annually in the mid-1880s by Michigan's 110 breweries. Possibly Detroit's and Michigan's oldest manufacturing activity (the city's first brewery was established around 1701), beermaking was greatly stimulated by the arrival of German immigrants in

the nineteenth century. One of these immigrants, Bernhard Stroh, continued a family brewing tradition dating back at least to 1775 by establishing a brewery in 1850 that was, at the time it shut down in 1985, the last of the Detroit breweries. However, the Stroh Brewery Company had grown into the third largest beermaker in the country and from its headquarters in Detroit it directed the operations of six brewing plants elsewhere in the country.

By the latter part of the nineteenth century, Detroit was also a leader in the pharmaceutical industry, which began when Frederick Stearns opened a drugstore in Detroit in 1855 and soon began manufacturing drugs. Stearns' company became one of the larger pharmaceutical firms in the country, but Stearns is best remembered today as a great collector—of Oriental art and baseball players. He bought Detroit's baseball team and purchased the contracts of the country's best available players, who brought the city its first national championship in 1887. By that date another Detroit drug firm, Parke, Davis, had moved ahead of the Stearns company and was claiming to be the largest pharmaceutical house in the country. The company originated in the 1860s and owed its growth largely

EUREKA IRON CO.

DETROIT, MICHIGAN.

Mills & Furnaces,
WYANDOTTE,
MICH.

General Offices,
DETROIT,
MICH.

MANUFACTURERS OF

Wyandotte BOILER PLATE and TANK IRON of all grades,

REFINED LAKE SUPERIOR (Equal to Norway) and Common BAR IRON.

CHARCOAL PIG IRON FROM LAKE SUPERIOR ORES

Especially for CAR WHEEL & MALLEABLE purposes.

Above: *Although the offices of the Eureka Iron Company were in Detroit, the real action was in Wyandotte, a town downriver which received its biggest boost when Eber Brock Ward located Eureka's mills and furnaces there in 1853. Ward's ships unloaded cargoes of iron ore from the Upper Peninsula and the ore was transformed into pig iron using charcoal made from Ward's timber holdings. The smoke belching from these chimneys announced heavy industry's arrival in the Detroit area. Courtesy, State Archives, Michigan Department of State*

Opposite page, bottom: *Although Michigan's auto pioneers showed virtually no interest in electrics, these vehicles, simple to start and quiet in operation, acquired a tiny but loyal following. Here in 1948 Mrs. Ernest Lloyd returns from shopping to her ancient Rauch & Lang electric which she drove around Ann Arbor for decades, becoming one of the city's most recognizable residents. Courtesy, Ann Arbor News*

to the management of Hervey C. Parke. Unlike the Stearns company, which is no more, Parke, Davis, now a division of the Warner-Lambert Company, remains one of the most familiar business names in Detroit and other Michigan communities where its branches are located. Some of those outstate areas were the sites of other nineteenth-century drug companies, both reputable and otherwise. Nearly all of them have long since disappeared, with the notable exception of Kalamazoo's famous Upjohn Company, which had its start in the 1880s with Dr. William E. Upjohn's search for a soluble coating for the medicine capsules he prescribed for his patients. From such humble beginnings emerged today's pharmaceutical giant.

One of Detroit's most famous and widely advertised products of the late nineteenth century was its heating and cooking stoves. The three big companies, the Detroit Stove Works, Michigan Stove Company, and Peninsular Stove Company, employed 3,000 workers and annually produced 125,000 to 150,000 stoves by the 1880s. In various ways they all owed their origins to Jeremiah Dwyer, who had learned the business in New York and had established a small Detroit company in 1857. By the end of the century the Michigan Stove Company, with its popular "Garland" stove, claimed to be the world's largest stove manufacturer. It certainly produced one of the world's largest stoves, a huge thirty-foot wooden replica which it displayed at the Chicago World's Columbian Exposition in 1893. The "Big Stove," as it was dubbed, then became one of Detroit's most familiar landmarks, standing on the grounds of the Detroit-Michigan Stove Company (the two largest stove manufacturers had merged), until the company closed down in 1957. Of course, stove-making was not confined to Detroit. No stove was better known than the Round Oak Stove, manufactured in Dowagiac from 1871 until the 1950s, while the Kalamazoo Stove Company, originating in 1901 and likewise continuing in that city until the 1950s, capitalized on the city's unique name with the slogan "A Kalamazoo Direct to You."

Although Michigan became the leading producer of iron ore, much of the iron used by its stove manufacturers was produced elsewhere. The Eureka Iron and Steel Company of Wyandotte, organized by Michigan shipbuilder and ship operator Eber Brock Ward and several associates in 1853, was a promising development. However, after the Eureka mill had produced America's first Bessemer steel in 1864, Ward's partners vetoed his plan to expand the Wyandotte operations to meet the anticipated demand by railroads for rails made of this improved steel. Ward, probably the richest person in Michigan at the time of his death in 1875, went instead to

Chicago, where his South Chicago Rolling Mills capitalized on the great postwar railroad boom to become the world's largest producer of steel rails.

If Ward's associates failed to recognize the business possibilities presented by an expanding national rail system, other Detroit businessmen did not make the same mistake. A few railroad cars were built in Detroit when the state's first railroads were being constructed in the 1830s, and in the 1850s a railroad equipment manufacturing business was started by Dr. George B. Russel which he and his sons would operate for four decades. More important, however, was the Michigan Car Company. Organized in 1864, the company provided great wealth for its fortunate founders and a base which its dominant leader, James McMillan, used to become the state's most powerful political figure in the years following Zachariah Chandler's death in 1879. In 1892 McMillan's company merged with its principal competitor, the Peninsular Car Company, along with the Russels' company and several

Above: *At the end of the nineteenth century, when the U.S. Senate was being called the Millionaires' Club, Detroit business tycoon James McMillan fit in well with the other wealthy members of that legislative body. Courtesy, State Archives, Michigan Department of State*

At the end of the nineteenth century when Ransom Olds and his family posed for this portrait, the automobile age had barely dawned and the Olds name was not yet linked with one of that age's best known automobiles. Courtesy, Gladys Olds Anderson

related firms, to form the Michigan-Peninsular Car Company. By that time Detroit was the nation's leader in railroad car production, employing over 9,000 workers who produced as many as 100 freight cars daily. Because railroad cars accounted for about a quarter of the annual value of the city's entire manufacturing output, it was not surprising that the city's papers were full of references to the cars Detroit was producing. The newsmen could scarcely know that they and the rest of the world would soon associate Detroit with cars that did not run on rails.

More has been written about the automobile industry than about any other aspect of Michigan's economic development, as would be expected of an industry that has dominated the area throughout the twentieth century to an extent not seen since the distant days of the fur trade. How this all came about, however, remains a subject about which most people, including

some writers on the subject, are poorly informed. Although it is easy to understand why so many assume that Detroit has always been the leader of the auto industry and that Henry Ford, the only one of the early leaders whose name is widely recognized, invented the automobile, neither assumption is correct. Most of the basic work in the development of self-propelled road vehicles occurred in Europe, well ahead of similar work in the United States, and the early leader in automobile production was not Michigan or any other area in the United States but France, where an auto industry was emerging by 1890. Within the United States, most of the initial experimental work with horseless carriages took place in the East and it was there, in New England, that the manufacturing of U.S. automobiles began in 1896.

In that same year, however, developments began in Michigan that would, within eight years, propel the state to the top of the industry. On the evening of March 6, Charles B. King test-drove on Detroit's Woodward Avenue an experimental automobile that he had built. Three months later on June 4, Henry Ford took his own version of an automobile out of a shed at the rear of his rented quarters on Detroit's Bagley Avenue and drove around several blocks of the downtown area. And on August 11, Ransom E. Olds took a Lansing newspaper reporter for a brief ride around the state capital in the horseless carriage Olds had just completed.

The fact that all three of these experimental vehicles were powered by gasoline engines is of great importance. Unlike many automotive pioneers elsewhere who wasted so much time on steam cars and electrics, Michigan's experimenters very early recognized the advantages gasoline vehicles had over the other two types. They therefore concentrated their efforts on the engine that the public soon indicated

was its overwhelming preference. Of the trio of Michigan automobile pioneers, Charles King, although probably the first person to drive a gasoline car in Detroit or anywhere else in Michigan, was never able to capitalize on this achievement. His friend Henry Ford, whose later accomplishments clearly entitle him to a preeminent position among the world's automakers, took a back seat at this time to Ransom Olds, who was primarily responsible for Michigan's initial development as the center of the industry.

Nearly all of Olds' work took place in Lansing, illustrating the need to recognize that Michigan's auto industry has never been confined to Detroit. Indeed, most of the state's actual automobile manufacturing has always been done not in Detroit but in other southern Michigan communities. In Lansing, Olds' father started P.F. Olds & Son in 1880, the direct ancestor of Lansing's giant Oldsmobile operations. In

1885, twenty-one-year-old Ransom Olds began playing a leading role in the family business, shifting its emphasis from repair work to manufacturing a small steam engine that he had developed. In the mid-1890s, he began producing gasoline engines with great success, making the Olds name a familiar one among those who bought and used engines. Although he recognized that "gasoline engines were our bread-and-butter business ... I knew," Olds later recalled, "that the car was my big venture." Experiments beginning in 1887 with a steamer had convinced him that steam engines were not a satisfactory source of power for horseless carriages. Consequently, after completing his first gasoline engines he built a vehicle driven by a one-cylinder Olds engine. With the successful test run of August 11, 1896, Olds announced that he intended to put the vehicle into production.

A few weeks later he applied for a

These thirteen curved-dash Oldsmobiles lined up in front of the Olds plant in Lansing in 1901 represented 3 percent of that year's total Oldsmobile production of 425, a minuscule figure by the standards of later years. Nevertheless, it marked the beginning of Michigan's emergence as the world's auto manufacturing center. Courtesy, State Archives, Michigan Department of State

The importance of the auto industry was being felt as early as 1907 when Lansing's rival automakers, Reo and Oldsmobile, fought for the honor of driving President Theodore Roosevelt out to Michigan Agricultural College where he would speak at the school's semicentennial. Reo won and Ransom Olds himself drove Roosevelt, college president Jonathan Snyder, and presidential secretary William Loeb, seated next to Olds, out to the college. An Oldsmobile brought Roosevelt back to Lansing. Courtesy, State Archives, Michigan Department of State

patent on certain features of this first Olds car (the registered Oldsmobile name would not appear for more than four years), explaining that his object was "to produce a road-vehicle that will meet most of the requirements for the ordinary uses on the road without complicated gear or requiring engines of great power and to avoid all unnecessary weight." Olds was essentially outlining the approach that would account for the Michigan auto industry's supremacy—concentrating on good, practical, relatively inexpensive cars, rather than the fancy, high-powered, expensive vehicles emphasized elsewhere.

Yet it was four and a half years before Olds was able to assemble and sell more than a handful of automobiles. Following an unsuccessful attempt to use the family's business resources to proceed with car production, Olds in the summer of 1897 joined with a group of Lansing businessmen headed by wealthy real estate investor Edward W. Sparrow to form the Olds Motor Vehi-

cle Company. However, the $10,000 that the Sparrow group invested was far too little, although half a dozen cars may have been produced, one of which survives today in the Smithsonian Institution. It was not until 1899, when Samuel L. Smith of Detroit invested $200,000 from the fortune he had made in the Copper Country, that the way was cleared for real progress in auto manufacturing. The Olds enterprises were reorganized as the Olds Motor Works, with the engine works continuing in Lansing and a new auto production plant on Jefferson Avenue in Detroit. Joining the original Lansing investors was a group of prominent Detroit investors, including Henry Ledyard, president of the Michigan Central Railroad and grandson of Lewis Cass, and two members of the Russel manufacturing family.

Olds tinkered with a dozen different models, including one or two electrics, none of which attracted much attention. In the fall of 1900, he finally settled upon a small, 650-pound, one-cylinder model that became the immortal curved-dash runabout, the first to carry the famous Oldsmobile marque. Despite a fire that destroyed its Detroit factory in March 1901, Michigan's first automotive manufacturer produced over 400 of the little cars in its first year—an astounding figure in those days of the industry's infancy. By 1902, when Olds' runabout sales rose to around 3,000 vehicles, the Detroit company clearly had the best-selling car in the country, and sales of 4,000 in 1903 and 5,500 in 1904 removed any doubts of its worldwide sales leadership. Never again would a non-Michigan company hold the top spot in U.S. auto sales, and only in recent years have developments elsewhere in the world seriously threatened to place a foreign company ahead of the top Michigan manufacturer. Although Oldsmobiles have remained one of the best-known cars on the market, the man after whom they were named had no connection with their production after the first weeks of 1904. Olds was forced out of the company as a result of policy disputes with his backers, especially Samuel Smith's son Fred, who gained control because the Smiths had held the majority of stock since 1899.

Later in 1904, Ransom E. Olds started a new automobile company which took its name from his initials. During the next several years he directed Lansing's Reo Motor Car Company to production records that put it well ahead of Oldsmobile, whose plant had been moved to Lansing. Once he had shown his old backers that he could get along without them, however, Olds seemed to lose interest in the day-to-day operations of his company. During the last forty years of his life he devoted most of his time to enjoying himself and to dabbling in a variety of other business activities. However, Olds' great success during his brief reign as the dominant figure in Michigan's auto industry stimulated its growth much like William Haldane's success spurred

Grand Rapids' furniture industry and Dr. Kellogg's activities pioneered Battle Creek's breakfast food industry. The Olds company also provided a training ground for young men like Roy D. Chapin and Howard E. Coffin, who used their experience to form the Hudson Motor Car Company in 1909. An important Detroit auto firm for many years, Hudson merged with the Nash company of Wisconsin in 1954 to form the present American Motors Corporation. Another Olds employee, Jonathan Maxwell, joined with Benjamin Briscoe in 1903 to form a company that produced a car Maxwell designed. It was the company from which today's Chrysler Corporation arose in 1925.

Briscoe and his brother Frank became involved in the auto industry when their Detroit sheet metal shop supplied radiators and other sheet metal parts for Oldsmobiles. The profits that Olds racked up gave the Briscoes what Frank described as "an itch to get into the big tent." Enjoying considerably more success in the big tent than the Briscoes were the owners of two Detroit

Twenty years older than most of the auto pioneers, Henry Leland was an impressive figure and a stickler for precision workmanship. He held Bible study classes for his workers and dealt sternly with any employee caught smoking or drinking. Courtesy, National Automotive History Collection, Detroit Public Library

Tom Dolson, second from the left, looks over a 1905 Dolson Model C about to be tested in Charlotte, home of the Dolson Automobile Company. One of many Michigan firms that sought to emulate Ransom Olds' success with automobiles, Dolson, like so many of these companies, failed after a few years. Courtesy, David W. Dolson

Latest Gents Styles at the Auto Show

1. JESSE FRENCH JR
2. ROGER D. M'MULLEN
3. D.W. TWYMAN
4. A.L. RIKER
5. LOUIS RAINBRIGHT
6. FAY HUSSEY
7. CHAS. E. DURYEA
8. ELMER APPERSON
9. FRED L. SMITH
10. E.R. THOMAS
11. ALEXANDER WINTON
12. GEO. W. BENNETT
13. H.S. FIRESTONE
14. CHAS. B. SHANKS.
15. JIM COUZENS
16. HENRY FORD
17. R.E. OLDS

Already in 1906, when Motor Way's artist made this fanciful sketch of auto industry leaders gathered for the Chicago Auto Show, Michigan dominated the industry. Henry Ford, wearing a tiny hat and an overcoat that partially hides the fact that he is not wearing trousers, stands to the right of Ford's bespectacled business manager, James Couzens. On Ford's right is Ransom Olds, wearing neither shoes nor socks. Harvey Firestone, complete with tire, is behind Olds. From the author's collection

machine shops. Henry M. Leland, whom one writer rather extravagantly described as "probably the most experienced, farsighted, and successful director of a machine shop in America, if not in the world," had made transmissions and engines for the Oldsmobile before he became involved in 1902 with the development of the Cadillac. Starting out as an inexpensive runabout on the order of the $650 Oldsmobile, the Cadillac under Leland's direction shortly became the high-priced prestige car that the Cadillac name has ever since denoted. The other machine shop

was operated by two brothers, John and Horace Dodge, who had also produced engines for the curved-dash Olds. In 1914 they would begin producing their own Dodge car, an immediate and lasting success. Until that time, the Dodges prospered by making parts for another Detroit firm, the Ford Motor Company, whose founder replaced Ransom Olds as the best-known figure in the industry.

Henry Ford was born in 1863 to an Irish immigrant farmer who settled in the Dearborn area. Young Ford's dislike of farm life led him to Detroit, where he applied his natural gifts as a mechanic, by 1893 becoming chief engineer of what is now the Detroit Edison Company. Like his mechanically minded contemporaries Ransom Olds and Charles King, Ford became absorbed by a desire to build a horseless carriage. Unlike their first self-propelled vehicles, however, the vehicle Ford tested on June 4, 1896, did not use an existing carriage for which an engine, rather than a horse, was the motive power. Instead, Ford not only built his own engine but he built the body as well, employing materials not of the carriage-maker but of the bicycle builder to create a "quadricycle."

Seven years elapsed between the appearance of Ford's first car and the time that cars bearing his name were available to the public. Even more than Olds, Ford was totally dependent on outside financial support in order to proceed with any manufacturing plans. Getting that support was not the cause of the delay, however. A succession of wealthy backers, including some of James McMillan's leading associates, financed Ford's continuing experiments and in 1899 and 1901 formed companies to manufacture Ford's cars. Yet Ford's backers had little or nothing to show for the money they invested, first because Ford was never satisfied enough with his vehicle to want to put it into production. Then Ford entered an automobile race at Grosse Pointe in the fall of 1901 to publicize his activities, and his unexpected triumph led him to devote all of his time to the development of what he said would be the most powerful racing machine yet built. With this news Ford's latest group of backers severed their relations with him. They turned to Henry Leland, who developed the commercially successful vehicle they had been seeking, the Cadillac.

Henry Ford, meanwhile, went ahead with the support of still others to complete a monstrous racer, the "999," which was Barney Oldfield's ticket to immortality when he drove it to victory at Grosse Pointe in the fall of 1902. Capitalizing on Ford's fame as the designer of fast cars, Detroit coal dealer Alexander Malcomson drew together a new group of investors, including the Dodge brothers, who on June 16, 1903, formed the Ford Motor Company. Ford, who was the company's vice president and general manager, had come up with a version of the car that Oldsmobile had popularized, but when the first of these Ford runabouts had been assembled Ford again found problems which he said would have to be corrected before they could be shipped out. He was overruled by business manager James Couzens, who pointed out that the bank balance was down to $223.65, and that they would be out of business if money from car sales did not come in immediately. The cars were shipped and within a few weeks the company was on solid financial ground.

In the following years, Henry Ford emerged triumphant in a patent infringement case brought against his company by those who claimed that they controlled the patent for all cars powered by gasoline engines. Within the company, Ford decided to concentrate on a low-priced model, despite the opposition of Alexander Malcomson. As a result Malcomson sold his stock

to Ford in 1906, giving Ford a majority of the stock and enabling him to move up to the position of president. Ford and his staff then proceeded with the development of a lightweight, durable car, and in 1908 they came up with the most famous car in American history, the Model T. During the next nineteen years, Ford's company produced over fifteen million of the homely but seemingly indestructible "Tin Lizzies," giving substance to its claim that the Model T was the car that put America on wheels.

Henry Ford's most enduring claim

By the second decade of the twentieth century, the always well-dressed Henry Ford was securely entrenched as the world's foremost automaker, leaving such competitors as Hudson's Roy D. Chapin, to whom Ford autographed this photo, far behind. Courtesy, Michigan Historical Collections, Bentley Historical Library, University of Michigan

William C. Durant, as suggested in this 1920s-era photograph, was a man whose shy, retiring manner on ordinary social occasions scarcely indicated his dynamic entrepreneurial abilities. Courtesy, Michigan Historical Collections, Bentley Historical Library, University of Michigan

to fame, however, lies in his company's successful application of mass-production techniques to the assembling of the Model T, bringing the car's cost down to a point where more and more people could afford it. At its high point in the early 1920s, about 60 percent of all cars sold in the country were Ford Model Ts. Yet, while Ford will always remain one of the most influential figures of the twentieth century, his company, which became the leading auto producer by about 1909, lost that position in the 1920s to General Motors. The new leader was the creation of the third great Michigan auto pioneer, Governor Crapo's grandson, Billy Durant.

Unlike Olds and Ford, Durant was largely ignorant of what made an automobile run, but few were ever his equal in knowing how to successfully make a business run. In 1904 he was ready for a new challenge. His Durant-Dort Carriage Company was in the capable hands of his associates, and although the stock market had begun to arouse his speculative instincts, he quickly accepted an offer to assume the management of the faltering Buick Motor Company.

The Buick had been developed by David D. Buick, a Detroiter who had earlier demonstrated skills in running a plumbing supply business. Inexplicably, he was unable to apply these skills to his gasoline engine and automobile business. The Briscoe brothers had backed Buick's new business, but they began to have grave doubts about the company's future under Buick's inept direction. In 1903 they unloaded their controlling interest onto the owners of Flint's second largest manufacturer of horse-drawn vehicles, the Flint Wagon Works. Although carriage and wagon sales had not yet been affected by the demand for automobiles, the Flint businessmen saw the acquisition of Buick as a way of insuring themselves against future changes in the market. When David Buick proved no more capable of managing the business in Flint than he had been in Detroit, the Flint owners in desperation asked their old competitor and business acquaintance Durant to take over and save the company.

After satisfying himself that the Buick was a good product that would sell itself if properly promoted, Durant

took control of the company. He then displayed a dazzling entrepreneurial talent that would have made his grandfather proud, transforming the anemic Buick company within three years into the foremost auto company in the country. Durant used his numerous contacts in Flint to provide Buick with an immediate transfusion of cash, and then built on Flint's north side a vast industrial complex where Buick and related manufacturing operations would be centered. Meanwhile, he moved Buick assembly work to a vacant plant in Jackson, Michigan, owned by his carriage company. Sales of the Buick, which had totaled perhaps thirty when Durant took over, skyrocketed after he beefed up the company's sales staff; Durant personally obtained orders for over a thousand Buicks when he attended the national auto show in New York at the end of 1904. He also brought the company and its car free publicity by hiring the best available road race drivers, who proceeded to win hundreds of trophies and half the races run in a two-year period.

Yet Durant's importance in automotive history does not rest with his

The Buick racing team poses circa 1909, with the stars of the team, Bullet Bob Burman and the brothers Louis and Arthur Chevrolet, standing respectively fourth, fifth, and sixth from the left. Burman would be killed in a 1916 race while Louis Chevrolet would become famous for the car that bears his name, but from which he received little financial reward. Courtesy, The Flint Journal

success in temporarily making Buick the nation's bestselling car. Rather, it was his vision of the volume of production that would soon be needed to satisfy the public's demand for automobiles. Durant thus saw the desirability of controlling more than one company in order to increase production capacity and offer the public a greater choice of models. Following the collapse of an initial effort by Durant and Benjamin Briscoe to create an automobile giant by merging their companies with Ford and Reo, Durant went ahead on his own in September 1908 to form the General Motors Company. A holding company, G.M. under Durant's direction soon acquired control not only of Buick, but of Lansing's Oldsmobile operation, Pontiac's Oakland company (G.M.'s future Pontiac division), Detroit's Cadillac company, and a host of other auto manufacturers and parts suppliers. Critics pointed out that Durant picked up a number of lemons along the way, but he defended himself.

They say I shouldn't have bought Cartercar ... Well, how was any one to know that the Cartercar wasn't to be the thing? It had the friction drive and no other car had it. How could I tell what these engineers would say next? Maybe friction drive would be the thing. And then there's Elmore, with its two-cycle engine. That's the kind they were using on motor-boats; maybe two-cycles was going to be the thing for automobiles. I was for getting every car in sight, playing safe all along the line.

It is unlikely that G.M.'s stockholders would agree that Durant was playing it safe: the company was forced to write off many of his acquisitions as losses, and his ambitious moves to expand Oldsmobile and Oakland brought G.M. to the brink of collapse during a slump in auto sales in 1910. To save the company, Durant arranged a loan from an eastern financial syndicate which insisted, however, that he be replaced by more conservative management. Consequently, Durant promoted a new Flint company, Chevrolet, whose success enabled him to regain control of G.M. in 1916. Durant then proceeded to add more companies to G.M.'s roster, including Chevrolet and parts makers such as Delco, before renewed financial problems late in 1920 led to his ouster for the second and last time. In the twenties, Alfred P. Sloan, Jr., directed a reorganization of General Motors that finally enabled it to capitalize on the diversity of its models, making it the industry's leader. It was Billy Durant, however, who had provided Sloan with the elements for an administrative structure that would be regarded thereafter as a corporate model.

During the prosperous twenties Durant's predictions of car demand were far exceeded by actual sales as America enthusiastically embraced the age of the automobile. In the mid-1920s ex-G.M. executive Walter P. Chrysler organized the company that still bears his name, and by the end of the decade the Michigan-based Big Three—General Motors, Ford, and Chrysler—produced 75 percent of the nation's cars. Other Michigan firms such as Packard, Hudson, Reo, and Hupmobile accounted for a sizable share of the remaining 25 percent. Michigan's older manufacturing activities continued to be important, but its auto assembly plants were now creating the state's twentieth-century image, replacing wheat, timber, and ore. It was a spectacular image, but the overwhelmingly dominant position that automobiles had now assumed in the state's economy, while promising bountiful returns when auto sales boomed, also raised the possibility of very difficult times when the demand for automobiles fell—a possibility that became a reality more than once in the years ahead.

THE END OF THE
HORSE-AND-BUGGY ERA

It may be difficult to imagine that the horse-and-buggy era is a part of the experience of a good many people still alive in a state internationally known for its role in promoting the use of motor vehicles. But such is indeed the case for some residents of Zeeland who can recall the grocery peddler's wagon coming around early this century (above left) or the milk wagon (left), *pictured here in 1920, which remained a familiar sight not only in Zeeland but in other communities throughout Michigan—including Detroit—as late as 1960. Courtesy, Zeeland Historical Museum*

Far left: *In Plainwell, the horse-drawn sprinkler wagon kept the dust down on the town's street in the summer—reflecting an age in which traffic did not seem to require paved streets. Courtesy, Regional History Collections, Western Michigan University*

Left: *Cement was a new paving material at the start of this century and it was some time before it would be used very extensively for the improvement of roads, which continued to be almost entirely dirt, built by and for the farmers. That was the case with this project near Hamburg, Michigan, being worked on by members of the DeWolfe family of that area. Courtesy, Mrs. Joyce DeWolfe Terry*

Far left: *Rural isolation began to subside with the establishment of the first experimental rural mail delivery service in 1896. For many years, however, the expansion of this service was limited by road conditions and by the fact that the mailmen, like Cap Foreman, the first rural carrier out of Plainwell, used horse-drawn wagons. Courtesy, Regional History Collections, Western Michigan University*

Middle left: *Farmers on a rural route out of Adrian in 1902 had a glimpse of the future when their mail was delivered for a short while by a carrier being driven in an automobile. The vehicle was a Murray, a runabout assembled from 1901 to 1903 in Adrian. Courtesy, Michigan Historical Collections, Bentley Historical Library, University of Michigan*

Left: *In 1906 in the tiny southwestern Michigan community of Mendon, a horse-drawn vehicle and an oxcart were lined up flanking three horseless carriages, and a photographer took this picture of the old giving way to the new. Courtesy, Regional History Collections, Western Michigan University*

CHAPTER IX

A NEW ERA SUCCEEDS THE OLD

A new era meets the old on a bridge in Genesee County circa 1905. Buicks made in Flint were said to be tough enough to stand up to anything, even a farmer's oxen, when it came to power. Courtesy, Genesee County Historical Society

An article in 1957 titled "The Real Michigan" marked a kind of literary homecoming for Bruce Catton, who was born in Petoskey and had spent his early years there and in Boyne City and Benzonia. Following World War I Catton departed to pursue a writing career in the East that culminated in popular and critical acclaim for his Civil War histories, one of which in 1954 received both a National Book Award and the Pulitzer Prize. During these years Catton maintained contact with his native state, eventually spending summers in the Benzonia area, but it was only in his later years that he turned his writing to Michigan themes, first in a memoir of his boyhood, published in 1972, and then in a history of Michigan published in 1975, three years before his death.

Although only the first months of his life fell in the nineteenth century, Catton's preference for that earlier time and his dislike for the twentieth century was reflected in the view of Michigan expressed in his later works. For him, the "Real Michigan" was not Detroit:

Its industrial empire spraddles over a good part of the state, to be sure . . . but the tremendous industrial nexus centered here is only half of the story. The other half is something very different—old times, the breath of bygone days and memories that went out of date before the men who remembered them were old—and as a man born out of his proper time I love this other Michigan a good deal more than I love Detroit.

And thus Catton hurriedly led his readers out of Detroit into northern areas where remnants of the Michigan he had known as a boy still survived. In his history of the state, this "man born out of his proper time" devoted a mere sixteen pages to the twentieth century, his tone reflecting a pessimistic view of what the century's developments promised for the future.

Catton's perspective, shaped by a childhood spent in the declining years of northern Michigan's lumbering era, was shared by others who had grown up in southern Michigan's farming communities or in the Upper Peninsula's mining towns. A state whose life had always revolved around the exploitation of its rich natural resources suddenly awakened to find that life giving way to one rooted in manufacturing. That in turn was leading to the growth of an urban population, particularly in the southeastern region. It was in 1920, precisely at the time Bruce Catton was leaving the state, that those who lived in what the census bureau defined as urban areas first exceeded those living in areas defined as rural. This trend, together with the economy's shifting emphasis, accounted for the sense of alienation felt by Catton and others who preferred the old ways to the new.

Until the latter part of the nineteenth century, Michigan's towns and cities had existed largely, if not entirely, to serve the needs first of fur traders, then of farmers, lumbermen, miners, and, in the case of Great Lakes ports, commercial fishermen and shippers. Since the start of the eighteenth century the largest concentration of population has been in southern Michigan, especially around Detroit. With the opening of the southern interior after the War of 1812, Detroit's share of the total population declined as farming promoted a rather even distribution of people across the lower half of the peninsula. Southern Michigan's share of the population, which was well over 90 percent in 1840, began dropping in mid-century as lumbering and mining drew people into the northern areas, which held about a quarter of Michigan's people by century's end. Houghton County in the Copper Country was the state's fourth most populous county in 1900, while iron mining towns such as Ishpeming, lumber towns like Cheboygan, and lake ports like Escanaba were among the northern communities whose populations compared favorably with most cities in southern Michigan's more heavily populated farming counties.

Yet residents of Ishpeming or Kalamazoo or Detroit were not typical of the majority of residents in 1900. Despite the declining proportion of people living in rural settings, 61 percent of the population of 1900 still lived on farms or in villages of less than 2,500, the figure used to separate urban and rural areas. Among Michigan cities, only Detroit, with 285,704 people, ranked among the larger cities in the country. Trailing far behind was Grand Rapids, with less than a third of Detroit's population, while Saginaw, with 42,345, was the only other city with more than 40,000 residents.

During the 1890s Michigan grew at only half the rate recorded in the previous decade, providing a warning of what lay ahead if the state continued to rely on traditional activities for its future growth. The decline already under way in the lumber industry by 1900 was certain to have an impact on Saginaw's future development, but because of that area's healthy agricultural economy, its prospects were not as bleak as those of towns farther north that depended almost exclusively on lumber production. In the Upper Peninsula, although mining output was still on the rise, officials were seeking ways of cutting costs to compete with the cheaper open pit mines of the West. However, they could see a day coming when the jobs would not be available to maintain the population levels that had been reached in Hancock, Ironwood, and other mining towns. That day was not long in coming. As fewer opportunities opened in the mines and the lumber camps, the northern two-thirds of the state witnessed an exodus that reduced its share of the population in the 1930s to half of what it had been at the start of the century. Yet the state as a whole, although growing at a rate below the national average from 1900 to 1910, saw that rate double in the next two decades, once again making Michigan one of the fastest growing states in the country.

A number of factors accounted for

THE "OTHER"
MICHIGAN

With his pipe, shotgun, shells, tattered hunting jacket, and a patiently waiting dog, John Henry Madden of Plainwell paused on a winter day in the late nineteenth century to have his picture taken. Usually, however, it was Madden who was taking the pictures, and he left a superb collection of photographs that recorded life in that western Michigan town of about a thousand people at the end of the Victorian era. A granddaughter, Mrs. Kathryn Gould, donated the collection many years later to Western Michigan University. Courtesy, Regional History Collections, Western Michigan University

Physically, much that is found in Plainwell today is seemingly little changed from Madden's time, almost a century ago. The beautiful Presbyterian church, built in 1872, still stands, looking basically as it did when Madden took this photograph. A window that has replaced the front entrance, however, suggests the extensive alterations that have taken place in the church's interior in recent decades. Courtesy, Regional History Collections, Western Michigan University

Right: *Much that is associated with the Victorian style of life is apparent in some of Madden's indoor shots. In this cluttered living room, the profusion of pillows, the heavy, wooden furniture, and the rope tassels serving as a room divider are features of Madden's day that would in later years increasingly survive only in antique shops or in historic house restorations. Courtesy, Regional History Collections, Western Michigan University*

Below: *Madden took his camera with him into the downtown businesses, perhaps while soliciting advertisements for his paper. During America's brief bicycle craze of the 1890s, Mel Gamble's shop was probably enjoying excellent sales. Courtesy, Regional History Collections, Western Michigan University*

Left: *Anson Reese's hardware store was obviously well-supplied with heating stoves and most of the other things hardware stores were supposed to carry—and the smaller items were not prepackaged for the customer who was expected to help himself. Instead, Mr. Reese waited on you. Courtesy, Regional Historical Collections, Western Michigan University*

Left: *The staff of Stilwell's 5 and 10¢ Store looks out from a doorway flanked by displays of pictures, dolls, jars, pans, and miscellany in an age before discount stores displaced such local businesses. Courtesy, Regional Historical Collections, Western Michigan University*

The iron bridge has since been replaced by a more modern structure, and the man, like the other subjects whom Madden photographed, is now dead, but the era in which he lived is preserved in these and other pictures in ways that no other kind of document could preserve. Courtesy, Regional History Collections, Western Michigan University

In the early 1900s, arches erected over Flint's streets trumpeted this carriage-making center's fame as "The Vehicle City." This 1910 view looks north on Detroit Street from the Flint River bridge. Courtesy, Genesee County Historical Society

this growth, but clearly manufacturing was the major attraction as Michigan became ever more an urban-industrial state. By 1930 those employed in manufacturing occupations numbered 833,789, 43 percent of the total workforce. By contrast, only 13 percent were engaged in farming and a mere 2 percent in lumbering, mining, and fishing. As recently as 1910 only 47 percent of the population lived in urban areas, but by 1930 it was 68 percent, higher than any state outside of the Northeast with the exception of Illinois and California. The impact of these developments was felt almost entirely in southern Michigan. There, the 1930 population of the counties containing the industrial cities of Grand Rapids, Kalamazoo, and Jackson was twice what it had been in 1900, while adjacent counties that remained primarily agricultural showed no gain or even lost population during the same period. But the most spectac-

ular gains were in southeastern Michigan, where auto assembly plants spurred population increases of five times or more in Genesee, Oakland, and Wayne counties.

Although Detroit was the center of attraction, Flint was one of the other cities in southeastern Michigan which Bruce Catton correctly declared "would be world-famous if it were in some other country." A satellite of the Saginaw Valley economy in the lumbering days, Flint made the transition into manufacturing so successfully that it far surpassed Saginaw and Bay City in the twentieth century. Carriage manufacturing made Flint a city of respectable size by Michigan standards, but the rise of Buick and Chevrolet caught the city totally unprepared for the explosion of its population: 13,103 in 1900; 38,550 in 1910; 91,599 in 1920; and 156,492 by 1930.

The excitement and discomfort

In "Scene on Farm near Kalamazoo," Robert Hopkin, one of
Michigan's foremost nineteenth-
century artists, suggests the problems pioneer farmers faced in
clearing their heavily forested
lands. Photo by W.D. Pieri III.
Courtesy, Grand Rapids Art
Museum

Right: *Much of the timber in southern Michigan was destroyed by farmers who were more interested in clearing the land than profiting by what was on it. Still, enough timber remained after the pioneer period to support small-scale lumbering operations, such as this one at Adams' Mill, near Plymouth, painted by an unknown artist on January 15, 1856. From the collections of Henry Ford Museum and Greenfield Village, Negative No. D-7079*

*White Lake lumberman W.
Frederick Nufer commissioned
Whitehall resident Frederick
Norman in the late nineteenth
century to do a series of paintings
on all aspects of lumbering. A
winter scene of a horse-drawn sled
of logs on Colby Street in Whitehall (opposite page) and the
Staples sawmill on White Lake
(above) are among more than a
dozen paintings Norman completed which now hang in the
First of America Bank of Whitehall, a gift some years ago from
Nufer's daughter. Courtesy, First
of America Bank, Whitehall*

Above: "Cliff Mine, Lake Superi-
or," a superbly detailed painting
completed by Robert S. Duncanson in 1848, depicts Michigan's
first producing copper mine. A
successful American landscape
painter, Duncanson spent most of
his professional life in Cincinnati
but died in a Detroit mental institution in 1872. Courtesy, F. Ward
Paine

Opposite page, top: In this 1863
painting by George B. Gardner, titled "View of the St. Clair River,"
the viewer is looking north and
east of what is now Pine Grove
Park in Port Huron. On the right
is what is now Sarnia, Ontario.
The steamship is the Forester,
which made as many as three
trips weekly between Port Huron
and Detroit. An excursion trip in
1860, with a band providing music
for dancing, cost twenty-five cents
each way. Courtesy, Museum of
Arts and History, Port Huron,
Michigan

Right: *Horse racing's popularity in Michigan extends back to the French period, and regular racing schedules began appearing in the mid-nineteenth century. This print records a matchup at the East Saginaw track in 1874 in which Goldsmith Maid, in the lead, set a record in the mile for trotters. Courtesy, Peters Collection, National Museum of American History, Smithsonian Institution*

Left: *The semiannual Grand Rapids furniture market, begun in 1878, was for many decades the great gathering place for furniture buyers, symbolizing the city's dominance in the industry. The markets ended in the early 1960s, but Grand Rapids' association with the manufacture of furniture remains strong. Courtesy, Grand Rapids Public Museum*

Right: *This poster, known as "Bavarian Girl," was done for the Stroh Brewery in 1890 by artist Louis Prang, who introduced the Christmas card twenty years earlier. Courtesy, Stroh Brewery Company*

This gentle advertising piece, probably dating from the late nineteenth century, leaves much to the imagination but perhaps symbolizes the soft-sell approach of a Dowagiac manufacturer whose stoves were considered by many to be the best, no matter what sales figures Detroit's Garland and Jewel stoves achieved. From the author's collection

"Painted from actual specimens" grown at Dexter M. Ferry's test grounds, these are examples of the fine artwork used on seed packets that the great Detroit seed company sold by the thousands throughout the country.

Right: *Howard Freeman Sprague, perhaps the greatest of the Great Lakes marine artists, painted "The Steamboat City of Alpena and City of Detroit II" circa 1889 at the age of nineteen. In the foreground is a rowboat in which a mail carrier delivered letters to the passing ships on what had become one of America's busiest waterways. Courtesy, Great Lakes Maritime Institute, Dossin Museum*

Below: *The small town of New Baltimore on Anchor Bay in southeastern Michigan represented a way of life that would soon be altered by the growth of industrial activities in the years following this 1890s painting by an unknown artist. Courtesy, Michigan Historical Collections, Bentley Historical Library, University of Michigan*

that had accompanied the boom town atmosphere of the pioneer days returned to the city on a far larger scale eighty years later. Excitement stemmed from the financial rewards that made the money generated in the lumbering days seem like small change in comparison. "Flint is rich," one visitor reported. "That is, it feels rich, it talks rich and it has a rich income." There were 182 men in the town in 1916 who reportedly had annual incomes between $50,000 and $3 million—or were the correct figures, as some insisted, $100,000 to $6 million? Downtown Flint, a product of the pre-automobile period, looked like any small midwestern city, but that was deceiving, as members of Chicago's Board of Commerce discovered in 1908 when they went on a tour of the new Buick industrial complex. The astonished Windy City businessmen confessed they "had no idea that the saying that Flint had the largest automobile

plant in the world was true, but it is for sure." Two years later a Boston financier, familiar with New England's well-established manufacturers, admitted that the Buick plant was the only one he had seen that made the United Shoe Machinery factory in Beverly, Massachusetts, "look small."

While booming auto assembly operations accounted for the city's prosperity, discomforts and inconveniences resulted from Flint's inability to meet the demands of tens of thousands of newcomers for housing and basic city services. During Billy Durant's feverish expansion of the Buick plant, the lack of living quarters in the winter of 1909-1910 forced many to live in tents. Land became a source of great wealth for real estate promoters, who subdivided tracts inside and outside the city and sold lots to prospective homebuilders for as little as a dollar down and payments of fifty cents a month. Yet in the summer of 1916 a writer for

The completion in 1908-1909 of Flint's new Buick factory, said to have been the largest automobile plant of its day, attracted a flood of job seekers and their families. Many lived in squalid conditions in shacks clustered outside the plant. Courtesy, The Flint Journal

145

Above: *In the boom that followed World War I, Flint again faced a desperate housing shortage. General Motors established the Modern Housing Corporation, which built one of the nation's first planned subdivisions, Civic Park, circa 1920. The houses looked identical, but they were a vast improvement over tents and shacks. Courtesy, The* Flint Journal

Right: *Around 1909 some of Flint's Buick workers lived in a tent community along the river, where these four proud young men posed for the photographer, looking their best and demonstrating how their life was not entirely deprived of its lighter moments. Courtesy, The* Flint Journal

a national magazine found that Flint was still suffering a critical housing shortage. He was told that "This is the town where they sleep them so thick that their feet hang out of the window." The visitor soon discovered that "they do 'sleep them pretty thick'—a family of seven in a two-room shack on the river bottom, a family of five in one inside room of a downtown block, three shifts in a Polish lodging-house in the North End." In 1916 about 2,500 houses had been built or started, but lack of housing forced nearly 3,000 workers to commute thirty or forty miles from homes in Saginaw and Bay City, while Durant was quoted as saying he would hire 5,000 more men if houses were available for them. The title of the writer's article, "Flint, When Men Build Automobiles Who Builds Their City?" raised a question to which the city and others facing similar problems had failed to find a satisfactory answer.

What happened in Flint was repeated with variations in Lansing, the state capital better known as the home of Oldsmobiles and Reos. Pontiac, once an important center of the carriage and wagon industry, also suddenly blossomed with production of the Oakland, a car that G.M. eventually replaced with the Pontiac. In Wayne County Henry Ford's decision to build an immense plant along the Rouge River transformed Dearborn from a tiny farm village of less than 1,000 in 1900 to a sprawling industrial center of 50,000 by the late twenties, swallowing up the sites of John and William Nowlin's nineteenth-century farms as well as Ford's own birthplace. Earlier, Highland Park's population ballooned from 425 to 46,499 within ten years after Ford opened a big assembly plant there in 1910. That same year the Dodge brothers opened their factory in nearby Hamtramck, and that town of 3,000 became a city of nearly 50,000

These thousands of workers pouring into and out of the Ford plant in Highland Park reveal the factory's impact on what had been a small town of only a few hundred residents. Courtesy, State Archives, Michigan Department of State

147

Horses and buggies stand along a commercial street in Detroit in the late nineteenth century. Courtesy, State Archives, Michigan Department of State

by 1920. Yet none of these developments matched the growth of Detroit.

At the turn of the century Detroit's appearance belied its ranking as the nation's thirteenth largest city. It called itself "Detroit the Beautiful," and one booster even contended that Detroit was "generally conceded" to be "the most happily located and most beautiful" of all American cities; among cities anywhere "perhaps" only Paris exceeded its beauty. The "noble Detroit river" was the city's most notable

physical asset but Detroit's undoubted charm also resulted from its retention of many small-town qualities. These included tree-lined streets, a downtown where few buildings were over three or four stories in height, and pleasant, well-kept residential areas. Cattle sometimes still grazed in vacant residential lots, and one writer reported in 1896 that "all good householders believe it their duty to keep chickens, spade a small garden, and maintain a small orchard." The writer noted that many businessmen continued to go home at noon to have dinner, as the noon meal was always called, with their families. "Time with them, as with the village craftsman, is a bountiful commodity, and the cheerful jest goes round, the food is passed and repassed, and the delights of life in the family circle enjoyed to their full."

Such a leisurely pace, so typical of the older way of life (this writer's father, a mining employee in Ironwood, for many years walked two miles every noon to eat with his wife and children), quickly became obsolete as Detroit was caught up in the whirl of automobile production. Having celebrated its bicentennial in 1901, the city was now born again, striving to live up to its new image which a visitor in 1920 found "almost overpowering"; Detroit became "one of the great cities, not only of the United States, but of the world." By 1903 outsiders were already commenting on the "sense of hustle and activity" they found: the stranger "soon falls into line with the rest of the folk and sets his watch a half-hour ahead of standard time to keep ahead of the outside world." City boosters scrapped "Detroit the Beautiful" in favor of "Detroit the Dynamic" as a more appropriate way of summing up "the intense desire for activity, the penetrating belief in the great destiny of Detroit, and the supreme joy of achievement."

Some Detroiters, of course, were unhappy with the developments. One woman, referring to an effort to enhance Detroit's big city image by giving it a symphony orchestra that at least excelled those in Cleveland and Cincinnati, declared she "would rather do without our fine new orchestra and have our nice old town back again." Quite different, however, was the sentiment of another resident who grew up in this era:

Not for us was any delight in our lovely old town. Tree-shaded streets, flagged walks, quiet lawns, the all-too-slow moving street cars and the leisurely pace of our parents were a pain in the neck to us. We found no music in the plodding clop-clop of horses' hooves. Even our stout young legs couldn't spin the two wheels of a bicycle fast enough. Ho, for a Brave New World—on four wheels—whizzed along by gasoline.

That "nice old town" was done in by those four wheels. An avalanche of people descended upon a city suddenly famous for jobs in an ever expanding auto industry, inflating Detroit's population from 285,704 at the start of the century to about a million in 1920 and 1,568,662 in 1930. The population explosion forced the relatively compact city of the nineteenth century to expand far out to Wayne County's northernmost regions, surrounding Hamtramck and Highland Park by 1916. New residential areas emerged at a furious rate as builders vainly sought to keep up with the rate at which older areas were absorbed by manufacturing and commercial developments. By the twenties Detroit's skyline was more in conformity with the public's idea of what a big American city should look like. A network of electric interurban lines fanned out into the interior, converting outlying towns such as Plymouth and Birmingham—once self-reliant, self-contained communities—

By 1920 the pace in Detroit was more than the camera's lens could handle as cars sped past on West Grand Boulevard. The opening of the General Motors Building, looming in the center, had greatly expanded the area of the city's business activities. Courtesy, Michigan Historical Collections, Bentley Historical Library, University of Michigan

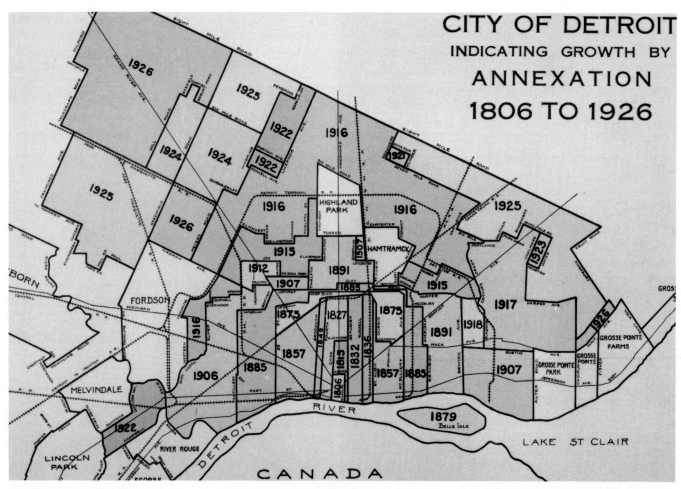

CITY OF DETROIT
INDICATING GROWTH BY
ANNEXATION
1806 TO 1926

Detroit's rapid geographical growth through annexation in the first quarter of the twentieth century is clearly indicated in this map. Courtesy, State Archives, Michigan Department of State

into suburbs dependent on Detroit. By the 1920s, however, new technology was undermining the use of interurbans, as well as streetcars, ships, and railroads. Henry Ford's airport in Dearborn was the site of some of the earliest developments of regular commercial airline service, which would have a disastrous impact on railroads and Great Lakes shipping. The widespread adoption of the automobile had a more immediate effect, closing down the interurbans by the end of the twenties, cutting deeply into public transportation revenues within Detroit and other cities, and compounding the woes railroads had been experiencing since the early years of the century.

Manufacturing also changed the mixture of peoples living in Detroit and other Michigan industrial centers. The Yankees who had been so dominant in the earlier farming, lumbering, and

mining activities remained an important element in the new age of manufacturing. The industrial boom of the early 1900s, coming when northern Michigan's lumbering and mining economies were declining or leveling off, prompted many from those areas to seek jobs in southern Michigan's factories. The factories' wage rates also lured increasing numbers of farm laborers. Webb Waldron recalled in 1920 that a few years earlier $25 a month was considered good wages for a farmhand. "One day a man who had been working on a Dakota ranch turned up at one of my uncles' farms and asked for a job; he wanted $30 a month. 'Go chase yourself!' my uncle exclaimed. 'No mother's son's worth $30 a month.'" But with the wages paid by many factories, particularly after the announcement in 1914 that Ford would pay most of his workers $5 a day, farmers who offered $75 to $100 a month plus board were getting no comers or, according to Waldron, "comers that might as well be goers." Farmers across the country were affected by the fact that workers could earn two or three times more in many factories than they could on farms, but Waldron believed the problem was felt "probably nowhere so acutely as here."

Some of the same immigrant groups so involved in Michigan's earlier developments continued to be prominent. For many years Germans were recruited by manufacturing plants because of their mechanical skills; similarly, Grand Rapids' expanding furniture industry sought the Dutch. Southern Michigan plants also attracted large numbers of Canadians who, because of their proximity, remained the largest foreign-born group in the state. Among other immigrants,

those who were from areas largely unrepresented earlier had by 1930 come to equal the number of those from the British Isles, Germany, the Low Countries, and Scandinavia who had constituted virtually all of the remainder of Michigan's foreign-born population during most of the nineteenth century. Some of the newcomers were from Asia, including several thousand from the Near East. By World War I more than 200 workers at Lansing's Reo plant were from Palestine, many of whose residents, referred to as Holy Landers, had converted Ransom Olds' initials into a word, "AR-REO," which meant variously the man, the machines he had developed, and the jobs their manufacture created. Around 1920 Islamic Near Easterners who had settled in the Highland Park area erected the country's first mosque; they were forerunners of the much greater num-

From the late nineteenth century until they were put out of business by the automobile in the 1920s and early 1930s, interurban cars provided cheap and frequent passenger service over a network of lines fanning out of Detroit and outstate hubs to communities throughout southern Michigan and neighboring states. Courtesy, State Archives, Michigan Department of State

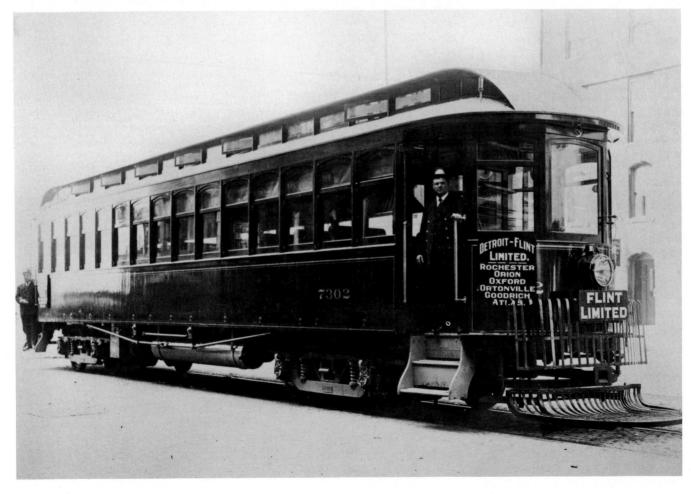

Every summer for many years in Michigan's Fruit Belt, families of migrants, most of them of Mexican origin, came to pick the fruit, as here in this cherry orchard. Courtesy, State Archives, Michigan Department of State

bers of Near Easterners who arrived in later years. The few hundred persons of Mexican birth living in Michigan in 1930 were also a modest indication of the number of Mexicans and other Latinos who would settle in the state in the latter part of the century.

Early in the century, however, the overwhelming majority of the so-called "New Immigrants" were from southern and eastern Europe. In 1930, 43,000 Italians and 34,000 Russians lived in Michigan, outnumbering residents of Dutch, Swedish, or Irish birth. In addition, Czechoslovakia, Hungary, Yugoslavia, Rumania, and Greece each contributed between 10,000 and 20,000 immigrants. But far outranking all of these and second only to the num-

ber of Canadians were the 119,228 residents of Polish birth.

Poles, probably Michigan's best-known ethnic group in the twentieth century, had begun arriving in the mid-nineteenth century, attracted by Michigan's pre-manufacturing activities. Evidence of a rural Polish influence includes the Thumb settlement of Parisville in 1857; Posen, in northern Michigan, settled in the 1870s by several hundred Poles who turned to farming when jobs in lumbering gave out; and Bronson, in southern Michigan, where an annual festival celebrates a Polish heritage dating from the 1870s. However, the Poles' rural activities have been overshadowed by their urban impact, resulting from the later arrival

of far larger numbers of Poles seeking manufacturing employment. They settled in cities such as Lansing, Muskegon, and Grand Rapids (where they became that city's largest ethnic element next to the Dutch), but considerably more than half of all Michigan Poles came to live in the Detroit area. There, Hamtramck became by 1920 the most predominantly Polish community in the country. In spite of major changes in the city's population, the Polish influence remains as evident in Hamtramck as is that of the Dutch in Holland or the Finnish in Hancock. The attention focused on Hamtramck, however, has obscured the fact that the largest concentration of Poles since the late nineteenth century has been in Detroit itself.

By the 1890s perhaps 15 percent of Detroit's population was Polish, although an exact percentage can not be determined because of the many Poles who were counted as Germans, Austrians, or Russians, after the three countries that controlled the Polish homeland. The hostilities and bitterness resulting from Poland's partition added to the difficulties that Poles, like any immigrants, encountered in a new country. Many of Detroit's Polish Catholics in the 1870s and 1880s, for example, felt that their diocesan bishop, a German, was not sympathetic to their needs. Suspicions toward those coming from different areas of divided Poland caused dissension among Poles

The barracks-like housing provided for these male farm workers was unfortunately not typical of all such housing, which was at times wretched. Mechanical means of picking many fruits and vegetables, plus higher labor costs, led growers to greatly decrease the use of migrant workers. Many workers, however, made their homes in Michigan, making Hispanics one of the state's largest ethnic groups by the late twentieth century. Courtesy, State Archives, Michigan Department of State

Opposite page: *In this portrait of Hazen Pingree, Detroit artist Percy Ives succeeded in depicting not only the Detroiter's impressive physical size but also the grim, unrelenting personality that made him such a formidable political adversary in the city and state during the 1890s. Courtesy, State Archives, Michigan Department of State*

themselves, leading to violence between rival factions on Christmas Day, 1885. The conflict originated with an order from Bishop Caspar H. Borgess prohibiting all religious services in the largest of Detroit's Polish churches, St. Albertus's, until Father Dominik Kolasinski, spiritual leader of one of the Polish groups, resigned and surrendered the church to the bishop.

Nine years later, shortly after new bishop John S. Foley had reluctantly accepted the controversial Kolasinski and his flock back into the church's good graces, new sources of trouble surfaced for the city's Poles. With Detroit—and the country—in the grip of its most severe depression to date, the jobless rate was highest among Poles and other eastern and southern Europeans who were generally unskilled workers and hence the first to be laid off. In April 1894, hundreds of workers, mostly Poles, were digging a trench for a city water project and objected to a decision which, it was believed, would pay them less than they had been promised. On April 18, when disgruntled workers sought to keep others away from the excavation site at Connor's Creek, rioting broke out between workers armed with picks and shovels and a handful of lawmen carrying guns. The riot, the most violent labor dispute Detroit had yet seen, resulted in the deaths of three Polish workers and serious injuries to at least twenty other workers and officials.

Newspapers denounced the rioters as "Polish-speaking cowards," "human hyenas," and "pitifully ignorant and not in sympathy with the American spirit." These descriptions reflected nativist sentiments that the "New Immigrants," with their strange names and different ways, had aroused among many of the population's older, more established elements. Although the nativists' anti-Catholic prejudices might seem to have been a reason for all Catholics to support their hard-pressed Pol-

ish brethren, the diocesan paper that reflected the established Irish-German Catholic leadership also attacked the rioters, calling them "howling Poles thirsting for blood." The violence did serve, temporarily at least, to draw Poles closer together, while some other immigrants with whom Poles had had differences voiced support for them. In addition, many Poles were now more receptive to the recruiting efforts of labor unions, even though the Polish workers' parish priests denounced union leaders as socialists and "foreigners."

Clearly, the new developments that were under way by the end of the nineteenth century were creating conditions that would demand new approaches. As mayor of Detroit and governor of Michigan from 1889 to 1901, no one did more to try to deal with the economic and social forces that had been unleashed than did Hazen S. Pingree. No one, including Pingree, could have guessed he would have such an impact when he entered the political arena. A native of Maine who came to Michigan after service in the Civil War (which included five months in the Confederates' dreaded Andersonville Prison), Pingree had built up a shoe manufacturing business that was said to be the largest of its kind west of New England. His success drew him into the inner circle of Detroit's business elite, and like many of his fellow businessmen, Pingree was a loyal Republican. After Grover Cleveland's election in 1884, the first victory of a Democratic presidential candidate since 1856, Pingree, James McMillan, Dexter M. Ferry, and others founded the Michigan Club out of their concern for Republican prospects.

The Republican party's control in Michigan had depended on its great strength in the outstate, rural areas to offset the Democrats' stronghold in Detroit, where that party had won the majority of city elections since the 1860s.

Well-publicized charges of corruption among Democratic officeholders in 1889, however, raised hopes among city Republicans that a good-government campaign, headed by a respected, honest businessman such as Pingree, could oust the incumbent Democratic administration. Pingree, whose political involvement had consisted mainly of financial contributions, at first rejected efforts to draft him for the mayoral nomination. "What in hell do I know about politics," he said. "I'm too busy making shoes." However, additional pressure, plus the promise of support from his business acquaintances, persuaded Pingree to enter the race.

From the outset Pingree's actions should have warned McMillan and his fellow conservatives that they had made the wrong choice. If elected, Pingree promised he would serve "not merely as the local figurehead of the Republican party, but as the mayor of the whole city, without regard to class faction or party." In keeping with that pledge, Pingree, whose poor speaking voice handicapped him in formal political rallies, kicked off his campaign at "Baltimore Red's" saloon. The act dispelled any notion that he followed the Republican temperance line that had attracted outstate Protestant Yankee voters but had been less than popular among Detroit's many foreign-born, Catholic residents. The latter voted Democratic because of the local party's anti-temperance stand and the representation Democrats gave to ethnic groups in their choice of candidates. Detroit Republicans in 1889 sought to offset their WASP image by including on their slate several Germans as well as the one Irishman who had been their top vote-getter in recent elections.

Pingree, however, went beyond these accepted ethnic constituencies to court support of the newer immigrants, particularly the Poles. This large bloc of voters, dissatisfied with the treatment they had received from the domi-

For these immigrant workers, the Americanization class sponsored circa 1915 by their employer, the American Seating Company of Grand Rapids, was clearly serious business. Their intent expressions are the best evidence one could find to refute nativist arguments questioning immigrants' desire and ability to become good citizens. Courtesy, Grand Rapids Public Library

nant Irish and German Democratic hierarchy, was ready for a switch to Pingree; his rough, down-to-earth approach offset the Republicans' anti-Catholic, temperance, silk stocking image that had repelled these immigrants. Reportedly with Father Dominik Kolasinski's support, Pingree captured most of the city's Polish districts, and his additional success among other ethnics, Germans especially, gave him the victory. By identifying with a broad spectrum of the new, divergent elements that comprised the urban population, Pingree pointed the way that successful candidates increasingly would have to follow in the future.

As mayor, Pingree initially did what his wealthy backers had expected—root out fraud and operate the city in a sound, businesslike manner. In one case he hired detectives to carry out a sting-like operation that proved several school board members were taking bribes from contractors. Walking into a school board meeting, Pingree announced: "There are quite a number of the members of this board who are going to jail tonight." He then read off the names of the implicated individuals and called in officers he had waiting outside. "It was like a scene from a

melodrama," the Detroit News observed, "for such things happen often on the stage but seldom in real life."

As mayor from 1889 to 1897 Pingree continued to fight for clean government, but by the end of his first two-year term he was concluding that the problem Detroit faced was not so much graft and corruption in city hall but special treatment accorded to a privileged few. With increasing enthusiasm Pingree took up the cause of the masses against the "bloodsuckers," as he termed the enemy in one of his more restrained moments. He fought the gas, power, and telephone companies over the rates they charged and succeeded in getting all of them to substantially reduce their fees, saving customers and the city millions of dollars. In his most famous campaign Pingree took on the traction companies who were, he said, guilty of providing the public with inferior services at grossly inflated prices. By setting up a competing streetcar line Pingree did improve the service, but the long-term charters a compliant city council had granted to the companies enabled their owners to resist many of the mayor's demands, leading him to press unsuccessfully for public ownership of the lines.

Senator James McMillan and Pingree's other business acquaintances, many of whom had interests in the utility and traction companies, denounced him as a traitor to his class but failed to secure his defeat. Pingree emerged as one of Michigan's most astute politicians, drawing upon the appeal his programs had among the common people of the city to win reelection by huge majorities. State law, which limited Pingree's ability to institute some reforms, especially those designed to correct gross inequities in property tax assessments, led him to seek the Republican gubernatorial nomination in 1892. In this case, however, Senator McMillan was able to defeat Pingree's bid with the control he had over party

delegates. In 1896, concern for Republican hopes in the presidential race led McMillan to hold his nose and approve Pingree's nomination in the correct belief that his presence would greatly strengthen the entire Republican ticket.

As governor from 1897 through 1900, Pingree came out in favor of a host of reforms associated with the Progressives of a somewhat later date, including nominations by direct primaries, popular election of United States senators, a graduated income tax, and strengthened controls over big business. However, Pingree had little success in securing the adoption of such reforms that lay within the power of the state to carry through. After an exhausting four-year struggle he did succeed in securing an amendment to the state constitution eliminating the exemptions that had prevented railroad and other corporate properties from being taxed at their true value, but the

majority in the senate that had fought him every step of the way delayed implementation of the amendment until after Pingree left office.

Pingree died in 1901, embittered by his defeats and by the manner in which his one-time friends had ostracized him and conspired to torpedo his reforms. But in his eleven years in public office he had revealed the Democratic party to be a spoils-oriented organization unable to hold the support of its ethnic constituencies in the face of an opponent who promised constructive programs. The groundwork was laid for the later Republican reform governors, Fred M. Warner and Chase S. Osborn. Between 1905 and 1913, they achieved some of Pingree's economic and political reform goals, solidifying a view of the Republican party as one that was able to deal with the problems of the new era. Not until the 1930s would the accuracy of that view be widely questioned.

On an unseasonably mild and sunny January 2, 1911, Governor Chase S. Osborn is inaugurated at the capitol in Lansing. For Osborn, the only Upper Peninsula resident ever to serve as the state's governor, it was an auspicious start to a term that would climax an era of Republican reform administrations. Courtesy, Michigan Historical Collections, Bentley Historical Library, University of Michigan

157

CHAPTER X

WARS, PROSPERITY, AND DEPRESSION

Between July 1917 and December 1918, the Aeroplane Division of Detroit's Fisher Body Corporation produced 2,005 "aeroplanes" for the nation's war effort. These men were among the 4,500 employees who applied some of the auto industry's mass-production techniques to aircraft production. Courtesy, Michigan Historical Collections, Bentley Historical Library, University of Michigan

Sarajevo in the Austro-Hungarian province of Bosnia was a city few Michiganians, other than immigrants from that part of the Balkans, had ever heard of prior to June 28, 1914, when the assassination of the Austrian Archduke Francis Ferdinand put the city on the front pages of Michigan's newspapers. Within a month events were leading Europe inevitably into what Michigan headline writers already were predicting would be the "Greatest War of History," but it is doubtful if anyone could have guessed that within two and a half years the United States would be drawn into the conflict and that life in Michigan would never be quite the same thereafter.

Like most Americans, Michigan residents generally felt that they were masters of their destinies, unaffected by foreign events. The wars in which America had been involved were all seen as arising from its need to deal with problems and issues resulting from its internal development and expansion. To be sure, a change became evident after the American acquisition of the Philippines in 1898, and particularly during the presidency of Teddy

Roosevelt from 1901 to 1909. As a newly recognized world power, the United States flexed its muscles and sought to influence developments in areas of the world other than North America. Sarajevo, however, marked the beginning of an age in which the United States would find that it was not always free to decide where and when it would be involved. Michiganians would have to adjust to an awareness of the possibly devastating effects of the overthrow of a Russian Czar, a German invasion of Poland, events in Korea and Vietnam, and an embargo by a group of oil-producing states in the Near East. Much as they might resist the idea, it was no longer possible to think of themselves as in control of their destinies.

The first reaction to events in Europe in the summer of 1914 included an assessment of the war's economic impact. A dispatch from Lansing on July 30 quoted state agricultural college authorities as saying that even if the war involved only the initial combatants, Austria and Serbia, it would "fatten the pocketbooks of Michigan farmers by at least $1,105,000" be-

159

cause of the war-related rise in wheat prices. If Germany and Russia were drawn into the conflict the resulting increases in market prices of other crops, the East Lansing experts agreed, would mean even more money in farmers' pockets. The war did spread, of course, and eventually Michigan farmers, who increased production during the war by an estimated 25 percent, benefited well beyond the experts' initial forecasts. War demands also drove Michigan's mines to new production records, while further depleting the state's few remaining timber reserves. Far more significant, however, was the dramatic demonstration World War I provided

of Michigan's emergence as a major manufacturing center.

Fighting was barely under way in Europe when Michigan companies began seeking war contracts both from the warring nations in Europe and from the United States government as expenditures for American defense increased. A Bay City manufacturer of pre-cut housing advertised its readiness to ship large quantities of buildings that could be used as "Barracks, Laundries, Mess Halls, Officers' Quarters, Field Hospitals, Store Houses, Field Kitchens," or for "Refugees or Emergency Buildings of any kind." Scores of merchant vessels were built for wartime service, particularly after the United States entered the war in April 1917, at shipyards in Ecorse, Wyandotte, and the Saginaw valley. Dow Chemical manufactured large amounts of mustard gas, the first of its controversial war products that would bring the Midland firm attention of a kind not always welcomed. The war, however, had its biggest impact on the auto industry. In addition to producing trucks, ambulances, and armored vehicles, the industry showed its adaptability by also turning out tanks, airplane engines, and at Ford's new Rouge plant, submarine chasers, called Eagle Boats.

Once the United States entered the war, the new method used to meet the armed forces' manpower needs illustrated the declining political importance of the states in the twentieth century. Albert Sleeper, the successful Republican candidate for governor in 1916, had expected the War Department in the spring of 1917 to call upon him to handle the recruitment of volunteers in Michigan. As recently as 1898 Governor Pingree had spearheaded successful efforts to raise the five regiments Michigan was asked to contribute in the Spanish-American War, repeating a role that governors Alpheus Felch and Austin Blair had played in the Mexican and Civil wars. But the federal government took over the job it had previously assigned to the states, and rather than relying on volunteers to fill the ranks, it turned to the draft. Sleeper's outspoken opposition to the change was attacked by many who charged that his criticism cast doubts on the state's willingness to do its patriotic duty in this time of crisis. Sleeper then reversed himself, cooperating wholeheartedly in the June registration that launched the draft process. The majority of the 135,000 Michigan men who served in the war entered as draftees, rather than as volunteers which in previous wars had served in units bear-

ing the Michigan name.

The opposition to Sleeper's views on the draft was not the first he had suffered as a result of intense wartime emotions. Anti-German feelings had led to widespread criticism of Sleeper when he campaigned for German-American votes in the 1916 election. German-Americans were one of the state's largest, oldest, and most respected ethnic elements, but after the United States declared war against Germany many questioned their loyalty. Educators, including nationally known university professors, led drives to eliminate the teaching of German in the schools, where it had been one of the most widely taught foreign languages. The town of Berlin, like a number of Berlins elsewhere in the country, changed its name, in this case to Marne, after the area in France where the German invasion in 1914 had been stopped. The loyalty of other ethnic groups was also questioned by many self-appointed guardians of Americanism, some of whom pressured people who had not bought war bonds by publishing their names in the papers or by splattering their homes with yellow paint.

Such ugly anti-foreign outbursts came at a time when the war halted the flow of European immigrants who for years had increasingly provided the labor that Michigan industry had needed. Now during the wartime boom the state's employers found in the South a surplus rural population that needed little encouragement to seek the opportunities available in the North. By 1916 the traditional east-west movement of peoples coming into Michigan from New York, New England, Canada, and Europe was being replaced by a migration from the South that would continue with little abatement for several decades, resulting in the century's most important demographic changes. Southern-born whites, previously an insignificant element in the state, by

John C. Dancy poses with his wife, Malinda, about the time he retired in 1960 after forty-two years as the head of the Detroit Urban League. Courtesy, State Archives, Michigan Department of State

1930 numbered 165,926, most of them from Missouri, Arkansas, Tennessee, and Kentucky. They settled mainly in industrialized southeastern Michigan, often in almost ghetto-like residential areas such as Flint's "Little Missouri." Derisively referred to by some as hillbillies, the southern whites, like all newcomers, often had difficulty in adjusting to their new surroundings and dreamed of returning to the South. Racial differences, however, made the southern blacks who came during this same period a much more obvious addition to Michigan's population, creating far more serious barriers to their acceptance.

From the Civil War to World War I Michigan's black population had shown relatively little growth, moving from 15,100 in 1880 to 17,105 in 1910, a mere six-tenths of one percent of the state's people. With the influx that began in 1916, the black community expanded to 60,082 in 1920

These excited Detroit-area children are about to board a bus in the summer of 1952 for a trip to the Green Pastures Camp near Jackson. The Detroit Urban League established the camp in 1931, when existing summer camps accepted only white children. Courtesy, Michigan Historical Collections, Bentley Historical Library, University of Michigan

and 169,453 in 1930, comprising 3.8 percent of the population. Flint, Jackson, Grand Rapids, and other industrial cities experienced a sharp increase in the size of their black populations, but the great majority of blacks came to Detroit. There, blacks had numbered 5,741 in 1910, slightly more than a third of all the blacks in the state. After 1916, they increased to 40,838 in 1920 and 120,066 in 1930, accounting for 71 percent of Michigan's blacks by that time. These blacks tended to come from areas farther south than did the southern whites, with those born in Georgia being the most numerous,

Camp Custer near Battle Creek was the World War I training ground for draftees in Michigan, but for these blacks, required to patronize only this "colored club," to live in "colored barracks," and to serve in all-black units, the experience demonstrated how universally segregation was accepted in the country. Courtesy, State Archives, Michigan Department of State

followed by natives of Alabama, Tennessee, and South Carolina. Many southern blacks were initially lured to Detroit, a city few of them had ever heard of, by the promotional efforts of company agents and the Employers' Association of Detroit, who painted an overly rosy picture of northern life and even offered to pay the migrants' travel expenses. But southern blacks, overcoming their skepticism and the efforts of alarmed southern leaders to persuade them to stay, soon needed no encouragement to make the move north. Although this migration began during the war, it continued in the twenties, with an estimated 3,500 blacks arriving monthly in Detroit in July and August of 1922.

These estimates were made by black civil rights leader John C. Dancy, a North Carolina native who came to Detroit in 1918 to head the local Urban

League chapter and remained in that post until his retirement in 1960. The Urban League, always interested primarily in the economic advancement of blacks, was supported by many of Detroit's businessmen who used it as a convenient hiring agency. Dancy cooperated, meeting the trains coming up from the South and often taking the arriving blacks directly to a place of employment before they had a place to live. In his effort to open new opportunities for blacks he succeeded in ingratiating himself with prominent Detroiters and got the jobs he was after, even if it meant going out of his way to chauffeur the head of Hudson's Department Store around town and, because that executive had a disabled arm, being sure to sit next to him at lunch so he could cut up the businessman's food for him. Dancy admitted that he had been called an Uncle Tom for stooping to such servile tactics and for his response to the terrible housing shortage created by the flood of new blacks. Rather than fighting the segregation that forced blacks to live in a limited area east of Woodward Avenue that ironically came to be called "Paradise Valley," Dancy led efforts to develop new housing on the city's outskirts where the white establishment would allow blacks to live.

In 1925 a black doctor, Ossian Sweet, defied the rules and moved his family into a previously all-white neighborhood. Someone in the Sweet home fired into the menacing white mob that gathered outside, killing one man. Dancy served as treasurer of the fund that was raised to defend the Sweets against the charge of murder. Clarence Darrow was brought in for the defense, and after two exhausting trials Darrow succeeded in getting the white jury to bring in a verdict of not guilty. After Darrow's closing argument, the Detroit judge in the case, Frank Murphy, told an associate, "This is the greatest experience of my life. That was Clarence Darrow at his best. I will never hear anything like it again." Forty years later, Dancy agreed. "Darrow was magnificent. I can close my eyes and see him, and hear his resonant, melodious voice, now sinking to a whisper that had everyone leaning forward breathlessly, now bursting out in a roar of indignation." It was a great performance, one of the highlights of Darrow's illustrious career. Yet although the Sweets were freed, the issues and attitudes associated with segregation remained to be solved.

For a good many years the newcomers from the South had little apparent impact on Michigan politics. A split between the Republican party's progressive and conservative wings in 1912 had enabled Democrat Woodbridge N. Ferris to be elected governor, and when he was reelected in 1914 he became the first two-term Democratic governor since the founding of the GOP sixty years earlier. But in 1916 the election of Albert Sleeper and the rest of the Republican state ticket signaled the

Alex Groesbeck, seated at his desk in the governor's office in Lansing, restructured the state government's administration during his tenure from 1920 to 1926. Courtesy, State Archives, Michigan Department of State

165

This circa 1905 view of downtown Lansing depicts a vintage automobile turning the corner at the right, previewing a mode of transportation that finally took hold in the 1920s and eventually supplanted the streetcar. Courtesy, State Archives, Michigan Department of State

party's reunification. From then until 1932 it dominated the state to a degree rarely if ever seen before. Except for the race for United States senator in 1922, won by Ferris because of personality differences among Republicans, Democrats had almost no success at the polls. In 1924 they were not only shut out in the race for state executive posts, but also could not elect a single member to the legislature.

Voting Republican had become a tradition for many in Michigan, but the party's triumphs are also attributable to the obvious competence of several of its top candidates in the twenties. One was Alex Groesbeck, whose Michigan roots went back to the time when the area was a French colony. Groesbeck, a Detroit attorney, rose through the ranks to gain the gubernatorial nomination in 1920. He went on that year

to defeat the perennial Democratic candidate, Woodbridge Ferris, and was reelected in 1922 and 1924 by huge margins. Groesbeck's major achievement was in imposing a more efficient administrative structure on a state government that had grown in a haphazard, unplanned manner. He created the state administrative board, headed by the governor, to enforce budgetary, purchasing, and accounting controls over previously independent departments and agencies. In addition, Groesbeck eliminated thirty agencies by combining their responsibilities in five new departments. These actions, which diminished the agency heads' ability to bestow favors on their friends and supporters, combined with Groesbeck's often brusque and tactless style of operating to alienate powerful members of the party. They combined to defeat his bid in 1926 for a fourth term, electing in his stead the conservative, stand-pat politician, Fred M. Green.

The twenties also saw the emergence of two of Michigan's most important United States senators, both of whom were appointed to serve the remainder of an unexpired term before being elected to full terms by large majorities. James Couzens, the onetime financial wizard of the Ford Motor Company, was appointed by Groesbeck in 1922. In Washington he quickly made his mark as a maverick who in spite of his business background was highly critical of the Republican administration's business-oriented approach. Although he clearly did not represent the thinking of the conservative Republican majority, Couzens was elected in 1924 and again in 1930, probably because many voters admired his independence.

Arthur H. Vandenberg, longtime editor of the Grand Rapids *Herald*, was appointed by Governor Green in 1928 to fill the remaining months in the term of Woodbridge Ferris, who died earlier that year. Ideologically, Vandenberg contrasted sharply with Couzens, but he would become one of Michigan's most influential senators not because of his conservative ideas on domestic policy but because of his stand on foreign policy.

Although the twenties began with Warren G. Harding's promise to lead the nation in a "return to normalcy," the decade was more notable for the breaks it made with past norms. The Nineteenth Amendment to the United States Constitution enabled Michigan women to cast their ballots in 1920, something that they only very rarely were allowed to do before that time. In the case of another 1920s innovation, prohibition, Michigan had jumped the gun by imposing a statewide ban on alcoholic beverages in 1918, a year before the Eighteenth Amendment paved the way for national prohibition. That

"Noble Experiment" was no more successful in Michigan than it was in other parts of the country, and the Detroit area became one of the major conduits through which liquor was smuggled in from Canada. Michigan breweries survived by producing soft drinks, malt extract (which enjoyed brisk sales to those who wanted to brew their own beer at home), and in the case of Stroh's, ice cream. Thanks in part to the efforts of Henry B. Joy, a retired head of Packard who became a national leader in the drive to repeal prohibition, the beer trucks were back on the road by 1933.

While the breweries struggled, the majority of the state's industries flourished following a postwar depression from 1920 to 1923. The prosperity of the Roaring Twenties triggered one of the greatest construction booms in the state's history. In addition to the resi-

Across the street from the state capitol, the 1920s ended with the opening of the Olds Hotel and the completion of the Olds Tower's steel frame. Both altered a landscape previously dominated by the capitol dome and symbolized the degree to which the auto industry had come to equal or surpass state government in the city's life. From Lansing and Its Yesterdays, *1930*

In 1928 Detroit Times *cartoonist Percy Cromwell expressed the prevailing view that scoffed at those few people who suggested that the good times resulting from the boom in auto sales might not last. Courtesy, Michigan Historical Collections, Bentley Historical Library, University of Michigan*

dential and commercial developments that completely altered the appearance of Michigan's burgeoning industrial centers, there were cultural developments that put the spotlight on something other than the economic achievements for which Michigan had generally been known. Detroit's new symphony orchestra was beginning to win national acclaim under the direction of Ossip Gabrilowitsch, while the public library and the Institute of Arts moved into magnificent new quarters on opposite sides of Woodward Avenue. Nearby, the establishment of the College of the City of Detroit in 1923 was the first step toward the eventual emergence of Wayne State University, one of the nation's largest urban universities. In 1927 the Jesuit-run University of Detroit moved to a new

campus, having outgrown its original downtown facilities. To the north in Bloomfield Hills, the Episcopalian-oriented Cranbrook educational complex was developed by newspaper magnate George G. Booth and his wife. To the west in Dearborn, Henry Ford opened the Henry Ford Museum and Greenfield Village, paying homage to an age he had had a major hand in bringing to an end while at the same time creating what would become one of the country's major tourist attractions.

Among state-supported institutions of higher education, the teachers' colleges at Ypsilanti, Mount Pleasant, Kalamazoo, and Marquette grew significantly, but the most attention centered on the schools at East Lansing and Ann Arbor. The enrollment of East

Above: *The massive Angell Hall that rose along Ann Arbor's State Street in the 1920s was an appropriate memorial to the late James B. Angell, president of the University of Michigan in the late nineteenth century when the university had become one of the nation's great schools. Courtesy, Michigan Historical Collections, Bentley Historical Library, University of Michigan*

Left: *The R. E. Olds Hall of Engineering, built during World War I with a $100,000 gift from the auto magnate, indicated the extent to which Michigan Agricultural College's name was no longer entirely descriptive of its curriculum. Although he never attended college, Olds was an ardent booster of the East Lansing school. Courtesy, Michigan State University Archives and Historical Collections*

REO ENTERS LOWEST-PRICE FIELD

with Brilliant New 1/2 and 3/4 Ton Truck!

★ 100% TRUCK CONSTRUCTION

*Built by Truck Engineers ·· Powered with Sturdy Truck Engine ··
Balanced Load Distribution ·· Exceptional Economy and Flexibility*

$555

SPEED DELIVERY—COMPLETE
F. O. B. Lansing, Michigan

Price includes all-steel top cab
with safety glass and option of 4-
cylinder or 6-cylinder Silver Crown
truck engine. Panel units, on short
or long wheelbases, at correspond-
ingly low prices.
Reo Speed Wagons and Trucks
range from 1/2 to 4-6 tons including
Tractor Trailers and Buses.
All models feature new
streamlined styling
with V-type wind-
shields. Prices start
at $555 f.o.b. Lans-
ing, Michigan,
plus tax. Special
equipment extra.

NOW see the new Reo Speed Delivery—
America's fine quality truck in the lowest price class and Reo's ringing answer
to "the challenge of a new day".
Brand new truck engineering makes scientific
load distribution possible in this new low-
priced Reo. Easier handling and greater
operating economy result. New engine and
axle locations permit the use of longer bodies.
Bulkier loads can be carried than
in conventional trucks of
corresponding size.
Typically Reo in every
detail — the new
Speed Delivery is
built by truck engi-
neers to do a real
truck job. Avail-

able in 1/2 or 3/4 ton models of 114 and 120 inch
wheelbase, it introduces a new conception of
value in the low-price truck field.
Two Silver Crown Engines are optional—6
cylinders for fast highway transport and 4
cylinders for economical multi-stop work.
Both handle capacity loads at high speed with
remarkably low gas and oil consumption.
All-steel cabs of roomier construction provide greater driver comfort. V-type safety
glass windshields assure unobstructed vision
and better ventilation. These features are
standard equipment on all cab models.
Check the new Reo Speed Delivery feature by
feature. Compare it with other trucks at or
near its low price. See for yourself that Reo's
Speed Delivery is America's highest quality
low-priced truck!

REO MOTOR CAR COMPANY, LANSING, MICHIGAN

America's Toughest Truck!

REO SPEEDWAGONS
TRUCKS AND BUSES

A casualty of the Depression, Reo automobiles were discontinued in 1936 after thirty-one years of production, but trucks bearing the Reo name continued to be produced in Lansing for nearly forty more years. The name has lived on through the efforts of a musical group that chose to call itself, for some unfathomable reason, the Reo Speedwagon. From the Saturday Evening Post, *November 14, 1936*

Lansing's agricultural college reached the 3,000 level by the end of the twenties, almost five times what it had been thirty years earlier. Much of the growth resulted from the school's expansion into new areas of study outside of those relating to agriculture. Beaumont Memorial Tower and numerous other new buildings were an indication of the new respect the school was receiving from the legislature and private donors, but for many of its alumni and supporters the football team's 63-0 loss to the University of Michigan in 1922 and the contrast between its new 15,000-seat stadium and the cavernous

new 87,000-seat stadium in Ann Arbor seemed a more important—and bitter—gauge of where they stood in the state. There can be no doubt that the University of Michigan, located in Ann Arbor since 1837 and long since recognized as one of the nation's top universities, garnered the lion's share of attention. Campus construction projects during the 1920s included Angell Hall, part of the Law Quadrangle, the exquisite Clements Library, the University Museums Building, the Michigan Union, and the University Hospital, as well as the stadium and Yost Field House.

The prosperity of the twenties that made these and many other projects possible resulted, in Michigan more than anywhere else, from the explosion in automobile sales. As financial institutions became willing to finance automobile purchases, middle and lower income families that had been unable to meet the previously customary cash-on-delivery terms now rushed to buy a car. Automobile registrations in Michigan alone rose from 326,000 in 1919 to more than 1.4 million by 1929, and automobile production more than doubled as the manufacturers tried to keep up with the demand. The state, particularly during Groesbeck's administration, launched a massive campaign to replace Michigan's dirt roads with a network of all-weather surfaced highways that automobile owners demanded and needed in order to travel with some sense of security. Beginning in 1925 the high cost of these roads was passed on to motorists through a gasoline tax.

The bubble burst in October 1929 when the stock market crash ushered in the worst depression in the country's history, one many believe was partly the result of high consumer debt levels encouraged by the practice of selling things like cars on installment plans. Although Ford tried to head off an anticipated drop in sales by cutting the

prices of its cars in November 1929, such tactics were to no avail. Auto production that had exceeded 5,000,000 vehicles in 1929 plummeted to 1,331,860 in 1932, and Michigan was treated to a sobering demonstration of what it meant to have an automobile-dominated economy. While the state had prospered from the heady heights to which that economy had carried it in the twenties, it now had to suffer through a depression whose depths in Michigan were much lower than the national average. Non-farm unemployment rates topped 20 percent in 1930 and by 1932-1933 had climbed to a staggering 50 percent. Hardest hit were the areas where auto production was concentrated and the mining areas of the Upper Peninsula where many mining operations were halted entirely, some never to be resumed. Nor were farmers exempt. The collapse of market prices led to an alarming rise in farm mortgage foreclosures and to tax delinquency rates that by 1933 were said to be the highest in the country.

Reduced property tax receipts made the task of providing relief for the Depression's victims all the more difficult. Frank Murphy, the judge in the Ossian Sweet case who was elected mayor of Detroit in 1930, exhausted the city's limited means and led efforts to persuade state and federal governments to provide the resources that local governments lacked. But President Herbert Hoover remained unpersuaded and favored more conservative measures. The Republican administration of Governor Wilber M. Brucker, Fred Green's designated successor, was as unprepared to effectively respond to this unprecedented crisis as was Hoover's administration. The result in 1932 was the biggest Democratic victory in many decades: all of Michigan's electoral votes went to a Democrat—Franklin D. Roosevelt—which had not happened in eighty years; William A. Comstock, a wealthy Detroit Democrat who had been soundly defeated in three previous runs for governor, was elected by a margin exceeding

These Democratic candidates in East Cohoctan on October 22, 1932, might already be sensing victory in a township and a state that had been solidly Republican for most of the preceding eight decades. Courtesy, Michigan Historical Collections, Bentley Historical Library, University of Michigan

Two of Michigan's greatest political figures, James Couzens (left) and Frank Murphy, belonged to opposing parties but shared the same humanitarian goals as they discussed the crisis that Detroit, the state of Michigan, and the nation confronted in the depths of the Great Depression. Courtesy, State Archives, Michigan Department of State

Roosevelt's victory in Michigan; and Democrats captured majorities in the state's legislature and Congressional delegation.

The election represented only a temporary lapse in Republican support in many outstate areas, which the party regained in 1934. The Republicans also elected Frank D. Fitzgerald as governor and returned Arthur Vandenberg to the Senate. But in the southeast, especially in Wayne County where Republican governors Pingree and Groesbeck had piled up huge vote totals, Republican defections among ethnic groups, blacks, and the working class were massive and long lasting. The same phenomenon occurred in the Upper Peninsula mining counties, where Democratic votes at one time had been nearly nonexistent. The change was revealed again in 1936 when Roosevelt once more won the state's electoral votes, Frank Murphy defeated incumbent Republican Governor Fitzgerald, and Prentiss M. Brown succeeded Senator James Couzens, who had been defeated in the Republican primary because of his support for Roosevelt's liberal programs. The Republican party's ability to get its supporters out to vote largely accounted for its victories in off-year elections, as in 1938 when Fitzgerald

regained the governorship by defeating the charismatic Murphy. The old-guard state Democratic organization was ill-suited for the new approaches needed to mobilize support for state and local candidates among those who had been won over by Roosevelt's New Deal. However, the encouragement the New Deal gave to labor would eventually provide the mechanism by which the Democratic potential would be fully realized.

Labor unions had existed in Michigan for a century, but aside from those who might belong to craft unions most Michigan workers were not unionized. Company and community opposition which had smashed efforts in the late nineteenth and early twentieth centuries to unionize workers in such areas as lumbering, mining, and the furniture industry helped account for Michigan's reputation as an open-shop state. Other factors helped explain the lack of a union among most auto workers. When a Detroit union organizer who was supposed to be recruiting members in that industry in 1920 was asked what grievances the union would redress, he replied, "Well, I guess we haven't anything to complain of. Everything's all right." Such a surprising response, which revealed the craft-dominated labor movement's disinterest in organizing workers who were mostly unskilled, also reflected conditions in an expanding industry that paid high wages to attract the workers it desperately needed.

Such conditions abruptly ended with the Great Depression. Those who were out of work or who were uncertain how long they would remain employed were more inclined to listen to organizers' appeals while the pro-labor attitude of the New Deal stimulated unions to renewed efforts. By 1936 the United Automobile Workers had emerged, affiliating with the Committee for Industrial Organizations which advocated organizing all workers in an industry in one union, rather than separating the skilled workers into their respective craft unions and ignoring the unskilled. Roosevelt's reelection and the election of the liberal Frank Murphy as governor convinced UAW leaders that it was time to proceed with plans for a strike against General

Motors as the first step in winning recognition as a bargaining agent for the industry's blue-collar employees. Although a number of G.M. plants in the country would be struck, union efforts were concentrated in Flint, for all practical purposes a G.M. company town. Only a small percentage of Flint's workers belonged to the UAW, but resentment toward the company was such that one union official, when asked if the men were ready to strike, replied, "They're like a pregnant woman in her tenth month!" Workers used the sit-down tactic that had been popularized that year to seize control of Flint's Fisher Body Plants Nos. 1 and 2 on December 30, 1936, and the great Flint Sit-down Strike was on.

The strike lasted until February 11, 1937. According to University of Michigan professor Sidney Fine, author of the definitive work on the subject, it was not only the most crucial labor con-

President Roosevelt's New Deal soon resulted in massive federal relief programs that would provide help to hundreds of thousands in Michigan. Here in the mid-1930s a Detroit street repair project financed by the Works Progress Administration provided work to scores of heavily-bundled men wielding picks and shovels. Courtesy, State Archives, Michigan Department of State

Probably the most famous photograph in the history of University of Michigan football, this 1940 posed shot by the Ann Arbor News' *Eck Stanger captured the exuberance of the backfield of (l. to r.) Forest Evashevski, Norm Call, Bob Westfall, and the immortal Tom Harmon. Better days lay ahead for the one-time "Champions of the West," who, like the state, had fallen on hard times in the thirties. Courtesy, Ann Arbor News*

As the United Auto Workers strike entered its second month, picketers, many armed with sticks or other potential weapons, marched around Fisher Body Plant No. 1 in Flint on February 3, 1937. Courtesy, The Flint Journal

frontation of the turbulent thirties but "perhaps in all of American history . . . The successful outcome of the strike helped to determine that the decision-making power in large segments of American industry where the voice of labor had been little more than a whisper, if that, would henceforth have to be shared in some measure with the unions in these industries, and the trade-union movement as a whole would enjoy a higher status in American life than it ever had before."

The union's victory, the first big breakthrough for the industrial union approach, came after a struggle that for many participants would be the most memorable event in their lives. General Motors, working through local authorities accustomed to following the giant corporation's dictates, attempted to remove the strikers through judicial proceedings. On the evening of January 11, however, violence erupted at Fisher Body Plant No. 2. Flint po-

licemen and sheriff's deputies, on whose orders it is not clear, sought to force their way past the plant gate using tear gas, but were driven off by pickets outside the plant and strikers inside who turned fire hoses on the lawmen and hurled door hinges, cans, milk bottles, pieces of pavement, and anything else they could lay their hands on. The retreating police drew their guns and fired at their tormentors. Fourteen strikers and sympathizers, eleven law officers, and two spectators were injured in the fray, which the jubilant strikers dubbed the Battle of the Running Bulls (bull, like pig in a later time, was a common slang term for policeman). Governor Murphy, who took office two days after the strike began, consulted city and union officials and then sent in the National Guard, but only to preserve order and not, as had been the case in the past, as a strike-breaking force.

For the most part, further violence was avoided as efforts to settle the dispute proceeded through negotiations. No one was more responsible for the successful conclusion of these talks than Murphy, who was the catalyst that brought the company and the union together in marathon negotiating sessions in Detroit. The talks concluded on February 11 as General Motors, under heavy pressure from many quarters including President Roosevelt, agreed to accept the union as bargaining agent for its members and, most importantly, not to hinder the union's efforts to en-

roll new members. Late that afternoon the strikers, after a month and a half, left the factories they had occupied and marched downtown, where they celebrated their victory with thousands of supporters. "These people," a CIO representative recalled, "sang and joked and laughed and cried, deliriously joyful . . . victory . . . meant a freedom they had never known before. No longer would they be afraid to join unions."

A few weeks later Chrysler also gave in to the union after a brief struggle, as did smaller automakers, but Ford held out. On May 26, 1937, company guards savagely assaulted union organizers who were attempting to hand out literature to workers at the end of their shift at the Ford Rouge plant. Not until four years later did

Henry Ford, nearly eighty years old and enfeebled by a stroke, surrender after a spontaneous walkout and a federally supervised election that showed an overwhelming majority of Ford workers favored the UAW. In the end, the old auto pioneer, ever unpredictable, gave the UAW a better contract than it had yet obtained from Ford's competitors.

One reason Ford may have wished to avoid further work stoppages was the fact that since the outbreak of World War II in September 1939, the United States, although not yet in the war, had been engaged in an increasingly large-scale preparedness program and was supplying aid to the British and their allies. Once the United States was involved in the conflict, Michigan's auto

With the announcement of the strike's settlement on February 11, 1937, strikers at the Chevrolet Factory No. 4 raise the flag and commence the celebration of their victory. Courtesy, The Flint Journal

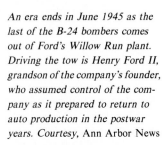

An era ends in June 1945 as the last of the B-24 bombers comes out of Ford's Willow Run plant. Driving the tow is Henry Ford II, grandson of the company's founder, who assumed control of the company as it prepared to return to auto production in the postwar years. Courtesy, Ann Arbor News

industry quickly became the mainstay of the nation's war production. Within two months after the Japanese attack on Pearl Harbor, civilian auto production was halted in order to funnel all the industry's resources into the war effort. At a new plant in Macomb County, north of Detroit, Chrysler would turn out over 25,000 tanks. General Motors also produced tanks at a plant in Grand Blanc and contributed a wide range of other war materials from its numerous plants. The greatest attention, however, was focused on the contract Ford received in 1941 to build B-24 Liberator bombers. An immense factory was built at Willow Run on the eastern outskirts of Ypsilanti, but as months went by and few bombers appeared doubts were expressed about Ford's ability to deliver. But the aging Ford staff overcame production problems and by the end of 1943 bombers were being assembled at a rate of more than one an hour, more than Ford production chief Charles E. Sorenson had originally promised. When production ceased in the summer of 1945 the Willow Run plant had turned out over 8,500 B-24s, a spectacular achievement.

Michigan's economy, which had never recovered from the Depression of the early thirties, was restored by the war to full vigor. Once again the state drew workers from around the country to fill the needs of its booming war plants, offsetting the loss of over 600,000 men and women who left for the armed forces. At its peak Ford's Willow Run plant alone employed 50,000 workers. By 1944 about four-fifths of the 254,485 migrants that had come to the Detroit area had come from out of state. As in World War I, the largest number were from the South. Southern whites had been coming to Michigan for three decades, but it was in the forties that many Michiganians first became aware of this group. Thinly disguised resentments were evident in some of the jokes that circulated: "How many states are there in the Union?" The answer was forty-six, because "Tennessee and Kentucky are now in Michigan." In Ypsilanti the influx of southerners was so great that some referred to the onetime quiet college town as "Ypsitucky."

Southern blacks also came in great numbers, as some 90,000 arrived in the four-county Metropolitan Detroit area between 1940 and 1944. The estimated 60,000 that moved to Detroit proper increased the city's black population by 40 percent. Housing for blacks, long in critically short supply, was now unbelievably overcrowded. When the city housing commission and Mayor Edward Jeffries attempted after much vacillation to open the Sojourner Truth housing project, providing 200 units for black defense workers in northeast Detroit, white residents of the area rioted on February 28, 1942, in an effort to keep blacks out. Black families eventually were settled in what proved to be at best a token gesture by the city, which did little thereafter to relieve the problem.

The Sojourner Truth episode should have been a warning of how the war was exacerbating tensions between the city's whites and blacks, but such trouble signs and the warnings of black leaders and white observers failed to head off one of America's worst race riots. Late on Sunday, June 20, 1943, fights broke out between white and black youths on Belle Isle, one of Detroit's few parks readily available and open to blacks. Inflammatory rumors spread through the city, and in the early hours of the following day violence broke out in all areas frequented by blacks. With the situation out of control, Mayor Jeffries called upon Governor Harry Kelly for help. When Kelly called for federal assistance, mistakes and misunderstandings in the handling of the request delayed the arrival of military police until ten o'clock that night. The soldiers quickly gained control of the city but in the meantime thirty-four persons had died, twenty-five of them blacks. Hundreds were injured, and property losses were substantial.

Mayor Jeffries and Governor Kelly defended the manner in which the city and state had handled the riot, but black groups, backed up by many outside observers, criticized the city's actions and charged that the police dealt with black rioters much more severely than with whites. Demands for a grand jury investigation were never heeded, but the violence of June 20-21,

1943, shocked the city and belatedly led UAW president R.J. Thomas and other civic leaders to propose programs to address black grievances and improve racial relationships. By 1945, with the end of a war fought to defeat oppressive regimes elsewhere in the world, hopes rose that Detroit—and Michigan—had learned a lesson from the tragic experiences of 1943.

In this 1942 print by Helen Johann, the elderly black woman's face, the star on the wall denoting a son or grandson in the service, and the Detroit News *with stories of an Allied victory and race riots in the* Motor City *combine to present a powerful indictment of a period when the nation fought for freedom abroad while denying full freedom to many at home. Courtesy, Library of Congress*

CHAPTER XI

THE POSTWAR YEARS AND A CHANGING WORLD

At San Francisco on June 26, 1945, Senator Arthur H. Vandenberg signs the United Nations Charter, which he had helped draft as a member of the American delegation to the U.N. Conference. Looking on are (l. to r.) President Harry Truman, Secretary of State Edward Stettinius, and Senator Tom Connally. Courtesy, Michigan Historical Collections, Bentley Historical Library, University of Michigan

On January 10, 1945, as the Second World War entered its final months, Arthur H. Vandenberg addressed the U.S. Senate on the subject of postwar foreign policy in the most important speech of his career and probably the most important speech delivered by any Michigan senator or representative. Vandenberg, once ridiculed by a colleague as the "only senator who can strut sitting down," had matured to become one of the Senate's most respected members. Because he had been a leading opponent of American involvement in the world problems that had led to the war, Vandenberg's remarks that January were awaited with great interest. The war had caused him by 1943 to alter his thinking regarding the desirability of an isolationist policy in the future, but he had not forcefully expressed his revised views.

Now he told the Senate that the time had come "for the straightest, the plainest and the most courageous

thinking of which we are capable." Leaving no doubt as to his "own personal viewpoint," Vandenberg declared:

I have always been frankly one of those who has believed in our self-reliance. I still believe that we can never again— regardless of collaborations—allow our national defense to deteriorate to anything like a point of impotence. But I do not believe that any nation hereafter can immunize itself by its own exclusive action. Since Pearl Harbor, World War II has put the gory science of mass murder into new and sinister perspective. Our oceans have ceased to be moats which automatically protect our ramparts . . . If World War III ever unhappily arrives, it will open new laboratories of death too horrible to contemplate.

Declaring that he intended to do all he could to see that "those laboratories

[were] closed for keeps," Vandenberg urged that the discussion of the nation's foreign policy goals and commitments be conducted with "honest candor" so as to achieve "the only kind of realistic unity which will most swiftly bring our victorious sons back home, and which will best validate our aspirations, our sacrifices, and our dreams."

The speech, widely praised and compared by some to the great orations of Daniel Webster and Henry Clay, established a new spirit of bipartisan cooperation in the development of an internationalist foreign policy. By appointing Vandenberg as one of the American delegates to the San Francisco conference that drew up the United Nations Charter, President Roosevelt confirmed the Michigan Republican's leadership of that bipartisan coalition. No Michiganian before or since has had the power that Vandenberg had over foreign policy from 1945 until his death in 1951, despite the fact that his party was in the minority in Congress during most of that time. In Michigan, too, Republicans were increasingly cast in the unfa-

miliar role of a minority party, as the potential that had existed since 1932 for the creation of a strong Democratic party in the state became a reality.

As was now so often the case, these developments were to a great extent an outgrowth of events in the auto industry. When the war ended in the summer of 1945 the industry and its customers looked forward to resuming the halcyon years of the twenties, which had been interrupted first by the economic collapse of the thirties and then by the halt in automobile production during the war. By the time the war was over there were scarcely any cars in the country that were less than four years old and most were considerably older. Consequently, for some years a sellers' market existed in which any car produced was snapped up at once by a public starved for new automobiles. The smaller companies—Detroit's Hudson and Packard and non-Michigan automakers like Studebaker, Nash, Willys, and Crosley—gained a larger share of the market than they had held in many years. New companies were started up, with the most promising being Kaiser-

In April 1951, this Willow Run parking lot crammed with new Henry Js, Kaiser-Frazer's early version of what were being called compact cars, was a sign of declining dealer orders that would soon force the company out of passenger car production. Courtesy, Ann Arbor News

Frazer, organized principally by Californian Henry J. Kaiser, who had gained fame during the war as a shipbuilder. Taking over the former B-24 bomber plant at Willow Run, Kaiser-Frazer in 1946 began producing the Kaiser and the higher-priced Frazer. Within two years the company had 5 percent of the market and appeared to have become the first successful newcomer in the industry in twenty years.

The postwar boom, however, was short-lived for the independents. By the early fifties Kaiser-Frazer was losing its fight to survive, and by 1955 its vehicle production consisted solely of the Jeep, which it had acquired when it bought out the Willys company of Toledo. In 1954 Hudson and Nash merged to form American Motors, and although the corporate headquarters remained in the Detroit area, production was concentrated at the Nash facilities in Wisconsin. After three years, the company dropped the Hudson and Nash names from its models. Packard, another of Detroit's famous cars, suffered the same fate when the company that had produced it for a half century merged with South Bend's Studebaker Corporation in 1954. Within four years the Indiana-based firm ceased making Packards, and with the demise of the Studebaker itself six years later, the last significant auto production by a non-Michigan company came to an end.

The independents could not stand up to Michigan's Big Three—General Motors, Ford, and Chrysler—whose vastly superior resources enabled them to regain and increase their dominance of the industry once they had made the transition from war work back to full-scale automobile production. Ford's recovery was also affected by a bitter fight for control of the company that followed Edsel Ford's death in 1943 and the obvious inability of Edsel's father, now in his eighties, to function effectively as head of the firm. By 1945 Ford's grandson, Henry Ford II, had

taken over the reins, and in the immediate postwar years he rejuvenated the company's management by recruiting experienced, able administrators. In 1950 Ford moved back into the number two spot, which it had relinquished to Chrysler during the Depression. Ford remained number two as Chrysler suffered recurring managerial problems that sometimes threatened the company's survival.

General Motors' plans to replenish its dealers' supplies of cars were delayed for some months at the end of 1945 and the beginning of 1946 when the industry giant was struck by the United Automobile Workers. Both sides looked upon this strike as a test of strength. A moratorium on strikes during the war had left labor and management about where they had been after the initial contracts were negotiated just prior to the war. As a result of this first postwar confrontation, the UAW held on to what it had gained earlier, killing industry leaders' hopes of regaining some of the control over their workers that they had held before the G.M. strike of 1936-1937. The union

In 1963 the Ford Motor Company observed the 100th anniversary of its founder's birth and the 60th anniversary of the company's founding. To cap it all off, the company, now headed by Henry Ford II (middle), produced its 60 millionth car. The fact that it was a Mercury, not a Ford, symbolized the company's later emphasis on providing a greater diversity of models. Courtesy, State Archives, Michigan Department of State

Nothing typified the automobile's overwhelming dominance in the postwar years than did the construction of expressways, such as Detroit's John C. Lodge Expressway, seen here in 1954. In rush hours it funneled thousands of commuters from their outlying residences and disgorged them at their place of employment in the city. (Rising on the left are units of the low-income Jeffries housing project, named, like the expressway, after a former Detroit mayor.) Courtesy, Library of Congress

further solidified its position in the latter part of the forties. In the years that followed, although the approaching expiration of a UAW contract inevitably led to the exchange of harsh-sounding words and threats of new strikes, the relationship between the companies and the union was actually much less hostile than it appeared on the surface. The companies increasingly viewed the union as a useful organization that was responsible for seeing that its members lived up to the terms of the labor contract, thereby relieving management of many administrative headaches.

Walter Reuther emerged in this period as the dominant figure in the UAW, a position he held until his death in an airplane crash in 1970. A native of West Virginia, Reuther had come to Detroit in 1927 to work in the auto plants. He was shortly joined by his brothers, Victor and Roy, and the

three became early members of the UAW and played major roles in the Depression-era strikes. At the time of the General Motors strike in 1945-1946 Walter Reuther headed the union's G.M. division. He charged that his failure to gain much of what he had been demanding at the start of that strike was mainly due to the union leadership's refusal to support his efforts. Labeling that leadership as pro-Communist, Reuther shrewdly played upon sentiments growing out of the Cold War to win the union's presidency in March 1946. He consolidated his control the following year when he succeeded in removing from the union's leadership the remaining members of the faction that had opposed his rise to power.

Reuther's anti-Communist beliefs, which led him not only to seek the ouster of Communists from the ranks of the

UAW but to become one of American labor's leading opponents of Communism wherever it was found, was not based on a conservative ideology. On the contrary, Reuther was a liberal, if not a radical, who had supported the Socialist party and had campaigned actively in 1932 for Norman Thomas, the party's presidential candidate. The fact that even in the depths of the Depression only 39,205 Michigan voters, slightly more than 2 percent of the total number of voters, cast their ballots for Thomas would eventually persuade Reuther that the two major parties offered the only hope of achieving the social and economic changes he favored. His postwar rise to power in the UAW offered him the opportunity to influence these parties through the votes of his union members.

Unlike older trade union leaders, whose interest in politics had been largely confined to efforts aimed at protecting their unions' interests, the leadership of the industrial unions that emerged in the thirties often looked at politics from a broader perspective. Few, however, rivaled Walter Reuther in the intensity with which he advocated humanitarian programs that were intended to benefit mankind and not simply UAW members. Because the Democratic party under Franklin Roosevelt and his successor Harry Truman supported many of the same liberal measures, Reuther and other labor leaders and unions that shared his interest in reform allied themselves with that party. They abandoned labor's earlier nonpartisan approach that had pledged support to any candidate, regardless of party, who promised to do nothing that would harm union interests.

In 1946 Democratic fortunes

The Lodge Expressway not only brought people into the city but also took them out to the suburbs that now mushroomed in size. Along with residential developments came huge shopping centers such as the giant Northland Center in Southfield, depicted in 1954. Malls continued to proliferate in outlying regions, leaving downtown Detroit without any large department stores by 1985. Courtesy, State Archives, Michigan Department of State

At Detroit's Eastern Market in
1966, G. Mennen Williams, running for the U.S. Senate, displays
the personal charm that made him
the envy of other politicians. He
lost this campaign, his only defeat
in a career that would be capped
in the 1970s and 1980s by his
election to two eight-year terms on
the state supreme court. Courtesy,
Michigan Historical Collections,
Bentley Historical Library, University of Michigan

across the country suffered a reverse as the party lost control of Congress for the first time since the early days of the Depression. In Michigan the situation was especially bleak for Democrats as a succession of Republican victories that had begun in 1942 culminated in 1946 with the GOP winning all of the state executive offices, 95 out of 100 seats in the state house, 28 of 32 seats in the state Senate, 14 of Michigan's 17 seats in the U.S. House of Represent-atives, and both of Michigan's U.S. Senate seats. The state Democratic party was in shambles, dominated by old-line political hacks who were unin-terested in expanding the ranks of ac-tive party workers for fear of losing their control of the organization and the occasional federal patronage plums that resulted from that control. These defeats on the national and state levels prompted efforts to revitalize the mori-bund state Democratic organization by labor leaders such as Walter Reuther and August "Gus" Scholle, head of the Michigan CIO Council, liberal Democrats such as Detroit attorneys G. Mennen Williams, Philip A. Hart, and Hicks Griffiths and his wife Martha, and Ann Arbor businessman Neil Staebler.

In 1948, with Hicks Griffiths and Neil Staebler supplying the organiza-

tional skills and Scholle and Reuther the resources of their unions, the nomi-nation of Williams for governor in that summer's primary election was se-cured, followed by his victory over the Republican incumbent, Kim Sigler, that fall. In the next several years this liberal-labor coalition consolidated its hold on the party: it unseated the old-guard leaders and their allies, the Teamsters union led by the contro-versial James Hoffa, while reelecting Williams to second and third terms in 1950 and 1952, in both cases by mar-gins so slim that the winner was not known until recounts had been held. In 1954, however, when Williams broke with tradition and ran for a fourth term, he was elected by a large margin. In addition, for the first time the entire slate of Democratic candidates for other executive offices was elected with him, indicating the Democrats' emer-gence as the state's predominant politi-cal party. Election returns through the remainder of the fifties simply served to confirm this impression.

The unquestioned standard bearer of a party enjoying its greatest success in over a century was G. (for Gerhard) Mennen Williams, perhaps the most effective political campaigner Michi-gan has ever known. The tall, powerfully built, handsome Williams possessed

The passenger pigeon became extinct at the start of this century, but in this fantastically detailed late nineteenth-century oil canvas, Lewis Luman Cross depicted a scene that had once been so familiar when immense flocks of the delicately colored birds darkened the sky, as here at Spring Lake in western Michigan. Little wonder that no one thought it necessary to protect them from the attacks of hunters. Photo by W.D. Pieri III. Courtesy, Grand Rapids Art Museum

*This circa 1910 impressionist
painting by Will Howe Foote depicts smoke belching forth from
factory chimneys next to Grand
Rapids' Bridge Street Bridge, tes-
tifying to the change that had
taken place since Sarah Nelson's
river scene painting of 1856 (see
page 75). Courtesy, Grand Rapids
Art Museum*

Ford's immense River Rouge plant, completed in the 1920s, attracted international attention and symbolized the Detroit area's dominance of the auto industry. In this 1932 painting and in numerous other studies of the Rouge complex, Charles Sheeler expressed his fascination with the physical characteristics of twentieth-century industrial operations. (*Charles Sheeler.* River Rouge Plant. *1932. Oil on canvas. 20 x 24 inches. Collection of Whitney Museum of American Art. Purchase. Acq.#32.43*)

Like the American, Charles Sheeler, the Mexican Diego Rivera was also fascinated by the vast Ford Rouge operations. But in contrast with Sheeler's almost totally dehumanized view of the subject, Rivera's famous murals on the walls of the Detroit Institute of Arts' Garden Court are teeming with people. The main panel on the court's north wall (right) deals with the production of the 1932 Ford V-8's motor at the Rouge, while on the south wall (below) the car itself is emerging from the assembly line. The murals were completed in 1932-1933 in the depths of a depression that had idled vast numbers of auto workers. The murals, possibly the Mexican master's greatest work, were commissioned by Edsel Ford. ©1987 The Detroit Institute of Arts, Founders Society Purchase, Edsel B. Ford Fund and Gift of Edsel B. Ford

188

A young Grand Rapids artist,
Armand Merizon, in the mid-
1940s captured this typical downtown scene in his hometown, featuring the Federal Building on the
left (now the Grand Rapids Art
Museum); St. Mark's Episcopal
Church, built a century earlier;
cars of the forties; and a recruiting poster. Photo by W.D. Pieri
III. Courtesy, Grand Rapids Art
Museum

Leland, which once prospered
through a combination of lumbering, fishing, and iron smelting activities, became a popular Lake
Michigan resort town in the twentieth century. Artists were attracted to Leland's waterfront and
the remnants of its commercial
fishing industry, making it a favorite subject of their work, as
with this 1962 watercolor by noted
Grand Rapids artist Reynold H.
Weidenaar. Photo by W.D. Pieri
III. Courtesy, Grand Rapids Art
Museum

In the 1960s, Michigan Bell commissioned Michigan artist Robert Thom to do a series of twenty-four paintings dealing with important developments in the state's history. In most cases, Thom relied upon meticulous research to re-create a scene as accurately as possible. For two scenes from the 1960s, however, Thom used live models. In this painting, an ore carrier of the Reiss Steamship Company of Sheboygan, Wisconsin, is loaded at the Soo Line dock in Marquette, reflecting the revival of iron mining in that area. Courtesy of Michigan Bell, An Ameritech Company

In his other scene from the 1960s,
Robert Thom went to the Detroit
Harbor Terminals on the Detroit
River, near the Ambassador
Bridge, which can be seen in the
distance. The Swedish ship Tris-
tan *is taking on a cargo of Chrysler automobiles, in knocked-down
form, to be assembled overseas.
Products of other companies that
also made great use of the Port
of Detroit are visible on the dock,
as a customs inspector in the
foreground checks a manifest.
Courtesy, Michigan Bell, An
Ameritech Company*

the physical attributes that had come to be of greater concern in judging a candidate than they had been in the days of Lewis Cass. With the increasing interest in candidates' wives, the presence of Williams's attractive wife Nancy on the campaign trail further strengthened his appeal to voters. An heir to the Mennen soap fortune who had had a distinctly upper class upbringing, Williams worked hard and successfully to develop among middle and lower income voters the feeling that he was one of them and that he had their interests at heart. With the green polka-dot bowtie that was his trademark, he encouraged people to call him by his boyhood nickname of Soapy (his brothers were apparently happy to be rid of their nicknames of Suds and Lather); he became adept at calling square dances; and he tossed in a phrase or two from the appropriate language when meeting with ethnic groups. His speeches and the manner in which he delivered them were rarely memorable, but what he lacked in oratorical abilities (something in short supply among Michigan politicians) was more than offset by the obvious sincerity and dedication with which he pressed for his programs.

A protege of Frank Murphy, the liberal governor of the 1930s, Williams resumed Murphy's fight for New Deal-type reforms, but unlike Murphy, he recognized the need for a strong party machinery if he was to succeed in obtaining those reforms in the face of Republican opposition. That machinery had begun to be organized in 1947 when Hicks Griffiths spearheaded the drive to bring many new, active workers into the party through the establishment of Democratic Clubs throughout the state. By the 1950s what was probably the most formidable political organization in Michigan history had been established first under state chairman Griffiths and then under his longtime successor Neil Staebler, ably

assisted by such astute and veteran political operatives as the governor's executive secretary, Larry Farrell, and his press secretary, Paul Weber. "Politics is a lot of people, good ideas, and coordination of the two," Staebler declared. "Participation, the widest possible participation, is the answer." Under the leadership of Vice Chairman Adelaide Hart, national committee-woman Margaret Price, and her alternate, Mildred Jeffrey, women particularly became active to a degree not previously seen in Michigan politics.

Yet no amount of organization and campaigning skills could smooth away some of the obstacles that would prevent the new Democratic leadership from achieving all of its goals in the 1950s. Nor could it help them achieve as impressive a record of election victories in the following decades. A major problem facing party leaders, Republican as well as Democratic, was the growing number of voters who no longer retained the kind of loyalty that would compel them to vote for a straight party ticket. Thus, during the years of victory for the Democrat Williams in 1948, 1952, and 1956, the Republican presidential candidates won in Michigan. In fact, Dwight Eisenhower's popularity enabled him to win in Michigan in 1952 and 1956 by majorities of more

A member of a prominent Ann Arbor family, Neil Staebler provided the organizational skills that combined with Mennen Williams' campaigning skills to make the Democratic party unbeatable in the state elections during much of the 1950s. Courtesy, State Archives, Michigan Department of State

In the mid-1980s, four decades after she came to Michigan to head the UAW's women's bureau, Mildred Jeffrey continued to be involved in a host of activities. Her position as an elected member of Wayne State University's board of governors reflected her longtime interest in education. But she remained best-known for her emergence as a leader of the Democratic party not only in the state but at the national level, where she played a major role in securing the nomination of Geraldine Ferraro for vice president in 1984. Courtesy, State Archives, Michigan Department of State

than 300,000 votes. This led Martha Griffiths, during her first, unsuccessful run for the Congressional seat which she would later hold for twenty years, to demonstrate in 1952 on Detroit television how voters could split their ticket. This action understandably disturbed many Democratic loyalists, especially because it came from the wife of a former state party chairman. Yet it illustrated a dilemma that would lead others to encourage the same kind of disregard for party labels by dropping references to their party affiliation from campaign billboards and bumper stickers.

Even before her celebrated 1952 television appearance, Martha Griffiths and her husband were under attack by the UAW and other labor leaders. They charged that Mrs. Griffiths as a state legislator had not been sufficiently pro-labor and that Hicks Griffiths, as state chairman, had failed to dispense enough jobs to union supporters. Although Mrs. Griffiths disputed the accuracy of these charges, she used labor's well-publicized coolness toward

her to win important support among the more conservative voters in her Detroit-area district, which had been Republican prior to her election in 1954. Her experience illustrated the dilemma many Democratic candidates faced in dealing with the popular belief that unions had too much influence over the party. Labor leaders denied that this was true, as Gus Scholle said with respect to Governor Williams, "The last thing Labor wants in public office is a man who is a stooge." Walter Reuther dismissed as "ludicrous" the idea that he controlled the governor. "I actually see him only three or four times a year, and then usually on a public platform. I have never sought to influence him and he has never sought my advice." Nevertheless, the belief in labor's control over the governor and his party was used to advantage by the party's opponents, who cited Reuther's Socialist past and the period in the 1930s when he and his brother Victor had worked in a factory in Russia as proof of the left wing nature of that control.

These claims added to Democratic difficulties in winning legislative seats in many traditionally conservative outstate districts, which continued to return Republicans to Lansing. Because the legislature had not been reapportioned to reflect the modern shift of population to the urban-industrial areas of southeastern Michigan, outstate representatives constituted the majority of the legislature. Thus, while virtually all statewide election contests were won by the Democrats by the end of the 1950s, the legislature was still controlled by Republicans. They consistently opposed Williams's proposals, especially those calling for a change in the state's tax structure, which for over twenty years had relied primarily on the sales tax. New revenues were needed to support escalating government expenditures that resulted from a population growth rate exceeded in the fifties only by that of Florida and

Richard Nixon (just call him Dick in this period when he had not yet assumed the role of a statesman) appeared with his wife, Pat, at the Ann Arbor train station in October 1952 on a whistle-stop swing through the state. Voters throughout Michigan supported the Republican ticket of Eisenhower and Nixon that year. Courtesy, Ann Arbor News

California. Then in the latter part of the decade a recession led to a sharp decline in auto sales, drastically cutting sales tax revenues while high unemployment resulting from auto industry layoffs forced greatly increased outlays for unemployment compensation and social welfare programs.

In the spring of 1959, with the state deficit exceeding $100 million and the state's available cash drying up, an impasse was reached. Diehard Republicans, particularly in the senate, saw an opportunity to torpedo the presidential ambitions harbored by Williams and his backers. They refused to budge on their opposition to Democratic proposals for corporate and personal income taxes, arguing instead for a sales tax increase. The continuing cash shortage caused the state treasurer to withhold the payments due state employees on May 5, and news flashed across the country that Michigan was broke. Soapy Williams's White House hopes, slim as they undoubtedly were, were dealt a knockout blow, but so were the reputations of many of his Republican opponents. The Detroit *News,* normally staunchly Republican, declared that although both parties had been guilty of stalling on the need to come to grips with the tax problem, "on the cash crisis issue the senate Republicans have made the Democrats look like paragons of political courage and virtue."

Before long, state workers received the checks they had not gotten on that infamous "Payless Payday," and following a series of stopgap measures and the return of a healthier economy the state made its way through the financial crisis. However, there remained those who felt drastic action was needed in order to strike at the underlying causes of that crisis. One such individual was labor leader Gus Scholle, a resident of Oakland County, which had a population of some 600,000 and one senator representing it in the upper

house of the state legislature. An area in the Copper Country with only a tenth of Oakland's population was also represented by one senator. This was the most extreme example of a situation that had left the senate and, to a lesser degree, the house of representatives with proportionately far more members from essentially rural districts than the population of those districts warranted. In 1959, therefore, Scholle asked the courts to declare Michigan's method of apportionment unconstitutional because it violated the Fourteenth Amendment rights of the state's urban residents to the equal protection of the laws.

Scholle's suit, designed to bring about a legislature whose membership conformed more strictly to existing population distribution, was supported by most Democrats because it would increase representation from areas where Democratic strength was the greatest. Rural areas, generally Republican strongholds, would lose representation, and thus Republicans were most often heard opposing changes in the existing apportionment. Moderate Republicans, however, wished to increase the party's support in urban areas and to lessen the influence of the conservative element so often found in the rural outstate party ranks. They agreed that the legislative inequities needed to be corrected but declared that this was only one of numerous defects in the state constitution, which, because it still reflected the conditions of a hundred years earlier, was totally unsuited to Michigan's needs in the middle of the twentieth century.

Seizing the leadership in the drive for a new constitution was George W. Romney, who had been born in 1907 in Mexico of American Mormon parents. Five years later they moved back to the United States, where Romney grew up in Idaho and Utah. He came to Michigan in the 1940s, heading up the Automobile Manufacturers Asso-

As head of the Michigan CIO Council, August "Gus" Scholle was one of Michigan's most powerful labor leaders, but he will no doubt be remembered primarily for his successful fight in the state and federal courts to overturn the state's system of legislative apportionment. Courtesy, State Archives, Michigan Department of State

Sitting behind his desk in the governor's office, Republican George Romney exuded a sense of dedication and self-confidence that had served him well as a business executive and which would enable him to score big in a state where the Democrats had seemingly become the majority party. Courtesy, State Archives, Michigan Department of State

ciation in Detroit. Later, as an executive with Nash, he helped bring about the merger in 1954 of that company and Hudson. In the late fifties, as president of the resulting American Motors, Romney became a national celebrity when he attacked the gas-guzzling monstrosities that other car companies were producing in order to promote, with great success, the merits of American's small, more efficient Ramblers. Then, in a move more typical of such nineteenth-century businessmen as Zachariah Chandler, Henry Crapo, James McMillan, and Hazen Pingree, Romney turned from the business world to a new career in politics.

In the spring of 1961, a tiny majority of the voters approved the calling of a constitutional convention. The four large urban counties in southeastern Michigan were the only ones voting in favor, but that was enough to offset the opposing votes of the seventy-nine outstate counties. Outstate Republicans,

who had opposed a convention, quickly regrouped and worked with those Republicans, like Romney, who had campaigned for a new constitution; together they won two-thirds of the convention seats. The delegates were elected from the existing house and senate legislative districts, and the results of the election reflected the split in the ranks of Democrats. Many Democrats, especially the union element, had opposed calling a convention until the reapportionment fight had been won and the legislative districts more closely mirrored Democratic strength. Other Democrats, however, felt the need for constitutional reform was too great to be delayed any longer.

During the convention's early weeks in the fall of 1961 it appeared that Democratic and moderate Republican delegates might work together to secure the adoption of the constitutional changes both favored. But in March 1962, Romney, leader of the moderate Republicans, and D. Hale Brake, the conservative Republicans' leader, agreed upon a compromise of the two factions' positions. Brake, a political veteran representing the outstate areas that wanted as little change as possible, got the best of the negotiations. Provisions that streamlined the state government and strengthened the governor's powers were in keeping with reforms advocated since the days of Chase Osborn and Alex Groesbeck, but conservative ideas prevailed with regard to state fiscal policies and an apportionment plan that continued to include factors other than population in determining legislative districts. Hopes of bipartisan cooperation were ended, as the final vote on the proposed new constitution, which followed the Romney-Brake guidelines, reflected almost without exception the partisan alignments of the delegates.

The convention propelled George Romney into the front ranks of Michigan political figures and gained him the

Republican gubernatorial nomination in 1962. A rugged, vigorous individual who possessed many of the same qualities that had made Soapy Williams such an effective vote-getter, Romney defeated Williams's successor, John B. Swainson, in a fairly close race. He then came back to swamp his Democratic opposition in 1964 and in 1966, when the new constitution's provision for a four-year term for the governor and the members of the state senate took effect. By emphasizing the provisions of the new constitution that were designed to provide more efficient governmental operations, Romney was able to place himself and the Republican party in the role of innovators seeking needed improvements while Democratic opponents of the constitution were pictured as selfish nay-sayers. It was, however, the support of some Democratic liberals who bucked labor's opposition to the new constitution that helped win voter approval of the document by a very small margin in April 1963.

Although a political neophyte when he took office, Romney was soon acting like a seasoned professional. In 1964, when United States Supreme Court rulings enabled Gus Scholle to win his five-year battle for reapportionment based solely on population, Michigan Democrats for the first time in over thirty years gained control of both houses, a majority of whose members now came from the heavily populated urban areas. The 1964 election saw Lyndon Johnson outpolling the Republican presidential candidate Barry Goldwater in Michigan by over a million votes, but Romney successfully bucked this Democratic tide by keeping his distance from the conservative Goldwater. Instead, he appealed to the ticket-splitting tendencies of many voters to defeat his Democratic opponent, Neil Staebler, by nearly 400,000 votes. Romney then demonstrated an ability to work with Democrats in the legislature to secure passage of programs not

unlike some that Williams earlier had vainly sought to persuade Republican legislators to approve. To finance the high cost of these programs he got the state's first income tax approved in 1967. It was not the graduated tax that Williams and the Democrats and liberals as far back as Hazen Pingree had favored, but a flat rate tax that conservatives had made sure was the only kind the new constitution would permit.

Romney's popularity only partially explained his reelection in 1966 by more than a half million votes, the return of a Republican majority in the legislature, and Robert Griffin's victory over former Governor Williams in the race for the United States Senate. Griffin was strongly opposed by labor leaders because of anti-labor legislation he had earlier sponsored in Congress; his victory indicated the declining ability of these leaders to control the votes of their members, many of whom were now enjoying life in the suburbs and were adopting middle class, conservative attitudes.

A good many younger people who earlier would have been attracted to the Williams-Reuther coalition were now impatient with its objectives. At the University of Michigan in the early sixties a student from Royal Oak, Tom Hayden, promoted a new radicalism through Students for a Democratic Society. The organization denounced the "old slogans" of liberals as well as conservatives, claiming that they were based on "conventional moral terms" which had little or no relation to reality.

The New Left's interests, as well as their ideas regarding morality, were often unrelated to those of the older liberals. Shortly before his death in 1970, Walter Reuther participated in an "Environmental Teach-in" at the University of Michigan, a format invented by the New Left to discuss a topic that essentially only surfaced in the sixties. With his customary intensity, Reuther delivered his typical speech which, it

One of the most visible and vocal leaders of the New Left in the turbulent sixties and early seventies, Michigan's Tom Hayden later settled in California, where he became active in the Democratic party but was best known as the husband of actress Jane Fonda. Courtesy, Michigan Historical Collections, Bentley Historical Library, University of Michigan

In the late 1960s and early 1970s the White Panthers were the best known element in Ann Arbor's rather extensive radical community. Here members of that group, obviously enjoying themselves, are engaged in 1970 in one of their numerous demonstrations to get their leader, John Sinclair, out of prison, where he was serving a nine-and-a-half-year term on a marijuana conviction. Sinclair was released in 1971 when the state supreme court reversed the lower court's action. The White Panthers soon disappeared and Sinclair became a successful manager of musical groups and night clubs. Courtesy, Michigan Historical Collections, Bentley Historical Library, University of Michigan

was said, always came around to the same exhortations to fight the good fight for progress and human freedom. The students, amused by this classic recital of what Hayden had called the old slogans and the tired morality, began shouting, "Right on, Walter!" The UAW president went on with his remarks, apparently unaware that his young audience was laughing at him. "It was sad as hell to watch," a Detroit reporter recalled.

Reuther, Williams, and other leaders of the liberal-labor coalition must have been puzzled by the new generation's reaction to the policies which they had so long fought to implement. These radicals, many from affluent families, realized that poverty still existed in spite of the Great Society reforms pushed through Congress in the mid-sixties by Democratic President Lyndon Johnson. Those reforms, they felt, were no more likely to end poverty than the earlier New Deal welfare programs. The civil rights gains that the liberal-labor forces had made at the state and national levels were rejected as far too inadequate not only by such impatient white activists as Tom Hayden but by blacks such as Malcolm X. The latter spent his boyhood in the Lansing area, where whites burned his

family's home and his father died as a result, many believed, of a white attack. Those experiences influenced his conversion to a militant philosophy that would no longer accept the integrationist stance of the NAACP, the accomodationist policies of John Dancy, or the nonviolent approach of Martin Luther King, Jr.

But it was the liberal-labor coalition's continued support of the bipartisan, anti-Communist foreign policy forged in the late 1940s by Arthur Vandenberg and Harry Truman that alienated the younger generation from the supporters of the Vietnam War in the 1960s. Opposition to American participation in that war by 1966 was responsible for a divisive primary fight for Michigan's Democratic senatorial nomination. Detroit Mayor Jerome P. Cavanagh was supported by New Left Democrats because his opponent, G. Mennen Williams, had been a member of the Democratic administration that got the country into the war. Williams's loyal union supporters enabled him to withstand Cavanagh's challenge, but the defection of antiwar Democrats in the fall assured his defeat at the hands of the Republican, Robert Griffin.

To a lesser extent, Vietnam also

divided the Republicans. George Romney, for example, probably forfeited whatever chances he may have had of gaining the Republican presidential nomination in 1968 when he alienated many in his party by coming out against the war. Earlier, in the summer of 1967, Romney's political hopes had been damaged by riots in Detroit. The racial violence that had erupted in 1943 during an earlier war broke out again in an equally violent fashion, as frustrations and hostilities growing out of economic and racial problems came to a head on the morning of Sunday, July 24, 1967. Rioting continued through much of the week, leaving 43 people dead, 1,700 stores looted, 1,383 buildings burned, and property damages of at least $50 million. Criticism of the manner in which Romney, Mayor Cavanagh, and President Johnson reacted to this tragedy had an adverse effect on their careers and forced Detroit's leaders, who had

prided themselves on their positive handling of racial issues, to recognize that new approaches were needed.

The Detroit riot, which was duplicated that summer on a smaller scale in several other Michigan communities, became a symbol of a violent era which also saw the assassination of John F. Kennedy, his brother Robert, Malcolm X, and Martin Luther King, Jr. A growing number of anti-war protests culminated in Chicago during the 1968 Democratic National Convention with riots, orchestrated in part by Tom Hayden, who had by this time left Michigan. The liberal-labor party establishment was able to secure the nomination of the old New Dealer Hubert Humphrey, and although he lost the election to Richard Nixon, the forces that had dominated Michigan's Democratic party for two decades mustered enough strength to bring Humphrey the state's electoral votes. The election, however, marked

With the kind of total devastation revealed in this aerial shot of one of Detroit's riot-torn districts in 1967, it is easy to see why early estimates placed the property losses at more than $100 million, not the more conservative figure of about $50 million arrived at by later appraisals. Courtesy, State Archives, Michigan Department of State

Throughout a political career that began in 1948 with his election to Congress, much of Gerald Ford's success can be attributed to an image of a clean-cut, all-American boy that befitted one who had starred in football at the University of Michigan in the mid-1930s. Courtesy, State Archives, Michigan Department of State

something of an end of an era in state politics. Democratic candidates for president would be defeated in Michigan in each subsequent election through 1984.

The race issue's impact on many blue collar whites who had long voted Democratic was immediately evident in 1968, as 10 percent of Michigan voters supported the third-party candidacy of Alabama's George Wallace. Nixon's half-million-vote margin over Democrat George McGovern in 1972 indicated Michigan Democrats' opposition to McGovern's anti-war stance and his ideas on domestic policy, considered by some to be too liberal. Gerald Ford's status as a long-time Grand Rapids political leader helped him win Michigan in his losing fight to defeat Democrat Jimmy Carter in 1976, but the 250,000 and nearly 700,000 margins by which Ronald Reagan swept Michigan in 1980 and

1984 again revealed the growing conservatism of much of the urban voting population, which no longer was inclined to go down the line for the Democratic ticket. This trend certainly benefited William Milliken, a moderate Republican who was reelected governor three times after succeeding to that office in 1969 when Romney took a job in Nixon's cabinet. Milliken's victories indicated the ticket-splitting actions of Michigan voters, who voted for a Democratic majority in the legislature during most of his tenure.

In 1982 James Blanchard became the first Democrat in twenty years to be elected governor. His victory was in part due to the Republicans' miscalculation in nominating conservative Richard Headlee as their candidate. Although Headlee was backed by George Romney, he lacked Romney's skill as a campaigner and the ability Milliken had had to attract the independents and ticket-splitters. Blanchard had also benefited, however, from the fact that the country under a Republican administration was suffering its most severe economic problems in a half century, which helped revive working-class ties to the Democratic party.

When he took office on January 1, 1983, Blanchard inherited a state government whose finances were in shambles, resulting in a plummeting credit rating that made it difficult to borrow the money needed to maintain basic services. Blanchard, who as a Detroit-area Congressman had vigorously supported a controversial federal program to help save the Chrysler corporation from bankruptcy, now pushed for and got an equally controversial temporary 39 percent increase in the state income tax rates. When combined with the return of a healthier economy and measures designed to cut the size of governmental operations and to hold the line on appropriations, the state's finances were in much better shape by 1984. But

William Milliken, behind the speaker's stand at his inauguration in 1970, was one of the state's most astute politicians who held office for fourteen years, longer than any other elected Michigan governor. Courtesy, State Archives, Michigan Department of State

the immediate reaction to Blanchard's tax increase was a revolt that led to an unprecedented recall of two Democratic state senators from Metropolitan Detroit districts who had voted for the new tax. Republicans were elected to replace them, giving that party control of the state's upper house.

By 1986 Blanchard's popularity had rebounded to new heights as national publicity referring to Michigan as the "comeback state" credited him with being the architect of that reversal. The Republican leadership's hopes of unseating Blanchard came to be centered on a Detroit black, William Lucas, who as sheriff of Wayne County and then as the county's first elected chief executive had won widespread recognition as an able administrator. With much fanfare, Lucas announced in early 1986 that he was switching his party affiliation from the Democratic to the Republican party, and that he would seek to become the first black governor of Michigan. Coleman Young and other black Democratic leaders denounced Lucas for his move, and hopes that Lucas's action would result in a sizable defection among black voters from the party they had supported in overwhelming numbers since the thir-

ties were not fulfilled.

Lucas's chances were further diminished when opposition to his nomination led to a bitterly fought four-way primary battle. Although he emerged the winner, it was more the result of his opponents' mistakes than of his surprisingly lackluster campaign. In the general election a combination of Blanchard's popularity, the inability of Lucas and his campaign managers to inspire much voter enthusiasm, and some lingering outstate hostilities toward Detroit and blacks resulted in Lucas going down to the worst defeat any Republican gubernatorial candidate had ever suffered. Blanchard picked up nearly 70 percent of the votes and won in eighty-two of the eighty-three counties. But Blanchard's victory did not signal a Democratic landslide. Confirming the now well-established ticket-splitting tendencies of so many voters, the legislature remained divided as Republicans held on to their control of the state Senate while Democrats remained in control of the lower house, but by a margin only slightly greater than they had held prior to the election. Clearly, party loyalty ceased to be the dominant influence over voters' choices.

CHAPTER XII

MICHIGAN AT AGE 150

A logger, gripping his chain saw, hurries away as the tree he has cut starts to go down in one of the stands of young timber that continue to support northern Michigan's limited lumber industry. Courtesy, State Archives, Michigan Department of State

The 150th anniversary of an event is not likely to be more noteworthy than the 149th, but it seems to be endowed with greater importance, especially when coupled with a term such as sesquicentennial. Thus in the mid-1980s the sesquicentennial of the actions that culminated in Michigan's admission to the Union aroused more than normal interest in the state's history, as Michiganians were encouraged to reflect on what had happened since 1837 to see what light such reflections might shed on the future.

This was the third time the state had ceremoniously marked the completion of a fifty-year chapter in its history. Michigan rather surprisingly chose to observe its semicentennial in 1886, on June 15, the date on which the federal government in 1836 proposed the compromise that Michigan had to accept before it was recognized as a state seven months later. Optimism pervaded the patriotic music and the speeches that made up the day-long festivities in Lansing. Michigan's abundant natural resources, the focus of the attention that had sparked a tenfold population increase during the

state's first five decades, were widely believed to assure continued growth for many years to come.

The state's centennial observances in the 1930s began on November 1, 1935, with the issuance of a three-cent commemorative stamp that signaled the federal government's belated recognition of the state government that had assumed office a hundred years earlier. The stamp's first-day sales at the Lansing post office broke all records for commemorative issues, but the remaining centennial celebrations were of a considerably more modest character as Michigan struggled to recover from the devastating effects of the Great Depression. Manufacturing, not farming, mining, or lumbering, had accounted for most of the growth that had expanded the state's population from less than two million to around five million in the fifty years since the semicentennial. But the thirties provided sobering evidence of the problems this new economic emphasis could present for the state. Symbolic of these problems was the fact that Governor Frank Murphy was unable to preside at the official windup of the centennial

The 1935 stamp commemorating Michigan statehood featured still another example of the complete absence of any firm guidelines governing the manner in which the state seal is to be depicted. Courtesy, Ned Brockington

on January 26, 1937, because negotiations regarding the Flint Sit-down Strike prevented him from being in the capital that day.

The World War II boom and the immediate postwar developments brought a quick resumption of rapid growth during the early stages of the third fifty-year phase in the state's history. By the end of that phase, however, Michigan had again gone through a period of economic difficulties that was the most severe and prolonged since the Depression, causing many to be pessimistic about the state's future prospects.

Any attempt to assess where Michigan stands must always begin with the recognition that it does not exist in a vacuum. A relatively small political unit within the United States and a much smaller part of the world as a whole, Michigan's development can not be separated from national and world influences which severely limit the efforts of its residents to control or change its course. At the same time, although Michigan may be small from a global perspective, it is made up of several regions, each distinctively different from the others, thereby increasing the difficulty of finding an approach that can satisfy all of the state's needs.

Michigan's regional differences were apparent as one examined the effect of the recession of the mid-1970s and the more severe recession of the early 1980s. These recent economic hard times had less of an impact in much of northern Michigan simply be-

In the 1960s a man fits comfortably in the rotted interior of this stump in the Upper Peninsula's Alger County, a testimonial to the enormous size of the trees that had once been found throughout northern Michigan. Without them, Michigan's twentieth-century lumber industry was a mere shadow of what it had once been. Courtesy, State Archives, Michigan Department of State

cause these areas, perennially hard up since the decline of the lumber and mining industries, had long since lived with unemployment as high or higher than the 17 percent figure that put Michigan ahead of all other states in the early 1980s. Lumber production in this century has never come close to the record years of the 1800s, but Michigan remained an important mining state, ranking sixth in the 1980s in production of non-fuel minerals. Mechanization, however, cut deeply into the number of workers employed in these billion-dollar activities. Iron ore remained the volume leader, as the giant Cleveland-Cliffs Iron Company achieved record production on the Marquette Iron Range with the processes it had developed to mine the ar-

ea's vast low-grade ore reserves. But the mining was now almost entirely of the strip mining variety, requiring only a fraction of the workers that earlier had been needed in the underground mines. On a smaller scale, similar low-grade ore processing kept iron mining alive on the Menominee Iron Range, but mining on the once fabulously rich Gogebic Iron Range ended in 1966. In the Copper Country, prospects for a return to prosperity seemed promising in the 1950s when the White Pine Mine employed new methods that increased the state's copper output to more respectable levels. But declining market prices for copper and bitter labor-management disputes ended the legendary Calumet and Hecla mining operations in the late 1960s. In the mid-

The Quincy Mine in Hancock, once famous as the "Old Reliable" among Michigan's copper mines, had ceased production years before this photograph of the mine's picturesque and weatherbeaten shaft house was taken circa 1950. This monument to the great days of Copper Country mining was destroyed by fire in 1956. Courtesy, State Archives, Michigan Department of State

Mrs. Potter Palmer, shown here with her entourage in the 1890s, was not the first Chicagoan to visit Mackinac Island. However, the appearance of the unchallenged queen of that city's society removed any doubt that the island and resorts farther south along the lower peninsula's western shore would be the favorite vacation spots of Chicago's in crowd. Courtesy, State Archives, Michigan Department of State

1980s hopes of saving the White Pine, the state's last significant copper producer, rested on a buyout of the mine by its workers, which would supply jobs to only half of those employed in the company's healthier days.

For many decades the tourist and resort industry had been looked upon as the savior of northern Michigan's economy. In the late nineteenth century Mackinac Island had already been spectacularly successful in making the transition from a fur trading economy to one that has prospered ever since on the trade of summer vacationers. In addition, the popularity of Great Lakes cruises in the same era helped the economy of such lake ports as Sault Ste. Marie and Marquette. In 1957 the opening of the Mackinac Bridge between Michigan's two peninsulas provided a solid link that was considered essential to the growth of northern Michigan tourism in the age of the automobile.

Tourism did indeed become big business in Michigan, although estimates of its size have varied greatly. This variance probably occurs because it is harder to calculate the income generated by tourists than from activities involved with more tangible products, as is the case with manufacturing and farming, which remain the two leading elements in the state's economy. By the 1980s, however, the estimated annual value of tourism to Michigan's economy was eleven billion dollars or more. Yet although tourism had become the mainstay of the economy in many northern Michigan communities, where as much as three-fourths of the work force were employed in tourist-related jobs, it did not prove to be an adequate substitute for mining and lumbering in the Upper Peninsula. The increasing popularity outside that area of Finnish saunas and Cornish pasties testified to the number of visitors who had become acquainted with those staples in that far northern culture, and the booming popularity of skiing helped reduce the seasonal character of the tourist trade, which earlier had been largely confined to the summer months. But none of this was enough to reverse the decades-old downward slide of population in much of the Upper Peninsula. Those who remained tended to be hardy souls, ever optimistic and sometimes viewing their lot with a sense of humor. "The economic situation has not shown much improvement, but we are still hopeful," commented a resident of Ironwood who was involved with the city's 1985 centennial observances. "Some folks around here complain because there is nothing to do. From where this writer is, that just is not so . . . The Milwaukee Symphony visited us in February. We were supposed to have a greased pig chase for the kids, but some folks felt it was cruelty to animals and stopped it. Apparently they have never seen such an event, or the animals they were thinking about were the kids . . . In balance, we think we are a pretty good place to live."

The tourist and resort business had a greater impact on the economy of the northern part of the lower peninsula, once the center of the great nineteenth-century lumber industry. In the latter part of that century railroads allied with Great Lakes shipping lines to promote this area as a vacationer's paradise. Fishing and hunting excursions lured sportsmen from around the Middle West, while others were attracted by resort hotels that the railroads built in such places as Charlevoix, Petoskey, and Harbor Springs. Those towns became rivals for the summer trade with Mackinac Island, where the largest of the resort hotels, appropriately named

Two thousand or more vacationers crowd the decks of the City of South Haven *as it completes the voyage that carried them from Chicago across Lake Michigan to that Michigan lake port circa 1906. New forms of transportation and more stringent safety requirements virtually eliminated such cruise ships from the lakes after the 1960s. Courtesy, Appleyards Studio, South Haven*

the Grand Hotel, was opened in 1887 and continues to operate according to the luxurious standards of that bygone Victorian era.

The railroads laid the groundwork for an explosion of development in the twentieth century when automobiles and improved roads opened the entire area to everyone. Michigan became the mecca for ski enthusiasts from around the Midwest, and since the 1930s ski resorts at Cadillac, Boyne Mountain, and elsewhere have grown into year-round operations, offering golf and other warm weather diversions during the summer. Also from the Midwest, which has always been the largest out-of-state contributor of tourist dollars, came those who wanted a second home where they might spend the summer or, when travel conditions permitted, simply the weekends. In the late nineteenth century, colonies of summer residences were built by people from St. Louis at Pointe Aux Barques on the eastern side of the lower peninsula and at Douglas and Saugatuck on the western shoreline. Chicagoans lived much closer to their summer homes, which stretched from Mackinac Island all the way down the Lake Michigan shore. These cottages proliferated in the twentieth century as the greater accessibility of these areas and a substantial increase in many families' disposable income led to residences of all types sprouting

on or near virtually any body of water in Michigan.

By the 1980s the new rage was condominiums, whose development was an especially notable feature of the Lake Michigan shore of the lower peninsula. They added further luster to an area which, because of its superb beaches and natural harbors, had come to be referred to as the "Riviera of the Middle West." Ironically, in much of this area tourism was not as vital to its well-being as it was in many other sections of the state. Fruit growing thrived from Berrien County in the south to Traverse City in the north, and agricultural production of all types remained the major component of the economy of much of west Michigan. There, visitors seeking relief from the heat of urban metropolitan communities were sometimes surprised to find local television and radio stations employing farm editors who aired daily reports on matters of concern to farmers. In addition, such west Michigan cities as Holland, Grand Rapids, Zeeland, Kalamazoo, Sturgis, Rockford, Greenville, and Traverse City were sites of well-established, diversified manufacturing activity largely unrelated to the auto industry. This combination of tourism, farming, and non-automotive manufacturing enabled west Michigan to be far less affected by the recessions of the seventies and the eighties than were other parts of the state.

In terms of people, however, difficulties in northern Michigan or even in the more heavily populated west Michigan are small in comparison to the numbers affected by the problems of southeastern Michigan and the extent to which these problems affect the state as a whole. This population disparity has long contributed to the sense of alienation felt by many northern residents, who find the state government to be far more concerned with the interests of the southeastern area. However, Michigan's recent economic problems

Already by 1900 these women had discovered some of the pleasures that South Haven's white, sandy Lake Michigan shore provided for nature lovers. Courtesy, State Archives, Michigan Department of State

have highlighted hostilities and jealousies among residents of the western part of the lower peninsula, also resulting from what they believe to be an excessive concern for Detroit's problems. These feelings go back to the state's beginnings, but in recent years one senses that the anti-Detroit rhetoric is rooted not only in the economic and political differences that have separated Michigan's two most populous areas in the past, but also in racial antagonisms. Detroit has become predominantly black, a race that, with notable exceptions, remains a small element, even a rarity, in large areas of outstate Michigan.

For a high proportion of southeastern Michigan's blacks, the recessions of the 1970s and 1980s could have been more accurately called depressions, since black unemployment rates were much higher than those for the state's population as a whole. Coleman Young, Detroit's first black mayor and one of the shrewdest and most capable politicians of recent times, teamed with other black leaders to fight for increased federal and state aid for victims of these bad times. The origins of the bad times themselves were to be found in southeastern Michigan's eighty-year economic dependence on the automobile industry. A sudden and unexpected rise in gas prices in the mid-1970s caught Detroit's automakers unprepared to meet demands by the public and the federal government for smaller, more fuel-efficient cars. Sales slumped sharply as more and more buyers turned to imports, particularly from Japan, where an emphasis on small and less expensive cars was already well-established. Michigan again had a painful reminder of the ripple effect on the state's economy created by declining auto sales.

Sales rebounded in 1977 and 1978 before the continuing rise in gas prices, growing consumer dissatisfaction with the quality of the Detroit-made cars when compared with that of the imports, and record high inflation and interest rates drove the Michigan Big Four companies' sales down to their lowest levels in many years. General Motors and Ford suffered staggering multi-billion-dollar annual losses while the red ink on the ledgers of the smallest company, American Motors, was proportionately as great or greater than that of the top two firms. Most attention was centered on Chrysler, which was rescued from complete collapse only by unprecedented $1.5-billion federal loan guarantees and additional financial aid from several states in which Chrysler operated. Of course, one of those states was Michigan, where the consequences of the corporation's bankruptcy were frightening to contemplate. Leading the fight to save Chrysler was its newly hired head, Lee Iacocca. Iacocca had earlier made his mark as a dynamic, innovative executive with the Ford Motor Company before being fired by Henry Ford II, who as he got older became almost as unpredictable as his grandfather had been. At Chrysler, Iacocca was a rare throwback to earlier days when colorful individuals, not faceless corporate executives, had been readily identified as leaders of the auto companies.

As the nation's economy improved, auto sales began to rise in 1983, and General Motors, Ford, and even Chrysler, all leaner and more efficient after employing various cost-cutting measures, were soon racking up record profits. But this time fewer people were lulled into believing their troubles were behind them. As University of Michigan business historian David L. Lewis noted, this latest recession had been longer and more severe than any since the thirties. During earlier recessions there had been talk of the need to diversify the state's economy but, he said, "by the time the study commission made its report, everything would be OK again. Before, everyone thought

For Coleman Young, shown here in the 1960s, election to the Constitutional Convention was the beginning of a career that would make him the most powerful politician in the state well before he began an unprecedented fourth four-year term as Detroit mayor in 1986. Courtesy, State Archives, Michigan Department of State

that the automobile industry would come back bigger than ever, and it did. No one believes that any more. That may be the biggest difference of all."

The search for ways of strengthening the state's economy was stepped up by state, county, and local governments and by private individuals and organizations. An effort was made to increase Michigan's attractiveness to outside investors and companies through a variety of tax breaks to new business developments, and through changes in such things as the workers' compensation system to reduce what had come to be viewed as unacceptably high costs to employers. Financial institutions sought to increase the amount of venture capital available to help new businesses get a start. Some labor unions showed a greater willingness to agree to concessions if they were needed, as they had been in Chrysler's case, to help a company stay afloat or to help persuade a new company to locate in this state.

Of course, the auto industry was not about to be replaced overnight as the number one factor in the state's economy. In fact, the most publicized business promotion efforts of Governor James Blanchard's administration were those aimed at keeping the auto industry as strong as it had been in the past. Late in 1984 the Japanese automaker Mazda agreed to locate its new American operations at a vacant Ford plant in Flat Rock, and in the same period Blanchard and his staff made a determined bid to persuade General Motors to use a Michigan site for its new Saturn small-car assembly plant. Plans by the auto companies and their suppliers to spend $2.8 billion on expansion projects in the state dwarfed other such investments cited by Blanchard in his 1985 State of the State address as evidence of Michigan's healthier economic condition. Blanchard also gave attention to other traditional Michigan manufacturing activities, noting developments tied in with the woodworking, paper, and food processing industries. But most promising for future growth was the governor's report that one-third of the country's robotics companies were located in Michigan and that over 500 "advanced technology firms have made their home in the research triangle formed by Ann Arbor, Detroit, and East Lansing."

Advanced technology was more popularly known as "high-tech," the "in" term of the eighties, and many felt that it was an industry Michigan should court in the years ahead. Although computer-age companies ap-

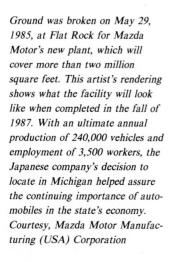

Ground was broken on May 29, 1985, at Flat Rock for Mazda Motor's new plant, which will cover more than two million square feet. This artist's rendering shows what the facility will look like when completed in the fall of 1987. With an ultimate annual production of 240,000 vehicles and employment of 3,500 workers, the Japanese company's decision to locate in Michigan helped assure the continuing importance of automobiles in the state's economy. Courtesy, Mazda Motor Manufacturing (USA) Corporation

peared throughout large sections of southern Michigan, they centered in Ann Arbor, boosting its population growth in a period when most Michigan cities' populations were declining. By 1985 over 200 high-tech companies had located in the eighteen technology parks in the city and at nearby sites in Washtenaw County. Ann Arbor's development was being compared with California's famed Silicon Valley and Boston's Route 128 corridor, as the University of Michigan provided the stimulus that Stanford and M.I.T. had given to those earlier advanced technology centers.

Perhaps the biggest boost to the new direction Michigan's economy was taking in 1984 and 1985 came when the patriarch of the state's business world, General Motors, dipped into its enormous cash reserves and came up with $7.5 billion to acquire the California-based Hughes Aircraft and the Dallas-based Electronic Data Systems. With Hughes, G.M. instantly became a major factor in the production of advanced weaponry and equipment for the armed forces, something in which Hughes specialized but which Michigan's auto industry had been largely unprepared to handle. At the 12,000-employee branch operations of E.D.S. that G.M. established in the Detroit metropolitan area, work began on the computerized car of the future. Meanwhile, at Ann Arbor, G.M.'s new high-tech division joined with the University of Michigan to establish a Center for Machine Intelligence, whose goal, straight out of the science fiction realm, was the creation of "thinking robots."

Although the University of Michigan's role was the most publicized, most of the state's colleges and universities were seeking to advance the high-tech cause. By so doing they were helping to keep in the state more of their science and technology graduates who had earlier gone elsewhere to find jobs. But in this new era there were hundreds

of thousands of older workers who did not have the skills or background required for the new approaches that were replacing the mass-production operations for which these workers had been hired. The familiar old factories of southeastern Michigan, like the underground mines of an earlier period in the Upper Peninsula, were on their way out, and the assembly-line workers, like the miners, had to try to adjust.

Management, too, was faced with the need to adjust, not only to deal with the need to modernize manufacturing facilities but also to meet the challenge of new managerial approaches practiced by the Japanese and by the new high-tech companies. In 1986 the public was treated to an extraordinary glimpse of corporate in-fighting as H. Ross Perot, founder of E.D.S. and still its head, now that it was a division of G.M., as well as a member of the corporation's board, openly criticized the huge automaker's policies. At the end of the year G.M.'s board of directors voted to pay Perot some $700 million for his stock in order to get him out of the company, an expenditure that raised some eyebrows since it came at a time when G.M.'s profits had dropped sharply because of lagging interest in many of its models.

In the same period G.M. announced the forthcoming closing of a number of its old plants, including several in Michigan. The thousands of workers who would be affected by these closings and the likelihood of similar announcements in the future from the other auto companies underlined the problems the state faced in adjusting to the declining importance of this long-dominant element in its economy.

Thus, as Michigan passed the milestone of its sesquicentennial and headed toward its bicentennial in the year 2037, adjusting to change was again, as had so often been the case during the preceding 11,000 years, the biggest challenge the state faced.

CHAPTER XIII

PARTNERS IN PROGRESS

Three hundred years ago the North American territory around the Great Lakes was coveted by longtime arch enemies, the British and the French. In their respective searches for riches from the New World to supplement their treasuries and augment their grandeur, the royal houses of Europe were heavily committed to colonial settlement and expansion.

From outposts throughout the Great Lakes chain, the French colonial empire—based almost exclusively on the harvesting and exportation of animal furs—thrived. Michigan's first businessmen were the French voyageurs, hearty trappers who adopted the ways of the Algonquian Indians who populated the region.

Michigan's colonial economy—fur trading—was supplanted in the early nineteenth century by farming. The state's rich land was opened to settlement under the new United States, and land-starved migrants from New England's rocky coasts flooded Michigan's land offices.

The 1840s saw the beginning of yet another business—mining. The rich copper and iron veins of the Upper Pen-

insula were as fabulous as local Indians and explorers had predicted they would be a century earlier. Michigan's mines led the country in output until the turn of the twentieth century.

Paralleling mining was lumbering, as vast tracks of virgin White Pine were harvested in a four-decade frenzy that closed the nineteenth century.

The twentieth century dawned to the noise of an internal combustion engine. The automobile era had come to Michigan, and by the 1910s Detroit became the world's auto capital. By the 1920s heavy industry dominated southeastern Michigan. Thousands flocked from the farms of the South or the joblessness of other states.

The 1930s brought depression and World War II brought only temporary economic stimulus. By the post-war years Michigan's dependency on manufacturing was a rough road. When times were good, they were very good; when they were not, matters became very difficult indeed. The industrial growth that spawned the auto industry is vulnerable to the ebbs and flows of the American and world economies. While it made possible wages and ben-

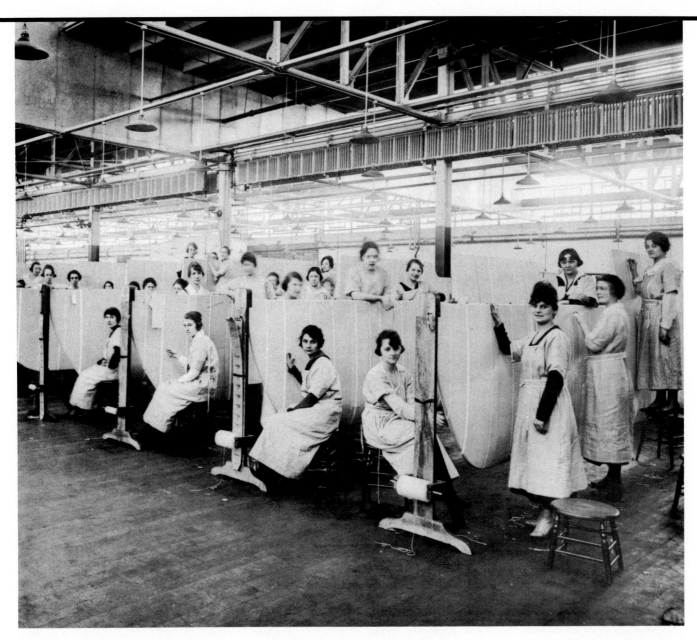

efits that are the envy of other industrial areas, it has extracted a price. Now, business and the leaders of organized labor are seeking solutions to problems in a nation and a world that have changed dramatically in the past half century.

These businesses, institutions, and associations represent an important part of Michigan's future. Presented here are the businesses that provide valuable consumer products to Michigan, and the institutions that are preparing the state's future leaders. And

here, also, are the various associations of professionals who ensure that the basic necessities and amenities are there for all to use and enjoy.

The following histories depict enterprises that make Michigan unique and a good place to work, study, and live. They have made this book possible, and continue to enrich the state of Michigan both with their presence and their civic involvement.

Thomas L. Jones

Any notion that it was Rosie the Riveter in the Second World War who brought women into the factories is dispelled by this picture of Fisher Body employees interrupted in their work during World War I. Courtesy, Michigan Historical Collections, Bentley Historical Library, University of Michigan

HISTORICAL SOCIETY OF MICHIGAN

A private home for more than 100 years, the Tuomy House serves as the Historical Society of Michigan's headquarters in Ann Arbor.

The Historical Society of Michigan was founded in the heady decade of the 1820s. Ten years before Michigan's statehood was a time of significant growth in Michigan's population and settlements. Territorial Governor Lewis Cass, along with noted scholar and Indian agent Henry Rowe Schoolcraft, believed that this new land needed an organization devoted to preserving its history—that was so rapidly changing—before the onslaught of settlers and development. Hence was born the Historical Society of Michigan.

Reorganized in 1874, the society exists today as Michigan's membership-supported organization devoted to the preservation and publication of Michigan's history. Although the organization's leaders, headquarters, publications, and membership levels have changed over the past century, the society remains committed to its original, simply stated goals.

In the late nineteenth century the society was charged by the state legislature to preserve the state's history. The result was the *Pioneer and Historical Collection,* a 40-volume compendium that is still a definitive source of vital information on Michigan's history. Since the early 1960s the society's *Chronicle* magazine has presented quality, illustrated articles to the society's members and readers across the state. And in 1987 the organization introduced to its members the *Michigan Historical Review,* co-published with the Clarke Historical Library, Central Michigan University. The society's reprint series, the Michigan Heritage Library, has currently four titles in print. Among them are Alan Nolan's *The Iron Brigade* and J. Lee Barrett's *Speedboat Kings.* The society's

Territorial Governor Lewis Cass (above, 1782-1866) and noted scholar and Indian agent Henry Rowe Schoolcraft (right, 1793-1864) founded the Historical and Pioneer Society in 1828.

Gillette Memorial Publishing Fund has brought forth *Fiery Trial,* the story of Michigan's great forest fire of 1881; *Backward, Turn Backward,* firsthand reminiscences of an early twentieth-century childhood on a northern Michigan farm; and, in production, the autobiography of Florence Cushman Milner, whose teaching career began in a Dowagiac, Michigan, one-room schoolhouse in the 1870s and culminated at Harvard University in the 1930s. The society also facilitates the production of books, such as *Mainstreet: A Portrait of Small-Town Michigan,* co-published with the *Detroit Free Press,* and *Stewards of the State: The Governors of Michigan,* co-published with *The Detroit News.*

Special programs sponsored by the

society include its award-winning Centennial Business Program, which honors 100-year-old (and older) businesses in Michigan. Among the organization's annual awards are the Ferris Lewis Award for excellence in teaching Michigan history, the Charles Follo Award for promotion of Upper Peninsula history, and the Awards of Merit, including the coveted Distinguished Service Award. These awards are presented at the society's statewide annual meetings, held continuously since 1874. The society has also

sponsored the annual Upper Peninsula Conference since 1952.

The Historical Society of Michigan's executive director is Thomas L. Jones. Supported by a five-person staff and advised by a 24-member board of trustees, Jones has headed the organization since 1980. The society's administrative offices are in the historic Tuomy House in Ann Arbor, Michigan. A private home for over 100 years, the Tuomy House was designated in Cornelius Tuomy's 1966 will to be used for historic and public purposes. The house is undergoing extensive rehabilitation during the celebration of Michigan's sesquicentennial. When completed, the Tuomy House will reflect the style of a bygone age while adequately adjusting to the modern needs of the society's administrative, editorial, and program responsibilities.

MICHIGAN MILK PRODUCERS ASSOCIATION

On May 23, 1916, a group of dairy farmers near Howell met at Michigan Agricultural College, now Michigan State University, to discuss ways to assure a stable market and a better price for their milk. For that ambitious and foresighted delegation, formation of Michigan Milk Producers Association 11 days later was a bold move; before Congress' passage of the 1922 Capper-Volstead Act, it was illegal for farmers to work together in that manner to improve the quality of farm life. Farmers who challenged the pre-1922 laws were subject to prosecution; some were jailed. The Capper-Volstead Act set forth the right of producers of many commodities to market their products without fear of violating antitrust laws.

"Dairy farm" is the name commonly given to a business enterprise wherein cows are raised for production of milk that is, in turn, sold for commercial use. That milk usually is marketed through cooperatives, such as MMPA, which are owned and controlled by dairy farmers. MMPA's impact on Michigan's economy is linked to the role of dairying in the state: Dairying is the top-ranked segment of the state's number two industry, agriculture. Michigan ranks sixth in the nation in milk production.

Among many other services and functions, MMPA arranges for the sale of its members' milk to processing and manufacturing plants in Michigan and elsewhere. At the plants, the milk is bottled for retail sale in fluid form or manufactured into such products as cottage cheese, butter, ice cream, or hard cheeses. The ultimate destination—consumers.

In the fall of 1916 MMPA began bargaining for a better price with processors in the Detroit area. Detroit was, and is, considered Michigan's principal milk market because that is where the heaviest concentration of population lives. Until the mid-twentieth century many communities—both within the Detroit metropolitan area and outstate—boasted their own "creameries." Each had a processing plant to which 10-gallon cans of raw milk from area farms were delivered for processing; the dairy products from it were usually sold locally. That was because neither roads nor refrigeration nor processing technologies then permitted long-distance hauling or long-term storage of dairy products.

Grass roots chapters of MMPA dairy farmers were formed near towns with creameries; the chapters, or "Locals," usually took the name of the town to which their milk was delivered, i.e., the Grand Rapids Local, the Houghton-Hancock Local, the Marlette Local. During those early years MMPA itself owned and operated creameries in many outstate communities. The Local remains MMPA's basic membership unit.

Advances in farming, transportation, and processing technologies—as well as dramatic changes in numbers and buying practices of consumers—resulted in a shift from numerous, small, community creameries to a handful of proprietary super-plants able to serve consumers in a large geographic area, even in surrounding states.

As consumer demographics were changing, life on dairy farms was changing,

Michigan Milk Producers Association's former Imlay City creamery in the early 1940s.

too. By mid-century a trend toward fewer yet larger and more productive dairy farms had gotten under way. In the mid-1950s MMPA consisted of about 17,000 farms. By the late 1980s that number had dropped to less than 4,000, but, thanks to advances in farm technology and in herd management practices, milk production per farm was more than triple that of 1955.

In 1979 MMPA acquired McDonald Dairy Co., adding fluid milk processing and retail sales to its range of activities. McDonald Dairy, through plants in Flint and Benton Harbor and distribution points in Alpena and Battle Creek, markets a full line of dairy products through some 5,000 retail stores in Michigan, Ohio, and Indiana. Another major processing and distribution company, Country Fresh, Inc., of Grand Rapids, bought McDonald Dairy from MMPA in 1986.

MMPA's statewide system of plants manufactures such nonfluid dairy products as butter, cheese, nonfat dry milk, and ice cream mix. The MMPA-owned manufacturing plants enable MMPA to preserve and expand its markets for nonfluid dairy products.

Through efforts of such cooperatives as the Michigan Milk Producers Association, dairy farmers pool strength with hundreds of other dairy farmers to provide a range of services no dairy farmer, operating alone, could afford or provide. Consumers benefit by being assured an adequate supply of wholesome dairy foods at reasonable prices.

LUDINGTON NEWS COMPANY, INC.

Ivan Ludington, Jr., president and chief executive officer of Ludington News Company, Inc.

and the business found new quarters on Fourth Avenue at West Forest Avenue in 1922. This location was home until 1960.

In the early years strong competition from nationwide firms such as American News Company and Harris News meant a struggle for Ludington News. All sorts of products were tried to bolster the basic distribution of magazines and paperbacks. Jigsaw puzzles, Hi-Li paddles, Woolfoam, yo-yos, TreeSweet Orange Juice, Universal Stove Cleaner, Wonder Water, Canada Dry, Kryptar film photofinishing, Gillette blades, and even Edelweiss beer were added to the line.

During the World War II era the competition was of a different sort. Finding tires, gasoline, trucks, employees, and, for the publishers, paper became a real fight and a problem, especially for distribution firms. Ivan Ludington kept it all together and moving.

The period following World War II was one of expansion, growth, and change. In 1951 the Ludington News Company-Flint, Inc., became affiliated. Six years later the American News Company closed its magazine warehouses across the

Ivan Ludington, Sr., founder of Ludington News Company, Inc., located at 1600 East Grand Boulevard in Detroit, was born October 16, 1897, in Alpena, Michigan. His father, Lewis, was a Great Lakes steamboat captain, and his mother, Fandira, a pioneer schoolteacher. The family moved to Detroit, and by 1912 Ivan and his mother had started their own business as distributors of the *Detroit Free Press*. Ivan dropped out of high school before his scheduled graduation in 1914 because he was too busy to continue. Besides, he was already making more money than his principal at old Central High.

The entry of the United States in World War I found him in officer's training at the University of Michigan, but

he commuted to Detroit to keep the business going. Just after the war, in June 1921, with his Liberty Bonds and some borrowed cash, he bought out Solomon Brothers, a magazine distribution concern, and the Ludington News Company was begun.

The first home of the Ludington News Company was a 3,000-square-foot building at 227 West Larned Street where the multistoried Hotel Pontchartrain currently stands. The firm employed six people, had three trucks, and an annual payroll of $7,500. Progress, experimentation, and a move were rapid, however,

The first location of Ludington News Company, Inc., on Larned Street in 1921.

The former Packard Building was acquired by Ludington News in 1960 and now serves as its headquarters and the center for all its operations.

country, and Ludington News became the sole distributor of magazines and paperbacks in its territory. Business grew tremendously, and larger quarters were required. Ludington News purchased the building at 1600 East Grand Boulevard that, when first erected, housed the Packard automobile company, then one of the nation's most prestigious names. The building offered 117,000 square feet, thus permitting the consolidation of all Ludington News Company functions under one roof.

Several innovations were developed by Ludington News by this time in various locations. Some of those now brought together included a company-controlled, nonprofit carpenter shop to supply dealers with modern display equipment; a company printing shop to turn out office forms, checkup sheets, invoices, and the like; a dealer news bulletin with promotional tips, personals about dealers, and pictures of rack installations; a separate merchandise department supplying dealers with razor blades, pens, postcards, and other notions; and a separate book department with its own personnel and its own specially equipped trucks that was one of the first book mobile plans in operation.

In conjunction with the opening of the new home of the Ludington News Company, the 1961 convention of Independent Distributors of the Great Lake Region was held in Detroit. Representatives of 78 cities gathered to honor Ivan Ludington, Sr. This was but one of many honors and awards presented to Ludington. Perhaps the presentation, in 1964, of his high school diploma from Central High School class of 1914 and the naming of the Ludington Middle School on Edinborough Street in Detroit were the most personally satisfying to Ivan Ludington.

His concern for education was lifelong. He originated the Ludington Plan, which found thousands of dollars for low-cost paperback books for Adventure Reading Rooms and for public and parochial schools and institutions in Detroit and throughout Michigan. Using his considerable persuasive powers in Lansing, he convinced the Michigan State Legislature to appropriate funds to help furnish low-cost books that would appeal to young readers.

From its inception in 1921 until January 1, 1958, the Ludington News Company was a partnership. Next it was a proprietorship of Ivan Ludington, Sr. On June 1, 1961, the Ludington News Company was incorporated. In 1985 the officers were Ivan Ludington, Sr., chairman; Ivan Ludington, Jr., president; William F. Penz, vice-president, Detroit; Nancy Donaldson, vice-president/retail sales; John T. Donaldson, vice-president, Louisville, Kentucky; David Persinger, vice-president, Dayton, Ohio; Lillian Santa, corporate secretary; and Richard J. Thomas, director and legal counsel.

Geographical expansion also occurred during this period. In 1969 a branch in Port Huron, Michigan, was opened, just after the 1968 acquisition of the agency in Louisville, Kentucky. Later, Dayton, Ohio, was added to the Ludington News territory.

Through many long years Ivan Ludington, Sr., was fortunate to have his son, Ivan Jr., in the company as president. Long before his death on November 18, 1985, Ivan Sr. had been assured of a smooth transition of management in the firm he had created. Moreover, the founder was pleased to observe the continued public service activities of his son, who serves on numerous university, hospital, business, nonprofit, and social organization boards.

Since Ivan Jr. joined the enterprise in 1951, he had been well prepared to assume the role of president and chief executive officer. His sister, Nancy Ludington Donaldson, is also in the family firm, and manages the Metro News Center at Telegraph and Maple roads in Birmingham, Michigan.

In 1985 the corporation opened a newly constructed 55,000-square-foot addition to its building on East Grand Boulevard. With employment at some 400 people and with revenues at about $65 million per year, Ludington News Company, Inc., is well positioned to continue its services to the reading public.

LA-Z-BOY CHAIR COMPANY

In 1923 Edward M. Knabusch built a garage at the rear of his father's lot at 912 West Front Street in Monroe. He was 23 years old and employed five days a week at the nearby Weis Manufacturing Company. He desired something more, however, and spent most of his earnings buying used machinery to build novelty furniture in his spare time.

Knabusch was raised on a farm near Scofield, and had attended school there. One-quarter mile away on another farm his cousin, Edwin J. Shoemaker, seven years younger than Knabusch, also attended school in Scofield. One fateful day Shoemaker bought a piece of yellow pine in order to build a radio. The board was too thick, so he borrowed his father's Model T and drove to his cousin Edward's garage to investigate the machinery there. Thus was begun a furniture industry legend.

The talents of the cousins meshed perfectly. Knabusch knew woods and had a knack for business. Shoemaker had a natural genius with metals and machines. Moreover, they got along with each other. Shortly thereafter Shoemaker left the farm to join his cousin in town. Years later he was to say his biggest motivation was to escape the rigors of the farm. For two years they built novelty furniture in the garage, but larger quarters were clearly needed.

In 1927 the cousins purchased a cornfield one mile north of Monroe on a wagon trail rumored to be a future state highway. The gamble paid off; Telegraph Road, constructed within a year, became U.S. 24, for many years the busiest highway in Michigan. This location was to prove fortuitous during the bleak days of the Great Depression. Soon the Floral City Furniture Company building was completed by the cousins—personally. From sewer to chimney the two designed and constructed the new factory.

Custom furniture, along with some ideas of their own, were the products; then, in 1928, they hit on the idea of a chair that would allow changing positions of the back and seat. They made a wooden porch chair with a seat that moved forward as the back reclined, and took the chair to the Lion Department Store in nearby Toledo, Ohio, to obtain a buyer's opinion. The buyer suggested an upholstered chair with

E.M. Knabusch (left) and E.J. Shoemaker (right), cofounders of La-Z-Boy Chair Company, have seen a lot of changes since they developed their reclining wood porch chair.

these features would be a winner. Defying upholsterers who said it could not be done, they created the chair. By April 1929 patents had been obtained and the La-Z-Boy chair was on its way to becoming one of the most popular types of upholstered furniture in the United States. At their first furniture market visit in May 1929 in Grand Rapids, more orders were received than could be filled.

The rosy start was not to last: By 1933 the desperate economic conditions forced the young firm to sell its woodworking machinery and to concentrate on the retail market. The Telegraph Road site was a good choice. Furniture shows in tents became annual events: Prizes were given, prices were rock bottom, and Floral City

Furniture Company survived. By the late 1930s conditions were improving. At the same time the decision to reenter manufacturing was made. Production started in September 1939.

By May 1, 1941, sales had increased dramatically, and a new corporation was formed with the name La-Z-Boy Chair Company. A new building, featuring the latest in manufacturing technologies, was completed just prior to the start of World War II. As a result, the new facility was leased to Woodall Industries for war

The La-Z-Boy product line has come a long way from that first wooden porch chair. Today a full range of products carry the La-Z-Boy name, including sofas, sleep sofas, and fashionable swivel rockers.

production. The old La-Z-Boy factory also converted to war production for the duration.

Growth of the company in the years since World War II has been phenomenal. New products, improvements in continuing products, and geographic expansion have all contributed. U.S. manufacturing facilities in Siloam Springs, Arkansas; Neosho, Missouri; Dayton, Tennessee; Newton, Mississippi; Florence, South Carolina; Redlands, California; and Tremonton, Utah, turn out a wide variety of chairs, sleep sofas, loveseats, and full recliners in styles that range from tradi-

tional to transitional and contemporary to country. A wholly owned subsidiary in Canada, and licensees in Australia, Italy, Japan, Mexico, New Zealand, and West Germany cover the rest of the world.

Industry recognition of La-Z-Boy quality and innovation has been a major source of satisfaction to founders Edward M. Knabusch and Edwin J. Shoemaker and the entire La-Z-Boy family of employees. At the 1970 International Home Furnishings Market in the American Furniture Mart in Chicago, La-Z-Boy Chair Company won the third annual Innovator Award for its creation of the

"Sofette," a multiple seating unit that will accommodate two individuals in a variety of sitting and reclining positions independent of each other.

Today the La-Z-Boy Chair Company has expanded its reach into fine furniture for the home and office and continues the heritage of quality and innovation it was founded upon.

LEONARD BROS. MOVING & STORAGE COMPANY

In 1880, the year Thomas Edison patented the light bulb, Samuel A. Leonard founded S. Leonard Company, now Leonard Bros. Moving & Storage Company. Today the concern is the oldest moving and storage firm in Michigan continuously operated by the same family.

The Port of Detroit was a stove and railroad equipment manufacturing center with unpaved and rutted streets when Samuel Leonard started his business using horse-drawn wagons to haul rail couplings, ties, and pins. Railroad, interurban, and streetcar construction projects were big business in Detroit and throughout Michigan in the 1880s. Samuel Leonard's traffic was brisk. His storage area was his backyard stable.

By 1900 S. Leonard Company was transporting a variety of commodities, including sand, hay, grain, and incoming freight for local merchants. As growing Detroit industries and services attracted more people to the rapidly expanding city, the demand for reliable movement and storage of household goods increased. Leonard began to specialize in the movement of household goods. In 1915 he was able to purchase his first motorized moving van.

Samuel Leonard retired in 1924, and his four sons, Charles, Fred, Leon, and Roy, assumed active management of the business. Under their direction Leonard Bros. continued to grow along with rapidly expanding Detroit—the nation's boom-town of the 1920s. In 1946 Jerry F. Leonard, Fred's son, became president. The enterprise continued to prosper as its national and international capabilities were expanded.

By the time Leonard Bros. Moving & Storage Company celebrated a century of service to Metropolitan Detroit in 1980, Jerry Leonard, Sr., was chairman of the board, and his sons, Jerry Jr., David W., and Larry, were all active in the management of the firm. Leonard Bros. offers "total transportation services," including household moves; office moves; special commodity moves; complete record storage and management; commercial, industrial, and domestic moving worldwide; moving of sensitive electronic equipment, displays, and exhibits; a modern transportation fleet; and special-

ized packaging, handling, and storage.

The first major portion of Leonard Bros.' operations is long- and short-distance shipments of both residential and commercial goods. On the commercial side, the company has the equipment, materials, and expertise to ship everything from sensitive electronic devices to light equipment. Many offices and industrial operations have been moved by Leonard Bros.

The S. Leonard Company was founded in 1880 by Samuel Alexander Leonard and eventually became a family-run business. Pictured here are the first and second generations of the Leonard family. Seated (from left) are Samuel Leonard, founder, and his daughter, Gertie. Standing (from left) are Leonard's four sons, Fred, Leon, Roy, and Charlie.

On the residential side, Leonard Bros. is an authorized agent of United Van Lines. Agents affiliated with United Van Lines are stockholders, and the board of directors are elective from the agents. This method provides a direct control of agents, thus assuring quality and uniformity. United Van Lines agents are nationwide, and through affiliates worldwide moves can be handled.

Leonard Bros. enjoys a large customer base. This has contributed to the development of a sophisticated record-keeping system using the latest in computer applications. All records, billings, and payroll operations are accomplished on the computer. All the branch offices are tied together and to United Van Lines headquarters in St. Louis, Missouri.

In addition to computers, Leonard Bros. has become a high-technology materials-handling operation: The latest in automated systems are employed wherever appropriate. One of the newer facilities

In 1924 the Leonard Bros. Moving & Storage Company used this moving van and tandem trailer for the family business.

features the extensive use of robots for material moving.

Leonard Bros. has also specialized in records storage. Household goods or residential moving is a cyclical business, busy in the summer and slow in the winter. By adding a storage service for hard-copy records in the 1970s, the company introduced a substantially less cyclical line to its storage operations.

Records storage and management is an interesting endeavor. Many kinds of businesses and services are required by law, and by desire in some cases, to maintain records for defined time periods, usually expressed in years. The capability for proper care and storage may not exist in many company plants and offices. Space itself possessing the proper qualities for storage such as fire protection, temperature control, moisture control, and the like may not be available. As a result, Leonard Bros. found a market niche storing records for others.

Many businesses, especially hospitals, legal, and accounting firms, have found the service convenient and economical for storing and servicing a variety of documents. Leonard Bros. has a computer control system to track the removal from storage for destruction cycles, and seeks the owners' final approval before actual destruction. Obviously having Leonard Bros. to take care of record keeping of this sort is a great service to those without such in-house capabilities.

Since records storage customers sometimes want the records returned rather than destroyed, Leonard Bros.

The first S. Leonard Company warehouse was located on West Fort Street in Detroit in 1930.

developed a messenger service to deliver documents from storage back to the customer. Small vans and station wagons are used in this operation, which has now branched out to serving other businesses by delivery between multiple firms.

International moves have become a Leonard Bros. specialty. All aspects of personal, commercial, and industrial moves are handled. By innovative boxing and crating of goods for shipment by land, air, and water, Leonard Bros. has attracted customers with shipping needs ranging from a 20-ton conveyer system and several hundred auto engines to the most delicate personal artifacts such as crystal, bone china, and expensive oil paintings. The company is an authorized agent for the International Air Transport Association and is a certified freight forwarder, which permits Leonard Bros. to provide total transportation services on a one-stop shopping basis anywhere in the world, a capability that was facilitated by the formation of Leonard Bros. International Ltd. in June 1980.

Metropolitan Detroit features a large number of manufacturing companies and service firms with worldwide operations. As a result, many international moves by personnel and their families occur regularly. Any move tends to be traumatic—the first international one even more

so. Leonard Bros. has developed a particularly well-qualified and experienced staff to help alleviate concerns about the international move. Moving is a service industry, and Leonard Bros. endeavors to "handle each person's possessions as if they were our own." In the international move, more extensive preparations are required. Household goods and personal effects to be stored and/or shipped must be carefully inventoried and wrapped or packaged. Bulky items such as sofas and pianos are individually padded and wrapped. Goods are then boxed in specialized, sealed, waterproof wooden lift vans, ship's containers, or air freight containers, depending on the mode of transportation. By working with a network of affiliates in other countries, Leonard Bros. can arrange for door-to-door delivery almost anywhere in the world.

Two major events occurred in 1985: David W. Leonard bought out his father and brothers to become sole owner of the company, and a terminal and warehouse were opened in Lansing.

Back in 1967, when Leonard Bros. opened its Troy operation at 1782 East Maple Road, David Leonard recognized the need to be active in the life of that fast-growing northern suburb. He personally has been active in the Rotary Club and the Troy Chamber of Commerce, serving as president of both organizations. In 1985 he was one of the appointed members of the White House Conference on Small Business. His company has been a good corporate citizen as well. Donations of time, equipment, labor, and money for charitable organizations have been commonplace.

Perhaps most notable is the Leonard Bros. Moving & Storage Company's part in the sponsorship of the Troy Cycling Festival race. This annual event now attracts top contestants from across the country, and includes an old-fashioned parade. As the *Troy Focus* communications magazine stated: "It wouldn't really be a parade without the Leonard Bros. fire engine."

Entering its second century of service, Leonard Bros. Moving & Storage Company is Michigan's oldest moving firm continuously operated by the same family. Seated (from left) are Jerry Leonard, Jr., and Jerry Leonard, Sr. Standing (from left) are Larry Leonard and David Leonard. David is the president of Leonard Bros. Moving & Storage and a great-grandson of Samuel A. Leonard.

FORD & EARL ASSOCIATES, INC.

Ford & Earl Associates, Inc., of Warren, Michigan, resulted from the 1964 merger of Harley Earl Associates and W.B. Ford Design Associates, Inc. Both companies had established enviable records in their respective fields, and in due time their imagination and vision drew them together. Their management realized that by joining forces, they could shake the design world.

Harley J. Earl had been appointed chief of design at General Motors in 1927. His contributions in industrial design, particularly in the automobile field, were so revolutionary that he is regarded as the father of modern automotive design, and a pioneer in the industrial design sphere. Most significantly, he was the first industrial designer given equal status with engineering as a vice-president in a large corporation.

This breakthrough gained designers a new image, enhanced their professional status, and created new avenues of opportunity. In addition to his own native talents, Earl possessed the instinct of spotting promising young designers. In 1945, with General Motors' blessing, Earl formed his own industrial design firm. The only condition imposed by GM was that Earl's venture not design products in competition with General Motors. Earl retired from GM in 1958.

During the same period Walter B. Ford II was focusing his architecturally

trained eye on creating new looks for bank lobbies, restaurants, and corporate offices. The Ford firm was a leader in package design and corporate identity programs as well. The open-office layout, considered a standard today, was an idea pioneered in this country by Ford. Industrial design was enjoying a successful emergence during the post-World War II period. Both Ford and Earl were at the vanguard of their fields. Pursuing their individual courses, the two firms grew and prospered.

Even the newspaper headline an-

nouncing that "Earl Joins Ford" brought international concern. General Motors executives on business in Paris were taken aback at this news of their famous, retired design leader, and were relieved to learn it was the merger of two independent design firms. Purveyors of design realized that competition would become tougher. By combining their talents, Ford and Earl established one of the first multidisciplinary design firms in the nation.

The Ford & Earl staff includes architects, interior designers, programmers, space planners, and product, graphic, and exhibit designers. Depending on the assignment, these professionals work individually or as a team, in architecture, interior design, facility and space planning, product design, and visual communica-

President Walter B. Ford II (left) and vice-president and director of design, Harley H. Melzian (right) at W.B. Ford Design Associates, Inc.

tions. The firm maintains a fully equipped shop for model making and prototype development. Programming and space planning is computerized with CAD capabilities.

Philosophically, Ford & Earl believes that by adhering to three precepts while incorporating analysis, good judgment, creativity, and good taste the firm can produce environments, products, and corporate images that are successful and excellent, by design. Those precepts are: Is it appropriate and functional? Is it interesting and aesthetically pleasing? Does it satisfy the client and the user?

The impressive client list that Ford & Earl Associates, Inc., has served is ample evidence that the concern has succeeded. Wally Ford commented some years ago that "Flights into the future are necessary for a designer. To succeed he must be able to accommodate, anticipate, or nudge the public's desires." The results of these efforts can be seen in Ford & Earl Associates' proudest achievements—designs that have endured and have enhanced people's lives.

Harley J. Earl (center, right) and his son James M. Earl (center, left) were the principals at Harley Earl Associates. In 1964 Harley Earl Associates and W.B. Ford Design Associates, Inc., merged to form Ford & Earl Associates, Inc.

MAZDA DISTRIBUTORS GREAT LAKES

The central atrium in Mazda Great Lakes' office building blends an exterior-type garden with an elegant reception area, and brings natural light deep into the center of the building.

facility in Grand Rapids to train Mazda mechanics and technicians. The firm also has on-site training programs in parts department management, business management, and sales. Mazda dealers can count on the company to be fair and straightforward. "We make no private deals with any individual dealer," says president Bob Hooker. "The arrangements we make are applicable to all, and our records are open to any of our dealers to show how we allocate cars."

Openness, in fact, is a key word in the Mazda Great Lakes business philosophy. "Our building makes a statement about how we operate—the open look and feel

The gleaming, pyramidal building at 618 Kenmoor SE that houses Mazda Distributors Great Lakes is symbolic of the company—contemporary, innovative, forthright, enduring.

Mazda Distributors Great Lakes is a Mazda automobile distributorship for five midwestern states—Michigan, Illinois, Indiana, Ohio, and Wisconsin. Representing one of the top-quality foreign-manufactured cars in the country, Mazda Great Lakes is a 10-year-old organization that was founded on the happy circumstance of being in the right place at the right time.

The company was formed in 1977 by Peter Cook, Robert Hooker, and Max Boersma at a time when the Japanese automaker, Toyo Kogyo, was seeking a more secure niche in the American auto market for its Mazda automobiles. Mazda then ranked among the top three in sales in auto markets in other countries, but only 17th in the United States. The firm was revamping its U.S. marketing strategy and looking for new, enthusiastic, aggressive distributors to handle its product.

Cook had owned a European-import auto distributorship for 22 years, but eventually, the parent company would take over the distributorship. Cook wanted to keep his own organization intact and was looking for a new business opportunity. Taking Hooker and Boersma into

Mazda's high-performance rotary engine is unique in the automotive industry. The driveway in front of the Mazda Great Lakes offices was designed to resemble the engine's triangular-shape rotor.

partnership, Cook formed an alliance with Mazda that has proven sound and rewarding for both.

In 1977 there were 65 Mazda dealers in the five-state region that Mazda Great Lakes serves; today there are 125. Mazda Great Lakes has developed a comprehensive support organization to serve those dealers.

In addition to supplying cars and parts, Mazda Great Lakes maintains a training

of the building reflect our approach to business and to our management style," says Hooker.

The same attitude that prevails toward the firm's dealers extends to employees. The loosely structured, informal organization, with easy access to management, makes for pleasant working conditions and little turnover among staff members. Innovative employee benefit programs add incentive to stay with the company.

The service philosophy also extends to the community at large. Mazda Distributors Great Lakes executives and staff members donate much time, energy, and money to community activities and causes.

VICKERS, INCORPORATED

The photograph illustrates the development by Vickers founder Harry F. Vickers of the first hydraulic power-steering pump, introduced in 1925. All of the components and tools pictured are of mid-1920s manufacture.

Harry Franklin Vickers was born into a large family in Red Lodge, Montana, on October 10, 1898. He attended public schools in Montana and later, California. By the time he was 14 years old, working in the nearby gold mines, he had begun to handle problems of business and working with people. At the same time his intense interest in the new field of wireless telegraphy, later radio, began to emerge. His penchant for the mechanical side of industry was furthered by working as a machinist during the day and assisting a master mechanic—at no pay—during the evenings in order to become expert in such things as cutting gears and cams.

When the United States entered World War I Vickers enlisted in the Army as a private with hopes of becoming a pilot. The Army discovered his skills in radio, and he was placed in the Radio Division of The Signal Corps, sent to Europe, and placed in charge of the construction and operation of field wireless telegraph stations.

Although the war cut short his formal education, Vickers, following his discharge in 1919, returned to Los Angeles, worked as chief engineer for a company that installed and serviced hydraulic hoists and bodies on motor trucks, and pursued

further education through correspondence courses and by private tutoring. In 1956 the University of Southern California conferred on him an honorary Doctor of Science degree.

In 1921 the 23-year-old Vickers formed the Vickers Manufacturing Company in Los Angeles. At first the firm rebuilt hydraulic pumps for replacement on motor trucks, but soon branched out into other hydraulic applications for special machinery such as forging presses and rail straighteners for the Southern Pacific, plus varied building, material handling, and machine tools.

Vickers altered the sluggish fluid power industry by the development of the Vickers balanced vane-type pump in 1925. That same year Vickers produced the first practical power-steering apparatus for heavy vehicles. Today his ingenuity is generally credited as the most significant

factor in the tremendous growth of the entire fluid power industry.

The startling innovations of the young manufacturing company caught the eye of Fred J. Fisher, oldest of the "Body by Fisher" brothers. In 1929 Vickers moved to a rented building in Hamtramck at Clay and Dubois. With financial backing from Fisher, Vickers, Incorporated, was formed to serve the fast-growing automobile industry. One of the first programs the company initiated was a packaged power-steering system experimentally applied to Hudson, Cadillac, and Oldsmobile automobiles; however, the onset of the Great Depression put a stop to any such "frill." In the early 1950s when power steering was finally offered on passenger cars, a split system of separate pump and steering booster was generally used. Today the trend is back to the packaged concept first envisioned by Vickers.

Through personal commitment, determination, and drive, coupled with superior products and applications, Vickers, Incorporated, continued to grow. In 1933 a new plant was constructed on Oakman Boulevard in Detroit, and two years later was more than doubled in size. In 1940 the building's area was again doubled. The physical capacity was necessitated by the several "firsts" developed, now standards

General Douglas MacArthur (center), newly appointed chairman of the board of Sperry Rand Corporation in 1955, with the two men who created Sperry Rand. Left is Harry F. Vickers, founder of Vickers, Incorporated, former president of Sperry Corporation, and former president and chief executive officer of Sperry Rand. Right is James H. Rand, creator of Remington-Rand.

of the industry: the balanced-piston, pilot-operated relief valve, pressure compensated flow control, traverse and feed panel, and piston pump and motor lines.

When the Navy had a problem in hoisting the powder for eight-inch guns in turrets, Vickers developed a prototype, shipped the sample to the Washington Navy yard, and, with a crew of Navy men, hooked the new hoisting mechanism to the powder car.

In 1937 yet another milestone was reached as Vickers, Incorporated, became a subsidiary of the Sperry Corporation through an exchange of stock. Founded by Elmer Sperry, the firm had acquired the Waterbury Tool Company in Connecticut in 1935. Waterbury had been founded in 1898, and created the oil hydraulics industry in 1903. Professor Harvey D. Williams of Cornell University and Waterbury chief engineer, Reynold Jan-

Harry F. Vickers (left) accepts this Army-Navy Production "E" Award on behalf of his company's employees during World War II. The firm went on to earn many such distinctions before the war's end.

ney, collaborated to create what became known as the Williams-Janney transmission, first installed on the U.S.S. *Virginia* in 1906. Thus Sperry joined the company that started the hydraulics industry with Vickers, the firm that had done the most to spur fluid power growth. Waterbury became a division of Vickers in 1940.

In 1942 the U.S. government built the Vickers Eight Mile Road plant for defense production. That massive facility is now a National Guard Armory used for many purposes including antique shows. To ensure a smooth transition to peacetime uses, the Vickers Hydraulics School was established in 1945, where thousands of students have been trained in the application, operation, and maintenance of hydraulic equipment.

Progress for both Vickers and Sperry advanced in the postwar years. In 1955 Harry Vickers engineered a Sperry Corporation merger with Remington-Rand, and was named the new Sperry Rand Corporation's first president and chief executive officer, a post he held until 1965, when he became chairman of the board and chief executive officer. Subsidiaries and partnerships for Vickers, Incorporated, a wholly owned subsidiary of Sperry Rand, were formed in many parts of the world. New plants in Jackson, Mississippi; Torrance, California; and an administration and engineering center in Troy, Michigan, were built. By the time Harry Vickers, inventor, entrepreneur, and

business leader, retired in 1967, the Vickers Division of Sperry Rand had operations in 24 countries.

Harry Vickers was to enjoy 10 years of "retirement" before his death at age 78. His company continues the rich traditions for care, concern, and opportunity that he established.

The Vickers Division continued to advance with a new line of miniature hydraulic valves, introduced in 1969, for use in low-power applications requiring fast, precise control. That same year the Vickers Hydraulic School moved to a new building in Troy, Michigan, that was double the size of the former facility; some 900 students per year complete their training at the school. Two years later the Vickers Division celebrated 50 years of service. In 1973 the Vickers Division name was changed to Sperry Vickers, and was restructured into North American and international groups.

In 1979 Sperry Rand Corporation changed its name to Sperry Corporation, while Sperry Vickers was exploring an exciting new dimension by concluding its first license agreement with the People's Republic of China for the transfer of industrial valve technology and manufacturing expertise.

In 1984 Libbey-Owens-Ford Company of Toledo, Ohio, acquired Vickers, Incorporated, from Sperry Corporation. Two years later the glass business of Libbey-Owens-Ford was sold, and the name of the company was changed to TRINOVA Corporation.

Today Vickers, Incorporated, is a successful and innovative operating company of TRINOVA with the world's most comprehensive facilities for fluid power systems research, development, engineering, and testing.

Headquartered in Troy, Michigan, Vickers, Incorporated, is a worldwide leading manufacturer of electronics, electrohydraulics, and fluid power systems and components with operations in 48 countries.

The plant and offices of Vickers, Incorporated, on Oakman Boulevard in Detroit. Building No. 1 (shown here) was later expanded and employed 12,000 Detroit area residents on three shifts during World War II.

METROPOLITAN DETROIT CONVENTION AND VISITORS BUREAU

The year 1896: Detroit was a bustling city on the verge of becoming the automobile capital of the world as the first horseless carriage was driven on its streets. Milton Carmichael, a reporter for the *Detroit Journal,* organized the nation's first convention bureau, originally named The Detroit Convention & Businessmen's League. Carmichael was an innovator and reported: "Originally the idea of spending money to bring conventions to a city was so unheard of that even a hotel man could not see it." Soon after the bureau was organized he further commented: "Now, even the bellboys are wise."

By 1914 the organization, renamed the Detroit Convention and Tourist's Bureau, was an astounding success. J. Lee Barrett, a former passenger agent for the Baltimore & Ohio Railroad, took over as secretary/treasurer. Referred to as "a man of great dreams," he was to run the bureau until 1952. By 1914 several other cities nationwide had formed bureaus modeled after the one in Detroit.

World War I interrupted the flow of convention business everywhere, but the rapid development of the automobile industry set Detroit apart as its population soared. Growth accelerated during the 1920s with many new hotels constructed

to accommodate the vast numbers of visitors. The bureau responded with an information booth on the Campus Martius to welcome the city's thousands of delegates and tourists, a monthly newsletter, and a massive advertising and promotional campaign.

The strong foundation established in the Roaring '20s helped sustain visitor activity during the Great Depression. Seeing the need for larger facilities, the bureau first lobbied in 1919 for the establishment of a civic center. The plans included a Veteran's Memorial Hall, a Labor Hall, and a combined city-county Administration Building, in addition to a Convention Hall, all to be built at the foot of Woodward Avenue on the Detroit River. In 1950 the first building, the Veteran's Memorial Building, opened.

In 1952 Herbert E. Boning succeeded J. Lee Barrett. Boning had just assisted in promoting a convention hall in Kansas City. By 1960 Cobo Hall was open; the following year Detroit enjoyed the biggest convention year in its history. Len Rolston took over as head of the bureau in 1963. He fought and was successful in reforming Michigan's Sunday liquor laws—now conventioneers could enjoy drinks on Sunday.

The first visitor information center of the Detroit Convention and Tourist's Bureau, circa 1923.

By 1977, when Ron Steffens was named president of the Metropolitan Detroit Convention and Visitors Bureau, Detroit was enjoying a Renaissance City image. This led to the successful bid for the 1980 Republican National Convention and the 1982 Super Bowl, held at the Pontiac Silverdome, while William McLaughlin was bureau president. Under McLaughlin's leadership the bureau grew. It soon had staff devoted to group tour development and corporate meetings, in addition to convention sales. All the departments had a common goal—to bring people to Detroit.

At the bureau's 50th anniversary, Charles B. King, an original member of the Detroit Convention League commented: "Perhaps there are two events which took place at the same time some 50 years ago that have made a lasting impression upon the City of Detroit and the nation. Namely, the formation of a convention and tourist bureau and the driving of the first horseless carriage on the streets of Detroit." Of course, King was the driver of that first vehicle!

AMWAY GRAND PLAZA HOTEL

The Amway Grand Plaza Hotel in downtown Grand Rapids is the fourth hotel to occupy the site. The first, Sweet's Hotel, built in 1868 by Martin S. Sweet, established a reputation for fine dining by featuring two famous chefs from the resort hotels of Newport, Rhode Island.

In 1870 T.H. Lyon, Jr., bought the hotel and had it raised about five feet to solve the recurring problem of Grand River floods. A fire, changes in management, and a default to the bank plagued the hotel until 1902, when J. Boyd Pantlind took it over, remodeled, and renamed it Hotel Pantlind. The operating plan was changed, making the Pantlind one of the first hotels outside the largest cities to adopt the European plan.

The new Amway Grand Plaza Hotel in downtown Grand Rapids now has a modern tower in addition to the former Pantlind Hotel (behind the tower).

Grand Rapids was a booming furniture capital, and the newly outfitted hotel opened in time for the June Furniture Market in 1902 with 97 well-furnished, spacious rooms. Two additions brought the number of rooms to 149 by 1909, but the growth of the Furniture Market and Grand Rapids led to the formation of the Pantlind Hotel Building Company. Following three years of study, a new hotel was started in 1912.

Built in two sections, the new north wing was completed before the old hotel was razed to make room for the south wing, affording continuous service. The new Pantlind Hotel opened on New Year's Day 1916 with 550 rooms. Pantlind's son, Fred Z., joined the hotel in 1916, became manager in 1918, and president at his father's death in 1922. Those were heady years in Grand Rapids, and by 1924 an additional 200 rooms were built. The Pantlind achieved many firsts, such as installing the initial cafeteria in a large hotel and an entire floor of oversize beds. By 1925 seasoned travelers were said to have proclaimed the Pantlind one of the 10 finest hotels in the United States.

For several years the hotel continued to flourish, but furniture styles changed and manufacturing moved south, and the US 16 and US 131 bypasses were built around the city. The proud old Pantlind showed its age.

In 1978 the Amway Corporation bought the Pantlind with plans to create

Sweet's Hotel, built in 1868, was the original hotel on the site of the Hotel Pantlind, which is now the Amway Grand Plaza Hotel.

(Inset) In 1925 the Pantlind was "one of the 10 finest hotels in America" as this clipping from The Grand Rapids Press *indicated.*

a first-class hotel complex that, combined with the new civic center, would transform that part of Grand Rapids into a major convention center. A restoration returned the "grand old lady" to its former elegance.

Carleton Varney "looked at the building with an eye toward preserving the Adam style and classic details." Composition gold leaf was used on the domed ceilings of the mezzanine, lobby, and ballroom at a cost of approximately $70,000. Two gracious 500-pound chandeliers with cast brass bodies and strands of Austrian-made crystal beads in the style of the early twentieth century were completely rehabilitated at a cost of $8,000.

Containing 287 rooms and a totally new 29-story tower with an additional 287 rooms, the Amway Grand Plaza Hotel had an opening on October 14, 1981, that was truly a worldwide event. Guests included U.S. President Ronald Reagan, Canadian Prime Minister Pierre Trudeau, and Mexican President Portillo, marking the first meeting of North American leadership in the United States.

ERVIN INDUSTRIES, INC.

On February 16, 1920, the late John F. Ervin (1883-1959) incorporated a jobbing foundry as Ervin Foundry and Manufacturing Company in Adrian, Michigan. The principal product of the new business with 35 employees was grey iron castings. The firm also produced tumbling stars, which were a popular medium for cleaning castings at that time. The enterprise quickly established a reputation for excellence in the products manufactured and service. In the 1930s the corporate headquarters was moved from Adrian, Michigan, to Ann Arbor, Michigan. That theme of excellence established at the outset by John Ervin continues to dominate the actions and thinking of those employed by the firm today.

Another of the noteworthy qualities of John Ervin was his expectation of change. When centrifugal blast-cleaning equipment was introduced, he adapted his business accordingly. In 1936 Ervin established the Alloy Metal Abrasive Division, later renamed the Amasteel Division. By so doing he diverted a substantial portion of his foundry capacity to the manufacture of shot and grit, which he recognized as the cleaning materials of the future.

The demand for shot and grit was so great that the production of castings and tumbling stars was soon abandoned. John Ervin recognized the rapid breakdown of chilled iron abrasives and the high maintenance associated with them. He was determined to find an alternative, and, on January 31, 1939, U.S. Patent No. 2,145,756 was granted. Amasteel, the original steel shot, was born and protected. The acceptance of Amasteel was rapid and, while many other manufacturers are producing steel shot today, the excellence and superiority of Amasteel have remained unchallenged. Indeed, Ervin Industries is the largest producer of steel shot in the world, with joint ventures in Mexico and South Korea, and licensees in Spain, South Africa, and Australia, as well as its own production facilities in the United States that ship more than 90,000 tons annually.

In the years following World War II the company introduced another first in the metalworking industry. It was an abrasive test machine that duplicated the actions of production blast-cleaning equipment in a

fraction of the time. The Ervin test machine is now the standard testing device for the industry. In 1952 Ervin pioneered and perfected the use of electric arc furnaces in producing steel abrasives. The process is still in use around the world.

In 1978, recognizing growth in the service economy, the company established the Ervin Leasing Division. Leases are written on a variety of commercial and industrial machinery, including medical and dental equipment, industrial lift trucks, computers, office copiers, and telephone equipment. Ervin Leasing Division branch offices have been established in Grand Rapids, Michigan, as well as in Ohio, Indiana, and Illinois. Diversifying into the

John F. Ervin, founder of Ervin Industries, Inc.

financial services area is an extension of the philosophy of the company's founder.

Under the leadership of former president James A. Pearson and current president William R. Penrice, Ervin Industries has continued to flourish. Since 1970 dollar volume has increased by 700 percent, and the company has tripled its manufacturing facilities and has extended its market base to every continent. By remaining alert to sweeping industrial development Ervin Industries, Inc., will continue to expand its role as a leading supplier of products and services to international industry.

FIRST FEDERAL OF MICHIGAN

The modest doors of First Federal Savings and Loan Association of Detroit first opened for business on October 2, 1934. Its quarters consisted of one small room at 150 West Fort Street, a site now occupied by the Federal Reserve Bank, and furnishings and fixtures were valued at $54.72. Two days later the company was granted Insurance Certificate No. 2 from the newly formed Federal Savings and Loan Insurance Corporation (FSLIC).

The establishment of First Federal was the vision and work of one man, Walter Gehrke, at the time president of Detroit Mortgage and Contract Company. Gehrke was troubled and discouraged by the virtual lack of credit for anything including the saving of one's home. Therefore, when he read in the *Detroit Free Press* of June 10, 1933, about the passage of the Home Owner's Loan Act by Congress, he moved into action.

Gehrke boarded the next train to Washington to find out about the new law. He returned to Detroit, managed to convince 60 friends to sign a hand-written petition believed to have been No. 1, then learned that the government had printed standard petition forms, and that it had to be done all over. Eventually he had a new petition with 104 signatures, and pledges for $8,000 in contributions. A charter was granted December 13, 1933, and shareholders met for the first time on January 10, 1934, to adopt bylaws and elect directors. The minutes of the April board meeting proudly noted that mortgage loans totaling $15,800 had been approved.

By October 1934, when the Fort Street office was opened, assets had climbed to $100,000. Progress continued during the hard times of the 1930s, and the first branch opened in 1939 in Highland Park. That geographic expansion, the first for a savings and loan in Michigan, set an example that has been followed since with great success. Soon after the branch was opened, First Federal took another major step and in 1942 moved its headquarters to a former bank building at the corner of Griswold and Lafayette. Assets at the time of the move were over $12 million.

First Federal continued to grow, and

First Federal opened its first branch on October 6, 1939, in Highland Park.

when Walter Gehrke died in December 1963, First Federal had passed the half-billion-dollar milestone. Larger quarters were clearly needed, and First Federal reaffirmed its commitment to downtown Detroit by purchasing the Majestic Building, Detroit's first skyscraper. The new landmark building, constructed of dark granite and glare-reflecting glass, was opened in August 1965. Overseeing the building and opening of the new headquarters as chairman of the board was Hans Gehrke, Jr., a nephew of First Federal's founder. When Hans Gehrke, Jr., retired in 1978, First Federal had nearly $3 billion in assets.

Branching represents a significant part of First Federal's growth. Initial branching occurred in Michigan both through opening new offices and through mergers. First Federal Savings of Owosso in 1976, Kalamazoo Savings and Loan Association in 1981, and Kentwood Savings and Loan Association in 1982 were added to give First Federal new offices in strategic markets. Branches have been added in Grand Rapids, Lansing, Ann Arbor, and Boyne City. Offices in Michigan now number 84.

In March 1983 First Federal became the first Michigan financial institution to venture out of state when it acquired and merged two savings and loans in Newport News, Virginia, to form Bay Savings Bank, FSB. Bay Savings operates 15 offices in Richmond, Southeastern Virginia, and suburban New Orleans, Louisiana. In October 1983 a savings and loan was acquired in Columbia, South Carolina. The new Omni Savings Bank, FSB, has

The First Federal Building today. Completed in 1965, it won a Design in Steel Award from the American Iron and Steel Institute.

five offices.

James A. Aliber became chairman of the board of First Federal in 1979. Growth has continued and, in a reflection of broader markets, the name was changed to First Federal of Michigan in 1982. The following year First Federal of Michigan converted to a capital stock form of ownership, netting new capital to support future growth, increasing funds available for lending, expanding customer services, and facilitating future acquisitions. Far from its humble beginnings with Insurance Certificate No. 2, First Federal of Michigan, with more than $11 billion in assets, has grown to be the largest savings and loan outside California, and one of the top 10 in the United States.

GSE, INC.

GSE, Inc., of Farmington Hills was founded in 1967. Its cofounders, Ralph S. Shoberg and Macit Gurol, started out in that classic American way—moonlighting engineers working in a basement.

By 1968 progress on the development of several inventions led to moving the fledgling company to a storefront location on Six Mile Road. Financial resources were gathered by lining up 23 shareholders. Shoberg knew the investors well, providing an early harmony and operational unity to the new firm. The original board of directors was chosen to provide a wide spectrum of technical and business knowledge. They were J. Lawrence Buell, Jr., Eugene Andre, Samuel E. Gawne, James K. Fulks, I. Macit Gurol, and Shoberg. A seventh major player was patent attorney Martin J. Adelman, now at Wayne State University Law School, who helped GSE, Inc., acquire the first of its many patents.

From its origin GSE, Inc., has been a high-technology, precision equipment builder, where engineering and research and development play the key roles. Attention to detail and carefully monitored procedures are essential. GSE, Inc., has gained a wide reputation as a lean and highly disciplined organization where each part fits precisely, similar to the equipment it builds.

Engineers tend to be conservative in general, and GSE, Inc., reflects that philosophy in its financial affairs. Borrowing has been held to a minimum, and expansions of product line and plant and equipment have been internally financed almost completely. Early successes with its product lines helped the company enjoy a 56-percent compounded growth rate over

a period of 13 years.

In 1973 a new, custom-built facility was constructed at 23640 Research Drive, Farmington Hills, to fit the needs of the rapidly growing enterprise. By 1987 the company employed 135 people.

The first rotary socket wrench torque transducer and portable peak meter for the testing of pneumatic nutrunners were developed by GSE, Inc., in 1968. Research with these new products led to universal acceptance of dynamic measurement of torque applied to fasteners. The art and science of electronic fastener monitoring on the production line began from this innovative combination.

Vehicle manufacturers in the United States, Europe, and Japan now standardize on GSE portable and automatic torque systems. More than 50,000 GSE reaction torque transducers are installed on air and electric nutrunners throughout the world.

Fastener force transducers are miniature strain gage load cells developed specifically for the measurement of fastener clamping forces. GSE, Inc.'s, patented design provides high stiffness in a small envelope, making these transducers ideally suited for static and dynamic measurement on fasteners, tie rods, and other similar structural test applications where space limitations exist. GSE, Inc., also manufactures fastener performance recorders for the ongoing measurement of torque, force, and pressure.

When GSE, Inc., developed and patented the "Floating Beam" weigh scale concept, it created a milestone in the history of scale technology. Other electronic flexure bases have used flexure straps (a concept patented in 1888) and summing levers to a load cell, or vibrating

GSE, Inc.'s, engineering and manufacturing staff and facility, where instruments, sensors, electronic weigh scales, and industrial automation process control systems are produced.

wire to measure an applied load to ground. The unsurpassed performance of the Floating Beam scale base is a direct result of the simplicity of the strain gage measuring section, which is isolated, hence "floating" with respect to all other elements of the scale structure. In addition to on-center and off-center accuracies unobtainable on conventional scales, the Floating Beam scales are engineered for rough industrial use, designed to resist overloading and impacting.

GSE, Inc., also manufactures and markets many other precision instruments for industry worldwide. Included are electronic weigh systems, torque/force monitors and controls, load cells, strain cells, seat belt transducers, tire rolling resistance sensors, and V-belt and parking brake tension-control systems.

In 1981 GSE, Inc., merged with CORE Industries, a New York stock exchange company located in Bloomfield Hills, Michigan. Today GSE, Inc., continues to prosper, providing innovative solutions for industrial automation and measurement requirements. Exports to Europe, Japan, and most industrialized countries of the world continue to be an important percentage of total sales.

Harold G. Munn has been vice-president of sales since 1972. The original engineer/innovator/inventor/manager, Ralph S. Shoberg, continues as president, actively working with the team of talented individuals who have all contributed to the successs of GSE, Inc.

DOW CORNING CORPORATION

"Silicones" is becoming a household word thanks to Dow Corning Corporation, a *Fortune* 500 company headquartered in Midland, Michigan. Known today as the technology pioneer and world's leading producer of silicone products, the business was formed in 1943 to discover and develop practical uses for a group of man-made materials known as silicones. Dow Corning's parents are both illustrious companies: Corning Glass Works in Corning, New York, teamed its silicone research with The Dow Chemical Company's manufacturing technology in a 50-50 joint venture.

The term "silicones" was coined by chemist F.S. Kipping of Nottingham University, England, during his nineteenth-century experiments with compounds made from silicon. There was no lack of raw material for Kipping's research as silicon is a component of silica, the main ingredient of quartz or common sand. Silica is one of the most abundant elements found on earth.

By the 1930s Corning researchers including Dr. J. Franklin Hyde—the father of commercial silicones—began investigating the practical applications of silicones with respect to their remarkable qualities such as water repellency, oxidation resistance, heat stability, and favorable dielectric properties. Scientists found they could successfully make silicones in a variety of forms: fluid, rubberlike, or hard as rock, with thousands of uses, from space exploration to spare parts for the human body. The versatility of silicones is re-markable; for example, they are used in cosmetics, antiperspirants, car polishes, textiles, electronics, food processing, and medical applications, to name a few.

One example of silicone's durability occurred when the company helped preserve the Statue of Liberty during a major restoration in 1986. Experts sought a sealant that would seal and protect the Lady's 80-ton copper skin. Independent researchers found only one sealant that would pass the test—a Dow Corning high-performance building sealant frequently used on skyscrapers. Dow Corning donated the product and company expertise.

As Dow Corning scientists have found new ways to benefit mankind with silicones, the firm has grown with more than 25 manufacturing facilities worldwide. However, Michigan continues to be important to Dow Corning's future. Its first and largest manufacturing facility is located in Midland, Michigan. The Dow Corning Center, company headquarters, and a specialty elastomers research and development center are located in Bay County. Two other key manufacturing facilities are found in Saginaw County—the Medical Products Plant and a joint venture company, Hemlock Semiconductor Corporation, a producer of poly-crystalline silicon, the basic raw material for electronic components.

There is another reason Michigan is important to Dow Corning. Much of the firm's research is done in Michigan, and this represents a substantial commitment to its future. "We have invested more in research and development in silicone technology," says Donald R. Weyenberg, vice-president and director of research and development, "than all the rest of the world's silicone manufacturers. Our future growth will continue to depend on new concepts from research."

From the company's inception, management and employees have believed in operating in a socially responsible way. Of particular note has been Dow Corning's long commitment to support education, including business education partnerships. One early example includes the Dow Corning Christmas Card Design Contest, a partnership that helped start Midland's community arts council and encouraged student creativity and artistic excellence.

Since the 1950s the firm has spearheaded many programs in support of education, including the formation of a nonprofit corporation between business and education to raise science and math understanding in lower Michigan, the Mid-Michigan Minority Pre-engineering Program.

Dow Corning Corporation recognizes that people are its ultimate strength and most valued asset. The lifelong partnership between innovative people and education holds the key for pursuing new and imaginative endeavors.

The Dow Corning Center—the firm's world headquarters, located in Williams Township, Bay County.

WKBD-TV50

During its brief 22-year history Detroit's WKBD-TV (Channel 50) has changed quite a few television viewers' minds about what to expect from an independent television station. "People thought independents ran nothing but 'Gilligan's Island' reruns, sign on to sign off," WKBD's program manager, Paul Prange, says.

The station, which debuted in 1965 with 30 employees and essentially an all-sports lineup, has grown through innovative programming and unique on-air personalities to become the nation's top-rated UHF independent television station.

Under the stewardship of the Kaiser Broadcasting Co., WKBD grew from its early format to the point in 1969 where it achieved better ratings than CKLW-TV in neighboring Windsor, Ontario, Canada. This occasion marked the first time a UHF independent station had pulled better overall ratings than a directly competitive VHF station.

WKBD gathered momentum in the late 1970s when its vice-president and general manager, George H. Williams, led a shift away from sedate evening talk shows to such popular syndicated programs as "M*A*S*H," "Three's Company," "Happy Days," and "Fame." The station's 8 p.m. to 10 p.m. time slot, one of three in which WKBD ranks at the top

WKBD-TV vice-president and general manager George H. Williams, responsible for a number of programming changes in the late 1970s, joined the station in 1975.

of the nation's independent stations, became the home for such movies as the critically-acclaimed *The Deer Hunter*, which WKBD aired unedited.

A bent toward unusual promotions was illustrated in WKBD's 1985 presentation of the movie *Godzilla '85*. Though not blessed with an Academy Award caliber film, the station scored a ratings coup by promoting Godzilla as "the ultimate party animal" with dolls and T-shirts.

One of the station's hallmarks has

been its history of colorful personalities, including controversial talk show host Lou Gordon and Bill Kennedy, who hosted an afternoon movie show. It was on Gordon's show in 1967 that former Michigan Governor George Romney said the generals and diplomatic corps in Vietnam "brainwashed" him during a trip there. One political observer said the remark cost Romney a shot at receiving the Republican Party's 1968 presidential nomination.

After years under the wing of Kaiser Broadcasting, Field Enterprises purchased WKBD in 1977, and Atlanta-based Cox Enterprises Inc. took over seven years later. Cox Enterprises, Inc., is a family-owned diversified communications company composed of newspapers, television and radio stations, cable systems, and Manheim auto auctions.

While poor signal reception by viewers without the proper UHF antennae hurt early ratings, the recent proliferation of cable television throughout Michigan has provided a solid boost for WKBD.

Currently based in the Detroit suburb of Southfield, WKBD-TV will triple its operating space as it is planning an imminent move into a new facility in early 1988.

Controversial WKBD-TV talk show host Lou Gordon featured guests ranging from Frank Sinatra, Jr., to former Michigan Governor George Romney. Gordon's show was syndicated in 1971.

The new WKBD-TV50 headquarters, featuring state-of-the-art technical facilities, is on West Eleven Mile Road. The Austin Company of Cleveland is responsible for the design, construction, and interiors of the 56,000-square-foot building, scheduled for completion in early 1988.

SPARTAN PLASTICS

Holt, Michigan, is a quiet little town just south of Michigan's bustling capital city, Lansing. Holt is home to many state government employees who enjoy the amenities of a small town with the proximity to all that Lansing and nearby Michigan State University offer. And it is also the home of Spartan Plastics, one of Michigan's success stories in its history of small, family-owned enterprises.

Spartan Plastics is one of the world's leading suppliers of pin striping, decals, and body molding. From automobiles to aerospace to speedboats, Spartan Plastics leads the way in developing, manufacturing, and delivering quality products for both the professional and amateur customizer. The company's various product lines are marketed throughout the United States and in 87 countries around the world. In fact, up to 15 percent of its products annually are for the export market.

That was certainly not the case, nor, for that matter, even the dream, when Chuck Krauss and his father, Leslie, started Spartan Plastics in 1960. That year they had put together $15,000 in capital and equipment and began operations in Leslie's garage. A year later they introduced their revolutionary auto striping tape to the

Chuck Krauss at an early 1960s display for Spartan Plastics.

Leslie and Chuck Krauss—where it all started—in Leslie's garage, circa 1960.

automotive aftermarket.

Now Spartan Plastics is housed in a 150,000-square-foot complex that has grown steadily in the past 20 years. Its 130 employees—plus 20 more at its Canadian affiliate—work in a recession-proof business, says Chuck Krauss. "Other than the local school system, we are the largest employer in the area," he emphasizes. "And outside of GM-Oldsmobile, we're the Lansing area's largest shipper of outgoing freight."

Spartan Plastics has six distinct divisions: Trimbrite produces items for the do-it-yourself customizer; Pro Stripe specializes in the auto repair shop area; Sport Stripe concentrates on recreational vehicles and marine trade; Spar-Cal is specifically for industrial products; McLean Screen Print is the company's graphics design subsidiary; and Extrusions, which are produced at the company's branches in Vancouver, Washington, and London, Ontario, Canada.

Spartan employees enjoy a well-supplied and pleasant working environment, where their suggestions are encouraged through employee committees. Krauss predicts a $28-million year for 1986-1987. "We're the type of employer," he stresses, "who represents the bulk of the state's employers. We're not big but we provide good, steady work. We pay our taxes and deliver what we promise."

Spartan Plastics has always operated on that premise, whether in the Krauss' garage in the 1960s or competing worldwide in the 1980s.

LIBERTY STATE BANK & TRUST

Liberty State Bank & Trust's main office in Hamtramck.

Joseph and Stanislaw Chronowski organized Liberty State Bank in July 1918 in the city of Hamtramck, Michigan. The bank was approved for operation with $100,000 in capital and opened for business on September 23, 1918.

The bank, originally located on Joseph Campau near Norwalk, moved to a location directly below the Chronowski family residence at the corner of Joseph Campau and Norwalk in 1920. The new headquarters had formerly been a saloon owned and operated by Joseph Chronowski, prior to Prohibition.

Liberty State Bank proved sound by surviving the bank run of 1930, when 50 percent of its deposits were withdrawn in two days. The bank was closed by the Banking Holiday, February 11, 1933, and relicensed to open on January 22, 1935. All assessments were met: Liberty State Bank was one of the few Hamtramck area banks to reopen.

The bank moved to its present main office location at the corner of Joseph Campau and Holbrook in 1936. The building, which provided additional space for the rapidly growing bank, was previously occupied by the North End General Market and a bank that closed in the early part of 1930. Brass doors, marble walls, and an ornate second-floor ceiling are reminders of a past era.

Joseph Chronowski died in November 1958 and was succeeded as president by his son, Alois. Liberty State Bank continued to grow and prosper. As of December 31, 1958, the capital of the bank had increased to $1.1 million.

Liberty State Bank began to expand in 1964. A $250,000 drive-in facility was added to its main office, and the first branch office outside Hamtramck was opened in Sterling Heights in 1965.

The controlling interest in Liberty State Bank was purchased by the Hamtramck Investment Company of Birmingham, Michigan, in April 1968. Alois Chronowski continued on as president, although the bank was no longer a family-owned concern.

Gerald M. Salkowski was hired in July of that year as vice-president of operations after previous banking experience with the National Bank of Detroit. He was promoted to executive vice-president in February 1969, and elected president at the end of the year. At age 28, Salkowski became one of the youngest bank presidents in the United States. The bank received approval from the Financial Institutions Bureau of the State of Michigan to change its name to Liberty State Bank & Trust in 1970.

A new era for the bank began when Morris Fenkell, a prominent Detroit businessman, and Salkowski, president of Liberty State Bank & Trust, spearheaded the formation of United Midwest Equity, Inc., the second bank holding company formed in Michigan: United Midwest Equity, Inc., acquired the bank on September 13, 1971. The holding company was comprised of local citizens, businessmen, employees, and officers of the bank. As of June 30, 1971, Liberty State Bank & Trust had total assets exceeding $60.8 million, total deposits over $56.3 million, and total capital in excess of $3.2 million.

The name of the holding company was changed from United Midwest Equity, Inc., to United Midwest Bancorporation, Ltd., in 1980. The impressive growth record of the holding company and its subsidiary banks, Liberty State Bank & Trust and Liberty Bank-Oakland, is attributable to sound financial management and a philosophy of providing quality service to customers.

Liberty State Bank & Trust opened six branches between 1971 and 1981, bringing its total offices in Wayne, Oakland, and Macomb counties to eight. Assets, as of June 30, 1986, were more than $250 million, return on assets was 1.2 percent, and return on equity was 17.1 percent. Liberty State Bank & Trust is ranked among the top 7 percent of all commercial banks in the United States in asset size. The bank is a member of the Federal Deposit Insurance Corporation and the Federal Reserve System.

Liberty Bank-Oakland, a subsidiary bank, opened on May 24, 1982, with almost $1.8 million in capital. Assets

Morris Fenkell, chairman of the board.

Gerald M. Salkowski, president.

reached $18 million and deposits totaled more than $15 million by the end of the year. Liberty Bank-Oakland was profitable within the first seven months of operation, exhibiting phenomenal success. Assets as of June 30, 1986, were approximately $73.8 million, return on assets was 1.3 percent, and return on equity was 19.5 percent. Liberty Bank-Oakland's president is Delbert F. Ruth. The bank is located at 801 West Big Beaver Road in Troy.

United Midwest Bancorporation, Ltd., opened a $10-million Operations Center office complex in Troy in 1982. Consolidated assets as of September 30, 1986, totaled $386 million. The six-story, 66,000-square-foot building, located at 801 West Big Beaver Road, is connected

to a three-story, 38,000-square-foot building by a common atrium. The building houses the holding company headquarters, executive and administrative offices, Liberty Bank-Oakland banking facilities, and the Operations Center for both subsidiary banks.

Morris Fenkell is chairman of the board of United Midwest Bancorporation, Ltd., Liberty State Bank & Trust, and

Liberty Bank-Oakland. He has been a member of the board of directors of Liberty State Bank & Trust since 1965, and was formerly a principal shareholder of City Foods Service Company, Inc., president of Fenkell Packing Company, and president of Raleigh House.

Gerald M. Salkowski is president and vice-chairman of the board of directors of United Midwest Bancorporation, Ltd., and Liberty State Bank & Trust, and vice-chairman of the board of Liberty Bank-Oakland. He has been in the banking industry for more than 22 years.

Liberty State Bank & Trust attributes its success to providing quality personal service to corporate and retail customers, and specializes in serving small- to medium-size business firms. Financial services include commercial, consumer, and mortgage loans; credit cards; personal and commercial checking accounts; time deposits and savings accounts; safekeeping and custodial services; specialized corporate services; and international services. The Liberty Investment Center provides discount brokerage and precious metals services, thus enabling customers to conveniently handle more of their investment transactions through the bank.

Liberty State Bank & Trust's Operations Center office complex in Troy.

THE DOW CHEMICAL COMPANY

In the 1890s Main Street in Midland, Michigan, featured boardwalks, saloons, and unpaved streets.

When Herbert Dow got off the train at Midland, Michigan, in 1889, the chemical industry of Michigan was not even a gleam in his eye. Today it is Michigan's fourth-largest economic resource in terms of jobs and income, only surpassed by automobiles, tourism, and agricultural products.

Planting a major new industry in the state was not what the 23-year-old Dow had in mind. He was looking for a way to use a process he had invented to extract bromine from the salt brines that underlie Michigan. Bromine was the main constituent of most of the popular medicines of that day and in demand for new uses such as photographic films.

His investigations indicated the brines in the Midland area—he had collected samples from the general Ohio-Michigan area—were best for his purposes. With borrowed funds from classmates and faculty friends at Case Institute in Cleveland, from which he had graduated the previous year, he set out for Michigan.

In the following eight years he founded three different companies, two in Midland and one in Ohio, with disappointing results. On his fourth try, in 1897, he hit pay dirt, establishing The Dow Chemical Company—today one of the largest chemical firms in the world, and the second-largest in the United States. The firm's world headquarters are still in Midland, and the original, or "home" plant, is the largest employer in its area.

He started with bromine, but Dow was already researching the possibilities of other chemical components of the Michigan brines—chlorine, calcium, iodine, magnesium—and soon began to use them as chemical building blocks for a widening stream of products. Today the company manufactures some 2,300 items, most of them still chemically related to the components of brine.

Dow put down deep roots in Midland. He married a Midland schoolteacher, Grace Ball, built a house, and settled down to building a family and a company.

In the World War I era, though the firm was barely 20 years old, it was thrust into national prominence. Midland was the nation's largest supplier of phenol, one of Dow's newer products, and with the war it became vital for armaments manufacture overnight. The government sent soldiers to protect Dow's phenol plant.

After the war Herbert Dow presided

Herbert H. Dow in 1897, the year he founded The Dow Chemical Company.

over another spectacular period of growth and continued his development of new products. He was showered with honors from fellow scientists, businessmen, and the nation. In 1930, barely 65, he was stricken with an illness that shortly proved fatal.

Midlanders stood in the rain and wept as the train bearing his body pulled in from the Mayo Clinic, where he had gone for an operation. They remembered how he had got off at that same station 41 years earlier and set about changing the face of east-central Michigan.

Those who mourned included the

distinguished corps of chemists, engineers, and executives he had assembled—E.O. Barstow, the "father of magnesium;" Earl W. Bennett, a onetime lumber camp cook who became Dow's financial genius; Charles J. Strosacker, developer of saran and other materials; Mark W. Putnam, who made the company into the nation's largest producer of aspirin; L.L. "Zip" Ryden, inventor of latex paint; John J. Grebe, who developed secondary oil recovery; and others. "I can find a hundred men to tell me an idea won't work," Herbert Dow once said, "What I want are men who will *make* it work."

He was succeeded by his son Willard. Willard Dow continued to organize new

Two Dow chemists on an outing, Lewis Ward and Charles Strosacker, look across the Tittabawassee River toward the chemical plant that was to become the world's largest. Circa 1908

research laboratories and build new plants to produce the products being invented: new families of plastics, everything from Styrofoam to Saran Wrap; modern farm chemicals; metals; textiles; and new products of all kinds that provide the chemical undergirding of modern life.

In the 1930s Willard Dow and his colleagues accomplished one of the most spectacular industrial feats of modern times—they succeeded in extracting the metal magnesium from seawater in commercial quantities. He built plants in Texas that now provide most of the nation's supply of that metal. It marked the first and only time the seas have been successfully mined for a metal. During World War II the ultralight magnesium was a key to U.S. air power, and so was Dow's development of styrene, without which there would have been no sty-

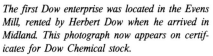

The first Dow enterprise was located in the Evens Mill, rented by Herbert Dow when he arrived in Midland. This photograph now appears on certificates for Dow Chemical stock.

rene-butadiene rubber.

When Willard Dow was killed in a plane crash in 1949, his brother-in-law, Leland Doan, took over the helm. He, in turn, was succeeded by his son, Herbert D. "Ted" Doan, in 1962. Throughout this period the firm continued to pour ever larger amounts of resources into chemical research, the building of new plants, and corporate growth.

Although its plants and offices now straddle the globe, with manufacturing plants in more than 30 countries and sales offices covering the civilized world, Dow Chemical's headquarters remain in Midland; in Michigan it also has plants in Ludington and Bay City.

Along the way the operation has dropped outmoded products as new ones are introduced: In Michigan's sesquicentennial year Dow will be dropping the original product that brought Herbert Dow to Michigan, and shutting down the brinewells that he scattered across some 2,500 square miles of Michigan as the major source of the nation's bromine. "Not to worry," current Dow president Paul F. Oreffice commented recently. "We have plenty of new products coming along to replace it."

Herbert Dow probably wouldn't mind either. He was a restless man, and he always said the worst thing a company can do is stand still.

237

INDUSTRIAL METAL PRODUCTS CORPORATION

Precision and quality have always been the goals of automobile producers, especially in the area of tool and die manufacturing. As the auto industry grew in Michigan, it created a constant demand for workmanship that was often met by small satellite shops. Industrial Metal Products Corporation (IMPCO) is a good example of this system at work.

Lansing, Michigan, is the state's capital, but it is also the home of a diversified industrial base, including the Oldsmobile Division of General Motors Corporation. In 1937 IMPCO started to supply Chevrolet with steel parts. Edward Judge, Sr., and Leonard Deason—along

The Industrial Metal Products Corporation (IMPCO) plant on West St. Joseph Street in Lansing.

with a handful of tool and die specialists—began operations in a converted dairy. By the 1940s World War II and the company's reputation spurred its growth. In 1951 it boasted 100 employees and a 24,000-square-foot building complex. Four years later the firm moved into even larger quarters.

Microfinishing is an essential element in auto parts manufacturing, and IMPCO has become a leader in the field. It also perfected nondestructive testing machines, eliminating the need to destroy parts to test for flaws. Both advances pushed the company's auto-related business to 60 percent of its total output by the 1970s.

The 1970s, however, were not good years in America's auto industry.

The owners and president of Industrial Metal Products Corporation. They are (from left to right, standing) James R. Clewley, vice-president/Ford sales and owner; Norman R. Judge, vice-president/marketing and owner; (seated) Edward E. Judge, Jr., vice-president/research and development and owner; Donald L. Judge, vice-president/estimating and owner; and John H. Greening, president and chief executive officer.

Nevertheless, despite some reverses, IMPCO continued to deliver what the auto builders wanted. But now engineering and laboratory skills came into play, and IMPCO brought Jack Greening on board to lead the company into the 1980s.

A Nikon microscope was installed in 1983, the same year a sophisticated surface finish measuring device was added to the growing technical work the company was asked to handle. In the next two years machines to measure circular and straightness accuracy were purchased. A permanent Quality Control Laboratory was constructed in 1985. Now the lab boasts a stereo microscope and detailed computer-aided testing equipment.

IMPCO is dedicated to microfinishing technology. It improves the geometry and surface condition of load-bearing parts. These alterations are measured in millionths of an inch, yet the results of IMPCO Generating Bearing Quality microfinishing are significant. They include microfinishing automotive crankshafts that increase horsepower, microfinishing small engine crankshafts that extend the lives of the product, microfinishing off-road equipment camshafts that permit superior warranties, and microfinishing compressor

crankshafts that boost energy efficiency.

In sum, IMPCO has responded to the demands of its industry. Moreover, its success emphasizes the belief of many that American skills in the area of precision tooling do not have to take second place to those of any other country's; among IMPCO's customers are enterprises in Germany and Japan.

Industrial Metal Products Corporation has maintained its reputation for

The research and development laboratory of Industrial Metal Products Corporation.

quality and skilled craftsmanship and even built on it. The results are in statistics everyone can understand; IMPCO's annual sales have grown from $7 million in 1984 to $17 million in 1986. And the future is as bright and clear as the finishes its machines create.

The computer-aided design facility—part of IMPCO's engineering department.

MICHIGAN ASSOCIATION OF SCHOOL BOARDS

The Michigan Association of School Boards (MASB) represents nearly 600 boards of education throughout the state, providing local governance for 99 percent of Michigan's schoolchildren. Guided by its 21-member board of directors, delegate assembly, and a variety of active committees, the association provides service, professional development opportunities, several sources of information, and a strong and unified voice for school boards throughout the state's K-12 system.

Representatives from K-12, intermediate (ISD), and primary/K-6 school districts, large and small, urban and rural, serve as the association's officers, representatives, and members. The organization has a staff of 26, headed by an executive director, Dr. Norman P. Weinheimer.

Over the past 50 years MASB's members and staff have worked closely with the legislature, the State Board and Department of Education, Michigan's colleges and universities, the federal government, and a variety of state and national educational associations to provide equal opportunities in education for Michigan's children.

A member of the National School Board Association, MASB stands out among other states in boardsmanship and other professional development programs and services. In its short history the Michigan Association of School Boards has been the innovator of many programs now considered essential by school board associations nationally.

MASB traces its roots to a small meeting, in 1940, at a kitchen table in Allendale, Ottawa County, Michigan. At that meeting a group of school board members from Kent, Ottawa, and Muskegon counties joined together to begin sharing resources and information for the betterment of rural schoolchildren. The kitchen table was in the home of Richard C. Tanis, a prominent figure in the history of the association, then a member of the Allendale Board of Education and later a 25-year member (24 as its president) of the Ottawa County/Ottawa Area ISD Board of Education.

Michigan's history of local school governance predates its statehood. Provisions for local control of public education were instituted by the Michigan Territorial

Council in 1837, when it abandoned centralized policy in favor of individual township-maintained schools. While neighboring school boards undoubtedly shared information on an informal basis, it was not until the 1940s, when an increasingly complex society required a more thorough education than small rural schools could offer, that school boards began to provide formalized, cooperative efforts to improve all schools.

The group of original counties grew slowly in its first few years. In 1945 the group organized as the State Rural School Boards Association. The following year some 600 rural school board members from the original Kent, Ottawa, and Muskegon counties were involved. That number grew to 29 counties in 1947, and 18 additional counties in the years shortly thereafter.

The association's general assembly voted in 1947 to change its name to the

From left are founder and longtime Michigan Association of School Boards (MASB) board member Dick Tanis, who was also MASB president from 1950 until 1952; Sid H. Sixma, MASB's first president (1948-1949) and longtime MASB executive director; and Everett Luce, who held the longest tenure as MASB president, serving from 1952 until 1956.

Michigan Rural School Boards Association, with the continuing emphasis "to protect and to promote the educational interests and welfare of the rural people of Michigan." The growth of the group required the hiring of its first executive secretary, William Speer of Caledonia. The president was Sid H. Sixma of Muskegon, who would become the executive secretary for many years, retiring in 1960. The acting secretary was Tanis, who would be president from 1950 to 1952 and remain with the association's board of directors until retirement in 1977.

The year 1947 was also a landmark

year for the association's communications efforts. MASB adopted "The Appleblossom" as its official publication. The monthly newsletter, produced by Central Michigan College (now University), Mt. Pleasant, was an information source for the wide range of organizations and individuals who had a particular interest in rural education in the state. "The Appleblossom" later became the "Michigan School Board Journal," and, after 40 years of continuous publication, it now reaches more than 9,000 school board members, educators, and others interested in education.

The association's communications today also include publication of the biweekly newsletter "Headlines," as well as many special topic publications and videotapes.

In 1948 the association held its first statewide conference. The annual Fall Conference celebrated its 38th anniversary in 1986 with more than 1,400 school board members, administrators, and others in attendance. The Fall Conference has been joined by the MASB-sponsored National Education Conference and a Mid-Winter Conference, as well as a series of four Boardsmanship Academies in the late summer to assist newly elected (as well as veteran) board members. A variety of special topic workshops of interest to board members and administrators is also offered. The Fall Conference is now held jointly with members of the Michigan Association of School Administrators every other year.

The organization's early emphasis on strictly rural youngsters was broadened in February, 1949, when its members voted to change its name to the Michigan Association of School Boards, and its purpose and goals to the betterment of *all* Michigan youngsters. Two factors contributing to this broadened appeal were the dwindling number of small rural schools in the state, which had decreased dramatically in the 1950s, and the impact the association had had on legislation and federal education laws: Urban school boards wanted to join!

MASB has always had a strong and continuing relationship with higher education in Michigan. Universities and colleges were instrumental in its early

In 1974 then-Governor William G. Milliken (at podium) took part in the dedication of the headquarters building for the Michigan Association of School Boards in downtown Lansing.

development, with Central Michigan College's part in "The Appleblossom" only one example. The association's headquarters, first in temporary quarters in Lansing, moved for a short time to the campus of the University of Michigan in Ann Arbor, and later moved to the campus of Michigan State University in East Lansing before moving off campus. In 1974 MASB occupied its current headquarters building at 421 West Kalamazoo Street in the heart of the state capital, Lansing.

In 1970 Dr. Norman P. Weinheimer, who had been superintendent of Grand Rapids Schools, assumed the position of MASB executive director. Much of the success and strength of the Michigan Association of School Boards is due to Dr. Weinheimer's long involvement, as well as that of officers and members, who have given many years of commitment to both the association and to their local and intermediate school districts.

In the past 15 years the executive committee has supervised a dramatic growth in school services. The MASB-affiliated insurance group, School Employers Trust/School Employers Group (SET/SEG), begun in 1971 to reduce skyrocketing school insurance costs, was the first such school board association insurance program in the nation. MASB's Legal Trust Fund, helping to pay legal costs

for local district court cases of statewide importance, was also a first in the nation, as was its Labor Relations Service, which assists local school districts in contract negotiations. The association's Superintendent Search Services assists school boards in finding the most appropriate replacement for superintendent vacancies.

In the wake of many reports on education beginning with "A Nation at Risk," MASB has led in providing education excellence for all children. The organization's membership—through MASB efforts and cooperation in county school board associations throughout the state—are the most informed, active, and knowledgeable school board members in the history of education in Michigan.

While many changes will undoubtedly take place in Michigan's system of K-12 education in the years to come, the Michigan Association of School Boards, guided by veteran members and an increasing number of dedicated newer members, will continue to provide strength, understanding, and a professional level of local school governance for future generations of Michigan's youth.

MICHIGAN HOSPITAL ASSOCIATION

Organized health care in Michigan dates back to 1832 with the establishment of the Wayne County Poorhouse, now Westland Medical Center.

St. Vincent's Hospital (later called St. Mary's Hospital), founded by the Daughters of Charity in Detroit in 1845, was the first hospital in the Great Lakes area, playing a major role in helping the sick and dying during Detroit's cholera epidemic in 1850.

Most of the hospitals established during this period were from church groups and religious orders: Protestant Presbyterian Society—Harper Hospital, Detroit (1863); the Ladies Christian Union—Women's Hospital and Foundlings' Home, and Detroit Hutzel Hospital (1868); The Daughters of Charity—The House of Providence (later Providence Hospital of Southfield), Detroit (1869), and St. Mary's Hospital, Grand Rapids (1875); The Lutheran Inner Mission Society—Working Woman's Home and Hospital (later St. Luke's), Saginaw (1888); and the Sisters of St. Joseph—Borgess Hospital, Kalamazoo (1889).

Other hospitals established during this period were set up in mining or lumber towns by companies for their own employees, like the Iron Cliff Company Hospital in Ishpeming (1872), today the Francis A. Bell Memorial Hospital. Others were established by city leaders who saw a great need for a hospital, such as the Port Huron Hospital (1882). And still others

were established as retreat facilities for those suffering from "chronic ailments," like the Sanitarium at Battle Creek (1866), established by J.H. Kellogg.

At the turn of the twentieth century there were approximately 30 hospitals in Michigan serving a population of 1,751,384. When the Hackley Hospital of Muskegon opened in 1904, the city called a full-scale holiday; banks, businesses, and schools closed.

Hurley Hospital in Flint was founded in 1908 with a bequest from James Hurley. When he died he left a major portion of his fortune to the City of Flint for the establishment of a hospital where anyone could be treated regardless of ability to pay.

A total of four hospitals were founded during the 1910s by the Sisters of Mercy, a religious order established by Catherine McAuley in Ireland in 1831. The first of their hospitals in Michigan was the St. Joseph Sanitarium in Ann Arbor (1911), now the Catherine McAuley Medical Center. The group today is the Mercy Health Care Corporation.

Other unique hospitals established during this period include The Michigan Mutual Hospital, Detroit (1916), established by an insurance company to treat patients suffering from work-related injuries (today Doctor's Hospital); Dunbar Hospital, Detroit (1917), established by black physicians for the care of blacks, who were not admitted to other hospitals at the time (today Parkside Hospital); and An-

drew Still Memorial Hospital, Romeo (1919), named for the founder of osteopathic medicine, today known as Detroit Osteopathic Hospital, the largest osteopathic health delivery organization in the country.

The first reconstructive plastic surgery hospital, Straith Memorial, was established in Detroit in 1952. The first Jewish-sponsored hospital, Sinai Hospital, was opened in Detroit in 1953. Ten years later 1,092,007 patients occupied 64,679 beds in 254 Michigan hospitals. By the 1970s medical centers encompassed many specialty areas of medicine, advanced research, educational components, and outpatient and satellite centers.

Today's multifaceted modern hospitals offer such services as burn centers, diagnostics, home care, psychiatric care, surgical services, physical and occupational therapy, and outpatient care. Community acute care hospitals in Michigan today have 37,546 beds serving 1,254,105 patients. In 1984 Michigan hospitals employed 129,556 persons, approximately 3.3 percent of the total labor force in Michigan.

The Michigan Hospital Association, located in Lansing, is a trade association representing more than 200 Michigan hospitals and health care facilities. Founded in 1919 to create a unified voice for the health care industry, the MHA has as its primary functions, advocacy, communication, and education.

MICHIGAN MERCHANTS COUNCIL

The Michigan Merchants Council, originally the Michigan Chain Stores Council, was founded by Wilfred F. "Bill" Doyle and a group of leading retailers who met in Lansing in 1934 to testify on legislation affecting the development of their businesses and the operating climate in the state. The council's purpose was to collect, analyze, and interpret all available data on retailing distribution and to communicate those facts to Michigan merchants, consumers, legislators, and governmental officials.

Doyle, born in 1897, served one term (1933-1934) as a Michigan State Senator prior to founding the Michigan Chain Stores Council. He is best known as an irrepressible booster of his beloved Mackinac Island. Dubbed the "King of Mackinac Island," Doyle was a shrewd politician whose maneuverings helped shape policies and laws boosting retailing to a dominant force in Michigan's economy. As a member of the Mackinac Island State Park Commission for over four decades, Doyle used that powerful post to promote Michigan retailing, shaping policy in Lansing from his home on the island.

The council has striven to meet the changing needs of its members representing 4,000 stores. Legislative action, administrative rules and regulations, court decisions, and an increase in political contact has made government an important partner in Michigan retailing. The pervasiveness of government means that now the association's major emphasis is on governmental affairs. While most large retailers have established public and governmental affairs divisions, small and medium-size retailers do not have the resources to do so. The Michigan Merchants Council gives all retailers a public affairs department.

Retailing remains one of the state's major employers. Retail employment in Michigan is over one million and, since 1970, the number of retail employees has increased by 66 percent compared with a 16-percent growth factor in manufacturing nationwide. In addition, retailers employ more than three times as many workers per dollar of capital invested than manufacturers.

Michigan is becoming a dominant

Michigan Chain Stores Council founder Wilfred F. Doyle (left) and current president and chief executive officer Christian H. Kindsvatter.

service state. During the 1970s Michigan lost 90,000 manufacturing jobs while gaining 456,000 service sector jobs. Retailing has also done its part to keep consumer prices down during the past decade. Retail prices nationally, for instance, have risen at a rate 40 percent below the rise in the Consumer Price Index.

Today wholesale and retail trade constitutes Michigan's third-largest industry, accounting for 24 percent of Michigan's gross annual product. Without the billions of dollars retailing spends in Michigan and elsewhere on transportation, advertising, postal services, printing, and countless other products and services many of these related businesses would be much smaller. Millions of items produced by tens of thousands of manufacturers pass through wholesale and retail centers every day.

Michigan's rich heritage has been marked by merchants' important role in its economic development. Michigan is the birthplace of some of the nation's largest retailing establishments and innovators in the retail trade, and also leaders in the

Michigan Merchants Council: J.L. Hudson Company, Cunningham Drug Stores, Winkelmans', K mart Corporation, Perry Drug Stores, Inc., Gantos, Jacobson Stores, Inc., Allied Supermarkets, Amway Corporation, Crowley Milner and Company, Damman Hardware, Highland Super Stores, Inc., Meijer, Inc., Arbor Drug, Inc., the Center-Companies, and the Taubman Company, Inc.

Retailing provides payrolls for thousands of employees, goods and services for hundreds of thousands of customers, and millions of dollars in capital investment. And with the use of modern computer technology, retailers direct the flow of goods, the billing of accounts, and the management of credit.

Retailing enterprises and the Michigan Merchants Council have grown in Michigan by representing the consumer, providing employment, and creating a favorable retail climate.

CONSUMERS POWER CO.

W.A. Foote (1854-1915), founder of Consumers Power Co., and his first office building, constructed in 1896 in Jackson, Michigan.

When Consumers Power Co. was in its formative years near the turn of the twentieth century, the now-routine process of transmitting electricity from its source to customers was not taken for granted. So in 1899, when the company built a 24-mile transmission line between Kalamazoo and a hydroelectric dam on the Kalamazoo River, Consumers Power founder W.A. Foote did not know what to expect from the new system until a rider on horseback returned from Kalamazoo to the dam yelling, "It's workin'. The lights is workin'."

Now supplying electricity and natural gas to nearly 6 million people in 67 of Michigan's 68 lower peninsula counties, Jackson-based Consumers has always had to be concerned with transmitting power over great distances to reach its far-flung customers. In addition to Michigan's rural regions, the operation serves some of the world's largest industrial giants, including General Motors Corporation, The Dow Chemical Company, The Upjohn Company, and Kellogg Company.

The 101-year-old utility, which now has 82,000 miles of transmission and distribution lines and pipelines, is the nation's 11th-largest investor-owned utility by revenues with 1986 sales of $3.1 billion.

The formation of Consumers Power dates to 1886 when Foote, a miller from

Adrian, asked the Jackson Common Council for permission to erect poles, string wires, and place streetlights in downtown Jackson. After forming the Jackson Electric Light Works, Foote developed electric companies in Battle Creek, Albion, and other Michigan cities. The Consumers Power Co. holding company was organized in 1910; all of Foote's various utility concerns were merged into Consumers Power Co. five years later.

Consumers' commitment to serving the farmer was articulated by Wendell Wilkie, the 1940 presidential candidate and president of the holding company that owned Consumers Power. He urged the firm to "get out front of the parade" by providing electricity to the farming community. The utility turned on power to its first farm family in 1927, and by October 1949 became the nation's first utility to connect 100,000 farms. That record has never been equaled.

An increased appetite for electricity and appliances led Consumers to develop its Traveling Showroom in 1935. The Showroom transported sample electrical appliances to anxious rural consumers.

The natural gas end of Consumers' business received a boost in 1941, when the company made its first connection with Panhandle Eastern Pipe Line Company's interstate gas transmission pipeline.

Pushed by Michigan's suburban boom, Consumers' electrical sales surged after World War II to the point where the firm built 19 baseload generating units between 1948 and 1971. The construction boom included the company's first nuclear plant near Charlevoix.

A proposed nuclear plant in Midland, however, almost proved to be the company's financial undoing in the early 1980s. Plagued by massive cost overruns in Midland, Consumers Power Co. halted work on the facility in 1984, concerned with bankruptcy. Current chairman and chief executive officer William McCormick took the firm's reins late in 1985 and has returned Consumers to profitability. He has spearheaded a joint venture with Dow Chemical and other investors to convert the would-be nuclear plant into one of the world's largest natural gas, combined-cycle cogeneration facilities.

The sales force of Consumers Power Co. in Muskegon in 1914. Here they are shown launching an electric iron campaign.

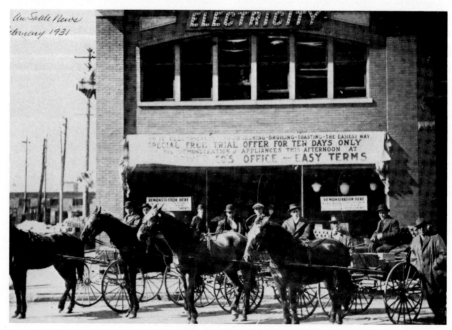

CROWLEY, MILNER & CO.

Crowley, Milner & Co., a venerable Detroit-based retailer with annual sales in excess of $100 million, owes its start to the Panic of 1907.

Shortly before the Panic swept through Wall Street and dumped the nation into a deep depression, Joseph J. Crowley formed Crowley Bros. Wholesale Dry Goods Co. in Detroit with his brothers, Daniel and William. A son of Irish immigrants, he was born in Detroit's Corktown section in 1862. Crowley quickly developed a thriving business with local retailers, including the downtown Detroit firm of Pardridge & Blackwell. As the depression worsened and Pardridge & Blackwell sunk further into debt, Crowley formed a partnership with Toledo, Ohio, retailer William Milner and they bought the ailing firm in 1908.

The new company immediately went to work renovating and improving Pardridge & Blackwell's six-level store. The Crowley, Milner & Co. store, while closing the old barbershop, grocery, meat, and liquor departments, featured "a complete house furnishings and china department, a sickroom for the use and care of any woman who may be taken suddenly ill while in the store," and a promise given in 1909 in *The Detroit Free Press* that "every dollar's worth of goods we sell will take with it our definite guarantee that it will give you proper satisfaction, a full measure of money's worth."

Detroit native Joseph J. Crowley (pictured here) and Toledo, Ohio, retailer William Milner founded Crowley, Milner & Co. in 1908.

Aided by the booming population and income growth spawned from Detroit's burgeoning industrial engine, Crowley's reaped sales of $39 million in 1928. By that time Crowley's 750,000-square-foot store had grown into a full-line department store featuring delivery service, a telephone order board, a mail order department, a nursery, a restaurant, a cafeteria, and a snack bar. One sale in May 1928 attracted 275,000 customers in a single day.

The 1920s also saw the end of management by the company's founders as Milner was killed in a 1922 automobile accident and Crowley died of pneumonia in 1925. Daniel Crowley, Joseph's brother, became president in 1927 and ran the company until his death in 1936.

After a lean period during the Depression, the company accepted script from City of Detroit employees and reorganized at the beginning of the 1940s. The firm's performance improved during the war years and continued under the leadership of general manager Jay D. Runkel, who retired in 1954.

The first branch store was opened in Dearborn in 1959, starting the suburbanization trend that gained considerable momentum in the 1960s and 1970s.

Crowley's and other downtown retailers suffered declining traffic and sales resulting in the closing of the downtown store in 1977. In 1986 the Detroit-owned chain opened a store in the New Center Area, across the street from the General

Motors headquarters.

Operating 12 stores, Crowley's continues to be headquartered in Detroit and employs about 2,000 people. According to Robert Carlson, president and chief executive officer, the company is currently engaged in a campaign to update its merchandise and total presentation.

The updating has meant designer fashions on the store racks and new display cases, special lighting fixtures, Italian marble accents, chrome, and mirrors for the stores themselves. A far cry from the bustling department store selling everything from washing machines to tea kettles during the 1920s, Crowley's is now positioning itself to be a leader in name-brand fashions, specializing in apparel for women, men, and children, and home furnishings.

Crowley's 750,000-square-foot downtown Detroit store, seen here in the early 1950s, served 275,000 customers during one day in 1928.

Crowley's downtown Detroit flagship store in the mid-1960s.

245

MICHIGAN BANKERS ASSOCIATION

When delegates from Michigan's banking community met in Detroit on October 26, 1887, to discuss mutual problems and concerns, they inaugurated an organization that not only would represent Michigan's bankers as the Michigan Bankers Association, but would also stand for an institution with roots extending back to antiquity.

Banking was practiced by the Babylonians, Assyrians, and Athenians. It was further refined by the Romans during the Middle Ages. The Bank of Venice dates to 1171, the Bank of Genoa to 1320, and the Bank of Amsterdam to 1609.

Banking in Michigan did not have a very auspicious beginning. In 1806 Michigan territorial officers authorized the incorporation of the Bank of Detroit. Its capital stock was minimal and the ambitions of its Boston-based leaders questionable. When the eastern promoters sold their stock, the innocent buyers were left with valueless notes, backed not by gold but only the unethical promises of the Bostonians. The bank's failure was inevitable once this scandal became public. Even though Congress revoked the bank's charter, it took years for Michigan to regain its status as a good place to invest.

By 1819, however, leading citizens established the Bank of Michigan. While it occupied the former headquarters of the Bank of Detroit, it differed in two important ways from its notorious predecessor: It was locally backed, and it had

One dollar note of The Bank of Washtenaw, Ann Arbor, 1836. When Michigan entered the Union, it had 15 chartered banks for every 3,500 people. Courtesy, the State Archives of Michigan

$10,000 in gold in its vaults. The Bank of Michigan continued for 22 years, closing under the direction of its trustees during the Panic of 1837. Other local banks were established during those formative decades before Michigan's statehood. Fifteen were in business in 1837, and combined capitalization was $7 million, although only $5.5 million of that was nominal, or authorized. Michigan's statehood brought about confusion and change for the banking industry.

Michigan's first banking law abolished legislatively chartered banks, thus opening up the industry to everyone. While there were certain requirements—subscription of stock and regular examinations—the law fostered the growth of banks, but not a banking industry. By mid-1838, 61 banks were in business or petitioning to open. "Wildcat" banks blossomed overnight, and while many of them legitimately met the needs of the populace, too many operated on the shady side of the law, causing the reputation of Michigan's banks to suffer. By 1839, 29 banks were in liquidation. The legislature stopped the practice convinced

that banks were a "great menace" to the state. From the 1840s to the late 1850s most banking in Michigan was in the hands of private bankers. Often called a "broker," the private banker was usually a person of considerable financial standing in the community who operated a mercantile or other business. Although insufficient, private banking did fill an important need.

When U.S. President Andrew Jackson killed, by veto, the Bank of the United States in 1832, the national banking system relied on a loose confederation of state banks. It was precisely during this tumultuous era that Michigan grew to statehood. Michigan's population had grown to over 200,000 by 1840, and development of its natural resources was on everyone's agenda.

Financing such endeavors, however, in the midst of a banking crisis proved dangerous to the planners' dreams. Many projects simply failed to materialize; others never reached public expectations. So much money was spent for so little that the state's leaders prohibited their government from investing in future internal improvements under the terms of the 1850 Constitution.

These years left divided opinions about banks in people's minds. There were those who felt banks were necessary, while others believed they only made their owners rich. Much of this feeling can be traced to the general instability of bank credit and money, especially the notes of some unethical "wildcat" banks. But

A sketch of the "Wildcat Bank" of Shiawassee. It was hard to find when it came time to exchange bank notes for specie, silver, and gold. Courtesy, the State Archives of Michigan

As banking grew more ornate structures were built, reaching Victorian elegance in furnishings and decor. The banking floor here is the main office of the Detroit Savings Bank in 1890. Courtesy, Michigan Investor

The Highland Park State Bank became Manufacturers' Branch #1 in 1933 and was referred to as its Woodward-Manchester office. An unusual feature of the bank was an underground tunnel that linked the bank and the paymaster's office at the Ford plant across the street. Employees of Ford were paid in cash, a certain group each morning. The tunnel was quickly dug to protect the payroll as it was transported from the bank to Ford headquarters across the street. Courtesy, Manufacturers National Bank

banking at this time was a reflection of the nation—diverse, disorderly, and growing unevenly and at a dizzying pace. The national crisis of the Civil War forced the nation's leaders to come to grips with the banking problem.

The federal government was very unprepared for war in 1861. The northern military forces were at low ebb, and no quick way to remedy the situation was at hand. There was no central bank to serve

as the federal fiscal agency. In that void a federal banking system developed. Out of the fiscal crisis facing Abraham Lincoln at his inauguration, namely a $60-million debt and $3.6 million in the treasury, came the National Bank Act of 1863. It created a system of national banks, issuing uniform national currency backed by government bonds. Confidence in paper money was restored. By the close of the Civil War 36 national banks existed in Michigan and the nation had uniform currency and, finally, some banking stability.

National banks and national currency proved a boon to business expansion. This was especially true in Michigan, where mining and lumbering were booming, aided by a perceptible expansion in the state's railroad system. The state had a dual banking system—the scattered 43 national banks plus seven state chartered banks. It

was during this era that the Michigan Bankers Association was founded. At the inaugural meeting the delegates called for a State Banking Department to oversee the burgeoning banking industry as Michigan was developing into one of the country's most highly diversified states.

Early success of MBA lobbying resulted in the passage and voter approval of the 1888 Michigan Banking Act. An independent banking commissioner was provided by the law, as were provisions protecting the dual banking system. The act allowed charter switches from national to state banks and six national banks did just that, while 27 new state banks were chartered. And all this activity was realized within two years of the act's passage!

The act also provided for the establishment of building and loan associations; by 1891, 27 local associations were organized. It created a strong banking system, one that was able to withstand the hardships of the Panic of 1893. In fact, there is evidence of intrabanking cooperation during the crisis. Only a few banks failed during the downturn.

An economic reversal in 1907 led national leaders to carefully review federal banking legislation, an item not formally reviewed at that level since the death of the Bank of the United States by Jackson's veto in 1832. In 1913, during Woodrow Wilson's first term, the Federal Reserve Act was signed into law. Although Detroit was not one of the original 12 district cities, its phenomenal growth caught the nation's attention. In 1918 the Detroit branch was formally opened.

The boom times of the 1920s disappeared quickly in the worldwide depression of the 1930s. And, by the 1930s, Michigan's economy had become totally industrially based, especially automotive-related businesses. Industrial employment in Michigan topped 530,000, and of that some 450,000 were dependent on the car building companies and their related suppliers.

Michigan banking was undergoing some changes at this time as well. A 1925

Michigan Bank Law allowed for the creation of holding companies. Two of the first were the Guardian Detroit Group and the First National. By 1932 both holding companies were in trouble, a situation facing newly elected Michigan Governor William Comstock upon his inauguration to the state's highest office.

Reorganization and careful evaluation were needed, but those would take time, and by February 1933 time was not easily found. The solution, backed by the Michigan Bankers Association, was a statewide Bank Holiday, extending the traditional bank holiday for Lincoln's birthday into a full eight days. During the "holiday" banks throughout the state were investigated and their solvency assessed. The two Detroit holding companies were not allowed to reopen. Meanwhile, the banking holiday became a national holiday when newly inaugurated U.S. President Franklin D. Roosevelt closed the country's banks for 14 days.

In March 1933 National Bank of Detroit opened; three months later Manufacturers National Bank opened. They replaced the closed holding companies and honored deposits: A full-scale

The MBA Centennial Committee authorized the publication of a book titled A History of Michigan Banking *to commemorate the 100th anniversary of the MBA. Standing, left to right, are John C. Shaffer, Ronald R. Gossett, Brandon C. White, Jr., Lowell L. Peacock, John D. Mertz, and Donald A. Booth. Seated are James R. Baker, Ralph L. Stickle, Mrs. Paul (Jean) Mann, George A. Harding, Donald B. Jeffery, and Herbert W. Corey. Committee members not present for the photo are Donald E. Green, Harold A. Elgas, Mrs. Robert M. (Betty) Perry, Judy Smith, James Cameron, R. Dan Musser, and Judith Daniels Sullivan.*

MICHIGAN BANKERS ASSOCIATION

SECRETARY
H M BROWN, DETROIT, MICH
FORD BUILDING

DETROIT, MICH.

November 10, 1917.

BULLETIN NO. 389

YEGGMEN ARE IN MICHIGAN

THE SEASON FOR BANK BURGLARIES HAS AGAIN ARRIVED

To the Member Addressed:

For several years Michigan has been free from the depredations of Yeggmen, having been quite active though in other States and being driven out of some States, have again turned their thoughts to Michigan, with much success.

The more recent NIGHT attacks have been on the following banks:

State Bank of Climax, Kalamazoo County, Climax Mich....Loss $ 7,000.00
Farmers State Bank, Barry County, Middleville, Mich......Loss 22,000.00
Farmers State Bank, Kent County, Alto Mich.............Loss 15,000.00
Farmers State Bank, Jackson County, Concord, Mich......Loss 18,000.00

DURING BUSINESS HOURS AND AFTER

A record should be kept of the description of all suspicious characters found prowling about the bank so that in case of arrest they may be identified. No one should be left alone in the bank during business hours or after business hours without carefully locking the safe and vault. It only takes a moment to unlock the vault and safe in case you need to get at the contents, and this precaution should always be taken. Keep a candle, matches, and a screw-driver always in the vault and know how to get out quickly with their aid in case you are locked in. **Be on your guard all the time.**

IMPORTANT

The Association can write for you additional Burglary Insurance for the winter months on the basis of

30 Days @ 20% of Annual Rate   90 Days @ 40% of Annual Rate
60 Days @ 30% of Annual Rate   6 Mos. @ pro rata of Annual Rate

Write at once if you need this extra protection.

Yours very truly,
MICHIGAN BANKERS ASSOCIATION.

panic had been averted. Further strengthening of the banking system came from a proposal to provide federal deposit insurance spearheaded by Senator Vandenberg of Michigan and others, later adopted by the Roosevelt Administration. Banking survived the crisis with its house in order.

The post-World War II boom years further expanded the influence and assets of Michigan's banks. In 1946 total resources of Michigan's 424 banks topped $5.14 million. Forty years later the assets were $64.6 billion. Furthermore, the introduction of new banking procedures —computers, automatic tellers, electronic funds transfers, credit cards, leasing—have changed the ways in which banking is conducted.

The recent decades have been ones of further national legislation. The deregu-

Banks became concerned over the number of burglaries in Michigan. The MBA mailed its Bulletin on November 10, 1917, warning of "the depredations of Yeggmen," a "yeg" being a safecracker or burglar, and the warning was timely.

lation act of 1980, followed by further legislation two years later, has opened up new challenges and opportunities for the banking community. At the same time the increasing national debt plus unbalanced federal budgets have created additional uncertainties among bankers. Nevertheless, as it has been since 1887, the Michigan Bankers Association is prepared for any eventuality.

The current MBA has some 327 affiliated bank members. Its primary duties include monitoring of state legislation, education of its members and the public at large, and service to those members. Banking schools, seminars, insurance programs, and legislative representation are but a few of the services provided from the association's Lansing headquarters. The MBA has progressed significantly in the past century. But one item remains at the top of its agenda—the continued leadership of Michigan's banks in a progressive and competitive Michigan.

The innovative leadership demonstrated by bankers in Michigan ensures the industry's place as a cornerstone of economic growth and development. (Derived from *A History of Michigan Banking* by T. Harry Gatton.)

SHEPLER'S MACKINAC ISLAND FERRY SERVICE

Michigan's Mackinac Island, a popular resort destination that was the hub of John Jacob Astor's fur trading empire in the early nineteenth century, has spawned a more recent business that is prospering from the tourist trade. Shepler's Mackinac Island Ferry Service has used its fleet of five hydroplaning diesel-powered ships to become the most popular way of getting tourists to the island from Mackinaw City or St. Ignace.

While the pre-World War II steam ferries took 50 minutes to one hour to chug the seven miles from Mackinaw City to the island, Shepler's promises its customers a brisk, 18-minute trip at speeds of up to 30 miles per hour. During the peak of the summer season Shepler's carries between 3,000 and 4,000 people a day. The boats, each carrying between 150 and 268 passengers, make 23 trips a day during this hectic period. The entire season lasts from May 1 to November 1.

Speed is the key element in the firm's success, says William H. "Cap" Shepler,

who founded the company with his wife, Marge, in 1955. "The fast ride brings them here," he believes. "We began the business with fast boats and we still have fast boats. Our advertising promises an 18-minute ride to Mackinac Island, and we do our best to deliver."

A 60-year veteran of the Great Lakes who started his career working on his father's tiny fishing dock, Cap Shepler and his wife started the company with two Chris Craft speedboats carrying six passengers each. These boats were fast, but larger vessels would be needed to meet the increasing passenger demand. So, after a long series of trials and errors, Cap Shepler commissioned J.B. Hargrave, a naval architect, to design and build a ship that could travel 30 miles per hour and carry 120 passengers.

This ship, named the *Welcome* after one of the first boats to sail the Mackinac Straits during the early 1700s, arrived in Mackinaw City with a flourish. Noting that a competitor operated on an adjacent

Shepler's Mackinac Island Ferry Service has five ships that ply the seven miles from Mackinaw City to the resort island in 18 minutes.

dock, Cap Shepler recalls that "when that *Welcome* came around the point full speed, I blew the whistle and flew the flag so he could see her."

Today Cap and Marge's son, William R. Shepler, is the company's president and general manager. He also serves as co-owner with his parents.

The business is not built on speed alone as the boats, dock, and crew are all known for their neat and clean appearance and for providing the best possible service. This does not happen by accident. Several weeks each year find William R. Shepler and his family at the Disney World complex studying that operation and adding elements he likes to his own business.

The combination of speed, neatness, and service has enabled Shepler's Mackinac Island Ferry Service to rule the Mackinac Straits.

249

AUTO-OWNERS INSURANCE

The evolution from birth to maturity of successful corporations is dependent on a number of factors. One of the most important is leadership.

It's not surprising, then, that Auto-Owners Insurance, a business resident of Lansing for all but the initial year of its existence, has evolved into the largest insurance company domiciled in Michigan.

Auto-Owners success can be traced back from its present management to the early leadership of Vern V. Moulton who, in 1916, organized Auto-Owners Insurance Company in Mt. Pleasant, Michigan. The infant firm had no capital and was housed in one room of a bank building.

Auto-Owners operated in Mt. Pleasant for a little less than a year. In 1917 V.V. Moulton literally picked the business up, placing it under his arm and in his pocket. (The company consisted of one book of policyholders' names and $174.25 in assets.) He moved Auto-Owners to the Hollister Building in Lansing—an environment that would prove to be ideal for future growth.

As the firm grew, both in volume and confidence, it also expanded physically. By 1922 Auto-Owners occupied part of the fourth floor of the Bauch Building in downtown Lansing, but soon filled the entire floor.

By 1927 Auto-Owners was writing in excess of one million dollars per year in insurance premiums and purchased one of Lansing's stately mansions on North Capitol Avenue for a home office. The young enterprise continued to grow by leaps and bounds, and in 1929 a two-story

addition was completed.

It wasn't long before the Depression began, and Auto-Owners weathered even the lowest point of that era—the bank holidays of February 1933. The company demonstrated its corporate toughness and financial stability by paying all claims promptly, daily, and in cash. The firm was then writing more than $2.5 million in

Auto-Owners Premium Income Growth

1916-	$	2,060
1926-		1,120,000
1936-		2,091,000
1946-		7,904,000
1956-		24,605,000
1966-		59,717,000
1976-		270,172,000
1986-		910,000,000

insurance premiums.

Despite the Depression, Auto-Owners continued to grow. In 1934 an additional building on East Shiawassee Street was leased, and in 1940 a two-story building on West Shiawassee was acquired.

Auto-Owners entered the general casualty insurance field in 1940 (only automobile insurance was written previously) and, during the next five years, found it necessary to acquire three more buildings in the vicinity of its main office on Capitol Avenue, due to continued

The Auto-Owners Insurance corporate headquarters building in Delta Township, just west of Lansing, anchors a 120-acre complex called Verndale. The development is comprised of a Sheraton Hotel, office buildings, a branch bank, condominiums, apartments, and single-family dwellings.

growth.

The first completely self-contained underwriting and claim office established outside of Lansing was in Detroit in 1947, when the firm purchased a nine-story office building at the corner of Shelby and Congress streets. This branch began servicing the Detroit area, southwestern Michigan, and Ohio. Today full-facility offices operate in St. Paul, Minnesota; Peoria, Illinois; Montgomery, Alabama; Marion, Indiana; Lima, Ohio; Lakeland, Florida; Brentwood, Tennessee; and West Des Moines, Iowa, with claim offices in 24 additional cities.

The original plans for building a home office to replace the five Lansing locations were begun in 1941, but World War II delayed construction until 1949. When the home office at 303 West Kalamazoo Street was built, it was constructed of reinforced concrete, faced with Indiana limestone, and was contemporary in design. This facility served as the home office from 1951 through 1976.

Auto-Owners growth didn't result from Michigan sales alone. The company wrote business in Michigan exclusively from 1916 until 1935, when it began writing insurance in Indiana and Ohio. In the 1940s Auto-Owners extended operations to include Illinois and Minnesota and, during the 1950s, Iowa, North and South Dakota, Florida, Missouri, Ala-

The three-story atrium is the most striking feature of Auto-Owners corporate headquarters building. Not only beautiful, this atrium is a means of efficiency and energy conservation within the building.

bama, Tennessee, and North and South Carolina. The firm began operations in Wisconsin in 1969, Georgia in 1973, Nebraska in 1978, and Arizona in 1982.

Because of Auto-Owners rapid growth in the 1960s and 1970s, the company outgrew the Kalamazoo Street quarters, and preparations were made to construct a new home office as part of a business and residential complex called Verndale, in Delta Township, west of Lansing. Construction began in 1975 and employees moved into the 207,000-square-foot facility in December 1976. By 1985 continuous growth produced a need for a major building addition to its corporate headquarters, so a three-story 50,000-square-foot addition was built onto the east side of the existing structure, with completion in early 1986.

The Lansing corporate office serves not only Auto-Owners Insurance, but its subsidiary companies: Auto-Owners Life Insurance, Home-Owners Insurance, Owners Insurance, and Property-Owners Insurance. The Michigan Branch Under-

writing and Lansing Branch Claims offices are also housed in the structure.

Auto-Owners growth evolves from its loyal employees, agents, and policyholders. The companies are represented by approximately 3,000 independent agencies marketing personal and commercial property/casualty and life and health insurance in 18 states. Total employees number more than 1,600 with over 700 in the Lansing area.

Since its beginning excellent employee relations has been an important business philosophy at Auto-Owners. As a result, there exists an atmosphere of team spirit that has enabled the firm to achieve above-average productivity from its employees.

Contributing to its reputation as being an employer that understands employee needs has been the company's employee benefits program. Auto-Owners was among the first organizations in the area to adopt pension and group life and health insurance plans for employees. An employee credit union has existed since 1948.

The Auto-Owners Insurance group of companies surpassed the one-billion-dollar-in-assets milestone in 1984. The group

ranks among the largest in the nation.

With more than two million policies in force, the group exceeded $910 million in annual premium writings in 1986, its 70th anniversary year. The companies also enjoy the highest possible ratings assigned by nationally recognized independent rating authorities.

SHERATON INN-LANSING

A highlight of Auto-Owners' Verndale complex, just west of Lansing, is the Sheraton Inn-Lansing. The five-story hotel and meeting and entertainment center was opened June 30, 1982, and features 221 guest rooms and 18 meeting rooms with facilities to accommodate up to 1,800 persons.

The Sheraton Inn (owned entirely by Auto-Owners as a part of its investment program) also features The Royale Ballroom, with banquet seating for up to 600; The Reo Theatre, seating 114; Scandal's nightclub; Christie's dining; and Cafe Carnaval for light dining and cocktails. Other hotel facilities include a swimming pool, racquetball court, exercise equipment, whirlpool, and sauna.

The Sheraton Inn-Lansing has earned the reputation of being Lansing's foremost hotel for quality entertainment, dining, and hospitality.

The Sheraton Inn-Lansing is located within Auto-Owners Verndale complex, adjacent to the Creyts Road I-496 exit, west of Lansing.

MICHIGAN STATE UNIVERSITY

Michigan State University is one of the most remarkable success stories in higher education.

The State of Michigan was only 18 years old when Governor Kinsley S. Bingham, on February 12, 1855, signed the law that founded the Agricultural College of Michigan. Carved out of 676 acres of unimproved woodlands just 3.5 miles east of the state's capital, what began as the nation's first college of agriculture has become one of the world's most important educational and research centers.

With 63 students, five faculty members, and the leadership of its first president, Joseph R. Williams, the college formally opened May 13, 1857. Historians ascribe the major credit for its establishment to John C. Holmes, merchant, nurseryman, member of the Detroit School Board, and editor. He and others organized the State Agricultural Society and watched over the legislation that brought this new school into existence.

Careful consideration was given to the curriculum. The schedule included such courses as chemistry, animal and vegetable physiology, geology, and veterinary science. Also, to assist with their expenses and to aid in the development of the young college, all students were required to work three hours per day. No one, regardless of financial status, was exempt from the work on the farms or in the gardens.

In the midst of the Civil War President

Abraham Lincoln signed the Morrill Act, providing for land grants to support a college in each "loyal" state. The new school in Michigan (called Michigan Agricultural College, or MAC) served as the prototype of the 72 land grant colleges and universities ". . .where the leading object shall be, without excluding other scientific and classical studies and including military tactics, to teach such branches of learning as are related to agriculture and the mechanic arts. . .in order to promote the liberal and practical education of the industrial classes in the several pursuits and professions in life."

Michigan received one-quarter-million acres of land, which were sold and the proceeds deposited in a perpetual endowment fund. MAC's financial future was secure and the faculty, curriculum, and enrollment expanded. Curricula in engineering (1885), home economics (1896), veterinary medicine (1909), and business administration (1925) were only the beginning.

It was during the tenure of John A. Hannah that the university saw its period of greatest growth; the enrollment on the East Lansing campus soared from 6,300 in 1941 to 40,820 in 1969. During Hannah's tenure and the institution's centennial year, in 1955, the name was changed from Michigan State College of Agriculture and Applied Science to Michigan State University of Agriculture and Applied Science by overwhelming vote in the Michigan legislature. The nation's first College of Communication Arts and Sciences was established; the university began attracting

more National Merit Scholars; the Honors College and College of Human Medicine were established; and 56 new buildings or major additions appeared, including a science complex with a cyclotron, food science building, the Eppley Center for the College of Business, the Abrams Planetarium, and the Kresge Art Center.

The school along the banks of the Red Cedar boasts one of the nation's most complete and finest athletic complexes. Spartan Stadium, constructed in 1923 to seat 14,000, was expanded for the third time in 1957 to accommodate 76,000 spectators, making it the 10th-largest university-owned football stadium in the country.

The latest addition to the athletic complex is the $40-million Jack Breslin Student Events Center. Set for completion in 1989, the 15,660-seat arena will be home of Spartan basketball and the site for commencements and other major campus events.

Under Coach "Biggie" Munn, the 1952 Spartan football team won the mythical national championship. MSU was admitted to the Big Ten in 1948 and competed in conference football for the first time in 1953. That year it shared the

During the early years of the university, all students were required to work three hours per day to assist with their expenses and to aid in the development of the young college.

Kellogg Center for Continuing Education is the first major facility erected specifically for adult residential education, and the first to be built with financial assistance from the W.K. Kellogg Foundation.

title with Illinois, qualified for the Rose Bowl, and gave Coach Munn a win over UCLA, 28-20. When Munn became athletic director, his assistant and successor, Hugh "Duffy" Daugherty, returned to the Rose Bowl in 1956, again defeating UCLA, 17-14.

Women's athletics gained varsity status in 1972 and Big Ten status in 1981. Star women athletes include 1983 Big Ten Women's Athlete of the Year Judi Brown in track and golfer Bonnie Lauer.

MSU had a banner sports year in 1979 highlighted by Jud Heathcote's basketball squad winning the NCAA championship. That year the Spartans won an unprecedented triple crown: Big Ten championships in football, baseball, and basketball.

Although ice hockey at MSU dates back to 1906, when a team was organized and played against Lansing High School on a local dam, it was not until the 1965-1966 season that Coach Amo Bessone and the team brought home an NCAA championship. Ron Mason and his squad repeated the feat in 1986.

Beginning with the basic agricultural research of more than a century ago, the MSU research program, with grants of $76 million in the 1985-1986 academic year, has expanded to include some 2,800 projects. MSU has become a world center for nuclear physics research. The world's first superconducting cyclotron was de-

veloped and went into operation at MSU in 1982. The chief designer and builder was Dr. Henry G. Blosser, codirector of MSU's National Superconducting Cyclotron Laboratory. His latest project is the world's most powerful cyclotron, a K800 superconducting "atom smasher" due for completion in 1987. He is also building the world's first superconducting medical cyclotron to be used for treatment of cancers.

Cisplatin, a potent, platinum-based anticancer drug that leads all other anticancer drugs in national sales, was discovered at MSU by Dr. Barnett Rosenberg and his colleagues. The drug has saved thousands of lives and is the drug of choice for testicular, ovarian, and bladder cancers.

Brucellosis, known as Bang's disease

RIGHT: Beaumont Memorial Tower stands on the site of College Hall (1857-1919), the first building in America erected for the teaching of scientific agriculture. The tower was constructed in 1928, a gift of John W. Beaumont, class of 1882.

BELOW: The Michigan State University campus in East Lansing occupies 5,239 continuous acres and has long been recognized as one of the most beautiful in the nation. This tract is graced by more than 19,000 trees and shrubs and is traversed by the scenic Red Cedar River. The developed campus comprises 2,100 acres and remaining 3,139 acres are devoted to experimental farms, outlying research facilities, and natural areas. The beauty of the campus is enhanced by a rich diversity of trees, shrubs, and woody vines representing more than 7,800 different species and varieties.

During Saturday home games football fans feel the excitement when Spartan Stadium reverberates with the sounds of the 300-member MSU Spartan Marching Band. The band also plays for selected away football games and for special concerts.

helped to found the state's sugar beet industry.

William J. Beal, one of the world's great botanists, was the first person to cross-fertilize corn to increase yields through hybrid vigor. Since then nearly 200 new plant varieties and hybrids have been created at MSU to increase production, improve quality, and benefit the state's agricultural marketing and processing industries.

The technological and environmental aspects of pest control are studied in MSU's Pesticide Research Center, which has helped identify substances in Michigan lakes and streams and assisted in pinpointing sources of contamination.

The largest research arm of MSU is the Agricultural Experiment Station and its 400 projects that are carried out in field stations throughout the state. Established in 1888, the station conducts and sponsors research in all phases of the modern food production and natural resources industries, and addresses human, environmental, and health problems as well.

One of the most extensive research sites, also a major visitors' attraction, is the W.K. Kellogg Biological and Forest Experiment Station at Hickory Corners. The station is a bird sanctuary, an experimental farm, and a research forest,

PRESIDENTS OF MICHIGAN STATE UNIVERSITY	
Joseph R. Williams	1857-1859
Lewis R. Fisk	1859-1862
Theophilus C. Abbott	1862-1884
Edwin Willits	1885-1889
Oscar Clute	1889-1893
Lewis B. Gorton	1893-1895
Jonathan L. Snyder	1896-1915
Frank S. Kedzie	1915-1921
David Friday	1921-1923
Kenyon L. Butterfield	1924-1928
Robert S. Shaw	1928-1941
John A. Hannah	1941-1969
Walter Adams	1969-1970
Clifton R. Wharton, Jr.	1970-1978
Edgar L. Harden	1978-1979
Cecil Mackey	1979-1985
John DiBiaggio	1985-

in animals and undulant fever in humans, is no longer a major public and animal health problem, thanks to the work of I. Forest Huddleson, MSU microbiologist.

Dr. Robert Kedzie, a physician, researcher, and professor of chemistry as well as an environmental and consumer activist, almost single-handedly ended trade in arsenic-laden wallpaper, highly explosive kerosene, and bogus fertilizers. He also

and is a national center for lake and land ecological research.

Michigan's major agricultural products such as soft wheats, peaches, sugar beets, and beans compete effectively against those of other states because MSU-developed varieties are used. In industry, MSU research on metal plating led to the development of the state chrome-plating industry.

The Michigan Biotechnology Institute, located in a new building on the western edge of the campus, is expected to be a major boon in building the state's biotechnology industry.

To analyze complex chemicals, MSU built a Mass Spectrometry Facility, supported by the National Institutes of Health. It can detect and identify chemicals present in amounts as small as one-trillionth of a gram.

The MSU College of Education is the site of the Institute for Research on Teaching and the National Center for Research on Teacher Education. It is also headquarters for the Holmes Group, an intercollegiate association that is championing sweeping changes in the training of teachers and the teaching profession.

The Clifton and Dolores Wharton Center for Performing Arts, completed in 1982, features a 2,500-seat Great Hall and a 600-seat Festival Stage. Music, theater, and dance programs are presented throughout the year.

MSU's research efforts have impacts far beyond the border of Michigan. Along with researchers from nine other American universities, MSU scientists are involved in a massive project to help prevent famine in 12 developing countries through improvements in the production and use of dry beans and cowpeas.

That small school that began in a woodland clearing has expanded to 5,263 acres with more than 41,000 students, the largest student body of any Michigan university.

Students come from every county, every state, and more than 100 foreign nations. They are high achievers: MSU has produced 10 Rhodes Scholars in the past 15 years, is a leader in attracting Merit Scholars, and boasts a number of students who win National Science Foundation Fellowships and Churchill, Marshall, and Truman scholarships.

Undergraduates may choose from more than 200 programs of instruction, and graduate study is offered through more than 75 departments and schools in 14 colleges: Agriculture and Natural Resources, Arts and Letters, Business and Graduate School of Business Administration, Communication Arts and Sciences, Education, Engineering, Human Ecology, Human Medicine, James Madison College, Natural Science, Nursing, Osteopathic Medicine, Social Science, and Veterinary Medicine. MSU is the nation's only institution with three medical schools.

Responding to the needs of increasing numbers of nontraditional students, each college or major academic division has an assistant dean or coordinator serving with Lifelong Education Programs in developing instruction, research, and public service activities, headquartered in Kellogg Center for Continuing Education, the first major facility erected specifically for adult residential education. Annually the center hosts 60,000 adults attending some 600 conferences and other educational meetings. It is the university's guest house and the nation's largest laboratory for hotel, restaurant, and institutional management students.

MSU reaches every county in the state through the Cooperative Extension Service. Created in 1914, it is a major

The 10.5-foot statue, "Sparty," guards the athletic plant and campus. Sculptured by Leonard Jungwirth and unveiled in 1945, it is said to be the largest free-standing ceramic in the world.

off-campus educational system offering programs in agriculture and marketing, family living education, natural resources/public policy, and 4-H youth development.

MSU's expertise and influence, however, extends far beyond Michigan. Through its study centers for Africa, Asia, Canada, and Latin America, and study programs for the Middle East, Russia, and Eastern Europe, MSU continues to be in the forefront of extending education and technical expertise throughout the world. MSU also conducts the largest number of academic programs offered overseas by any American institution—65 programs in 24 countries.

The university is addressing the needs of other segments of society through its urban affairs' programs and schools of journalism, labor and industrial relations, music, nursing, packaging, and police administration.

Supporting the entire educational system are the MSU libraries, which include the Main Library with a growing collection of more than three million volumes; the G. Robert Vincent Voice Library, the largest academic voice library in the nation with more than 40,000 recordings; and 15 branch libraries.

In 1986 a $29-million Plant and Soil Science Building, one of the largest structures at MSU, was opened. Several facilities in the new building are shared by both the Crop and Soil Sciences and Horticulture departments. The building's greenhouse complex covers three-fourths of an acre and features computer-controlled temperature and ventilation systems.

KELLOGG COMPANY

When Battle Creek, Michigan, was in the midst of its "cereal boom" of the early twentieth century, Will Keith Kellogg knew his Kellogg's Corn Flakes® had the potential to satisfy the nation's newfound hunger for cereals. But with such products as Malta-Vita, Egg-o see, Try-a-bita, Per-Fo, Flak-Ota, and Cereola all competing for the same market, Kellogg quickly discovered he would have to undertake extraordinary measures to get the Kellogg name out to the notice of the public. He appreciated the value of good marketing strategy. So, when Kellogg founded the Battle Creek Toasted Corn Flake Company in 1906, the firm spent one-third of its working capital on a full-page advertisement in *Ladies' Home Journal* and gave away four million sample boxes labeled "The original bears this signature—W.K. Kellogg." His campaign proved successful; production increased that year from 33 to 2,900 cases per day.

Today Kellogg leads the $4.35-billion ready-to-eat cereal market with a 40-plus share. The company manufactures products in 17 counties, distributes its cereals in 130 countries, employs 17,000 people,

and now produces more than 30 cereal varieties. By 1986 Kellogg had achieved 42 consecutive years of increased sales, 35 years of improved earnings, and 30 years of increased dividends.

W.K. Kellogg's original product—corn flakes—dates back to 1894 when his older brother, a Battle Creek Sanitarium superintendent, Dr. John Harvey Kellogg, was looking for a healthy food for his patients. That year he turned wheat grains into the world's first flaked cereal. The Kellogg brothers experimented with various breakfast cereals until 1898, when they produced their first corn flakes.

Thanks to a healthy advertising budget that reached one million dollars by 1911, and such packaging innovations as the patented Waxtite package liner, the Kellogg Toasted Corn Flake Company blossomed as more families craved the quality and convenience of the firm's ready-to-eat cereal. American doughboys carried Kellogg's cereals through Europe's

Kellogg Company and the people of Battle Creek celebrated their partnership in developing a "city of the future" when the company's new corporate headquarters, built in the heart of downtown, was dedicated in 1986.

muddy trenches during World War I, and the company launched Canadian, British, and Australian production plants by 1924.

Beginning in the 1950s Kellogg used the television era to introduce Tony the Tiger® and such popular ready-sweetened cereals as Corn Pops®, Kellogg's Frosted Flakes®, and Honey Smacks® to millions of young TV viewers.

The following decade Kellogg began a major worldwide expansion program that included the acquisition of Salada Foods Ltd. By the mid-1960s the average annual sales jumped to 490 million pounds.

With the recent trend by consumers toward convenient, healthy food products, the Kellogg Company is the ready-to-eat cereal leader, offering a wide variety of good-tasting, nutritious products to meet a broad range of dietary needs, including fiber, vitamins and minerals, and whole grain.

®*Kellogg's,* product names, and character design

"We are a company of dedicated people producing quality products for a healthier world." W.K. Kellogg cared deeply for the health and welfare of other people. In 1930, about the time of this photo, he established the W. K. Kellogg Foundation, which today is among the world's largest philanthropic organizations.

CENTRAL MICHIGAN UNIVERSITY

Arthur Ellis, president, 1986- .

Mt. Pleasant, a small mid-Michigan city blessed through the years with both a timber boom and a major oil strike, today looks to an educational institution that started on 10 acres of orchard and swampland as its major employer. Central Michigan University has grown from its modest beginnings as Central Michigan Normal School and Business Institute with 31 students to become a major state-assisted university with 16,734 students and 80 major facilities on 854 acres.

Though it now offers 24 academic degrees ranging from bachelor of fine arts to doctor of psychology, Central Michigan's earliest mission was to train teachers. Organized in 1892 by a group of Mt. Pleasant residents responding to a teacher shortage, Central Michigan became the

Warriner Hall, Central Michigan University's administration building, opened in 1928 during the presidency of Eugene Warriner.

state's second state-assisted normal school five years later.

Growth continued at a deliberate pace into the current century until Eugene Warriner took over as Central Michigan's fourth president in 1918. Before he stepped down 21 years later, Warriner saw Central Michigan's conversion from a normal school to a college, the dedication of the administration building now bearing his name, and the beginning of the so-called Copeland Program in 1935. Named after U.S. Senator Royal Copeland from New York, the program stressed the importance of "character education" in the nation's schools. As Warriner explained it, the Copeland Program was designed to "improve our teacher training to provide a richer curriculum, to develop creative activity in our students, to give back to the state teachers better fitted for character training and building." Vestiges of the Copeland Program remained in Central Michigan's elementary education and mathematics program for several years.

The school's next president, Dr. Charles Anspach, served during a 20-year period in which Central Michigan expanded from 50 acres and seven buildings to reach 235 acres and 40 buildings by the end of his tenure in 1959. Enrollment had doubled from the fewer than 2,500 students that were on campus in 1939. Equally important, Central Michigan College became Central Michigan University in Anspach's last year as president.

While continuing to cling to its roots as an institution for educating prospective teachers, Central Michigan, during the 1960s, broadened its educational focus to "foster intellectual, cultural, and moral development by providing a liberal education." That trend continued through the mid-1970s and 1980s with the implementation of a doctoral program in psychology, the creation of a strong liberal arts requirement for all programs, and an affiliation with the Midland-based Michigan Molecular Institute.

Today, as Central Michigan University heads toward its centennial under current president Arthur Ellis, students pursue programs in such diverse areas as marketing, management information systems, sports medicine, communication disorders, anthropology, and recreation.

Eugene C. Warriner, president, 1918-1939.

Charles Anspach, president, 1939-1959.

257

WEBER'S INN

The Mobil Travel Guide Four-Star Award and the Four Diamonds designation of the American Automobile Association are coveted honors in the hotel and restaurant business. The Mobil Four-Star rating means "outstanding—worth a special trip." Fewer than 10 of these distinctions are awarded in the State of Michigan by either of the rating services. Therefore, Weber's Inn, located at 3050 Jackson Road, Ann Arbor, is justifiably proud of having received these awards every year since the opening of the new Weber's Inn in 1969.

The Weber's Inn of today had humble beginnings. In 1937 Herman Weber launched the Hi-Speed Inn, a hamburger stand, and the Hi-Speed gasoline station at the corner of Washtenaw Avenue and Platt Road. Weber had grown up on a farm near Chelsea. His family sold fresh, butchered meats and chickens to area restaurants, including Ann Arbor's oldest establishment, Metzger's German Restaurant. Weber's first restaurant job began one spring at Metzger's, as dishwasher and busboy. Later he worked at the Michigan League as an elevator operator. His original objective was to accumulate enough earnings to buy a car; but later he decided to go into business with an older brother. Soon the brother enlisted in military service, and Weber was on his own. He found a lifelong partner in marriage and business in Sonja.

In 1937 Washtenaw Avenue was a residential street, and the local governments wished to retain that characteristic. As a result of their pressure, Weber moved to a rented building on Jackson Road, west of Ann Arbor, in Scio Township. He created the Oak Grove, a new tavern with beer, wine, and his famous hamburgers; it lasted until his lease expired.

Deciding that building ownership added stability to a business, the Webers purchased some property on Jackson Road, just west of Wagner Road. Since Jackson Road at that time was US 12, the busiest highway between Detroit and Chicago, the location was ideal for the new, sprawling, ranch-style roadhouse named Weber's Supper Club. The new establishment soon became a favorite eating spot for Ann Arborites and travelers alike. Some of the patrons from out of town wished to make Weber's an overnight stop or weekend excursion. Soon an eight-unit motel, Weber's Holiday House, was constructed adjacent to the supper club. Weber's traditional concern for diners' and travelers' well-being led to continued growth. The demand for additional space coincided with moves to bring over-the-bar liquor sales to Ann Arbor and Scio Township.

Scio Township's residents refused to permit liquor sales. As a result, Weber purchased land in Ann Arbor, which had approved drinks in restaurants and bars. Weber's Restaurant opened in 1962 at 3050 Jackson Road, near the interchange with Interstate 94. The brand-new Weber's Restaurant, though in a new building, retained the flavor of the former supper club. This ambience was achieved by moving employees, equipment, and furniture to the new location. Weber's Holiday House was kept open, but as the new restaurant became more and more popular with celebrities, politicians, students, and the public, Weber devoted most of his time to it.

By 1968 ground was broken for a new motel with 126 rooms. The area's first four-season swimming pool was an attraction that soon garnered a loyal following. Throughout the 1970s Weber's Inn continued to prosper. By 1980 the restaurant was ranked by *Restaurant Hospitality Magazine* as the 17th-largest independent restaurant in sales of food and beverages in the nation.

Expansion was not long in coming. In June 1984 a 3,000-square-foot Atrium Ballroom was opened, at the same time all the guest rooms were refurbished and a second-level deck overlooking Ann Arbor's Dolph Park nature area was added. The inn now had meeting spaces that could be combined to serve as a reception hall for 1,000 guests. Soon a new South Wing featuring the "Suite Life" was constructed. Poolside suites were the latest innovation to be introduced to the area by Weber's.

Herman Weber has been described in many ways. "He's a maverick and a real people person. He's an American success story. He's modest but determined and not easily intimidated." All of these qualities, combined with the Weber family "philosophy of perpetually upgrading the business," have led to the long string of hospitality awards.

Weber's Inn as drawn by noted Ann Arbor artist, Milton Kemnitz.

MICHIGAN RAILROADS ASSOCIATION

One of the many freight trains that serves shippers throughout Michigan carrying commodities essential to Michigan's economy, with Detroit's Renaissance Center in the background.

private industry responding to the needs of its shippers.

From the introduction of the steam locomotive in 1837 on the Erie and Kalamazoo Railroad, through the incredible expansion of the rail industry at the turn of the century as Michigan's vast white pine, iron ore, and copper reserves were harvested, the state's private-sector railroads have met the challenge. At its

serve shippers on 4,700 miles of track, carrying hundreds of commodities essential to Michigan's industrial, chemical, commercial, and agricultural economies. Thanks largely to the deregulation of the industry by passage of the Staggers Act of 1980, Michigan's railroads now are able to compete freely among themselves and with other freight carriers in an open market. The result of this new freedom has been a 20-percent increase in tonnage between 1980 and 1985.

The introduction of the steam locomotive in 1837 on the Erie and Kalamazoo Railroad.

The history of Michigan and its railroads began together. In 1836 the railroads had developed a 50-mile network of track in the Great Lakes peninsulas. One year later Michigan gained statehood. From there the state has seen its railroads develop from primitive, horse-drawn wagons on wooden rails to the modern, computer-assisted trains. Each step in Michigan's railroad freight history represents the effort of a

peak in the 1920s, Michigan's railroad industry had 9,000 miles of track.

The state's railroads have responded not only to the economy but also in times of national crisis. The Civil War, World War I, and World War II all tested the railroads' abilities to move personnel and material efficiently. Again the railroads met the challenge.

Today Michigan's freight railroads

John H. Burdakin, chairman of the Michigan Railroads Association, puts the future in focus: "The railroads have responded to the demands of the past and will continue to be competitive and efficient in the future."

Double-stacking of containers on trains, popularized in 1983 for ship/train movements and economics, has become a normal procedure and an efficient means of carrying cargo.

Computerized traffic-control equipment permits railroad dispatchers to safely control train movement over hundreds of miles of track.

MICHIGAN EDUCATION ASSOCIATION

Michigan's tradition of educational innovation predates its admission to the Union as the 26th state in 1837. Not only did its first state constitution contain a provision for a superintendent of public instruction—the first such post in the nation—it also confirmed the state's support for a school system that had been established four years earlier. Michiganians' early commitment to education was part of a New England tradition settlers brought with them to the new Michigan territory in the 1820s and 1830s. Most immigrants to Michigan in those decades were "Yankees," often the second- or third-generation stock whose ancestry stretched back to the colonial era.

That New England tradition imbued Michigan with many distinctive social concerns: Prohibition—Michiganians debated the matter as early as the 1850s; abolitionism—Michigan became the terminus for the Underground Railroad; and educational reform—schools and schooling were among the first issues discussed at Michigan's early constitutional conventions.

Out of that tradition of educational innovation the Michigan Education Association (MEA) was created. In 1852, a scant 16 years after Michigan's statehood, the MEA was established. It was then called the Michigan State Teachers Association (MSTA). The founding site was the State Normal (Teachers) School at Ypsilanti, now known as Eastern Michigan University, the oldest teachers' college west of the Alleghenies. The association's initial 20 members agreed to levy annual dues of 25 cents. Once again Michigan pioneered in the educational area, for it would still be five years before the National Education Association (NEA) was founded.

Higher education was not ignored by Michiganians. In their first constitution in 1837, they established a state university at Ann Arbor (now the University of Michigan). In the 1850s the state legislature established Michigan Agricultural College (now Michigan State University) at East Lansing.

The MSTA was in the forefront of educational reform. Long before U of M became coeducational, the association was on record supporting the right of women to attend the institution. And in the 1870s,

with the dawn of industrialization, it supported the teaching of science and industrial education. Yet it also reinforced its long-held position that the ultimate goal of education is to turn out well-trained minds, not trained technicians.

The organization's call for more teachers' colleges was heeded: Another normal school was established at Mt. Pleasant in 1893 (now Central Michigan University), at Marquette in 1889 (now Northern Michigan University), and at Kalamazoo in 1904 (now Western Michigan University).

By the turn of the twentieth century association membership topped 800, and included administrators, superintendents, and principals. Six years later that number swelled to 4,488. Its members supported a mandatory teacher retirement system. In 1911 annual dues were one dollar, and membership had doubled from the 1906 level. Meanwhile the state extended mandatory attendance to age 17, and in 1917 adopted a retirement fund plan.

By the 1920s differences within the association's ranks called into question the continued presence of administrators on its membership roster, but final resolution would take more years. That same decade saw the introduction of the *Michigan Education Journal* (now called the *Voice*) as the association's house organ. In 1926 the MSTA changed its name to the

In 1852 the Michigan Education Association was created to establish a tradition of educational reform and innovation within the state. Here an early school, the Amasa Mine School in Hematite Township, was an example of that education tradition. Photo circa 1897

Michigan Education Association (MEA).

The 1930s were times of more advances in Michigan's education profession. The MEA took a stand for four-year, college-level work for teaching certification. A refined retirement bill was enacted, recognizing particularly the vulnerability of teachers due to their ineligibility for Social Security benefits. Credit unions sprouted up in the 1930s, 36 of them by decade's end.

World War II depleted teacher ranks, as many were drafted and still others left for lucrative jobs in the war industries. MEA membership stood at 30,000. The association supported the sales tax diversion amendment to the State Constitution, a move that is generally recognized as the financial salvation for Michigan's schools during the lean years of postwar reconversion (1948-1950).

The 1950s marked the association's centennial. Its membership neared 35,000, and its staff 30. Improvement in retirement plans and liability insurance marked the early years of the decade. And, in 1955, teachers were finally covered under Social Security. By decade's end MEA membership topped 50,000, a gain of more than 12,000 since 1950.

The association started the 1960s off with a significant legislative victory—passage of a mandatory statewide tenure bill. Its census showed nearly 1.8 million students in the state's public schools; average salaries were $6,600, the fourth best in the nation. Fully 31 percent of its teachers had advanced degrees. And the cost of educating a student rose to $352 annually.

In 1964 the association's current headquarters building in East Lansing was dedicated, and its membership swelled to 66,000. A year later the state gave teachers the right to organize and negotiate through their exclusive bargaining agency. This landmark act required public employers to negotiate with their employees. Its passage also required the association to campaign against the Michigan Federation of Teachers (MFT), an affiliate of the American Federation of Labor (AFL). School administrators and principals voted to disassociate themselves from the MEA, a move that had been reviewed 40 years earlier.

Labor issues dominated the headlines in the late 1960s, as the state counted 12 strikes in 1968 alone. Meanwhile, the association supported further consolidation as the number of school districts in the state dropped to 712 from more than 2,000 in the late 1950s. In addition, the matter of state aid to parochial schools dominated public opinion. The MEA was strongly opposed to any such measures. A state referendum marked the 1970s, and the "parochiad" proposal was soundly defeated by a 14-percent margin.

By 1971 MEA membership topped its all-time mark at 71,400. The decade was also a time of teacher shortages and economic reversals. Busing for integration purposes was endorsed by the MEA. Moreover, the hot issue of accountability began to dominate conversations and negotiations. Any plan for the MEA and MFT to merge was dashed. The association rejected the federation's insistence on

continued AFL membership for any joint organization.

The MEA's leadership role in establishing equality in the work place was recognized as it received, in 1977, a federal grant to organize workshops on Federal Title IX, outlawing sex discrimination. At the same time the association adopted a statewide bargaining plan to meet the needs of contract bargaining in the future. Such foresight was a pioneering position nationally.

MEA research on the costliness of teacher firings and hiring of nonaffiliated teachers ("scabs") showed that such tactics often cost districts more money than the original costs of the contracts they sought to reject. However, economic ills continued to affect teacher contracts. Exacerbating the problems statewide were declining enrollments and reduced state-federal funding.

The whole matter of support for schools became hotter, as districts found themselves more and more dependent on property taxes as a way to counteract drops in state aid. The association's political voice was heard as it supported Congressman James Blanchard in the 1982 gubernatorial election. After his election, the MEA supported his move to increase the state income tax to offset Michigan's economic ills. In turn, Blanchard promised to increase state aid to education, and he kept to his word.

It was a historic moment in 1984 when MEA broadened its membership to include educational support personnel. By 1987 school support staffs, such as cooks, bus drivers, custodians, and office personnel, represented 16,000 of the more than 100,000 MEA membership.

MEA recently lobbied successfully for an improved retirement bill that truly ensures retirement with dignity and in past years led statewide efforts to defeat tax-cutting ballot proposals it argued would devastate public school finances.

MEA's top-priority item for the 1980s was equitable pay for teachers and school support employees as a way to maintain and achieve educational excellence in school districts throughout Michigan. MEA will continue to tackle this problem and many more in coming years, just as it has done in its 135 years of existence.

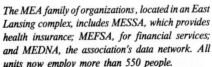

The MEA family of organizations, located in an East Lansing complex, includes MESSA, which provides health insurance; MEFSA, for financial services; and MEDNA, the association's data network. All units now employ more than 550 people.

FRANKENMUTH BAVARIAN INN

The William Zehnder, Jr., family—proprietors of the Frankenmuth Bavarian Inn.

Over 100 years ago the Union House Hotel was built in Frankenmuth, Michigan, some 90 miles north of Detroit. Unlike other hotels of the lumbering era in mid-Michigan, it was destined to become famous as the Frankenmuth Bavarian Inn—the 10th-largest restaurant in the United States. No one could have predicted that guests would still be enjoying good food and friendly hospitality at that location an entire century later.

The Frankenmuth Bavarian Inn in Frankenmuth has a tradition of hospitality dating back to the late 1800s. Today it is the 10th-largest restaurant in the United States.

The Union House was built in 1888 by Theodore Fischer, who had four years experience operating Frankenmuth's Exchange Hotel across the street. The Union House was larger than its neighboring hotel and catered to lumbermen and salesmen who traveled the Flint to Saginaw route.

By the early 1900s the town had seven hotels, which were really boardinghouses. Frankenmuth's reputation for good food was well established. Theodore Fischer was the first to specialize in "all you can eat" family-style chicken dinners, and soon there was rivalry among the hotelmen in Frankenmuth to serve bigger and better plates. At the Union House, a meal for one

diner and a horse was 75 cents.

Before he died, Theodore renamed his restaurant Fischer's Hotel, and it remained in the Fischer family for 62 years. His wife, Katherine, took over the business after Theodore's death. At first their son Henry helped too, but later he bought his own hotel, so another son, Herman "Tom," stepped in. In 1941 Tom sold the restaurant to his son Elmer. It was Elmer who sold Fischer's to the William Zehnder, Sr., family in 1950.

By this time the Zehnders had 23 years of experience in the restaurant business in Frankenmuth. The large family of William Zehnder, Sr., and Emilie (Bickel) included six boys and two girls—too many people to support during the Depression years by farming in rural Frankenmuth. So William sold some farmland in 1927, bought the boarded-up Exchange Hotel, and opened it as a family business on May 12, 1928, Mother's Day.

Although the Zehnders had no experience in the business, they figured they could run the restaurant like they did the farm. Mother would do the cooking and the children would help. The plan worked well, and they served a whopping 312 people opening day at one dollar per dinner. But beginner's luck did not hold.

The Union House became the Fischer Hotel during the early 1900s and stayed in the Fischer family for 62 years until it was sold to the William Zehnder, Sr., family in 1950.

The Depression hit soon after the business began, and city folks from Saginaw, Flint, and Detroit could not afford the trip to Frankenmuth for Sunday dinner. William Sr. took a job at the county courthouse where a steady paycheck was guaranteed. The oldest son, Fred, and other children got outside jobs to help pay the bills. Emilie Zehnder died in 1941, and her children continued to operate Zehnder's Restaurant. On March 10, 1947, William Sr. signed over the business to his children—debts and all.

With the younger generation of Zehnders at the helm, things changed. Brothers Edwin and William "Tiny" Jr. decided to buy out their only real competitors across the street—Fischer's. The deal was signed in 1950, and family-style chicken the "Zehnder way" was served on both sides of Main Street. Eddie and his wife, Marion, stayed at Zehnder's Restaurant as managers while Tiny and his wife, Dorothy, became the new managers at Fischer's.

But a monopoly on chicken dinners did not double the profits. The second restaurant drained the assets. By the recession of the 1950s Fischer's was drowning in red ink. Something had to be done to make Fischer's "different."

The German family drew on their strong heritage for a game plan. In 1958 they built a new Bavarian addition and renamed the restaurant the Frankenmuth Bavarian Inn. The new restaurant was introduced during a week-long grand opening that was repeated each June. The celebration continues today as the annual Frankenmuth Bavarian Festival. More than 250,000 visitors come to celebrate each year.

The Bavarian theme set the table for more than a long line of hungry dinner guests. The William Zehnder, Jr., family incorporated Old World traditions in every imaginable way. Waiters and waitresses were costumed in colorful dirndls and lederhosen. German food was added to the menu. Even the air was filled with the German polka beat. Outdoor attractions were added, including a hand-carved maypole, Wetterhaus for weather forecasting, and the glockenspiel—one of the community's most popular attractions. The story of the Pied Piper is told as wooden characters depict the famous legend high above the chiming clock tower.

More dining rooms were added. Now there are seven—each with a German name like Edelweiss, Bavarian, Austrian, Alpine, Heidelberg, Family Crest, and the new Roof Garten. All have their distinctive German motif. The restaurant currently seats 1,200 people.

Recent marketing has included other features besides the food. There is an expanded Gift Shop, Bake Shop, Candy Corner, and Wine Shop. Just completed is a Doll and Toy Factory, where German dolls are assembled on view to visitors. It is a total German experience.

Both restaurants operated as one family corporation and built a reputation for Frankenmuth as Michigan's number one tourist destination. They also built, in 1979, the largest wooden covered bridge crafted in the twentieth century as yet another major Frankenmuth attraction.

Now the third generation of Zehnders is involved in the restaurant business. The family holding company was disbanded January 1, 1985. The Frankenmuth Bavarian Inn and Zehnder's Restaurant currently operate independently.

In 1986 the Bavarian Inn family of William Zehnder, Jr., diversified its business even more by opening a 100-room Frankenmuth Bavarian Inn Motor Lodge with small convention facilities. William and Dorothy's daughter, Judith Zehnder Keller, operates the motor lodge while their son, William A., manages the restaurant. Together they employ about 750 people.

For all of the extras the Frankenmuth Bavarian Inn offers guests, the good food remains the single most important reason visitors come back year after year. Breads, pastries, tortes, pies, and other delicious desserts are homemade in the expansive Bavarian Inn bakery. The restaurant also operates its own food-processing plant for vegetables such as locally grown squash and fruits like Michigan apples, cherries, and berries. Some beef served is locally raised on the Bavarian Inn farms.

Mention the Frankenmuth Bavarian Inn to Midwesterners and there immediately comes to mind visions of golden premium spring chicken, savory dressing, hearty chicken noodle soup, rich giblet gravy, bowls of creamy mashed potatoes, buttery noodles, salads, vegetables, and fresh homemade fruit bread and preserves. The atmosphere, shops, and other attractions are just the icing on the apple strudel.

The Union House Hotel (the site of the Frankenmuth Bavarian Inn today) was built in 1888 by Theodore Fischer and served as a boardinghouse/hotel to lumbermen and salesmen who traveled through the area. At the Union House a meal for one diner and his horse would cost about 75 cents.

HYGRADE FOOD PRODUCTS CORP.

Hot dogs and baseball have always gone hand in hand, and nowhere has that combination been more compatible than in Detroit's venerable Tiger Stadium, the home of the famous Hygrade Ball Park frank.

The stadium's official hot dog since 1957, these franks have become so popular that the Detroit Tigers' general manager, Jim Campbell, once observed of the enthusiastic fans that "They're not eating hot dogs, they're eating tube steaks." Over the years Hygrade Food Products Corp. has sold 36 million tube steaks at Tiger Stadium and an average of 600 million a year to the general public, as the franks are widely available.

Ball Park franks, the nation's second-most-popular brand with 7 percent of the market, is the flagship product of a company that dates back to pre-World War I New York City. Soon after Samuel Slotkin founded the Hygrade Provision Co. in 1914, he used pure beef frankfurters and brand-name recognition to capture a strong hold on the New York hot dog market. Slotkin formed Hygrade Food Products Corp. in 1927 through a combination of nine New York-based companies.

In addition to his hot dogs, Slotkin was known for his voracious appetite for acquiring meat-packing companies. Hygrade purchased the Chicago-based Allied Packers, which included Parker Webb Co. of Detroit, in 1929, even though Allied's annual sales of about $54 million were six times those of Hygrade's. The acquisition binge continued despite the Great Depression of the 1930s; Hygrade acquired plants in Australia, New Zealand, French Morocco, Ireland, South America, and Europe.

After moving the company headquarters to Detroit in 1949, Hygrade made its most important acquisition by purchasing Indianapolis-based Kingan & Co. in 1952, thus becoming the nation's fifth-largest meat-packing company. The combined companies had annual sales of $351 million. The next major acquisitions

Hygrade Food Products' current plant at 38200 Plymouth Road in Livonia. Built in 1968, the plant produces Ball Park franks, West Virginia hams and bacon, and Hygrade-brand processed meats.

Hygrade's major Michigan plant for a number of years was located at 2811 Michigan Avenue in Detroit. The plant was acquired by Hygrade in August 1929 and ceased operations in September 1965.

included the West Coast packing firm of Carstens Packing Co. in 1954, several companies producing meat casings for the industry, and the I.J. Grass Noodle Co. of Chicago in 1963.

Though strictly a processed meat company now, Hygrade at one time was in such other food businesses as ice cream and coffee. A group of New York investors purchased the firm in 1968, and by 1977 Hygrade had merged with Hanson Industries USA, a part of Hanson Trust PLC of London. Hanson's other U.S. holdings include a leading manufacturer of indoor and outdoor florescent and incandescent lights, tool and building materials companies, and firms producing shoes, textiles, and furniture.

Through the years Hygrade, like many

of its competitors, closed or sold its fresh meat operations and concentrated on processed meats. The company closed its classic multistory slaughtering and processing facility in Detroit during the late 1960s to make way for a modern one-story processing plant in the Detroit suburb of Livonia. The new 120,000-square-foot facility serves 16 to 18 states and features Hygrade's largest ham operation; it also produces frankfurters and luncheon meats with state-of-the-art equipment.

Since the Hanson merger Hygrade's processed meat business has grown to reap annual sales of $275 million with 1,000 employees based in Livonia, Pennsylvania, Maryland, Illinois, and Washington.

Hygrade's current food lineup includes West Virginia-brand bacon and ham; chicken-based Grillmaster frankfurters and luncheon meats; such Ball Park brand products as franks, bratwurst, bologna, and knockwurst; and meats prepared for supermarket delicatessens under the Hygrade and Broadway brand names. Now based in Southfield, Hygrade sells its products nationwide.

The company's recent momentum nearly came to a halt before Halloween in 1982, when news reports circulated that razor blades, nails, pins, and tacks were being found in Ball Park franks. As Hygrade recalled the franks in Detroit and outstate Michigan, the firm's dedicated workers volunteered to pass recalled franks through a metal detector. This helped Hygrade return its product to store shelves.

The City of Livonia, the site of Hygrade's Michigan plant, showed its appreciation of the company by holding a Livonia Loves Hygrade Week in which its residents consumed 148,000 hot dogs.

Though what turned out to be a hoax cost Hygrade an estimated one million dollars, sales recovered within six months after the scare. Having survived the hoax, Hygrade's current goals are to pass the leading frankfurter brand and become the nation's leading producer of frankfurters and for its other brands to gain wider recognition around the country.

But despite its push to promote product sales in supermarkets nationwide, Hygrade will probably always be best known in Michigan for its sales to hungry Detroit Tiger fans.

265

BLUE CROSS AND BLUE SHIELD OF MICHIGAN

Though a catastrophe, the Great Depression of the 1930s was in many ways a boon to innovation. While families and businesses endured unprecedented hardship, government and private enterprise invented safety nets to meet the challenges. Some of the steps taken in the private sector would eventually lead to today's Blue Cross and Blue Shield of Michigan.

During the Depression even many employed people could not afford health care. They might have health insurance, but it paid limited benefits—and only for the policyholder, not for his or her family. As a result, millions simply did without needed care. Hospitals went bankrupt as financial support dried up.

Against this bleak backdrop the forerunners of Blue Cross and Blue Shield of Michigan emerged on the scene in 1938 with the promise of available and affordable health care for the employed and their families. Today Blue Cross and Blue Shield of Michigan's 4.86 million subscribers—including 450,000 in seven health maintenance organizations—take this prepaid health delivery system for granted.

In 1986 the company's 8,500 employees serviced 20,000 customer groups and made benefit payouts of $3.65 billion for private coverage and $3 billion for Medicare. Blue Cross and Blue Shield of Michigan's customer groups range from the Sisters of Mercy to the City of Detroit,

John C. McCabe, chairman and chief executive officer, Blue Cross and Blue Shield of Michigan.

from the Flint Board of Education to K mart to United Parcel Service.

Over the years Blue Cross and Blue Shield of Michigan (BCBSM) has grown to be more than just a name on a health insurance card. The company offers traditional prepaid health care coverage, a preferred provider organization, and a health maintenance organization network.

Health Service Company, a BCBSM subsidiary, includes a seven-entity statewide health maintenance organization network, the Dental Care Network, and the Michigan Health Care Education and Research Foundation.

The Michigan Medical Service subsidiary includes firms that handle administrative and risk management services, claims processing and administration, benefit and risk management, financial services, office furnishings, real estate brokerage, construction, maintenance, and design.

Compared with 16 other consolidated Blue Cross and Blue Shield plans with more than one million members, BCBSM ranks first in subscription income and second in benefit payout. It has the fourth-lowest operating expense level as a percentage of subscription income.

The concept of prepaid health care dates to 1929 when Justin Ford Kimball, the vice-president of Baylor University in Dallas, developed a program in which a group of 1,300 school teachers made small monthly payments to a Baylor medical facility in return for assured hospital care. Though not called Blue Cross at the time, this and other programs are considered prototypes.

After a group of Newark, New Jersey, hospitals developed the first Blue Cross plan serving more than one institution in 1932, Michigan's versions of Blue Cross and Blue Shield were born in 1939. Unlike commercial health insurance, the Blue Cross and Blue Shield plans provide benefits based on service rendered, not a fixed dollar amount.

The hospital prepayment plan, Blue Cross, developed as the Michigan Society

Customer service representatives at Blue Cross and Blue Shield of Michigan answer more than 6 million inquiries annually, using the largest communications terminal network in the state to quickly access information.

for Group Hospitalization with a $10,000 loan from three Detroit hospitals. Private citizens, including the Oldsmobile automobile founder, Ransom Olds, advanced an additional $5,000. Blue Shield, the plan for doctors' services, was created by the Michigan State Medical Society. Michigan Blue Cross and Michigan Blue Shield consolidated in 1975.

Despite the obvious need for a prepaid health care system, the fledgling plans were so new to the public that doctors in some states sued Blue Shield for practicing medicine without a license. That concern was addressed when the Michigan Hospital Association and the State Medical

Society sought regulatory legislation for their new entities. Two Michigan bills were signed in 1939.

The following year the Ford Motor Co. became the first of Detroit's automobile companies to sign up with the plans. When General Motors Corp. and Chrysler Corp. enrolled in 1941, Michigan Blue Cross and Blue Shield were well on their way to becoming two of the nation's largest plans.

In 1945 Blue Cross and Blue Shield sold their first contract to an individual subscriber not affiliated with a group. Three years later the plans enrolled their one-millionth member.

New ground was broken in 1957 when the plans began paying for surgery in a doctor's office and hospital outpatient facilities. In 1966 the federal government selected Blue Cross and Blue Shield to administer Michigan's Medicare program.

After decades of fast growth, Blue Cross and Blue Shield has faced a new set of challenges in recent years. As all prepayment programs became increasingly popular, so did appeals from group customers to control the rapidly rising cost of health care.

Blue Cross and Blue Shield of Michigan's downtown Detroit headquarters building was dedicated in 1971.

Blue Cross and Blue Shield, which started addressing the cost containment issue in the 1950s, has developed a number of programs to discourage the provision of unnecessary services and to encourage a more efficient health care delivery system. Most of the cost avoidance programs are designed to keep people out of the hospital whenever possible because that is where most health care costs arise. Other elements have included encouraging same-day surgery and the seeking of second medical opinions for certain surgical procedures. In 1986 Blue Cross and Blue Shield recovered $194 million through

Blue Cross and Blue Shield of Michigan sponsors fitness events in communities across the state to help build a healthier Michigan.

these programs. Total cost containment savings topped $1.6 billion that year.

While the plans provided a unique service back in 1939, Blue Cross and Blue Shield today faces an increasing number of competitors in the nation's $466 billion health care market. Those new entrants include commercial insurance companies, health maintenance organizations, preferred provider organizations, for-profit hospital/insurance combines, and third-party administrators. That competition, which cost Blue Cross and Blue Shield 20 percent of its members in the late 1970s and early 1980s, has spurred the Blues to fight back with its own HMOs and the relatively new preferred provider organizations. Blue Cross and Blue Shield's 1983 annual report spelled out this challenge:

Group Health Service of Michigan Inc., in Saginaw, is one of seven health maintenance organizations in the statewide Blue Care Network developed by Blue Cross and Blue Shield of Michigan.

"Our market is changing. We must grow and change with it."

In meeting that goal, chairman John C. McCabe said in a 1984 speech, "We've become the standard by which other health plans are judged. People refer to 'Blue Cross' when they mean any type of health coverage or insurance. That's good! It means our 45 years of service have achieved a measure of recognition many organizations only dream of. But it also places on us an obligation to continue doing what we do best—provide the finest-possible health care at the lowest-possible cost."

AAA MICHIGAN

Founded in 1916 to serve the motoring public, the Detroit Automobile Club (now AAA Michigan) has grown along with the automobile industry and responded to its inherent challenges. From marking roads in the 1920s to offering wartime travel advice in the 1940s to advocating the use of safety belts in the 1980s, AAA Michigan has never lost sight of its responsibility to motorists.

In the early days of motoring, un-

Marking roads and offering safety tips were part of the club's early services to its members.

marked roads were an adventure and a hazard. In 1916 William B. Bachman, later to be known as the "Father of Modern Highway Marking" was chairman of the club's Signs and Road-Posting Committee. Taking buckets of paint and whatever help he could find, Bachman painted bands of color on utility poles along major highways. By 1920, 19 different routes covering 1,500 miles were marked, making it the first comprehensive road sign system in the United States.

Travel planning was a logical step for the club, and it began providing free maps, brochures, and advice to motorists. Parking instructions and routings to popular events, such as football games in Ann Arbor, began in the club's early years and continue to be offered today by AAA Michigan.

Motorists and pedestrians have benefited from the many programs instituted by AAA Michigan. They include the school Safety Patrol, started in 1919 to reduce the number of deaths among young pedestrians, and the "Bring 'Em Back Alive!" Holiday News Service now in its 23rd year of informing drivers of road conditions during the three major summer holidays.

Emergency Road Service and automobile insurance were added in 1922, and

commercial airline tickets were issued to AAA customers in 1929. The AAA Travel Agency is now the largest in the state.

The club magazine, *Detroit Motor News,* dropped the city designation from its title in 1931. Renamed *Michigan Living* in 1981, the publication now has the largest circulation of any magazine in the state.

In 1961 AAA Michigan became the first auto club in the nation to serve an entire state. It is one of 166 affiliates, and, except for affiliation agreements with National AAA, is autonomous.

AAA Michigan serves its members in many other ways, such as offering discount auto leasing; finance plans for purchasing new or used cars, campers, and boats; money market funds; AAA/Visa credit cards; and home, boat, and life insurance.

In 1983 the 272-acre Boblo Island amusement park in the Detroit River was purchased, adding a new facet to AAA Michigan's recreation services, which include ticketing for sports and entertainment events.

AAA Michigan's current officers are Lawrence B. Lindermer, chairman; Dean E. Richardson, vice-chairman; Jack Avignone, president; and Robert B. Janks, executive vice-president.

Thousands of passengers each summer ride the historic SS Columbia and her sister ship, the SS Ste. Claire, to Boblo Island, an amusement park in the Detroit River purchased by AAA Michigan in 1983.

THE AMBASSADOR BRIDGE

On November 11, 1929, tens of thousands of U.S. and Canadian citizens jammed the waterfront on the Detroit River to witness ceremonies opening the Ambassador Bridge. The longest suspension bridge in the world at that time, it connected Detroit, Michigan, and Windsor, Ontario, over a narrow stretch of the Detroit River, thus providing convenient travel for motorists and a burgeoning trucking industry.

The completion of the bridge did not take place without a long struggle between politicians, railroad barons, and Great Lakes shipping magnates. As early as the 1870s James Joy, head of the Michigan Central Railroad Company, petitioned the U.S. Corps of Engineers for permission to build a bridge across the Detroit River and thus eliminate the slow, unreliable, and costly ferry service. Opposing the railroads, however, was the powerful Great Lakes Carriers Association representing the shipping industry in the Great Lakes. That organization successfully blocked the construction of any bridge on the Detroit River that required the construction of piers in the river. Finally, after repeated failures to get approval from the U.S. Corps of Engineers, the Michigan Central Railroad Company built a tunnel under the river. This alternative met the immediate needs of railroads when it opened in 1909, but did nothing to eliminate the bottleneck facing the steadily increasing number of motorists and truckers who traveled constantly between Michigan and Ontario.

Mayor James Couzens of Detroit announced plans in 1919 to build a bridge across the Detroit River as a memorial to the U.S. and Canadian soldiers who served in World War I. But nothing tangible was accomplished until 1920, when Charles Evan Fowler, a prominent New York civil engineer, developed a plan for a two-tier suspension bridge to accommodate automobiles, trains, streetcars, and pedestrians. He won approval from the Corps of Engineers, Parliament, and Congress, and organized the American & Canadian Transit Companies to raise funds from public and private sources.

The Fowler plan failed because the high costs of constructing a railroad bridge with its need for long inland approaches was prohibitive. Only $500,000 of the required $28 million was raised. Fowler

had the engineering experience but was not an experienced fund raiser.

This role was filled by Joseph A. Bower, a New York financeer who was contacted by J.W. Austin, an official of the American Transit Company. Bower was a Detroiter by birth and had lived there until 1914, when he was lured to New York to join the J.P. Morgan financial empire. He had developed a reputation for rescuing and reorganizing declining or mismanaged

companies. He eagerly accepted the challenge.

Bower scrapped the Fowler design as too costly and eliminated the railroad tier of the bridge. He hired the distinguished engineering firm of McClintic and Marshall of Pittsburgh and several bridge experts as consultants. After a bitter battle

The Ambassador Bridge

with Mayor John Smith of Detroit, who opposed a privately owned bridge, and a successful fund-raising campaign, construction began in September 1927.

The span was 152 feet above the Detroit River at the center and 135 feet at the harbor lines. The grade was 3 percent on the American side and 4 percent on the Canadian side. The two main towers rise 363 feet above the base of the piers; the main span stretches 1,850 feet between the towers.

The construction proceeded well ahead of the three-year schedule with arrangements made for an opening in July 1929. These plans changed suddenly in February of that year when it was discovered that a number of broken wires were found on the cables of the nearly completed Mount Hope Bridge in Rhode Island. This bridge shared with the Ambassador Bridge the dintinction of using newly developed heat-treated wire. Bower and officials of McClintic and Marshall immediately halted works on the Detroit bridge; removed the center span, suspenders, and cables; and started anew with time-tested cold-drawn steel wire. Despite this setback the bridge was ready for opening on Armistice Day, November 11, 1929.

The completion of the Ambassador Bridge was not the only challenge to Joseph Bower and his staff. Two weeks prior to its opening the stock market crashed, heralding a long economic recession. In 1930 the Detroit and Canada Tunnel, connecting downtown sections of Detroit and Windsor, opened, providing intense competition for motorists. With the start of World War II, gas rationing, a shortage of cars, and the decline of tourism, the bridge continued to struggle. It was not until the 1950s that the bridge witnessed a steady growth in revenue and traffic. The U.S. Canada Auto Pact, passed in 1965, also provided a tremendous increase in truck use of the bridge.

To meet the increased volume of traffic bridge officials have conducted a continuous maintenance program, replacing the roadways when needed, enlarging customs and warehouse facilities, and in 1981 installing a beautiful necklace of lights on the cables to give greater visibility to the structure.

The fact that the service of the Ambassador Bridge has expanded tremendously since it opened in 1929, without major reconstruction, is a tribute indeed to those with the vision to plan for its future usefulness. Its 57-year history is marked by the leadership of men who planned the structure, the expertise of engineers who built and maintained it, and the competence and resourcefulness of those who managed it.

Joseph A. Bower skillfully guided the fortunes of the bridge until he retired in 1965. R. Bryson MacDougald and C. Clinton Campbell managed the company until 1961 when Roy G. Lancaster took over the reins of leadership, first as vice-president and secretary, and in 1967 as president.

Although the success of the enterprise has, too often, been measured in terms of profit and revenue margins, the benefits from the bridge extend far and wide. It has done more than facilitate crossing of the Detroit River for people and vehicles. Reaching skyward, the Ambassador Bridge's magnificent towers give the populace of Detroit and Windsor, as well as traveling newcomers, a sight perhaps as awe inspiring as that witnessed by Father Louis Hennepin, the Jesuit priest, who reported on the remarkable beauty of the natural Detroit River scene more than 200 years ago.

Laying of the cornerstone of the United States Administration Building, early 1929.

MICHIGAN 4-H FOUNDATION

4-H has been a part of Michigan since 1914. Once a youth program to help teach rural children, 4-H now reaches more than 170,000 young people in every Michigan county.

For more than 70 years the 4-H clover has been the familiar symbol of a thriving program for the nation's young people. It began as a youth program to help teach home and farm practices as well as skills for living. It has blossomed into today's 4-H—a contemporary youth-serving organization with diverse programs aimed at meeting the needs of young people and their families in every part of Michigan.

It was in 1914 that 4-H became the official youth program of the nation's land-grant universities. Since then Mich-

The Michigan 4-H Horseback Riding for Handicappers program has given more than 10,000 special children the chance to learn to ride horses. The program helps the riders improve balance and coordination and gives them the chance to be in control of a large animal.

igan State University in East Lansing, the nation's premier land-grant university, has been the home base for Michigan 4-H Youth Programs. It is administered through the Cooperative Extension Service.

Thanks to the connection between

Michigan State 4-H Directors (1914-present)

Eduard C. Lindemann
Ray A. Turner
Arne G. Kettunen
Russell G. Mawby
Gordon L. Beckstrand
Norman A. Brown
Barbara S. Stowe
Michael J. Tate

4-H and the university, MSU faculty and staff develop curriculum and activities in such areas as family and child development, foods and nutrition, career exploration, agricultural sciences, the arts, and computer technology. From Cooperative Extension Service offices in all of Michigan's 83 counties 4-H staff members help thousands of adult volunteer leaders work with local young people. County government and local advisory groups provide essential financial commitment and grass roots orientation to program emphasis.

The Michigan 4-H Foundation, founded in 1952, is one of the major support mechanisms by which 4-H develops and expands its programs to children and communities throughout the

state. The foundation, organized by business leaders and educators, is governed by a 24-person board of trustees who give time and talent at quarterly meetings, through active committee work, and by obtaining financial contributions for 4-H work. As a public foundation it invites charitable gifts and grants from everyone who is interested in its purposes. Effective management and application of these resources has been credited with helping Michigan 4-H become recognized as one of the nation's most successful, most innovative, and most popular youth programs. The foundation also owns and operates Kettunen Center, the state's

---

Michigan 4-H Foundation Executive Directors (1952-present)

Howard S. Worthington
Benjamin Westrate
Ralph E. Kirch, Jr.
Edward C. Miller
Donald R. Jost

---

popular 4-H retreat in northwest Michigan.

A secret of Michigan 4-H success is its 4-H volunteer leadership—recruited, trained, and sustained by paid staff. Working directly with children and teens, 4-H provides opportunities for thousands of caring adults to give testimony to their keen interests in the education of youth. All 4-H activities are designed to complement and supplement the learning offered in schools. 4-H is helping more than 173,000 Michigan young people experience success—the gratification that results from taking on responsibility, following through with projects, doing the very best they can, and thereby building confidence.

Ultimately 4-H makes a difference at

A Selection of Events, Michigan 4-H History

1908 Boys' and Girls' clubs begin.
1914 4-H becomes the youth program of the Cooperative Extension Service.

1925 Arne G. Kettunen begins a 31-year career as Michigan 4-H director.

1942 The first of 27 annual State 4-H Shows is held on Michigan State University campus.

1952 Michigan 4-H Foundation incorporated to marshall private support and donations for 4-H development.

1961 Kettunen Center (originally named Camp Kett) is constructed entirely with donated money. It becomes the training facility for 4-H volunteer leaders and the symbol of Michigan 4-H's commitment to excellence.

1970 4-H Youth Exploration Days becomes an annual event for 4,000 teens at Michigan State University.

1975 Michigan 4-H Horseback Riding for Handicappers program is established as one of 4-H's most innovative activities.

1977 Michigan legislature funds special expansion project.

1978 Superior Service Award of USDA comes to Michigan's state 4-H leadership.

1980 The nation's first packaged stress management program for youth is developed by 4-H and the MSU College of Human Medicine.

1986 Enrollment tops 173,000 youths. Over 27,000 people are volunteer 4-H leaders.

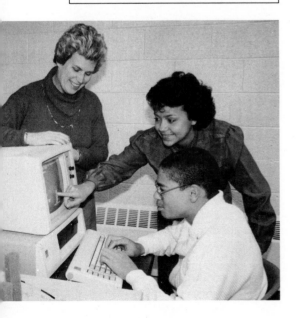

the community level. 4-H'ers in the Thumb, for instance, research the rich heritage of one-room schools and interview former students of all ages, while a club near Three Rivers devotes a winter season to mastery of the microwave oven, learning good nutrition and food preparation skills. The McClellan 4-H Center in Detroit operates in a former youth gang stronghold. Now young people are in groups that spend time learning home economics, nutrition, drama, and dance—programs that develop self-esteem and positive leadership.

The array of popular 4-H projects available includes video production, fashion design, bicycle safety, and outdoor adventure. Youths also gravitate toward programs focused on stress management, substance abuse prevention, building family relationships, and international understanding.

There is no one ingredient that makes 4-H the prominent and effective youth-serving organization that it is. Rather it is the blending of competent county staff members, expert program design by Michigan State University specialists, community leaders who serve on planning

RIGHT: Kids and animals are an unbeatable combination. Through their large and small animal projects, 4-H'ers have responsibilities and learn about animal behavior, health, and life cycles.

LEFT: Today's 4-H means helping kids get in touch with the future. Programs in career exploration, computers, robotics, and electronics help 4-H members explore the multiplicity of high-tech careers.

Symbolic of Michigan 4-H programming excellence is Kettunen Center. Its modern buildings and 140 acres are ideal as the setting for training the 4-H volunteer leaders corps. Located at Tustin, south of Cadillac, the conference center hosts 4-H workshops plus meetings of many other nonprofit groups.

committees, the support of the Michigan 4-H Foundation, and the invaluable efforts of thousands of volunteer 4-H leaders from all over the state.

The most important ingredient, however, is young people. As it has for more than 70 years, 4-H allows youngsters to discover themselves and explore their world, and have fun in the process!

EASTERN MICHIGAN UNIVERSITY

The Eastern Michigan University campus occupies 420 acres on the northwestern side of Ypsilanti.

Prior to 1849 the concept of establishing special schools for teacher training was still a novel idea; only Massachusetts and New York had launched normal schools. Michigan, with fewer than 400,000 residents scattered around the still rural state, joined those enterprising states that year with the founding of The Michigan State Normal School. Now known as Eastern Michigan University, the new school was the first teacher training institution west of the Allegheny Mountains, the sixth such college in the nation, and only the second normal school to offer a four-year baccalaureate program for teachers.

Eastern Michigan has maintained its leadership in training teachers through the years, and it is currently among the nation's top five schools in the number of professionals it prepares in all areas of education.

The Ypsilanti-based university has branched out quite a bit since those early days. Located on 420 acres, state-supported Eastern Michigan is comprised of the colleges of Arts and Sciences, Business, Education, Health and Human Services, and Technology. Eastern Michigan has over 23,000 students including 16,739 undergraduate students and 6,356 graduate students in the fall of 1986.

Early on the normal schools distin-

guished themselves from other institutions by their emphasis on practical training or student teaching. During Eastern Michigan's formative years this training was conducted at a special school called The Model, which featured a curriculum of "object lessons and the elements of natural science. . .arithmetic, grammar, and elementary history, thorough training in reading, penmanship, spelling, drawing, composition, singing, and moral lessons." The aspiring teachers took such courses as psychology, history, the philosophy of education, and the legal basis and structure of Michigan's public school system.

Eastern Michigan developed a special niche in special education when it became the nation's first teacher's college to prepare instructors of handicapped children and developed Michigan's first program for teachers of the mentally impaired.

Despite the fact that teacher training was the school's bread and butter, Eastern Michigan also developed a fine arts department that helped lay the groundwork for a broader liberal arts program. By the 1930s students could take programs in stage decoration, sculpture, commercial art, etching, and art appreciation.

Dr. John W. Porter became Eastern Michigan University's 17th president in 1979 after 10 years as Michigan superintendent of public instruction.

Even though it was so successful Eastern Michigan had to fight off threats of being closed during the Great Depression and during World War II when there existed a growing demand for housing for factory employees who worked in a nearby military supply plant. Eastern Michigan's image changed

Opened in 1982, Eastern Michigan University's Olds Student Recreation Center contains the largest indoor swimming pool in Michigan.

programs as computer-aided design technology (CAD), computer-aided manufacturing technology (CAM), plastics technology, and polymers and coatings technology. Eastern Michigan graduates in these areas have gone on to work at Hewlett-Packard Co., Dow Chemical Company, and other corporations on the cutting edge of applied research and development.

"The problem we're having in the United States is not a lack of knowledge," the College of Technology's dean, Alvin Rudisill, told the *Ann Arbor News.* "I think institutions like Eastern have to play a fairly large role to apply knowledge and skills."

As it approaches its 140th anniversary, Eastern Michigan has continued to update its physical plant with such developments as the Olds Student Recreation Center. Opened in 1982, the complex features the state's largest indoor pool. Construction is now starting on the university's $4.5-million Corporate Education Center, which is part of a $30-million development. Land acquisition is under way for a $17-million College of Business building in downtown Ypsilanti.

As Eastern Michigan University has remained true to its teaching heritage, it has also found the resources and made the commitment to branch out and serve Michigan's changing needs.

markedly from that of a "woman's teaching school" with the development of industrial arts and physical education programs and the massive influx of war veterans returning to school after 1945.

Michigan State Normal College became Eastern Michigan College in 1956 and attained university status three years later. Since then the university has continued to broaden its course selection and to develop the distinct educational niches that have distinguished it from the University of Michigan, its larger and better-known neighbor in Ann Arbor.

Under the leadership of the university's 17th president, Dr. John Porter, Eastern Michigan has been on the forefront of Michigan's efforts to shift its economic base from one heavily concentrated on manufacturing to a more diverse economy. To further these ends Eastern Michigan's College of Technology has developed such

Eastern Michigan University's Corporate Education Center is currently under construction. The complex will include a Radisson Hotel and a golf course.

WDIV-TV

When WWJ-TV began broadcasting in Detroit on March 4, 1947, it was Michigan's first television station, only the sixth in the nation, and part of a natural progression for its owner, the *Detroit News.* Because the *News,* Detroit's evening newspaper, already owned the city's first AM radio station and the nation's first FM band, a television station would cement the newspaper's goal of becoming a communications and media leader.

Once on the air, WWJ-TV—first called WWDT and now known as WDIV-TV—reeled off a string of television firsts, including the first telecast stage show, the first televised bowling match, and the first complete university extension courses by television.

But the *News'* desire to lead the pack and an almost zealous interest in sending remote crews to cover football, boxing, hockey, and baseball led to financial losses

The WWJ-TV in-house orchestra played back-up music for television shows and occasionally performed on its own.

in the first few years. WWJ-TV crews would often shoot two or three of these remote shots in a given day.

The early studio programming included "Romper Room," "Church at the Crossroads"—one of the first religious shows on television—and "At the Zoo," hosted by Detroit comedian and television personality Marvin "Sonny" Eliot, who took viewers on trips around the Detroit Zoo. The early WWJ-TV even featured an in-house orchestra that occasionally performed on its own during specials as well as playing background theme music for various shows.

The station joined the National Broadcasting Company network in 1948 and became one of the broadcasters forming NBC's first coast-to-coast television network three years later.

WWJ-TV became WDIV-TV in 1978, when the Evening News Association, the parent company, exchanged television stations with Post-Newsweek Stations Inc., which then owned WTOP-TV in Washington, D.C.

In 1982 the station moved next door from its old art deco-style building in downtown Detroit to a new $13.5-million, 79,500-square-foot facility complete with rooftop helicopter landing area, four studios, and 100 pieces of artwork throughout the structure. In addition to its modern studios, WDIV-TV has continued WWJ-TV's tradition of innovative remote broadcasting by being the only station in southeast Michigan with mobile production capabilities.

WDIV-TV continues its historic in-

From its inception in 1947 WWJ-TV (now called WDIV-TV) featured remote broadcasts. Here the station documents a physical therapy session for a polio victim.

WDIV-TV's $13.5-million downtown Detroit studios are among the most technologically advanced in the nation. The new building opened for business on December 6, 1982.

terest in sports by broadcasting numerous Detroit Tiger baseball games each season. The television station has also reached out to new frontiers in local programming. The nationally syndicated music show, "Saturday Night Music Machine," is produced at WDIV and distributed to other cities. WDIV-TV annually produces the Easter Seal Telethon. The Detroit telethon has a tradition of generating the second-highest total of pledges. And, in a unique approach to fund raising, WDIV-TV, in partnership with Children's Hospital, produces the "Salute to Excellence" each year. The program honors a Detroiter in a fun-filled roast that is broadcast and, in turn, raises money for important research and services at two Michigan hospitals serving children.

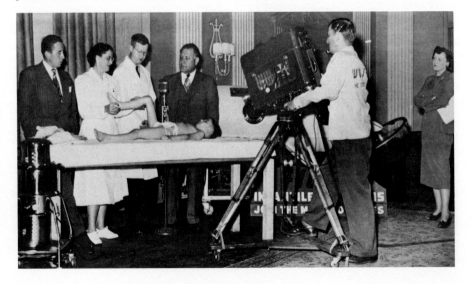

GRAND VALLEY STATE COLLEGE

Grand Valley State College was chartered by the Michigan State Legislature on April 26, 1960, in large part because a group of West Michigan citizens, led by L. William Seidman, believed a public baccalaureate institution was needed to serve the state's second-largest population center. In addition to acquiring a beautiful 897-acre site on the Grand River seven miles west of Grand Rapids, the founders had to raise in excess of one million dollars to give the institution its start.

In September 1963 GVS first opened its doors with 226 freshmen and 14 faculty members. Dr. James Zumberge from the University of Michigan served as the first president. In 1967 the pioneer class graduated and the college earned its first accreditation from the North Central Association. Arend D. Lubbers became president in 1969, coming to GVS from the presidency of Central College in Iowa.

College enrollment has since grown to more than 9,000, with faculty and support staff numbering nearly 650. Under the leadership of Lubbers the college introduced new professional programs in response to regional needs, including business; nursing, physical therapy, and health sciences; social work; computer science, engineering, and technology; and communications.

In the 1960s a unique federation of colleges came into being at GVS, with Thomas Jefferson College, William James College, Seidman College, and Kirkhof College joining the original College of Arts and Sciences. By 1983 the institution had completed an administrative reorganization into a traditional single-college system with four divisions: Arts and Humanities, Science and Mathematics, Social Sciences, and Business and Economics, offering 75 baccalaureate degrees as well as several master's programs: business administration, education, health sciences, nursing, public administration, social work, taxation, and joint programs with Michigan State University in engineering.

More than 11,000 individuals each year participate in classes, conferences, and workshops on GVS's main campus, through its downtown Grand Rapids Center, or through its Lakeshore Center at Muskegon Community College. In addition to serving students from nearly every county in Michigan and from 44 other states, the college hosts students from foreign countries around the world.

From an old farmhouse designated as an administration building and a single-story home housing the library in 1962, the college's facilities have increased to 43. Among the most recent additions are a new nine-story high-tech Grand Rapids Center and four buildings adjacent to the center donated to the college by Steelcase Inc.

The center, on the west bank of the Grand River in downtown Grand Rapids, includes 43 classrooms and laboratories, as well as teleconference and seminar rooms, the college's public broadcasting operations, the GVS Office for Economic Expansion, and the Institute for Office Productivity. The facility is becoming the hub of a major research and technology park, encompassing the approximately 10 acres of property and buildings owned by the college at the site.

As Michigan adapts to changing technology and a changing national and international economic structure, Grand Valley State College looks to the years ahead with the same intellectual energy and resilience that has characterized its first quarter-century.

The college's high-tech center in downtown Grand Rapids delivers graduate courses and other professional offerings—including workshops and teleconferences tailored for business, industry, government, health and human services, and higher education.

In less than 20 years Grand Valley State's Zumberge Library has become an important regional facility, meeting the needs of students, scholars, and researchers in business, industry, and government.

EDISON SAULT ELECTRIC COMPANY

"Water is power" is a fitting corporate motto for Edison Sault Electric Company. Few natural water formations in the world have lent themselves so readily to hydro development as the St. Mary's River, which drops some 19 feet in less than a half-mile while connecting Lake Superior with lakes Michigan and Huron.

The shallowest point in the spillway of the St. Mary's River is the rapids area, named by the early French missionaries as Le Sault de Sainte Marie, or Falls of St. Mary. A gathering place for native tribes who fished and traded in the Great Lakes area, when the first Europeans arrived in the early seventeenth century, land at the edge of the rapids became one of the interior frontier's first settlements. Sault Ste. Marie, regarded today as the third-oldest settlement in the United States, is headquarters for Edison Sault Electric Company.

In the late 1800s local investors formed the Edison Sault Light and Power Company and developed the first hydroelectric generation in the St. Mary's River. In 1892 William Chandler and Harris T. Dunbar formed Edison Sault Electric Company to take over the operation of the small hydro plant. In 1907 the company, to meet a growth in the demand for electricity, built a second plant on the St. Mary's River. That same year the International Joint Commission (IJC), consisting of parties from the United States and Canada, was formed to clarify the ownership of water rights in the St. Mary's

River. In 1909 the U.S. Congress passed the Rivers and Harbors Act—boundary waters such as the St. Mary's River belonged to both countries and thus had to be shared.

This act also authorized acquisition by the U.S. government of the land, rights, and powerhouse owned by Chandler and Dunbar, deemed necessary in order to better control the lakes' waters for navigation purposes. This Supreme Court case, *U.S.* v. *Chandler Dunbar Water Power Company,* resulted in a decision that provided a cash payment to the Edison Sault Electric Company for the plant. As part of the consideration the hydroelectric plant was to be leased to the Edison Sault Electric Company for a period of 30 years. In addition, similar leases were to be granted for any new power plant constructed in the rapids by the government.

In 1952 the government completed a new, 16,000-kilowatt hydroelectric facility in the St. Mary's Rapids, and Edison Sault Electric Company entered into an agreement to lease the power that is not required for the Soo Locks. Under this contract, which expires in the year 2000, Edison Sault Electric Company provides some of this power to Cloverland Electric Cooperative.

Edison Sault Electric Company purchased its 30,000-kilowatt hydroelectric plant in 1963 from the Union Carbide Corporation. In operation today, the plant has been designated as a National Historical Mechanical Engineering Land-

The Edison Sault Electric Company hydro plant facility.

mark. The power plant and canal were constructed in the late 1800s by Francis Clergue and completed in 1902. The plant itself is a full one-quarter mile long. Water is diverted into the plant from Lake Superior through a 2.25-mile-long man-made water canal that averages 200 feet wide and 20 feet deep. Power from this plant is also distributed to Cloverland Electric Cooperative. Edison Sault Electric Company has secured water rights to keep the plant operational by a lease that expires in the year 2050.

The water rights secured by the government contracts have enabled Edison Sault Electric Company to provide the lowest electric rates in the State of Michigan among investor-owned utilities. The company purchases the balance of its needs from Consumers Power Company over submarine cables in the Straits of Michigan.

Today the utility serves approximately 16,000 residential and commercial customers in the eastern upper peninsula. Its employees number approximately 100, with operational crews at St. Ignace, Mackinac Island, and Manistique. The firm is owned by approximately 1,000 shareholders spread throughout the United States. Close to 50 percent of the stock is held by Michigan shareholders, the majority of which reside in the service territory of Edison Sault Electric Company.

AMWAY CORPORATION

Amway Corporation's two founders, Richard DeVos and Jay Van Andel, developed a friendship in the early 1940s while attending Grand Rapids Christian High School in keeping with their Dutch heritage. Van Andel owned a Model A Ford, and the first deal between the two paid Van Andel 25 cents per week for transportation.

They chose the Air Force for World War II service. At the end of the war the two went into business together in a flying school and air charter bus service, The Wolverine Air Service at Comstock Park. The venture was rocky at best, and, following attempts in fast food, bread baking, and toy manufacturing with time out for a yearlong cruise down the East Coast to South America, the two returned to Grand Rapids. The friends started a new business selling a line of food supplements, called Nutrilite Products, direct selling through a group of distributors. Van Andel and DeVos decided to break out on their own, and in late 1959 the Amway Corporation of Ada was organized.

The fledgling firm had humble beginnings in the basements of the two founders' homes. Wives Betty Van Andel and Helen DeVos provided support, understanding, and suggestions on what products should be offered to the consumer. The first was Liquid Organic Cleaner Concentrate (LOC), an all-purpose liquid that could be used for washing windows, dishes, walls, appliances, and cars. One year later another cleaning product, S-A-8 Laundry Detergent, the first biodegradable product, was introduced.

After a brief stint in a former Masonic Temple in Ada, the growing company purchased an abandoned gas station on M21 near the bridge over the Grand River. Growth was explosive.

The decade of the 1960s witnessed the first Amway convention of distributors in 1961; additional household cleaners added to the Amway products line; Amway of Canada, Ltd., opening at London, Ontario; and Queen Cookware items added in 1963, Amway's fifth birthday. Five new regional warehouses were added in 1965 to improve service to the independent distributors, the research and development staff was doubled, and a new cosmetology laboratory was fully equipped to evaluate personal care products.

Several automated production lines were in place by 1971, the installation of a giant color press brought in-house printing capability, and the "World of Amway" symbol was introduced when Amway of Australia Pty. Ltd. opened. In 1972 Amway purchased Nutrilite Products, Inc., the food supplement firm for which the founders had once worked. Amway purchased the Mutual Broad-

In 1959 Richard M. DeVos (left) and Jay Van Andel (right) combined their business experience and creativity to create Amway Corporation, which today is one of the world's largest network marketing companies with operations in more than 40 countries and territories.

casting System, Inc., and announced the acquisition of both the Pantlind Hotel in Grand Rapids, now the Amway Grand Plaza, and a luxury hotel/resort on Peter Island in the British Virgin Islands.

By 1986 Amway's estimated retail sales had soared to $1.3 billion. Operations of the network marketing company were conducted in more than 40 countries around the world by more than one million distributors, who were independent business persons. More than 300 items carried the Amway name in the fields of home care, personal care, home technology, health and fitness, and commercial lines.

When Amway Corporation purchased the "Hall of Free Enterprise" exhibit shown at the 1963-1964 New York World's Fair, which became the nucleus for the Center of Free Enterprise at the firm's world headquarters at Ada, the American Economic Foundation noted that "Amway and the Amway distributors provide an excellent example of free enterprise in action."

Amway Corporation's world headquarters is in Ada, Michigan, where DeVos and Van Andel started the company in 1959.

RENAISSANCE CENTER

To understand the saga of Renaissance Center, you must first appreciate the fact that these five towers consist of 11,500 windows, with 16,000 people on one side looking out and 4.5 million metropolitan Detroiters on the other side peering in.

The visions through both sides of those windows—the cityscape of downtown Detroit and the internal meanderings of Renaissance Center—tell a story of a mixed-use development unlike any other in America, a single massive construction of concrete, steel, and glass in which a major metropolitan community focused its hopes for the future: a complex that was created to be the major catalyst in the rebirth of a faltering central city.

Renaissance Center opened in 1977, after six years of planning and construction. In the early 1970s Detroit was a community that was on the verge of losing its heart. The civil disturbances of the late 1960s had intensified residential and business flight to the suburbs. And not unlike other major metropolitan areas, the city was becoming poorer while its surrounding neighborhoods became richer, amplifying urban-suburban tensions. Retailing was leaving the central city for outlying shopping centers.

A visitor to the central business district in the evening hours would find it dark and empty. Its pulse weak and its lifeblood draining to the suburbs, downtown Detroit

An artist's rendering illustrates the dramatic five-story reflective glass facade planned for the Jefferson Avenue entrance of Renaissance Center.

This aerial photograph of Renaissance Center shows the 73-story hotel, four 39-story office towers, and two 21-story office towers overlooking the Detroit River, the international border between Detroit and Windsor, Ontario, Canada.

was being deserted by many.

But one man in particular was not ready to give up on the area. Henry Ford II was determined to see a rebirth of vitality in Detroit, a rebirth that would begin right at the very roots of the city, its riverfront, on a site where its first settlers had established farms and trading posts. In November 1971 Ford announced his plans to build Renaissance Center. Through the sheer force of his convictions, he gathered 51 companies as partners, led by the Ford Motor Company, putting together the largest privately financed development in the history of the United States, selecting John Portman as the architect.

On April 15, 1977, the $350-million center was dedicated. It consisted of four 39-story office towers surrounding the world's tallest hotel and Michigan's tallest building, the 73-story Westin-Renaissance

Center. A 14-acre, four-level podium served as the base for the four office towers containing 2.2 million square feet, while the hotel provided more than 1,400 guest rooms. Included in the podium area was room for 360,000 feet of retail space.

In 1981 two additional 21-story towers were constructed on the east side of the center, again privately financed, this time as a joint venture of Ford Motor Land Development Corporation and Rockefeller Center, Inc. These two towers were subsequently purchased by American Natural Resources, put under a master lease, and syndicated.

As the people of Detroit invested their hopes and aspirations for the city in Renaissance Center, it became the symbol of the city. It represents Detroit as the Eiffel Tower represents Paris or the Empire State Building once represented New York. For example, two years after Renaissance Center construction was completed, the regional chamber of commerce incorporated it into its logo. The local public TV station focuses on the center in its opening visuals for Detroit-produced PBS programming. Everything from book bags to coffee mugs bears the logo of the center as the image of Detroit.

Renaissance Center's office towers are now 97-percent occupied. Tenants include the city's major financial institutions, all the Big Eight accounting firms, Michigan's largest law firm, Michigan's largest public relations firm, and many, many other key companies. Ford Motor Company demonstrated its commitment by leasing one entire tower, which came to include the headquarters for Ford Division, Lincoln-Mercury Division, and Ford Aerospace. General Motors and Honda expanded into the center, as well. Office space occupancy and the concentration of major corporations are the outstanding success story of Renaissance Center.

In 1986 Renaissance Center began implementing a $27-million redevelopment plan created by Rubloff, Inc., which now markets and manages the center.

A spectacular marquee was placed over the outside entrance to the hotel

Before (top) and after (left) views of Detroit's downtown riverfront show the dramatic change that has occurred with the construction of Renaissance Center. The earlier view was taken before site clearance began in 1972.

lobby. Then the lobby itself was redefined by large glass walls. A new registration area reflected a classic sytle with Brazilian granite, marble, brass, and earth tones, with this motif carried through the lounge and elevator lobby to further define the hotel's boundaries. Plush carpeting throughout the lobby area added to the comfort of the hotel entrance, as did comfortable chairs, intimate seating areas, and more pleasing surroundings. Colonnade pillars guide guests to the hotel elevators.

Stores were designed with large show windows opposite mirrored pillars. Colorful canopies top each entrance.

The second level was converted into a unique Professional Plaza, with 125,000

square feet of space for professional services. Michigan's largest law firm, Dykema, Gossett, Spencer, Goodnow & Trigg, and Manufacturers Bank are among the tenants of the plaza.

Ford Motor Company has further increased its commitment to Renaissance Center by leasing 35,000 square feet above the prime retail area for "The World of Ford," a public display of new Ford products and technology that opened in December 1986.

The most visible and revolutionary changes were carried out in 1987. A new main entrance for the center was constructed as a five-story reflective glass facade. Large display windows line the sidewalk from the front entrance around

the sides of the building.

A sleek, brightly lit pedestrian bridge now extends from the center across broad Jefferson Avenue to the Millender Center hotel/apartment/retail complex. It, in turn, is linked by a similar bridge to the City-County Building. Another bridge connects with a people mover elevated train station. The track makes a large loop at the berms bringing riders right to Renaissance Center's doorstep.

The Jefferson Avenue lobby houses a two-story atrium containing a new information center and two new escalators to transport tenants and guests to the people mover station, the Millender bridge, the Professional Plaza, and office tower elevators.

Hundreds of millions of dollars of development have been launched and planned since Renaissance Center took its place as the symbol of renewal on the riverfront.

When Detroiters peer into Renaissance Center's windows, they show smiles and a curious satisfaction. When tenants gaze out, they see an increasingly vibrant and bustling downtown and take pride in the knowledge that they are playing an important role in helping lead the city back from the brink of a smudged and murky future to a sparkling clear success.

WESTERN MICHIGAN UNIVERSITY

East Hall in 1910, at the top of Prospect Hill, which at the time was Western's entire campus. The building was entered in the National Register of Historic Places in 1978.

This double-track trolley was operated at the northeast corner of Prospect Hill, leading to East Hall, between 1908 and 1948.

"School Means Much To This City," shouted the headline in the *Kalamazoo Gazette-News* on August 30, 1903, two days after the state board of education announced its decision to locate a normal school in Kalamazoo. In fact, the decision to locate the state's fourth institution for the education of teachers was big news indeed.

And it should have been. The location of what would become the only comprehensive state university in West Michigan in a community would mean much—culturally, socially, economically, of course, and more.

To be precise, it took big money to get what would, in five name changes, become Western Michigan University—now one of the state's leading institutions for graduate education and research as well as for undergraduate education. To get it, Kalamazoo city fathers put up $40,000 in cash. They guaranteed that a site of at least 20 acres would be provided. And they promised to connect the institution to the city's utilities system without charge.

And it meant big money to have that institution as a "good neighbor" in the community. City fathers figured the facility would be worth $300,000 per year to the town in expenditures. That number has grown to what is conservatively estimated to be $150 million in revenue annually to its home community and to the region it serves. Not only would Western's presence contribute to the economic development of the region, but its programming would

almost from the start be focused on regional education and economic development.

Enrollment would grow from 117 students to nearly 22,000 students, more than 20 percent of them at the graduate level—the third-largest percentage of total enrollment in the state. Programs would grow from three—teacher education, rural education, and manual training—to nearly 170, including eight at the doctoral level. From its roots in teacher education, Western would emerge as one of the most successful institutions of its kind in the United States to make the transition to multipurpose university.

Western would grow from being one college to an institution encompassing nine colleges, a "multiversity" with nationally recognized stature as the fourth-most-complex and diverse institution of higher education in Michigan. That diversity is expressed in the names of the colleges: arts and sciences, business, education, engineering and applied sciences, fine arts, general studies, health and human services, the Graduate College, and the Honors College.

Western has carved out a unique national identity for itself by raising up centers of excellence—programs, many of

them pioneering ones, that are ranked today among the best in their fields. Such programs include paper and printing science and engineering, blind rehabilitation and mobility, mathematics and statistics, accountancy, psychology, speech pathology and audiology, educational evaluation, creative writing, computer literacy, occupational therapy, aviation, medieval studies, and Michigan's only doctorate in public administration.

That excellence is often expressed in the creation of knowledge. Research and other sponsored programs, which had their roots in a bureau of educational measurement and research begun in 1926, now approaches $5 million per year. From 11 faculty members, a principal—Dwight B. Waldo, who would become Western's first president—and his secretary, Western has grown to 770 full-time faculty members and a staff of 1,530.

It was fortunate, then, for Kalamazoo that those early civic leaders offered the state board of education a deal it did not refuse. Kalamazoo, with characteristic verve, was successful in its bid, at least in part because it demonstrated a very early awareness of, interest in, and commitment to securing the normal school for itself. On

June 3, 1903, exactly one week after Governor Aaron T. Bliss signed legislation authorizing the state's fourth normal school, Kalamazoo city council members, local school board members, and other influential citizens met to form an organization to seek the prize.

The group had to move quickly to accomplish what would become one of the major cultural and economic coups in the city's history, a stroke that would help to assure its relative economic security to the present day. In just 20 days, on June 23, 1903, the board of education would make its official inspection visit to Kalamazoo. When it arrived, it found a community that was both eager and prepared to make big promises, including the $40,000 in cash, the pledges of land, and a utilities connection—and that half the salaries of the training-school teachers would be paid by the city for up to five years.

Some of the cities that had competed for the school would soon benefit directly from the location of the institution in Kalamazoo. In 1905 Dr. John T. McMannis of the school's department of education and psychology was appointed to head an extension department that by 1909 would be operating centers in Grand

Sprau Tower, which houses faculty offices, stands today as a symbol of the university's commitment to excellence and the success of its students in some 170 academic programs, including eight at the doctoral level.

Rapids, Kalamazoo, Muskegon, and Niles. By 1929 no fewer than 57 classes were being offered to students throughout West Michigan. It was the beginning of what has become the second-largest university extension service in the state.

By the fall of 1986 the WMU Division of Continuing Education was offering 215 courses through 40 academic units to 17 communities through six regional centers: Battle Creek, Benton Harbor-St. Joseph, Grand Rapids, Kalamazoo, Lansing, and Muskegon. That "extension" of the university's effort and expertise has been characterized this way by Western's fifth, president, Dr. Diether H. Haenicke: "Nothing is more important to Western Michigan University than meeting the educational and economic development needs of the citizens of West Michigan and the state."

While Western has been delivering continuing education to communities throughout its region for many years, at first only in education but eventually through every one of its colleges, it was not until 1957 that Western appointed its first off-campus-based coordinator of extension programs—in Muskegon. A new emphasis in noncredit programming was added the same year. It was more than coincidence that 1957 was the year Western was granted university status in legislation signed February 26, 1957, by Governor G. Mennen Williams, and so became the state's fourth public university.

Governor G. Mennen Williams (seated) signed legislation on February 26, 1957, designating Western as the state's fourth public university. With him is university president Paul V. Sangren.

As Western Michigan University continues to reach out to the people of West Michigan and toward the next century, even more significant "extension" of the university is planned—through a reach into the heavens. It has been announced that Western is to be a charter member of a group of universities to offer educational resources by satellite television through the planned Michigan Information Technology Network. But no technology could meet the educational and economic development needs of the people of West Michigan and beyond without the long-standing prior commitment of Western Michigan University to be of abiding and increasing value and service—a commitment its history has demonstrated from the beginning.

PATRONS

The following individuals, companies, and organizations have made a valuable commitment to the quality of this publication. Windsor Publications and the Historical Society of Michigan gratefully acknowledge their participation in *Michigan: An Illustrated History of the Great Lakes State.*

AAA Michigan*
Judith Dow and Robert H. Alexander
The Ambassador Bridge*
Amway Corporation*
Amway Grand Plaza Hotel*
Auto-Owners Insurance*
Barfield Mfg. Co.
Battle Creek Adventist Hospital
Blue Cross and Blue Shield of Michigan*
Central Michigan University*
Consumers Power Co.*
Crowley, Milner & Co.*
Doubleday Bros. & Co.
The Dow Chemical Company*
Dow Corning Corporation*
Durametallic Corporation
Eastern Michigan University*
Edison Sault Electric Company*
Ervin Industries, Inc.*
First Federal of Michigan*
Ford & Earl Associates, Inc.*
Frankenmuth Bavarian Inn*
Grand Valley State College*
GSE, Inc.*
Hygrade Food Products Corp.*
Industrial Metal Products Corporation*
KAR Laboratories, Inc.
Kellogg Company*
Koenig Fuel & Supply
The Kroger Co.
Bill & Margaret Kruger
Laboratory Research Enterprises, Inc.
La-Z-Boy Chair Company*
Leonard Bros. Moving & Storage
    Company*
Liberty State Bank & Trust*
Ludington News Company, Inc.*
McPhail Corporation
Mazda Distributors Great Lakes*
Metropolitan Detroit Convention and
    Visitors Bureau*
Michigan Association of School Boards*

Michigan Bankers Association*
Michigan Education Association*
Michigan Elementary and Middle School
    Principals Association
Michigan 4-H Foundation*
Michigan Glass Coatings Inc.
Michigan Hospital Association*
Michigan Merchants Council*
Michigan Milk Producers Association*
Michigan Pharmacists Association
Michigan Railroads Association*
Michigan State University*
Montgomery and Associates
Morleys Travel Service
Parker Hannifin Corp.
Renaissance Center*
Saginaw Products Corp,
Severance Tool Industries Inc.
Shepler's Mackinac Island Ferry
    Service*
Smith & Smith Associates Architects,
    Inc.
Spartan Plastics*
Vickers, Incorporated*
WDIV-TV*
Weber's Inn*
Western Michigan University*
WKBD-TV50*

*Partners in Progress of *Michigan: An Illustrated History of the Great Lakes State.* The histories of these companies and organizations appear in Chapter XIII, beginning on page 212.

ACKNOWLEDGMENTS

Many individuals contributed in a variety of ways to this book and it is for me both a duty and a pleasure to acknowledge their help, without which it would not have been possible to carry this project through to completion.

First of all, my deepest thanks go to my wife Tish for her encouragement and help and for putting up, once more, with the inconveniences that work on a book often create.

I am indebted to Tom Jones, executive director of the Historical Society of Michigan, the society's board of trustees, and to Windsor Publications for entrusting this work to me. The members of Windsor's editorial staff with whom I worked—Annette Igra, Lynn Kronzek, and Jerry Mosher—were unfailingly helpful. Jerry Mosher's handling of the final editing of the manuscript and the illustrations greatly improved the quality of the work.

The following individuals took the time to help, particularly in acquiring materials which were either in their possession or which they helped to make available:

John Tobin of Plymouth; Glenna and Richard Kaiser of Canton Township; George Wiskemann and Geneva Kebler Wiskemann of the Lansing area; Ned Brockington and the late Henry Hopper from Saugatuck; Julian DePree of Castle Park, Holland; Toni VanKoevering of Zeeland; Jim Nice of Niles; John W. Leddick of Montague; Burton H. Boyum of Ishpeming; Lawrence Gustin of Flint; Congressman Mark D. Siljander; Margaret R. Bogue of Madison, Wisconsin; Betty Fladeland of Carbondale, Illinois; and F. Ward Paine of Portola Valley, California.

Equally important were the following individuals who helped open doors to materials or information available through the agencies or organizations in which they were employed:

Amway Grand Plaza, Grand Rapids: Nancy Hopkins

Ann Arbor Area Chamber of Commerce: Jim Taylor

Ann Arbor *News*: Bruce Moore and Mary Jane Hampson

Burton Historical Collection: Alice C. Dalligan

Detroit Historical Department: Patience A. Nauta

Detroit Institute of Arts: Michele Smith Peplin and Nancy Rivard Shaw

Dossin Great Lakes Museum: John F. Polacsek

Eastern Michigan University: Richard Oltmanns and Dick Schwarze

Ella Sharp Museum, Jackson: Mildred Hadwin and Ted Phelps

First of America Bank Muskegon, Whitehall Branch: Carol D. Mines

Flint *Journal*: David Larzelere

GeoSpectra Corporation: Peter K. Pleitner

Grand Rapids Art Museum: Cheryl L. Poole

Grand Rapids City Historian: Gordon Olson

Grand Rapids Public Museum: W.D. Frankforter and Marilyn Merdzinskissp,0,0

Henry Ford Museum and Greenfield Village: Kenneth M. Wilson, Cynthia Read-Miller, David Crippen, Win Sears, Jr., Walter E. Simmons II, and Wanda C. Karavas

Holland Tulip Time Festival: Pauline Vander Koog

Longfellow National Historic Site:

Stephen Whitesell

Mazda Motor Corporation: Joan M. Antista

Michigan, State Government:
Bureau of History, State Department: John Curry, Leroy Barnett, and Saralee R. Howard-Filler
Department of Commerce: Patty Jo Clouse
Department of Natural Resources: James F. Wieber
Governor's Office: Julia Wiles

Michigan Bell: Ralph R. Barber

Michigan Technological University: David Halkola and Jim Lutzke

Minnesota Historical Society: Bonnie Wilson

Museum of Arts and History, Port Huron: Sarah E. Larsen

Museum of Fine Arts, Boston: Carol Troyen

New Yorker: Grace Darby

St. Adalbert's Church, Grand Rapids: the late Rt. Rev. Msgr. Maksymowski

Smithsonian Institution, National Museum of American History: Patricia E. Geeson and Roger B. White

University of Michigan:
Bentley Historical Library: Francis X. Blouin, Jr., Nancy Bartlett, and Marjorie Barritt
Museum of Anthropology: John M. O'Shea and Mike Shott
William L. Clements Library: Arlene Shy

Western Michigan University Regional History Collections: Wayne Mann and Phyllis Burnham

Whitney Museum of American Art: Nancy Heine and Nancy McGary

SELECTED ADDITIONAL READINGS

GENERAL HISTORIES AND REFERENCES:

Bald, F. Clever. *Michigan in Four Centuries*. Revised ed. New York, 1961.

Catton, Bruce. *Michigan: A Bicentennial History*. New York, 1976.

Dunbar, Willis F., and George S. May. *Michigan: A History of the Wolverine State*. Revised ed. Grand Rapids, 1980.

Fuller, George N., ed. *Michigan: A Centennial History of the State and Its People*. 2 vols. Chicago, 1939.

May, George S. *Pictorial History of Michigan*. 2 vols. Grand Rapids, 1967, 1969.

Sommers, Lawrence M., ed. *Atlas of Michigan*. East Lansing, 1977.

Verway, David I., ed. *Michigan Statistical Abstract*. Detroit, published annually.

Writers' Program of the WPA. *Michigan: A Guide to the Wolverine State*. New York, 1941.

SPECIALIZED STUDIES:

Bald, F. Clever. *Detroit's First American Decade, 1796-1805*. Ann Arbor, 1948.

Barnard, Harry. *Independent Man: The Life of Senator James Couzens*. New York, 1958.

Capeci, Dominic J. *Race Relations in Wartime Detroit: The Sojourner Truth Housing Controversy of 1942*. Philadelphia, 1984.

Carson, Gerald. *Cornflake Crusade*. New York, 1957.

Chase, Lew Allen. *Rural Michigan*. New York, 1921.

Clive, Alan. *State of War: Michigan in World War II*. Ann Arbor, 1979.

Dain, Floyd R. *Education in the Wilderness*. Lansing, 1968.

_____. *Every House a Frontier: Detroit's Economic Progress, 1815-1825*. Detroit, 1956.

Dancy, John C. *Sand Against the Wind: The Memoirs of John C. Dancy*. Detroit, 1966.

Disbrow, Donald W. *Schools for an Urban Society*. Lansing, 1969.

Dorr, John A., Jr., and Donald F. Eschman. *Geology of Michigan*. Ann Arbor, 1970.

Dunbar, Willis F. *All Aboard: A History of Railroads in Michigan*. Grand Rapids, 1969.

_____. *Lewis Cass*. Grand Rapids, 1970.

_____. *The Michigan Record in Higher Education*. Detroit, 1963.

Farmer, Silas. *History of Detroit and Wayne County and Early Michigan*. 2 vols. Detroit, 1884.

Fine, Sidney. *Frank Murphy: The Detroit Years*. Ann Arbor, 1975.

_____. *Frank Murphy: The New Deal Years*. Chicago, 1979.

_____. *Frank Murphy: The Washington Years*. Ann Arbor, 1984.

_____. *Sit-down: The General Motors Strike of 1936-1937*. Ann Arbor, 1969.

Fitting, James E. *The Archaeology of Michigan: A Guide to the Prehistory of the Great Lakes Region*. Revised ed. Bloomfield Hills, 1975.

Fladeland, Betty. *James Gillespie Birney: Slaveholder to Abolitionist*. Ithaca, N.Y., 1955.

Formisano, Ronald P. *The Birth of Mass Political Parties: Michigan, 1827-1861*. Princeton, 1971.

Fuller, George N. *Economic and Social Beginnings of Michigan: A Study of the Settlement of the Lower Peninsula During the Territorial Period, 1805-1837*. Lansing, 1916.

Gates, William B., Jr. *Michigan Copper and Boston Dollars*. Cambridge, 1951.

George, Emily. *Martha W. Griffiths*. Washington, D.C., 1982.

George, Sister Mary Karl. *Zachariah Chandler: A Political Biography*. East Lansing, 1969.

Gilpin, Alec R. *The War of 1812 in the Old Northwest*. East Lansing, 1958.

Hamilton, Raphael N. *Father Marquette*. Grand Rapids, 1970.

Hatcher, Harlan. *A Century of Iron and Men*. Indianapolis, 1950.

Havighurst, Walter. *The Long Ships Passing*. New York, 1943.

Hemans, Lawton T. *Life and Times of Stevens T. Mason*. Lansing, 1930.

Holbrook, Stewart H. *Holy Old Mackinaw: A Natural History of the American Lumberjack*. New York, 1938.

Holli, Melvin G. *Reform in Detroit: Hazen S. Pingree and Urban Politics*. New York, 1969.

Innis, Harold A. *The Fur Trade in Canada: An Introduction to Canadian Economic History*. New Haven, 1930.

Katzman, David M. *Before the Ghetto: Black Detroit in the Nineteenth Century*. Urbana, 1973.

Kellogg, Louise Phelps. *The British Regime in Wisconsin and the Northwest*. Madison, 1935.

_____. *The French Regime in Wisconsin and the Northwest*. Madison, 1925.

Kinietz, W. Vernon. *The Indians of the Western Great Lakes, 1615-1760*. Ann Arbor, 1940.

Knauss, James O., and Charles Starring. *The Michigan Search for Educational Standards*. Lansing, 1969.

Levine, David Allan. *Internal Combustion: The Races in Detroit, 1915-1926*. Westport, 1976.

Lewis, David L. *The Public Image of Henry Ford: An American Folk Hero and His Company*. Detroit, 1976.

Lewis, Martin D. *Lumberman from Flint: The Michigan Career of Henry H. Crapo, 1855-1869.* Detroit, 1958.

Lucas, Henry S. *Netherlanders in America: Dutch Immigration to the United States and Canada, 1789-1950.* Ann Arbor, 1955.

McNaughton, Frank. *Mennen Williams of Michigan.* New York, 1960.

Martin, John Bartlow. *Call It North Country: The Story of Upper Michigan.* New York, 1945.

May, George S. *A Most Unique Machine: The Michigan Origins of the American Automobile Industry.* Grand Rapids, 1975.

——————. *Michigan and the Civil War Years, 1860-1866.* Lansing, 1964.

——————. *R.E. Olds: Auto Industry Pioneer.* Grand Rapids, 1977.

Maybee, Rolland M. *Michigan's White Pine Era, 1840-1900.* Lansing, 1960.

Murdoch, Angus. *Boom Copper: The Story of the First U.S. Mining Boom.* New York, 1943.

Nevins, Allan, and Frank Ernest Hill. *Ford.* 3 vols. New York, 1954-1963.

Orton, Lawrence D. *Polish Detroit and the Kolasinski Affair.* Detroit, 1981.

Parks, Robert J. *Democracy's Railroad: Public Enterprise in Jacksonian Michigan.* Port Washington, N.Y., 1972.

Peckham, Howard H. *Pontiac and the Indian Uprising.* Princeton, 1947.

Porter, Kenneth W. *John Jacob Astor, Businessman.* 2 vols. Cambridge, Mass., 1931.

Quimby, George I. *Indian Life in the Upper Great Lakes, 11,000 B.C. to A.D. 1800.* Chicago, 1960.

Rae, John B. *The American Automobile.* Chicago, 1965.

Rector, William G. *Log Transportation in the Lake States Lumber Industry.* Glendale, Cal., 1953.

Rintala, Edsel K. *Douglass Houghton, Michigan's Pioneer Geologist.* Detroit, 1954.

Rowe, John. *The Hard-Rock Miners: Cornish Immigrants and the North American Mining Frontier.* New York, 1974.

Sarasohn, Stephen R., and Vera H. Sarasohn. *Political Party Patterns in Michigan.* Detroit, 1957.

Schwarz, Richard H. *John Harvey Kellogg, M.D.* Nashville, 1970.

Stieber, Carolyn. *The Politics of Change in Michigan.* East Lansing, 1970.

Sweeney, J. Gray. *Great Lakes Marine Painting of the Nineteenth Century.* Muskegon, 1983.

Tompkins, C. David. *Senator Arthur Vandenberg: The Evolution of a Modern Republican, 1884-1945.* East Lansing, 1970.

Tyler, R.L. *Walter Reuther.* Grand Rapids, 1973.

Vander Hill, C. Warren. *Settling the Great Lakes Frontier: Immigration to Michigan, 1837-1924.* Lansing, 1970.

Vinyard, Jo Ellen. *The Irish on the Urban Frontier: Detroit, 1850-1880.* New York, 1976.

Whitehead, Don. *The Dow Story: The History of the Dow Chemical Company.* New York, 1968.

Woodford, Frank B. *Alex J. Groesbeck: Portrait of a Public Man.* Detroit, 1962.

——————. *Lewis Cass.* New Brunswick, N.J., 1950.

——————, and Arthur R. Woodford. *All Our Yesterdays: A Brief History of Detroit.* Detroit, 1969.

Wright, K.T. *The Changing Scene in Michigan Agriculture.* East Lansing, 1978.

NOTES
. . . . .

Chapter 1, p. 15, "a region of perpetual snows . . . , " quoted in Willis F. Dunbar and George S. May, *Michigan: A History of the Wolverine State,* revised ed. (Grand Rapids, 1980), 257.

—p. 15, "It would have been idle . . . ," Thomas M. Cooley, *Michigan: A History of Governments* (Boston, 1905), 224-225.

Chapter 2, p. 19, "an impoverished Hopewell . . . , " James E. Fitting, *The Archaeology of Michigan: A Guide to the Prehistory of the Great Lakes Region,* revised ed. (Bloomfield Hills, 1975), 98.

—p. 23, "to more effectively manage . . . ," Leslie Eger, speaking for the Sault Ste. Marie Tribe of Chippewa Indians and Bay Mills Indian Community, in *Natural Resources Register* 5(May 1985):6.

Chapter 5, p. 47, "He said it was impossible . . . , " William Nowlin, *The Bark-Covered House, or Pioneer Life in Michigan,* reprint ed. (Chicago, 1937), 4.

—p. 47, "was a beautiful country . . . ," Nowlin, *The Bark-Covered House,* 7.

—p. 47, "The thought of Indians . . . ," Nowlin, *The Bark-Covered House,* 5.

—p. 50, "Don't go to Michigan . . . ," quoted in Dunbar and May, *Michigan,* 187.

—p. 50, "was a very fertile country . . . ," Nowlin, *The Bark-Covered House,* 4.

—p. 50, "four feet deep . . . ," quoted in Douglas H. Gordon and George S. May, eds., "Michigan Journal, 1836, John M. Gordon," *Michigan History* 43(Sept. 1959):269, footnote 177.

—p. 50, "deep & rich loam . . . ," Gordon and May, eds., "Michigan Journal," *Michigan History* 43(Sept. 1959): 269.

—p. 57, "the magnificent harbor . . . ," Bela Hubbard, "A Michigan Geological Expedition in 1837," *Michigan Pioneer and Historical Collections* 3(1881):200.

—p. 59, "been more fortunes made . . . ," John T. Blois, *Gazetteer of the State*

of *Michigan,* reprint ed. (New York, 1975), 154.

—p. 59, "particularly odious . . . ," Gordon and May, eds., "Michigan Journal," *Michigan History* 43(Dec. 1959):452.

—p. 60, "Then come ye Yankee farmers . . . ," quoted in Dunbar and May, *Michigan,* 193.

—p. 61, "as a wheat country . . . ," quoted in Blois, *Gazetteer,* 418.

—p. 62, "One for the blackbird . . . ," quoted in Lew Allen Chase, *Rural Michigan* (New York, 1921), 188.

Chapter 6, p. 68, "occasionally seen . . . ," Blois, *Gazetteer,* 155.

—p. 70, "intelligent, imbued more than is common . . . , " quoted in Betty Fladeland, *James Gillespie Birney: Slaveholder to Abolitionist* (Ithaca, N.Y., 1955), 213.

—p. 72, "to take such measures . . . ," quoted in Henry M. Utley and Byron M. Cutcheon, *Michigan as a Province, Territory and State* (New York, 1906), 3:381.

—p. 72, "That in view of . . . ," quoted in Utley and Cutcheon, *Michigan,* 3:383.

—p. 73, *Chief Shoppenegons* (19th Century) by Eanger Irving Crouse (American, 1866-1936). Paint on canvas, 6 feet, 6 inches x 36 inches. Accession No. 11.4. ©1987 The Detroit Institute of Arts, Gift of Charles Willis Ward.

—p. 74, *Sault Ste. Marie, Showing the United States Garrison in the Distance* (1836-1837) by George Catlin. Oil on canvas, 19 5/8 x 27 5/8 in. (49.7 x 70.0 cm.) L.1965.1.339. National Museum of American Art, Smithsonian Institution, Gift of Mrs. Joseph Harrison, Jr.

—p. 77, *First State Election in Detroit, Michigan* (1837) by Thomas Mickell Burnham (American, 1818-1866). Paint on canvas, 24 1/2 x 30 3/4 in. Accession No. 57.267. ©1987 The Detroit Institute of Arts, Gift of Mrs. Samuel T. Carson.

—p. 79, *View of Detroit in 1836* (1836) by William James Bennett (American, 1787-1844). Paint on canvas, 17 1/2 x 25 in. Accession No. 34.24. ©1987 The Detroit Institute of Arts, Gift of the Fred Sanders Company in memory of its founder, Fred Sanders.

—p. 83, "Some of the manufacturing states think . . . , " quoted in George

S. May, *Michigan and the Civil War Years, 1860-1866* (Lansing, 1964), 5.

—p. 83, "late president . . . ," document in the possession of Pritchard's grandson, Dudley Pritchard, Allegan, Michigan.

—p. 84, "To treat this enemy gently . . . ," quoted in May, *Michigan and the Civil War Years,* 20.

—p. 85, "Freedom reigns . . . ," quoted in David M. Katzman, *Before the Ghetto: Black Detroit in the Nineteenth-Century* (Urbana, 1973), 50.

Chapter 7, p. 87, "inseparably linked . . . ," quoted in George S. May, comp., *"Let Their Memories Be Cherished": Michigan Civil War Monuments* (Lansing, 1965), 31.

—p. 91, "a gorgeous incident . . . ," Stewart H. Holbrook, *Holy Old Mackinaw: A Natural History of the American Lumberjack* (New York, 1938), 82.

—p. 94, "The modern saw mill . . . ," James W. Bartlett, in *The Semi-Centennial of the Admission of the State of Michigan into the Union* (Detroit, 1886), 342.

—p. 95, "to render the evenings . . . ," quoted in Edsel K. Rintala, *Douglass Houghton, Michigan's Pioneer Geologist* (Detroit, 1954), 10.

—p. 95, "even of those who . . . ," quoted in Rintala, *Douglass Houghton,* 12.

—pp. 97-98, "As we looked at the instrument . . . , " quoted in Harlan Hatcher, *A Century of Iron and Men* (Indianapolis, 1950), 24.

—p. 101, "contributed more than any other . . . , " John Bartlow Martin, *Call It North Country: The Story of Upper Michigan* (New York, 1944), 109.

—p. 103, "far richer . . . ," quoted in Angus Murdoch, *Boom Copper: The Story of the First U.S. Mining Boom* (New York, 1943), 147.

Chapter 8, p. 107, "I never expected Michigan . . . , " William Saroyan, *Short Drive, Sweet Chariot* (New York, 1966), 44.

—p. 110, "All that Michigan wants . . . ," quoted in Martin D. Lewis, *Lumberman from Flint: The Michigan Career of Henry H. Crapo, 1855-1869* (Detroit, 1958), 252.

—p. 112, "made more traction engines . . . ," quoted in George S. May, *A Most Unique Machine: The*

Michigan Origins of the American Automobile Industry (Grand Rapids, 1975), 156.

—p. 115, "You and I thrive . . . ," quoted in May, *A Most Unique Machine*, 81.

—p. 119, "gasoline engines were . . . ," quoted in George S. May, *R.E. Olds: Auto Industry Pioneer* (Grand Rapids, 1977), 57.

—p. 120, "to produce a road-vehicle . . . ," quoted in May, *R.E. Olds*, 67.

—p. 121, "an itch to get into . . . ," quoted in May, *A Most Unique Machine*, 300.

—p. 122, "probably the most experienced . . . , " Allan Nevins and Frank Ernest Hill, *Ford: The Times, The Man, The Company, 1865-1915* (New York, 1954), 211.

—p. 126, "They say I shouldn't have . . . ," quoted in May, *A Most Unique Machine*, 325.

Chapter 9, p. 131, "Its industrial empire . . . ," Bruce Catton, "The Real Michigan," *Holiday* (August 1957). Reprinted in Robert M. Warner and C. Warren Vander Hill, eds., *A Michigan Reader, 1865 to the Present* (Grand Rapids, 1974), 6.

—p. 136, "would be world-famous . . . ," Catton, "The Real Michigan," in Warner and Vander Hill, eds., *A Michigan Reader*, 7.

—p. 145, "Flint is rich . . . ," John Ihlder, "Flint, When Men Build Automobiles Who Builds Their City?" *The Survey* 36(Sept. 2, 1916):549-557. Quote reprinted in Warner and Vander Hill, eds., *A Michigan Reader*, 116.

—p. 145, "had no idea . . . ," quoted in May, *A Most Unique Machine*, 77.

—p. 147, "This is the town . . . ," Ihlder, "Flint . . . ," in Warner and Vander Hill, eds., *A Michigan Reader*, 115.

—p. 148, "the most happily located . . . ," quoted in May, *A Most Unique Machine*, 77.

—p. 148, "all good householders . . . ," quoted in May, *A Most Unique Machine*, 78.

—p. 149, "one of the great cities . . . ," quoted in May, *A Most Unique Machine*, 347.

—p. 149, "sense of hustle . . . ," quoted in May, *A Most Unique Machine*, 345.

—p. 149, "intense desire for activity . . . ," quoted in May, *A Most Unique Machine*, 345.

—p. 149, "would rather do without . . . ," quoted in May, *A Most Unique Machine*, 347.

—p. 149, "not for us was any delight . . . ," quoted in May, *A Most Unique Machine*, 347.

—p. 150, "One day a man . . . ," Webb Waldron, "Where Is America Going?" *The Century* 100(May 1920):58-64. Quote reprinted in Warner and Vander Hill, eds., *A Michigan Reader*, 139.

—p. 154, "Polish-speaking cowards . . . ," quoted in Lawrence D. Orton, *Polish Detroit and the Kolasinski Affair* (Detroit, 1981), 176.

—p. 154, "howling Poles . . . ," quoted in Orton, *Polish Detroit*, 177.

—p. 155, "What in hell . . . ," quoted in Melvin G. Holli, *Reform in Detroit: Hazen S. Pingree and Urban Politics* (New York, 1969), 17.

—p. 155, "not merely as the local . . . ," quoted in Holli, *Reform in Detroit*, 17.

—p. 156, "There are quite a number . . . ," quoted in Holli, *Reform in Detroit*, 28.

Chapter 10, p. 159, "Greatest War of History," headline in *Marshall Weekly News-Statesman*, July 31, 1914. Reproduced in George S. May, *Pictorial History of Michigan: The Later Years* (Grand Rapids, 1969), 136.

—p. 159, "fatten the pocketbooks . . . ," *Marshall Weekly News-Statesman*, reproduced in May, *Pictorial History of Michigan: The Later Years*, 136.

—p. 160, "Barracks, Laundries . . . ," advertisement of the Lewis Manufacturing Company of Bay City, reproduced in May, *Pictorial History of Michigan: The Later Years*, 137.

—p. 165, "This is the greatest experience . . . , " quoted in Irving Stone, *Clarence Darrow for the Defense* (Garden City, N.Y., 1941), 284.

—p. 165, "Darrow was magnificent . . . ," John C. Dancy, *Sand Against the Wind: The Memoirs of John C. Dancy* (Detroit, 1966), 32.

—p. 172, "Well, I guess . . . ," quoted in Webb Waldron, "Where Is America Going?", in Warner and Vander Hill, eds., *A Michigan Reader*, 135.

—p. 173, "They're like a . . . ," quoted in Sidney Fine, *Sit-down: The General Motors Strike of 1936-1937* (Ann Arbor, 1969), 116.

—p. 174, "perhaps in all of American history . . . , " Fine, *Sit-down*, 338.

—p. 175, "There people . . . ," quoted in Fine, *Sit-down*, 312.

—p. 176, "How many states . . . ," quoted in Alan Clive, *State of War: Michigan in World War II* (Ann Arbor, 1979), 179.

Chapter 11, p. 179, "only senator . . . ," quoted in C. David Tompkins, *Senator Arthur Vandenberg: The Evolution of a Modern Republican, 1884-1945* (East Lansing, 1970), 46.

—p. 179, "for the straightest, the plainest . . . , " Arthur H. Vandenberg, "A Speech Heard Round the World," in Warner and Vander Hill, eds., *A Michigan Reader*, 250-253.

—p. 188, *Detroit Industry* (1932-1933), North Wall, by Diego M. Rivera (Mexican, 1886-1957). Fresco. Accession No. 33.10.N ©1987 The Detroit Institute of Arts, Founders Society Purchase, Edsel B. Ford Fund and Gift of Edsel B. Ford.

—p. 193, "Politics is a lot . . . ," quoted in Frank McNaughton, *Mennen Williams of Michigan* (New York, 1960), 197.

—p. 194, "The last thing Labor wants . . . ," quoted in McNaughton, *Mennen Williams*, 153.

—p. 194, "ludicrous . . . I actually see . . . ," quoted in McNaughton, *Mennen Williams*, 152-153.

—p. 195, "on the cash crisis issue . . . ," quoted in McNaughton, *Mennen Williams*, 23.

—p. 197, "old slogans . . . conventional moral terms," quoted in "Tom Hayden," *Current Biography Yearbook, 1976*, Charles Moritz, ed., (New York, 1976), 182.

—p. 198, "It was sad as hell . . . ," quoted in R. L. Tyler, *Walter Reuther* (Grand Rapids, 1974), 76.

Chapter 12, p. 207, "Some folks around here . . . , " form letter to George S. May dated March 11, 1985, from the Ironwood High School Reunion Committee.

—pp. 209-210, "by the time the study . . . ," quoted in Gary Blonston, "The Down-sizing of Michigan's Economy," magazine section, Detroit *Free Press*, Feb. 12, 1984.

—p. 210, "advanced technology . . . ," excerpt from Governor Blanchard's 1985 State of the State Address, Detroit *Free Press*, Jan. 24, 1985.

INDEX
· · · · ·

The Ford Tri-motor was part of Henry Ford's venture into the aviation field, which resulted in some of the nation's first commercial airline service in the 1920s. However, the automaker did not make a permanent commitment to this new form of transportation. Courtesy, State Archives, Michigan Department of State